A Virginian in Yankeeland

OWEGO, NY
May 4, 1991

To: Olympia J. SNOWE
of the U.S. House of Representatives
and
all members of her staff
studying the ways & means
of filling a big hiatus
in Americana
— with best personal
regards
Benjamin Evans Dean

A Virginian In Yankeeland

Volume Three

Of Monkeys, Quinine, and Magnetos . . . . Linked

By

Benjamin Evans Dean

As

An Unaware George Washington VI

B. E. DEAN, Co.
Owego, New York

Dedicated to all of those hearties who yearn to get away on a long dangerous voyage yet resist such temptation so that they can keep bringing home the bacon, raising their families, while earning their pay at Monkey Ward's, Norwich Pharmacal, Scintilla, Link Aviation, and other great American industries, while they work together under the auspices of management teams making inspired applications of W. Edwards Deming's ways and means of making America competitive with foreign competition.

Contents

VOLUME III

Introduction

In January 1942, just over a month after Pearl Harbor, a hundred U.S. Army volunteers shipped out from Binghamton to Fort Niagara. In charge of the contingent was an unaware George Washington VI, thus also referred to in this tome as your Virginian. Although your scribe is a resident of the so-called Yankee Tier (roughly the area orbiting Owego, county seat of Tioga County, N. Y., and running along the border of Pennsylvania and New York between Binghamton and Bath, New York), the saga of *A Virginian in Yankeeland* (this being Volume III) is told from the unique viewpoint of an author unaware that he is a great-great-great-grandson on the male line of our First President, George Washington.

As detailed in Volume I, your Virginian had unsuccessfully planned to study medicine at Harvard, but thereafter settled for Cornell, earning a bachelor of arts degree majoring in economics. Since George Washington left vast estates, his secret son, Israel Dean, by virtue of the laws of descent and distribution, became the titleholder but didn't know it. Also unaware were Israel's descendants. A *per stirpes* line, pertinent to this tome, now passes down through Israel's younger son, Pierce Dean, the father of Frederick Wellington Dean, who was the father of Clifford Pierce Dean. He now sees his only son off for his first post-college job, entitled trainee for store manager with Montgomery Ward & Company at its retail operation in Ann Arbor, Michigan.

From Monkey's we fortuitously leapfrog some quinine business at a pharmacal company, to some conscription-exempt magneto making, all phases finally being fatefully linked (for the purposes of this saga) while serving at a last peacetime job at Link Aviation Devices, a fine company that gets kissed goodbye when your Virginian enlists.

So here's what it was like as your Virginian, fresh out of four years of rowing substantially all crew races at Cornell, left the Yankee Tier to try out for a captaincy of industry, his first attempt to win a cigar being under the overall tutelage of that kingpin of nationwide merchandisers, Sewell (The Great) Avery.

Acknowledgments

My thanks go to friends known and unknown who have encouraged my literary efforts by contributing words of helpfulness and living lives of inspiration during their long wait for this the third volume of my saga. Also, before I name a few of them, many thanks to those who have helped by their acts, preachments or deeds enhance the author's required abilities to focus on his literary task: Frances Hobbs, the George Washington Office, Winchester, Virginia, Jim Burchard, Jack Bartlett, Nancy Williams, David M. Walsh, Matilda Ehlers Burke, Henry Kingman, Glendora Wiegand, Wallace R. Foster, Jr., Betty Duckett, Harold Kinch, Stella Bell, Walter B. Peyton, Helene De Lamater, John A. Barbour, Joyce Sibbald, Austin H. Kiplinger, Irene Johnson, The *Journal-News* of Rockland County, N.Y., Howard Orcutt, the Board of Selectmen, Falls Village, Connecticut, Wellington Stanley Evans, Doris Cunningham-Ryan, Joe Shortino, Joyce Palmer, Arthur D. Hopper, June Barkerding, Edwin Van Ness Barrett, Catherine Sanders, Alan J. Tucker, Margaret Flagg, Francis De Cator, Mrs. Ray C. Goodenough, Richmond Snyder, Harold H. Corbin, Jr., June Peterson, Joseph E. Murphy, Urico Rossi, Diane Ely, Rev. Walter M. Higley, John T. Swing, Stella Catlin, Arthur T. Myers, Ensley M. Llewellyn, Egbert White, Joseph H. Lindsley, Barbara Wood, Charles Hibberd Bassett, William O. Lay, Tioga County Historical Society, Charlotte Bartow, Webster Ellsworth, Eileen Riseley, James S. Truman, Doucette Charbonnier, George Boldman, Nathan Turk, Elaine Kelleher, Lewis B. Parmerton, Mary Elizabeth Vona, Joseph Hobbs, Pauleen Overlander, Robert V. Gilfillan, Jr., Lee Brady, John H. Bartow, Peggy London, Leonard Pozzi, Bessie Mentz, Russell Rawley, Richard D. Barton, Frances Kren, Rev. Gordon B. Kierstead, Catherine Turk Truman, *Tioga County Courier*, Burton H. Blazar, Len Ellis Jones, Ralph Hanford, Margaret Douglass, Chester Majka, Mary Rawley, Lennart Hesselman, Edvin B. Johanson, Barbara Majka, Emile M. Holzenthal, Lorraine Lyons, Jimmy Carter, Richard C. Lounsberry, Barbara Bowman, Charles P. Ayres, Jr., William F. Fuerst, Jr., Hugh Carey, Albert London, Mario M. Cuomo, Albert C. Neimeth, L. Cunynghame (Ted) Robertson, Philippe Jutras, Beverly Halversen, Matthew F. Mc Hugh, Richard Thomas Franz, Peter Lawson, *State Line Free Press*, Dale Carnegie Courses, Ralph Telfer, Erwin J. Baier, Richard G. Smith, Leon Halstead, Francis J. Clohessy, Richard L. Franz, Syracuse Law School, Ruth Telfer, Richard W. Moore, Ed Hubbard, Thomas J. Ash, Robert Ritter, Howard Ward, Carl W. Klett, Nicholas Kovalchick, Dean F. Klett, William S. Alexander, Everett A. Reynolds, Robert F. Ball, Elaine Ely, Allan D. Bishop, Jr., Gerald E. Rothwell, Wilbur Georgia, John Carr, Adam Auth, Patrick McDonald, Joseph G. Terry, Ernest B. Beisner, Elias Karban, Faxon Dean, and Meryle Hutchinson. Also to those who may be saying kind things about my first two tomes, this and upcoming volumes—the critics, readers, historians, booksellers—they will make it possible for me to transpose a great dream into actuality. They have forced me to keep going forward in spite of all obstacles.

Chapter 1

Called to Michigan by Monkey's

Hooking Up as a Retail-store Trainee for Monkey's

It was July 5, 1939. All harbingers of war had been put on the back burner. Your Virginian thus commenced his stereotyped peacetime pitch to become a captain of the merchandising world.

From the SAE house at Ann Arbor, where a friend from Cornell, now a summer student at the University of Michigan, had fixed me up for a term of several weeks with a room, I outed on Washtenaw Avenue. My easy-going gait masked a spiritual charge. A mile to the west on the business end of the campus, I saw a higher cause in waiting—Monkey's.

I was fresh out of Cornell, and in my mind's eye I toted under my left arm my combined degrees (A.B. and rowing). Tucked under my right arm was the volume entitled *The Young Man in Business*, by Howard Lee Davis. The A.B. sheepskin carried with it a major in economics and a minor in geology (this latter element being relegated temporarily to the proverbial pigeonhole). The rowing

1

degree, as mentioned in the preceding volume, was hypothetical, yet consisted of my having participated in practically every crew race during my just-past four years at Cornell. As for my now being about to become a young man in business, here was the exciting objective—my appearance in work duds for my first day's application of principles taught by the professors at Ithaca's land-grant college. And the current conduit was Howard Lee Davis' book as I approached the portals of Monkey Ward's Ann Arbor, Michigan retail store.

Years earlier, after my having saved some money raising chickens, I had thus been enabled to purchase some wanted products. Through Monkey's catalog department, I had purchased items such as a button accordion and, more importantly, a full-size, rebuilt Underwood typewriter that I had brought along with me to Michigan. Since my father had thereafter confiscated my early seed money, such loss meaning that I couldn't buy a car required were I to become a salesman for Sheaffer Pen Company, this warm spot that my having done business with Monkey's had generated had led to my current reach for the stars.

Excepting perhaps Julius Rosenwald of Sears, the merchandising world's great Merriwell of the day was Sewell Lee Avery, born in Saginaw, Michigan, on November 4, 1874. Here at Ann Arbor he had graduated from the University of Michigan Law School in 1894. When U. S. Gypsum Company was organized in 1901, he had become its eastern sales manager and, four years later, its president. In 1931 Avery was appointed a director of U. S. Steel. During the same year he had joined Montgomery Ward and Company at a yearly salary of $100,000 plus certain stock purchase options. Opposition faded when Avery put the company back in the profit column and the stock again started paying dividends pleasuring owners to the tune of higher share prices.

Hoping to follow in the footsteps of Sewell the Great, your unaware George Washington VI found himself spending fewer and fewer moments looking back. First I had wanted to study medicine, then law or, for that matter, even art. But now your young man in business, knothole by knothole, readied to cram his spirit through the various steps that had been outlined by Howard Lee Davis in his how-to lectures regarding employment when he had appeared during our junior and senior years at Cornell. With such clues nicely boiled down in his book now tucked hypothetically under my right arm, here go the applications!

On Wednesday, the day following the Fourth of July, overshadowed by Burton Tower, and to a Swedish classical tune pealing forth from the high and mighty campus carillon, I entered the portals of the business district, where I continued westerly along the main drag lined with retail establishments that included the leading local movie house, a smoke shop, a drug store, etc. As I walked along enjoying the warm seven A.M. July morning, I couldn't help but ruminate over my previous career plans, in particular these two more recent aspects. Chronologically, they had gone something like this:

After boyhood dreams first of being a locomotive engineer, then an aviator, by the spring of 1934, just over five years before my current go about to commence as trainee, I'd intended to enter Harvard, embarking on a premedical course. Had I done so, by combining my senior year on the Charles with the first year of medical school, by now I'd have just passed the halfway mark. When overconfidence had led to a lack of success on college boards, my father had talked me in to starting out at Cornell. But there an additional bout of self-assuredness had stopped me just short of qualifying for my senior year as an undergrad as a double registrant in law school.

Worse yet, because my father (the unaware George Washington V, also referred to as CPD) was back home running for county treasurer, and thus had urged me to get a job and go to work, I wasn't even thinking about returning to Cornell in September to start my first year of law.

And then there had been my dream of going to South America. But during a question and answer session with Howard Lee Davis, the visiting job counselor at Cornell, it was this same Mr. Davis who'd talked me into perishing all thought of leaving the U.S.A. "The economic opportunities will be just as good right here," Howard Lee Davis had, in part, stressed so convincingly that at once we'd accepted it. Otherwise, by now, instead of for Ward's, I'd be on my way to work in Spanish-speaking territory with lots of interesting social life, lots of young ladies, awaiting any off hours to perk up my morale. But now, instead of South America, when from my father I still hadn't recently been able to retrieve my previously confiscated $500 chicken-money nest egg to use to buy a car to get a traveling salesman's job with Sheaffer Pen Company, I'd taken my alternative ladder in stride. Forgetting that such a nest-egg recouping problem was lurking in the background (and not yet realizing that the political dirty tricks to which my father had been subjected had caused him to con me out of my seed money), just to show off to my father by displaying the industriousness of his only son, here I was about to step up and take my first time at bat with Ward's.

Last but not least, back at Cornell, any time I'd found class attendance boring, with pen and ink I'd sketched my various professors. This constant snatching at any passing opportunity to make a sketch of most anything on any old scrap of paper, without my having then realized that I had a strong tendency to become an artist—a quick sketcher of various and sundry mugs as well as a painter of landscapes and seascapes, rough seas in particular—had led to my having launched out on that extra college course in freehand drawing early on during the fall of my senior year at Cornell. But, before I'd given it enough time to discover that I was a natural, and without an inkling that more than a couple of decades later I'd get gripped by art to the effect that I'd discover that I had a special knack for handling color and could paint after the fashion of a French impressionist—I'd dropped the college art course. Contributing to such decision had been the long hike to the ag campus after I had lost my only means of transportation in the freak accident at Springdale. As detailed in the preceding volume, the collision had wiped out my late open-air taxicab. Thus on this fine 1939 day after the Fourth, besides being about to cram myself into the disciplines laid out and advocated respectively in Howard Lee Davis' book and lectures, without my realizing what I was doing to myself, I was also about to jam my personality's artistic quality, the very existence of which I was generally unaware, into a relatively dull-looking but otherwise efficiently contrived distribution scheme— a retail establishment generating almost a million a year in sales, which said firm had the mission that we unquestionably had to accept and go all out to bolster—keeping up its well-regarded status of moneymaker.

Before I'd left the East for the Midwest, I'd psyched myself into thinking of the mountain of hard work that I'd now be facing. But I had foreseen as a reward (on the obstacle's lower slopes) a

decorative enchantment—garden spots in the Michigan wonder-
land—big executive cookouts, swimming pools (but only after a
few years) lined with maidens in waiting . . . an idyllic recreational life. Now for the real world.

After a hearty breakfast of oatmeal, toast and coffee at the counter
of Teed's restaurant, Mr. Allen, the assistant manager and Harvard
Business School graduate, greeted me at quarter of eight when he
opened one of the front doors of the big retail establishment and
conducted me along one of the aisles lined with counters brimming
with fresh softgoods to the landing at the top of a short flight of
stairs in the rear. We never reached the enchanting second floor
with all of its big-ticket items—furniture, major electrical appli-
ances, gas stoves, and floor covering. Stopping short half a flight
up, we entered the command post that opened off the landing.
There the fortyish store manager of medium height, slightly ro-
tund, with a fair but slightly reddish complexion and dark hair,
whom we'll affectionately call Bosso McCarty, displayed the dynamic Irishman's personality of the Indiana farm boy who'd worked
his way up through the dime stores to Ward's. As he greeted this
raw recruit, Bosso McCarty's personality contrasted sharply with
the grim dourness of his assistant, who spoke but briefly and then
only with well-chosen words, and now took his leave.

Previously, at the behest of Chicago GHQ, I'd sent Bosso
McCarty written notice of my time of arrival, now taking place
substantially ahead of the dot. After my being introduced to the
head office staff and our group's otherwise exchanging formalities,
Bosso McCarty explained:

"Dean," as he would always call me, "any time you have any
questions feel free to contact me or our assistant manager or any of
our department heads, with whom you soon will be getting acquainted. Since you've already told us that you've had no retail
experience other than selling eggs and other poultry products from
chickens that you once raised to villagers along your own bicycle
route and, later on, selling programs at football games at college, I
can tell you now that one of your chief missions here in a very busy
retail store at first will be to learn to 'see things to be done,' [a
preachment that would be oft echoed amongst the store's staffers].
But, aside from that, just now I've got a special introductory assignment for you." Bosso McCarty hesitated and took note approvingly of my work duds. "When you get to be a store manager," he

stressed, and your Virginians's ego was somewhat puffed by the way the bait was dangled, "you're going to have to become by then familiar with many various aspects of this business. One of the most important of mandatory aspects of the expertise that you will develop is the handling of our receiving room operation, also called our stockroom, where all incoming merchandise is checked off, priced against orders, and then turned over to the respective department heads who originally made the requests. Right now I am going to introduce you to our receiving clerk. Perhaps you'll hear that he's got the reputation of being a wild man. But he gets things done. I'm sure that you'll understand and won't ever forget that he's an expert at this intake part of the merchandising business. He's greathearted and he'll show you the ropes, and I want you to learn all that you can from him about this vital section of our business."

"Yes, sir," said your Virginian.

By eight A.M. (as we recall it) we were descending the short flight of stairs, the front doors were being opened, and eager buyers were streaming in. To purchase some softgoods, some of Monkey's good old customers stopped on the main floor, where ladies' dresses were in the department to their right, men's suits in another section including the haberdashery on the left. At the rear of the main floor, the catalog order desk was at the head of the stairs that led down one easy flight to the basement. There effervesced popular departments such as automotive, sporting goods, paint and wallpaper, plumbing, heating and hardware. Exciting, huh?

Now back to Monkey's main floor. At the foot of the stairs at the rear, through swinging doors Bosso McCarty led your Virginian. In a stall on the left, where there was a little built-in desk and stool, sat Wes Eisley, the delivery clerk, with a friendly Ypsilanti-type smile of greeting. Just then, from the door opening on the back alley there came a high-pitched shout. "You can't unload. I told you not to come back today," Louie Sinelli, Ward's astute receiving clerk, was shouting at a tough truck driver. "Look at how I'm all jammed up," complained Sinelli as he explained: "Don't you see, even the freight elevator is jampacked? Now come back tomorrow," Sinelli commanded. Then he turned and spotted Bosso McCarty. Instantly, the store manager and the receiving clerk huddled.

"I'd like to have you meet Dean," said Bosso. "He's going to

assist you checking in that load of paint. Maybe with Dean here,"
Bosso told the harried truck driver, whose face suddenly brightened,
"we can soon get around to doing something about unloading you."
For some confirmation, Bosso then looked at Sinelli.

The short, stocky, blue-eyed blond Italian proffered a hand
and took a good imaginative look at your long drink of water and
saw us moving gallon cans of paint like mad. "OK," said Sinelli.
But it all depends on how fast Dean can move this stuff, checking
it off first, then getting it on into the store. Otherwise, we'll have
the fire inspector on our backs for jamming up the freight elevator
and the aisles." The now very happy trucker saw the green light.

So it was that your Virginian was off to a racing start. Two tons
of paint (from Ward's own factory), much of it in one-gallon cans
(four to a cardboard box), was soon being boosted from truck to
receiving room where, after being checked in to fill the ongoing
demand, it was stacked on a four-wheeled cart, rolled onto the
freight elevator, motored down a floor to the basement level, then
rolled forward and delivered to one Stetler, head of that pertinent
department, who soon got busy ticking off the items on his copy
of the requisition, making sure that his order was all there. His
assistant, one Teeter, stepped up, and the three of us, so long as
either of them had no waiting customers, got busy sliding the cans
into their allotted shelf space. Together with handling all sorts of
other incoming merchandise, this baptism of your Virginian into
the receiving room took four days. Then Bosso McCarty said: "Dean,
another chore you're going to have to know how to handle when
you become a store manager is, if necessary, to teach employees
how to take an inventory. So now I want you to come to work
Monday in good clothes and help Stetler take his weekly inventory
in the paint department. Then, based on it, he'll show you how he
makes up his weekly order that goes in to Chicago. While you're
breaking the ice . . . learning our basement merchandising operation, you can also make sales to customers. Later on our store will
have filmed educational programs, but for now the clerks will show
you our procedure for selling up, counting out change, and handing
each customer a sales slip. Yet for the moment, if you make a sale,
have one of the other clerks ring it up until we get a chance to
make sure that you're fully aware of Ward's procedure in closing
out a sale to an individual customer."

As my merchandising career was slowly picking up speed, on

my first Sunday evening in Michigan, the first classmate from Cornell's boathouse world stopped off. Chicago Rep, en route home to the Windy City, dropped in at the fraternity house where I roomed. As fellow members of the crew squad back at Cornell, we'd participated in many of the same regattas as freshmen and, later on, in both junior varsity and varsity crew races. Chicago Rep was about to commence hacking the hundred-a-month life as a trainee. But his engineering job with Erie Forge on the Niagara Frontier had some labor-law advantages. Situated in the Empire State, he was working but five days a week for a total of forty hours whereas, for Ward's, I was working six longer days plus a couple of nonpaid evenings restocking shelves while the store was closed, plus the customary one Saturday evening when the store stayed open. And there was more. As I would eventually learn, an occasional unpaid Sunday would be an add-on.

Back at our retail store, did that basement with all of its paint, sporting goods, hardware, plumbing and automotive supplies ever heat up at the onset of the muggy mid-July weather! From the dead end at the front of the basement, a tall heavy-duty fan pushed lots of extra-stuffy air back towards the stairwell and elevator shaft at the rear. This afforded some relief and, at the end of one extra-hot day, Stetler invited your unaware George Washington VI to go fishing. But an hour later his assistant, Teeter, who wasn't much older than I, came up and invited me to go swimming at the public beach on the nearby Huron River. Swimming won. Perhaps I wasn't yet dry enough behind the ears. With proper explanations and apologies I canceled out with Stetler, one of Ward's expert local-level merchandisers, who was several years older than I. Afterwards, once I'd cooled off in the currents of the Huron River, I was sorry that I'd broken the fishing engagement with Stetler. After all, he'd asked me first. Furthermore, he was the senior employee in that section of the sales floor to which your Virginian had first been assigned. As Howard Lee Davis would have pointed out: I'd missed an opportunity to get new insights into the business from right out of the horse's mouth. Otherwise, it happened that both Stetler and Teeter would soon be gone—promoted to other stores, respectively, in the Michigan sector of Ward's coast-to-coast chain.

One by one, many of the experienced clerks sashayed up and volunteered some words of advice. From Stetler came soto voce: "Don't ask anyone any personal questions."

From Teeter came a briefing on just how tough it was to expect to get ahead with Ward's. Then, topping it all off, he warned: "Watch out for the Wilmark shoppers. When you get to clerking regularly on the sales floor, one of them will come in and profess an interest in buying a certain item. It's just about impossible to spot one of them so you can be sure that they're going to take you by surprise."

"What's their target? Trying to catch a thief?"

"Only rarely," said Teeter. "But you've got to be sure to count back their change and make especially certain that you give each and every customer his or her cash register receipt. Everyone who works here has been so thoroughly checked out that it's most unlikely that any of our employees would ever pocket any merchandise or any money."

"What else can these Wilmark shoppers be after?"

"Stuff like seeing whether or not you are alert enough to sell up," explained Teeter. "That Wilmark shopper in the disguise of an ordinary customer will pick some lowest item off the counter where there are three levels of quality and price. The clandestine shopper will feign an interest in the low-ball item. Then if you don't sell up to the middle, and further attempt to finally sell up to the top quality and thus the top price level, the Wilmark shopper, for that particular element on the score sheet, will give you a low mark. That means that Monkey's first makes you feel guilty, then exploits it by not giving you a raise even though, otherwise, your work is excellent." Teeter aired a beef as he tipped me off.

Thanking Stetler's assistant, I told myself that once I got to selling regularly on the sales floor, no Wilmark shopper was ever going to catch your Virginian with his pants at half-mast. Perhaps I was overconfident, but with any Wilmark shopper, I was ever so certain that I had sufficient personality, and by the time of any attempted entrapment, I would have developed sufficient sales-clerk skill so that were I to eventually become *the* mark, I would make requisite points whether aware or unaware of any upcoming clandestine test. It was all part of getting hooked up as a trainee with Monkey's.

A Change of Scene to Softball

Then, as though they simply didn't exist, I forgot all about Wilmark shoppers when Louis Sinelli soon had a different and more colorful change of scene to explain. As though this new occasional backdrop were being fatefully programmed for your Virginian's later benefit, Sinelli's suggestion would help your Virginian over a very rough spot coming up four years later at Casablanca, Morocco, as will be detailed in the upcoming volume. This new colorful angle was, of all things, softball!

When your young man in business was pinch-hitting as assistant to the receiving clerk, Louie Sinelli forgot work for a moment and briefed me: "Until this year we had a Twilight League for softball operating under the auspices of the Ann Arbor Recreational Department. But this year Walter Frey has completed a beautiful new enclosed park erected primarily for softball on Stadium Boulevard near West Liberty Road. It's called Sportsman's Park, and Walter Frey is getting most of the top teams of the former Twilight League to move their operations to take advantage of the floodlights on his new softball diamond. I manage one of the teams and I've got a hot dog stand there. When you're not tied up working overtime nights here at the store, you can come down to the park evenings and make some extra bucks selling hot dogs, popcorn, and soft drinks," Sinelli suggested.

Having at once some misgivings about whether this would be a proper moonlighting occupation for the young man in business, I wondered what Howard Lee Davis would have had to say about it. Because I was unable to look sufficiently well into the future, the upshot was that this opportunity by your Viriginian to substantially and practically enhance his hundred-a-month life while getting a bird's-eye view of the goings-on in the softball world—that in turn would enhance his skills of observation that would come in fatefully handy four years hence at Casablanca—was turned down. Grounds were that I surmised that Howard Lee Davis would have said: "As the lucky holder of a trainee's post, forget earning that extra money selling hot dogs and soft drinks. After working all day plus some certain payless overtime evenings restocking shelves for the heads of other departments, go back to your room, study the store manuals, then get your rest and reappear all bright-eyed and bushy tailed in the morning to continue concentrating on improving your merchandising skills with Ward's."

Nevertheless, this introduction of softball into the trainee's background was a big plus that was fated to play a major role in one very important military segment of our next volume. Thus a word here is in order about the doings that I saw when I intuitively attended some few games here in the Ann Arbor softball world during the summer of 1939:

Eight teams in all competed in the new Triple-A League at Sportsman's Park. Old Bru won the league, followed by Ty's Market, St. Thomas CYO, and Dhu Varren Farms. Pitching was a big part of the game. Jack Kett was the Old Bru pitcher as well as one of the heaviest hitters Ann Arbor ever turned out. In a few years he would go to the Dow Chemical team at Midland, Michigan, which would compete with the best league of the nation. Playing first base there, because of the way he'd hit the ball for distance, he would become known as "The Babe Ruth of Softball."

Amongst the other pitchers, Ty's Market had two—Bob Leneberg, a right-hander, and Dick Bucholz, a left-hander. St. Thomas CYO, managed by our good friend Louis Sinelli, had Frank Burke (fated to become the latter-year eastern Montana newspaper magnate), who graciously reviewed these many softball reminiscences. Besides being rated as the fourth best pitcher in the league, Frank provided impressive public relations (PR) coverage, running a sports column in the local Ann Arbor daily. Decades later Frank would surface as the editor-publisher of *The Ranger-Review*, of Glendive, Montana, with interests in other western newspapers.

Frank Burke would recollect: "Incidentally, Sportsman's Park was the finest lighted softball field in Michigan at the time. When some of the Midwest's top teams were brought in, Sportsman's Park drew huge crowds. The Brown Bombers aggregation out of Detroit was sponsored by Joe Louis, the heavyweight boxing champ. At least four thousand people would turn out at Ann Arbor where Joe himself usually played an inning or two at first base, but as a ballplayer he was a terrific boxer."

Enough said for the softball backdrop. The next scene returns to the young man in business.

A GOP Hoax Orbiting the County Treasurership: Dismasked!

In 1930, after my father (your unaware George Washington V) had been hornswoggled by the freak recount (as detailed in Volume I) out of his six-vote GOP primary victory for the Tioga County treasurership, it had become apparent that his estimated half of the countywide Republicans wanted my father to run as an Independent. When he hadn't gone along, it quickly had become evident to the county's GOP sounder-outers of the populace that CPD's followers intended to vote for the Democrat in the general election of November 1930. This meant that a member of the minority party, thus a Democrat, would become county treasurer-elect.

How to hoax my already-victimized father into helping out E. Burt?

First the Owego Old Guard, through the good offices of the GOP county chairman Old Dingle (who was also my father's counselor), asked CPD to endorse E. Burt.

But the backers of the hornswoggled victim rejected such a blatant request. Finally the leaders of the Owego Old Guard toned down their bizarre demand and merely inveigled CPD into writing a "No Hard Feelings" letter. Although Owego's GOP weekly had refused to publish CPD's early announcement of his candidacy in early summer, in good time before the November election, the same Main Street sheet had seen the "No Hard Feelings" letter in a different light and had published it promptly on the front page.

After such a publication subscribed by my father had enabled E. Burt (even though he had become the beneficiary of the freak recount at my father's expense) to defeat the Democrat by a narrow margin and thus be first touted as county treasurer-elect, the next problem for the political occultists: how to further hoax the victimized CPD into not again running against E. Burt for the time that it would take them to chop into my father's fifty percent of the countywide GOP vote. With the objective of stalling the unaware George Washington V for three terms of three years each, or for a total of nine years (thus until this current spring-summer campaign of 1939), the E. Burt backers worked it in two steps. First they let the GOP weekly mention it. Then they expanded it by bandying it about—E. Burt only wanted the job for three terms of three years each. Then, at the end of 1939, he would retire and leave the field wide open for the unaware George Washington V to win the summer-1939 election either unopposed or against some lesser-known candidate.

Keeping CPD occupied for an effective part of the first three years, Old Dingle had had him appointed receiver of an important local firm (a small yet important political plum).

Implementing the wet blanket, CPD was next slotted into a public relations (PR) trap by the Owego Old Guard. The political occultists exploited a most unusual and age-old feature in the charter to the village from the state legislature. Villagers elected a member of the county board of supervisors. To date, many important Republican politicos had held the job, including the Senator, who provided most of the political brains behind E. Burt. And never had any bizarre problems arisen.

In contrast: After CPD completed his first two-year term, he was returned to office by the voters. When he had most of the last year left to go of the second year of his second two-year term, with the PR attribution being slickly focused by the print media on the Democrats, a so-called sneak bill was passed in Albany, eliminating the few-hundred-a-year elective post. This dirty trick had taken place in the spring of 1935. During the same fall CPD commenced putting two children through the college of arts and sciences at Cornell (meaning that he didn't see his way clear to announce for the treasurership in the spring of 1936).

The extension of the hoaxing thus had run into the third three-year term (that would wind up with the last day of December of this current year of 1939) for E. Burt. But a year before E. Burt (were he to timely retire as the politicos had bandied it) was slated to step down, there had come the game of musical chairs in the Lodge, a political ambush by secrecy and surprise, that had left the unaware George Washington V losing face without an office, some of E. Burt's friends reputedly being behind the ploy.

Came the spring of 1939. Both of the children of the aspirant who'd been hornswoggled out of the treasurership in 1930 were up for graduation from Cornell. Relieved of that economic burden, and feeling that the bandied retirement of E. Burt would now become a reality, in mid-May, as mentioned in the preceding volume, CPD as your unaware George Washington V had announced for the county treasurership. In contrast to 1930, the GOP weekly published his announcement that had included, as mentioned, a long list of accomplishments.

What about E. Burt? Would the bandied word of his retirement become a reality or a hoax?

Hoax it was! One week after CPD announced, E. Burt formally announced. As mentioned, the published list of accomplishments of the unaware George Washington V were formidable. E. Burt's were of equal note. Whereas CPD had graduated from Strouds-burg, later to become a state teachers college, the incumbent E. Burt had graduated from the local high school, known as Owego Free Academy. And such a home-town root (as it had worked for E. Burt in 1930) could again be presumed to mean lots of votes generated by the influence of former classmates.

Some of the principal differences between the two men were these: CPD was primarily a self-employed individual who had moved down the Susquehanna watershed forty miles from New Milford, Pennsylvania, to Owego, New York, almost twenty years earlier (in September, 1919), whereas E. Burt was a lifelong resident of the village and a long-term employee of the Main Street Bank.

The unaware George Washington V's holding off for nine years had not been appreciated. This meant that were soundings by the E. Burt cohorts to indicate that CPD was going to win the GOP primary in September, more unseemly ploys after the fashion of the freak recount of 1930 could be expected.

Although the political manipulation by use of the pretense of noncandidacy and possible retirement was now dismasked and its usefulness was thus ended, only the upcoming GOP primary on Tuesday, September 19, would tell whether the retirement rumors had done their job. And were the now-completed stalling hoax to be sounded out as insufficient, the unsuspecting CPD, while feeling entitled to at least a pretense of fair play, might well find his candidacy targeted, especially in the public relations (PR) sector, by some newer and even more unique political dirty tricks.

The Dark Streak

At Ward's, the built-in routine took up a full nine-hour working day plus a couple of unpaid evenings a week and some occasional unpaid Sundays. Although I would have much liked to contact some of my cousins, there was no opportunity for me to make any quick side trips to see branches of our Dean family, descendants of Israel Dean by his two sons and by some of his five daughters, some of whom had been in Michigan since the very early days of the state. In response to family information forwarded to me by my father, I did manage to carry on some correspondence. My great-grandfather's older brother Julius Dean, previously mentioned, after serving in the state militia at Albany, New York, and then after spending some time at Ann Arbor before 1840, had settled at Pontiac where he had operated a drug store. One of his descendants was Ernest Parr (with whom I exchanged notes), an official at Ferris Institute at Big Rapids, Michigan. Another descendant was Ernest's brother, Lyman Parr, who worked for the Chevrolet division at Flint, Michigan. We were all descendants of Israel Dean but didn't realize that he was George Washington's secret son. At my first possible opportunity, I intended to go have a yarn with these two of my father's second cousins. What was the holdup? Since Monkey's was devouring just about all of my waking hours, there just wasn't time to get over the road by bus to see such two of my various long-lost Michigan cousins for a little reunion of unaware descendants of George Washington.

While putting off such trips was a disappointment, I had no choice but to put up the best possible front that a young trainee could muster up. Soon I was gung-ho about my carrying out some higher duty—working for Ward's for the hundred a month. Having no idea of the slowness of progress that was in the cards for me, and displaying that I had a lot to learn, both from personal experience and from a much closer study of Howard Lee Davis' book about the workings of big business on the young trainee just starting out, instead of carousing, I gave precedence to getting back to my room and typing up a chronicle for the home folks. Already, without my realizing it, I was a reporter. When we'd just completed five working days on the job, the imaginative dreamer segment of our personality went slightly out of control. The visionary in me outed as your Virginian wrote home:

"Bosso McCarty is gradually taking Stetler out of the paint department and easing me into his place. [Keep in mind that the more-mature Stetler was a very seasoned and skilled merchandiser and big business wasn't about to replace him with any greenhorn.] Within two or three more days I probably will have complete charge of the paint and sporting good departments," I waxed enthusiasm. Then, as though giving any recipient of my letter—in this case my parents—who might just happen to be sufficiently more experienced than your unaware George Washington VI—a clue that I didn't realize, but that they would dig the eventuality that in all reality was more likely to soon happen, I gave it away: "Today, back in white-collar duds, I waited on customers for the *first* time. I am not yet allowed to operate the cash register but am instructed to have the other clerks handle the ringing up. During the few conversations I have had with Bosso, he has frequently used the words: 'When you, Dean, get to be store manager.' "

In all of this was the clue. In sharp contrast to my envisioning managing, right crack off the bat, paint and sporting goods, Bosso McCarty now came up with a new department—a far cry from paint and sporting goods—for your Virginian to explore. Said Bosso: "Now, Dean, you've had a glimpse into operations of our receiving department and into operations of some of our other sections including paint, wallpaper, and sporting goods in the basement, and you've gotten acquainted with our various department heads. Next, I want you to see how the warehouse works. So come back in the morning in work clothes and I'll introduce you to Bill Wilkens, who's in charge there. For a week or so you'll be his assistant."

That nice little presentation, in the morning, was duly made and within the hour, Bill and I were proceeding to move a mixed bag of mostly nice heavy stuff—refrigerators, stoves, sofas, dinettes, etc., as incoming freight trucks from the factory dropped them off at our warehouse. Up on the heavy-duty elevator we'd transport all of these incoming household items, warehousing them in various corners of our spacious storage building to await delivery orders from the second-floor house furnishing, top-generating star sales producers a few blocks away at our primary Ward's retail establishment. While Bill and I were busy most of the time, on a midafternoon break during dog days, I could step down the street a few doors and pick up a nice cool bottle of chocolate milk at a farm-outlet store. Back on the job, when Bill was looking for something for your Virginian to see to be done, his eye lit on some accumulated trash in the bottom of the relatively shallow pit of the freight elevator shaft. As though Ward's had been saving it up to test the incoming trainee, Bill said: "I'll run the elevator up while you get down in there and clean that all out." In a jiffy the job was completed . . . some more Brownie points with Ward's *maybe* were racked up in favor of your Virginian!

Deliveries to retail store customers out of inventory from the warehouse were another part of the ball game. When it would come time to get this heavy stuff to customers, out would go, by virtue of Wilkens' and your Virginian's horsepower, such heavy warehouse-type items as refrigerators, etc., onto the big red truck operated by Lyle Hurd and his son Junior. With Ward's big sign emblazoned on the truck's side, Lyle and Junior would then make the deliveries. As a result of moving stuff into inventory from big cross-country freight trucks and then moving sold items out, and helping boost heavy items up onto Hurd's big local truck for delivery to retail customers, my erstwhile oarsman's muscular system got a new type of tune-up. Every night when I'd leave the warehouse, then hie back across the campus for my room at the fraternity house, on Ann Arbor sidewalks behind me, I saw that I was leaving a dark streak. But what of? The streak was left where your Virginian's tail was dragging the ground!

The Nine-Year Wait Yields More Smoke for the Real Horse Race

Those members of the Owego Old Guard who had been interested in stalling CPD nine years for E. Burt's benefit were now anxious to keep the voters from identifying the real horse race early on. And did the promoters of the waiting game ever have lots of smarts!

The nine years during which the politicos had hoaxed the unaware George Washington V into holding back provided lots of raw material to the political newshawks engaged in redirecting the voting public's attention onto some other contests that were races, but not such close ones.

In 1930 when CPD had won the GOP nomination for county treasurer (only to thereafter have been hornswoggled out of it by the freak recount), his contest with E. Burt, although played down by the print media and in all practicality covered up, had been the solo horse race.

Now, nine years later, his second challenge to E. Burt was shaping up again as the one real horse race. But this time, including the treasurership, there were four (instead of one as in 1930) major contests at county level. And this time the fourth estate would do its best to cover up the attempt by the unaware George Washington V to make up for his having been hornswoggled in 1930. Then, the newshawks had redirected the voting public's attention onto a couple of minor contests for membership on the county GOP committee. But now, nine years later, the scribes had three other contests to write up and thus deflect public attention from CPD's second try for the treasurership.

Early on, George Andrews of Owego, next-to-last DA who'd retired, curiously came out of the woodwork and challenged the incumbent DA. Surfranc, as detailed in the preceding volume, had pulled a surprise in 1936. Taking note that the Owego Old Guard was running the Senator against the well-entrenched incumbent county judge, Boilerplate, to throw the county judgeship to Eaton of Waverly (for the purpose of softening up CPD's strength in the village of Waverly and the Town of Barton, should he run in 1939 for the treasurership . . . and as he now was doing), Surfranc, in a surprise, last-minute move (his first shot at the DAship), had obtained requisite designating petitions. In a spectacularly short time, Surfranc had then not only qualified, but also had gone on to win the GOP primary over the incumbent, tantamount to winning the November election.

Making it look as though the scales for DAship would be tipped back to Owego, Senior Rep of Waverly, when he threw his hat in the ring, made it two from Waverly against one from Owego. So much for DA.

Upstaging (in the number of contestants) the contest for district attorney, the county sheriff's post was also a much sought-after position. So in 1939, four men (of whom Doug Grant looked like the strongest) went after that particular GOP nomination.

And back in the category of two-way races, matching CPD vs. E. Burt for the treasurership, it was Charles Haywood against incumbent Beck for the county clerkship.

As though three contests (in addition to CPD vs. E. Burt) didn't provide the newshawks with sufficient distractive stuff, in early August, the Lake Street's political scribes wrote, "A few weeks ago the GOP county committee amended the rules of the party by giving the enrolled voters of the town of Nichols an opportunity to make the nominations in the primary election rather than by the caucus system.

"This [belated] request came to the [GOP] county committee from the voters of the town of Nichols, because in the past the caucuses were so largely attended that much confusion arose, which in the case or two, a candidate who sought nomination to office lost out because all of the voters were unable to express their preference before the closing of the caucus. In the town of Nichols, almost as many voters attend the town caucus as go to the polls for the election.

"In eight other towns of Tioga County, nomination of town officers will be made in caucuses as has been done for many years.

"The petitions of Nichols candidates show—there will be two [town of Nichols] contests: 1. town clerk; 2. superintendent of highways."

What was the result of the hoaxing of CPD to wait nine years? At the early-campaign mark, the addition to the contest between CPD and E. Burt for the county treasurership (the one most likely to turn into a real horse race) of these other three county-level GOP primary battles wasn't enough. So the GOP county committee fixed up the overall rules enabling the hiking of two town-level contests to the GOP primary ballot, whereas the county-level contests had been the originally intended monopolists of the spotlight. E. Burt's PR partisans thus had plenty of ammunition for use in manipulating the print media into covering up the real horse race.

CPD: "You Made Your Bed....Now. Lie In It!"

Probably because my father's great-uncle, followed by a couple of his regular uncles, had migrated to Michigan, my father liked having me out here (where I was less likely to push for a professional career—medicine, law, etc.). And I was getting a big kick out of keeping the home folks posted.

At mid-July I received from Chicago, through the local store's GHQ, my first confidential paycheck. Adjusted for days worked it came to just under forty dollars but . . . What a very great thrill! It was sealed in a blue envelope marked "personal," which in turn was sealed in a regular envelope with my name on it that came out of the Chicago pouch. The reason for all this secrecy about my hundred a month was this: as I now joined class with them in the school of hard knocks, I was making more than some of Ward's experienced merchandisers who hadn't been blessed by a college education.

By July 19, two weeks after my arrival on the big Ann Arbor retail merchandising scene, in a letter home, I was hinting that I might not stick with Ward's very long (just the opposite of what the book by Davis said) briefly as follows: "Here it costs a good share of my paycheck just to live. Food costs eight dollars a week and I pay three for my room. Now I can realize that, had I stayed home for my first job, I might have been better off. During my six-day workweek, I take three-quarters of an hour for the break at lunch, thus donating an extra quarter of an hour to the company each day. I take my time leaving the store at six P.M. Maybe it sounds tough. Yet there are good pickings here if I can ever get at them. For instance, in this world of big business, this particular link in the coast-to-coast retail chain comes close to a $1 million annual retail sales volume. Depending on the bonus formula, the store manager makes between eight and eleven thousand dollars a year. The assistant manager, even though he's a crackerjack graduate from Harvard Business School, makes just thirty-five dollars a week, and he's already been racking up experience in the chain store business for a substantial number of years. Among the outstanding departments in the store are: furniture, major electrical appliance, and automotive supply. Volume in each of such departments runs between sixty-five thousand and a hundred thousand dollars a year, and the respective department heads for these three departments that look somewhat choice make around three thousand dollars a year."

Then, hints of impatience against which Howard Lee Davis warned in his book and lectures, and perhaps a bit of homesickness commenced to bubble up to the top as I continued: "The business statistics and data that already I have gotten wind of here make me itch to get into business for myself. Who knows, maybe I'll yet be home in time to vote for Dad in the GOP primary for the county treasurership just after mid-September."

Curiously, at this juncture, there's no mention made by your Virginian of his disappointment, a year earlier, of not having commenced law school, the point being that, had I decided to take advantage of my previously guaranteed entry at Cornell and start law school in rapidly upcoming September, the former missing of the boat could now soon be remedied. But would any encourgement be forthcoming from my father? Instead of making such a suggestion, your Virginian kept telling the home folks all about the situation at the big retail store. And, needless to say, had we had more information about the workings of commercial intelligence as well as about leaks from letters and postcards, we'd have clammed up and we'd have told our parents little or nothing through the mails. But, being young, callow—and a chapter on such matters, along with another preachment that we'll soon mention, having been forgotten or otherwise omitted by Howard Lee Davis from his book— here we continue to expound about Monkey's for the folks back in the Yankee Tier.

"With the exception of certain other more successful department heads, the remainder of the help gets paid between a little over sixteen dollars up to almost twenty-eight dollars a week." And I couldn't help but point out that my coworker in charge of the warehouse soon had let out the amount of his salary. Although he had a wife and child to support, and although he had put in three years at this position of very substantial responsibility at the warehouse, his pay was just a shade less than your Virginian's. I had good reason to feel lucky.

Maybe, as Howard Lee Davis, in his book, indicated that I should, I did! Certainly I had to realize that I was luckier with this job than a lot of other chaps. But that to me didn't seem to be the issue. Let's say I was lucky . . . But . . . already I was penning to Papa, in part: "Being at the top would be fun. But being at the bottom isn't so hot. Already I am gradually getting fed up on the idea of working for others. Still, even though my ideas are gradually changing about this business of working for a big corporation four hundred miles away from home, I keep showing plenty of enthusiasm over my job. I get to work fifteen minutes ahead of time every morning and do everything that I am told and more, too. If I should quit, I want to be able to be sure of getting a good recommendation from the store manager."

Then, reminding the unaware George Washington V of his going-away prediction that he'd made on the station platform back in the Yankee Tier on the day before the Fourth, just before I'd hopped the Pullman for Michigan, I wrote: "You seemed to think that I wouldn't be out here in the Midwest for so very long. Maybe you weren't so far wrong after all. I haven't definitely made up my mind, nor do I intend to do so for at least three weeks or a month." Without realizing it I was keeping the door open psychologically for law school. I let my father know in no uncertain terms that I was a long way from settling down into this trainee's job with Wards. "If I come home soon, I'll be able to campaign for you for the county treasurership while I'm lining up the traveling salesman's job that was offered me—provided I'd buy my own car—last spring by the Sheaffer Pen Company."

In the meanwhile, had I been able to retrieve my $500 chicken-money nest egg from which I'd been parted by my father just over four years earlier, I'd now be able to buy a car with which to qualify for that traveling salesman's job. In spite of my father's thus having blocked me out from this available job option, at this point I was taking the fall of 1936 confiscation of my $500 chicken-money nest egg in stride. Never once did I press my father to return it, even though a couple of hundred dollars that I'd inherited from my grandfather was involved in that clever transfer of my money on loan to him that had taken place on April Fools' Day of 1935 when, ahead of time, I should have gotten my pockets sewn up. Instead of now pressing to get my money back, when I'd been on my trainee's post for twenty days, I was writing my father that for a new car, for a down payment, I had almost half of the six hundred dollars cash that it would take to buy a brand-new Chevrolet or a Plymouth business coupe. And, instead of demanding the return of my $500 chicken-money nest egg, I asked my father whether, for the new car, he'd loan me the difference.

Actually, since he'd simply be loaning me back some of my $500 chicken-money nest egg that during the fall of 1936 he'd con-fiscated after parting your Virginian from his purse in the spring of 1935, it now wouldn't be practical—from my father's viewpoint—

to become my banker. If he were now so to do, I'd then have every right to retaliate by finding some excuse to return the favor and confiscate the monies that would be loaned from him to me. Thus did my proposal for a loan get quite the negative response. Like some incredible wise guy, my father as he wrote back came on with such a tone that would make it much more difficult for me to ever stretch my imagination to see that he was an unaware George Washington V. After refusing the automobile loan and stressing the valuable experience that I was getting as a trainee with Wards, my father got behind one of his favorite artillery pieces and pulled the lanyard: "You made your bed—now lie in it!"

The Psychological Roller Coaster

"Although I continuously display plenty of spirit about my work, I am fed up with Wards and the Midwest," I was writing home even before I'd completed my third week as a trainee. "If this job with the fountain pen company doesn't soon come through, I intend to quit Monkey's sooner or later anyway," I asserted as again I stressed to my father that if I wound this thing up well before the September GOP primary for the county treasurership, I could get home in time to help electioneer for him for the county treasurership.

How come I didn't mention law school? My aspiration was not exactly dying on the vine. From lack of encouragement, it was pigeonholed. And through all of the sweat and grime that I was taking back evenings to my room at the fraternity house, I was just starting down a psychological roller coaster. Going into my fourth week on the new job, after acknowledging for the umpteenth time that I was well-aware that I was getting valuable experience, to my father I elaborated some more on my young-man-in-business thinking, in part, like this: "Do you think that I should stay with Ward's even if the Sheaffer sales spot looks like a better opportunity?" This question, though, would never get answered because the traveling opportunity hung on my furnishing my own car which, for the time being, because my father had borrowed then confiscated my nest egg, appeared to be out of the question. While I'd been at Cornell, I'd stepped out of the arts and sciences department a few times to take a couple of business administration courses in the engineering school. Stressed by the profs had been this point: "If you don't want to wait a long time to make real do-re-mi, get into sales." And it was sales on which now, at least subconsciously, I was targeted. "If I got this job with Sheaffer's," I wrote, "if progress would turn out to be too slow, I could switch to Sloane-Blabon, the company that manufactures linoleum floor coverings, etc. Their sales organization might turn out to be similar to Sheaffer's, and Sloane-Blabon's president—Houlder Hudgins—was the college roommate of my college roommate's big brother."

One of the business magazines such as *Fortune* had recently sketched out just how well Mr. Hudgins was doing as head of Sloane-Blabon. An interesting sidelight soon developed. When I wrote Houlder Hudgins, introduced myself, and stated my problem (one key element of which was my opinion that by now instead of a hundred a month, I should be making forty a week), he called in his secretary and dictated in reply a nice explanatory letter. It followed the tenets that had been previously laid down for me by Howard Lee Davis in his lectures and in his previously mentioned book that looked down from a shelf in my room. The important parts still remembered from Hudgins' letter to your Virginian were points such as these: "With Ward's you are in one of the best positions available for learning the ropes in big business. Considering all of the facts and circumstances, that hundred a month that you are getting is very reasonable." Mr. Hudgins, same as Howard Lee Davis' book, confirmed my fortunate situation with Wards. But, in closing, Mr. Hudgins left it like this. "Should you eventually still desire to go to work for Sloane-Blabon, should the opportunity avail itself, we will set up a job interview."

When a deer rushes past the hunter who, out of deer season but during bird season, just happens to be armed with a shotgun, he doesn't fire at the deer. Instead, when he spots the oncoming pursuing hounds, the hunter turns the dogs around. Temporarily, to say the least, this letter from Mr. Hudgins turned your Virginian around. From that moment on I commenced to forget getting back East when summer school on the Michigan campus would let out and rides with students homeward bound to the vicinity of the Yankee Tier would become available. Likewise, I commenced to let slide back there the Indian Princess. Intelligence had it that during my absence, one of her compatriots had gotten the inside track. I'd now let this situation cool off in the hope of being able to run more successfully some other day.

Suddenly, as though concerning our merchandising career there had been some winds of change, I was writing my father: "The first objective on which I am going to target is assistant to the two crackerjacks running the automotive supply department. At the feet of these two first-rate merchandisers there I can sit and learn. In charge is Epperson and he's assisted by Boyer, who once owned his own retail tire outlet but got clobbered during one of the financial panics earlier in the decade, and now says that working for Ward's is better than running your own business. Still, even though Epperson made well over three hundred dollars for the month of June and makes around three thousand a year, there's still this other factor to consider. Such inside work is usually in a stuffy basement. On the other hand, though, I am finding out that work just for the sake of work, if for nothing else, is the thing. If I didn't have a job, I'm sure that I'd miss work."

Whether your Virginian liked it or not, he couldn't help but settle down, if only for a goodly term of months, for a ride on Monkey's psychological roller coaster.

Little Reminders of the Military Alternative

With war clouds hovering over Europe, at the nearby university library, on Sundays I'd keep posted up on developments that might soon embroil the United States. According to one officer writing in one of the military journals, the United States before very long was going to have to go to war. He saw the increasing probabilites of upcoming hostilities as a contest about to break out between two gigantic banking systems. By now this wasn't news to your Virginian. One of our visiting lecturers back in class at Ithaca had filled up a blackboard with numbers distinguishing the haves from the have-nots. After our speaker had demonstrated that such countries as Germany, Italy, and Japan were short of raw materials (while we weren't), he had left our class with something to chew on. Now that it commenced to appear that Monkey's might be merely filling the gap as part of a waiting game, I now found myself being treated more like a roustabout than as a trainee. Maybe the military life with something to run would be better than all of this heavy work in the warehouse that was soon making me wonder what I was doing out here in the Midwest.

Passing a Navy recruiting station on the campus after work one day, and sensing that the current undercurrents of unrest in the western Pacific would eventually provide a more exciting life, and thinking that an officer's life might be a relief from Monkey's, I dropped in. (In the western Pacific a new-order-for-Asia policy in 1940 had aligned Japan with Germany and Italy in the tripartite pact. Although no immediacy of conflict appeared here at home, you could feel the increasing disquietude. By now Japan's Combined Fleet was being gradually readied for war as the faction increasingly getting the upper hand saw preparedness for conflict with the United States the only answer.) The Annapolis product in charge, as he looked with wonderment at my work duds dirtied after a rough day in the warehouse, had mostly "yes" answers, to wit: yes, he knew my good big brother-type of friend from my home town in the Yankee Tier—Robert V. R. Bassett. Yes, Bassett now was with the Pacific Fleet after having graduated some years earlier from Annapolis. Yes, your Virginian, with his degree from Cornell, was eligible to apply for a Navy commission. Yes, that rowing degree we'd obtained at Cornell was impressive to the navy . . . Then came a "No." That rowing degree didn't cut enough ice to get your Virginian past that old bugaboo, that roadblock—the requirement of twenty-twenty vision. Tough.

It soon looked as though I had no choice but to forget joining the Navy. And if I didn't learn that trick of memorizing charts and hiding my glasses, were I to eventually apply to the Aviation Cadets to become a fighter pilot, this roadblock might leave me no further alternative other than to enlist in the Army Air Corps. So it was so long to the Navy recruiting officer and back to the fraternity house for a night's rest, then to make my reappearance in the morning to lock horns at the warehouse with lots of nice heavy refrigerators, stoves, and sofas, etc.

On Saturday, when July had only two more days left to run, I was in the middle of my fourth week on the brand-new job, and I looked more like a hot and grimy coal miner coming off shift from the bowels of the earth than a trainee for store manager. For delivery to a retail customer, from an upper level at the warehouse I was lowering by freight elevator a modest load made up of a sofa that was furnishing me with a rare sitting moment. As I turned the control lever, slowing down the elevator and finally stopping it level with the main floor, I looked out through the wood slats of the protective gate. I had visitors! Here at Ward's warehouse in Ann Arbor now stood the cool-looking former varsity rowing mates on the Cornell crew—Wisconsin Slim and West Hooker in crew shirts, slacks and black and white saddle shoes. We had participated in intercollegiate varsity competition on the Severn, Housatonic, Charles and Hudson Rivers. We had raced other colleges on Lakes Carnegie and Cayuga. As we renewed our old camaraderie, I couldn't help but sense that to them your Virginian, in dirty sweaty work duds, was presenting a scene that would later on put these two upcoming seniors in readiness for what might well also be in store for them should they ever opt to also go the route of trainee—the young man in business. For Wisconsin Slim, I presume, this viewing of your Virginian in action in the grimy scene at the warehouse would help him, eventually, to decide to give up engineering and instead to follow in his father's footsteps and study law. By the same token, Hooker, after a stint as movie producer, would eventually be inspired to become a self-employed overseas soft-drink executive.

What brought them through town? The military alternative was again cropping up. For a couple of reminders here at Ward's warehouse in Ann Arbor now stood these two Army reserve officers in mufti. En route to their midwestern homes from their recently completed ROTC summer training course at Pine Camp, they had first checked with Ward's store, from whence they'd been directed to the warehouse by Bosso McCarty. Although they were under pressure to get on down the road toward their respective home towns at Stevens Point, Wisconsin, and Winnetka, Illinois, the shortness of this visit was nevertheless a big morale booster. But when these two trainees (but focused on the officer corps of the U.S. Army) were getting ready to leave, the growing question surfaced. I asked: "Are we going to have to go to war? Is there going to be one!"

"Not right away," Wisconsin Slim answered.

But Hooker, perking up, implemented Slim's remark. "From

all of that hustle that we've just been through at Pine Camp, we're sure getting ready for something!" Hooker left the question wide open.

This dangling of the militaristic leftovers from the Kaiser's war was the chapter that Howard Lee Davis hadn't seen fit to add yet to his book about the young man in business. With war clouds seeming to be off-again, on-again, just how was a trainee such as your Virginian to assess their impact on his relationship with Ward's or whatever other employer with whom he might wind up during these days of such great uncertainty? In any event, it was impossible to talk Wisconsin Slim and Hooker into staying over. Out front at the curb awaited Hooker's four-door Ford V-8 convertible sedan with the top down, as my two former rowing mates in midafternoon under Australian-type blue skies soon climbed aboard the nifty sled. Commitments in Chicago mandated their late-evening arrival. Yet, they were just as disappointed as I that we couldn't get together for an ovation, and Slim yelled out from the copilot's seat: "Watch our racing start!"

Hooker gunned it. On two wheels they kept it down to a dull roar as the fancy Ford screeched around the first corner and out of sight. It would be years and years before I'd see either of them again. But just now how I'd have liked to hop aboard with them and head west! Both of them would soon be returning to Cornell, Wisconsin Slim to complete his senior year of engineering and participate in a much improved—without all of the previous year's boathouse politics—varsity crew, and Hooker, as incoming prexy of the university student council, to complete his senior year in the college of arts and sciences.

Your unaware George Washington VI, in the meanwhile, proceeded to dig in some more with Monkey's at the warehouse while my two ongoing friends would cook up and pass along a yarn that would make everybody forget the potential bugle call on land or sea. Eventually tying still another of my classmates, Double-A, in knots of mirth, the runner-up to your unaware George Washington VI for top participation in number of races rowed for the Class of 1939 during four years on the Cornell crew would hear Monkey's warehouse yarn with this embellishment: As seen through the slats by Hooker and Wisconsin Slim, your Virginian had been sound asleep on that sofa in that descending elevator!

Pressing the Trainee Into Davis' Pattern

By Sunday, the next to the last day of July, I was writing my parents: "I haven't yet heard from the fountain pen company. The offer they made me last spring was two hundred a month for a drawing account, which had to be made up in sales commissions. Of course, for a starter, I'd have to furnish my own car and then would have to pay expenses out of commissions . . . ."

So it went, In contrast to Ward's, a job with the pen company would have been more like being in my own business with some substantial incentive that would improve my abilities as a self-starter.

While it would take me almost three decades to become aware that I was a George Washington VI, now, with an Ann Arbor dateline, bravely I penned my parents: "Don't worry about my getting discouraged, as I might yet end up as a college professor or the president of the United States."

About do-re-mi, I told them: "I have managed to commence rebuilding a small bank account out of the one that I had before I went to college." (Although I never now reminded my father, this account had been the previously touched upon $500 chicken-money nest egg that during the fall of my sophomore year had been massacred—in all actuality, confiscated—by my father.)

My letter indicated that getting back to the Yankee Tier for a quick gander at the home town . . . actually it was to go knock on the door of a certain beauteous young maiden . . . was still much on my mind. Thus I had to keep my parents from feeling too surprised should I show up. After telling them that I was making my new bank account grow, I reminded them that if and when I returned home, I expected to have some money saved up to use to finance myself until I found new employment. Making it clear that in spite of all of the Howard Lee Davis-inspired enthusiasm I displayed on the job, I didn't intend to become a permanent fixture at Ward's (or in the chain-store business), I said: "You know that I was a bit skeptical about this job before I started. Ken Duff, one of my older friends in Owego, tipped me off so if you want to know how I really feel, just talk to him. He graduated right out here from the University of Michigan. But the talent scouts hired him to work for Lincoln Stores at Waterville, Maine, where he walked down the street in midwinter and froze an ear. [This bit about the ear may sound like a non sequitur, but just wait until the Michigan winter soon rolls around and your Virginian freezes up something else.] Ken knows this gamut that I'm going through. The same as I'm now thinking about doing, he pulled up stakes and now has his own business in our home town in the Yankee Tier, where he makes a good forty a week and doesn't have to work as hard as I do.

"But whatever the developments here at Ward's Ann Arbor retail store—like The Man said: 'interesting women, they're everywhere,'—they are keeping me just yet from quitting Ward's and returning home." Additionally, I told my parents: "I have two chances for rides to upstate New York on August 18 when summer school on the campus here lets out. But I do *not* think that I will come home at that time even though I know that, back in the East, I can always get a job."

While all of that sounded as though I were ready to quit, just then I reverted to reading Davis' book to the effect that a little bit later on, by early August, just after I'd been hooked up with Ward's for a month, displaying that I was getting more interested in my work, I was writing to my parents: "I'm learning a lot that I never before knew about general merchandise. You ought to buy a twenty-nine dollar Ward's studio couch and put it in place of the daybed." (This was a somewhat worn-out and very uncomfortable lounge that had been purchased more than ten years earlier so that my father, by relaxing on it after lunch, could speed his recovery from his stomach operation.)

While continued gleanings from Davis' book brought me back up on the psychological roller coaster, not so down at Ward's retail establishment at Marion, Ohio. There my former college roommate was getting ready to pull up stakes as trainee and return to Ithaca to commence his second year of law school. No more, though, of last year's encouragment to me to study law. My fraternity-house waiters job would be waiting for Si. He sent a note: "Monkey's was first-rate, but only for the purpose of educating me to keep out of the chain-store business for the rest of my life."

Ward's at Ann Arbor must have gotten wind of it. The assistant manager assigned me to help one Jordan (a seasoned sales clerk who was about to be promoted to another of Ward's retail stores) to do a little woodwork chore. As we got together at the warehouse and boxed up a small defective pump for shipment to the factory for repairs, as he'd probably been instructed, Jordan, while I served as carpenter's helper, sounded out your unaware George Washington VI about law school. Later that afternoon, when I returned from the warehouse to the retail store, the assistant manager intercepted me. Ordinarily untalkative, this time, after conjuring up some remarks by which he laid a foundation for his probe, he asked: "Maybe you intend to start law school next month?"

Without my realizing that starting my first year of law school in rapidly upcoming September was just exactly the plan for which I should now have been opting, to the contrary I suddenly let the preachments out of Davis' book help me see Monkey's as a higher cause. As a result, I replied: "No, sir. Going to law school is the farthest thing from my mind. I intend to make a career with Ward's . . . to become a store manager."

Gruffly, the assistant manager nodded assent, then, as though he'd extracted the correct answer, hurried off, perhaps to report— orally and/or in writing. With your Virginian there was hardly a contrary thought left. Yet, had I pursued my first plan (it wasn't law but medicine, from which in 1934 I'd been stonewalled by college boards) in upcoming September of 1939, I'd be commencing my third year of medical school! And had I become a double registrant in Cornell Law School during my senior year last past as an undergrad, I'd soon be back in Ithaca commencing my second year at law.

But after that little probe by Jordan, followed up by the assistant store manager's question, medical school and law school, temporarily, to say the least, slid down the tube. And I got on with the questionable business of pressing myself into Davis' pattern of the young man in business.

World War Sure to Come . . . Within Five Years

Having a psychological effect on the west, back on the eastern end of the Owego-Ann Arbor axis, Hon. George Pratt of Corning hied from the westerly end of the Yankee Tier to Owego, where he told the Rotarians (and the Democratic weekly headlined it on page five), "World War is Sure to Come . . . Within Five Years."

Pratt pointed out that Hitler was copying Napoleon. He was making an alliance with Mussolini that included fortifying the toe of Sicily. "Hitler will go into the Ukraine next for mines and natural resources."

On the bright side, Pratt thought that the people of Germany and Italy, not wanting war, would soon revolt against the dictators.

What did all of this mean? From your Virginian's viewpoint, it generated a sigh of relief as blue skies chased away the war clouds, translating "within five years," to a breathing spell to be measured by a similar stretch of time within which, perhaps, your unaware George Washington VI could get to be the youngest store manager in Monkey's chain.

As Pertaining to Monkey's: Pennala Tries to Debunk Davis

Not long after I'd completed my first month as a trainee, the counseling from a distance by Howard Lee Davis commenced to take hold. When I commenced uttering preachments, very subdued at first, about what a great future a career with Ward's held in store for all involved—your Virginian, in particular—Art Pennala pricked up his ears.

An opportunity soon arose to do some Sunday sightseeing in the great state of Michigan. Art Pennala, who was one of Ward's best young all-around, first-rate sales clerks, got a day's domestic leave while his wife was on duty as an RN at the university's big, important hospital. To make sure that your Virginian early on got acquainted with some nearby areas of great natural beauty while hacking it with Ward's, and to check out one of his, Pennala's old stomping grounds—the Irish Hills, a goodly drive southwesterly from Ann Arbor—Pennala, who had the wheels, organized this motor trip on which your Virginian was invited to see the sights, including the country belles who would soon be turning out at a tea dance there. All of such ballroom dancing activities would make your Virginian's Michigan sojourn that much more bearable and acceptable. But now back to some points of wisdom emanating from the astute Finn.

Art Pennala was a product of one of the Finnish colonies that had planted roots in Michigan's Upper Peninsula. Seeking his fortune, he'd first looked for it at Harlingen, Texas. As to what it had been like way down there along the Mexican border, when folks from the northern climes waxed eloquent about the Rio Grande area of southeastern Texas, Art said, "Maybe the weather down there is warm and the big sky beautiful. But just start watching that barometer commence to drop like an elevator come September." To sidestep the threat of annual hurricanes, Art, when he'd eventually returned to his native state, had stopped at Ann Arbor. Working first for Hoover Ball and Bearing, he'd eventually gravitated to Ward's, where by now he'd racked up some few years of experience and had gotten the hang of selling paint, sporting goods and hardware in the stuffy basement. About such of his own contrasting insights, after having heard some of my preachments (out of Davis' book) about the great days that were waiting for all of us—your Virginian, in particular—with Ward's, Pennala, as we drove down the road to the Irish Hills, said: "Dean, you're supposed to be a trainee for store manager. But don't get any idea that you're going to get there fast with Monkey's. Look at Bosso. He came up from an Indiana farm through the dime stores. He's fortyish, has a wife and child and only within the last few years did he become store manager. That means that if you stay and work hard for Monkey's for fifteen years, you'll be lucky if by then you'll get to be assistant store manager. And they're liable to make you wait even longer, let alone getting to be store manager."

"No," I tried to argue with the astute Finn, "it's not going to take me any fifteen or twenty years."

"Look at those war clouds in Europe," said Pennala. "If a conflict breaks out, even if we sit on the sidelines, it's going to mean shortages. Any kinks in the flow of merchandise from the factories will stop Monkey's from being able to expand. So it will take them just that much longer to grow a new position for you to fill as store manager," he continued his pitch.

But refusing to allow Pennala to debunk Davis, I came back with, "President Sewell Avery is hoarding all of that cash and when the time is ripe, he'll expand." Having already been turned around—the psychological roller coaster was commencing its ascent—I was being led by my "right" constructive attitude into more and more enthusiasm about the great opportunities that I psyched myself into thinking abounded for your unaware George Washington VI in making a career of it with Ward's.

The GOP Ladies Work Against an Unaware George Washington V

While I continued to devote myself to Monkey's in Michigan, back in the Yankee Tier at Owego, over the weekend, one of my father's best friends passed away. Mentioned during the close of our previous volume, he was Charles Ballou, the president of the cooperative fire insurance company of which my father was secretary-treasurer. For seven of his earlier years Charley Ballou had served as GOP county chairman. His continued political presence would have been good for a minimum of an extra two hundred votes in the upcoming September primary. But although his passing would have a negative effect on my father's campaign for the county treasurership, the overall strength of CPD in the Waverly area of the town of Barton would still keep the unaware George Washington V on the vote-getting pace. Yet, Charley Ballou's recent inability (for health reasons) to circulate designating petitions had to be factored into the oscillating evenness of the odds.

My father, as mentioned, was now making his second try for the county treasurership after having seen his six-vote GOP primary victory wiped out in 1930 by the freak recount.

Thereafter, as noted in a separate chapter, the unaware George Washington V had been hoaxed by the GOP leaders of the Owego Old Guard into thinking that were he to wait nine years, then run again for county treasurer, E. Burt would retire, leaving the field wide open to my father. But one week after CPD had announced, E. Burt had declared that he would run once more, this time for his fourth three-year term.

Tuesday, August 15, was the deadline for the filing of GOP

designating petitions. The Owego Old Guard had indicated that since my father had waited faithfully nine years before running again, they would support him even though E. Burt by now (thanks to my father's "No Hard Feelings Letter," before the general election of 1930, allowing E. Burt to win the November election that had followed the freak recount of October 1930) had become the incumbent.

On deadline day for filing designating petitions that would put his name on the ballot for the GOP primary, my father walked into the election board offices in the tall orange-red brick Georgian Tioga County courthouse at Owego. He carried with him a stack of signatures totaling 1,447 names of registered Republican voters. But E. Burt, who had for nine years been dropping lots of little hints that he'd not now during the summer of 1939 run again, continued to unmask. Confirming his previous announcement, E. Burt dogged my father's footsteps into the same election board offices and plunked down an even larger stack of 2,242 names of registered Republican voters! Although the ploy of pretense of noncandidacy and possible retirement was now seen as a clever hoax and its usefulness was thus ended, it had well-done its job. It had kept my father waiting nine years before he now tried to get redress from the hornswoggling impact of the freak recount of October 1930.

Both candidates, my father and E. Burt, had procured well over the required number of petition signers. E. Burt's procurement of about thirty-five percent more names dramatized the carrying over of the secretiveness and the slyness that had characterized the freak recount of October 1930, when his side had managed to focus the recount on selected election districts where E. Burt votes could be picked up. As one of a number of places where CPD might have gained enough votes on a recount to maintain his six-vote victory, E. Burt's side, curiously in control of the recount (as detailed in Volume One), had preserved E. Burt's lead in the Owego area as an unrecounted sacred cow.

Even though E. Burt seemed to have the inside track in this current contest (because he'd lived in the county—the site of this potential horse race—all of his life, while my father had only arrived to the site of the contest from forty miles up the watershed at New Milford, twenty years earlier), E. Burt, in spite of his thirty-five percent lead in designating-petition signers, was really running scared. Secret soundings indicated that CPD's customary fifty percent or more of the countywide vote was still very much intact in spite of his lesser percentage margin of designating signatures.

Helping generate E. Burt's margin of almost eight hundred petition signers had been the inclusion of two more key factors. First, my always very energetic but now temporarily bedridden mother had been unable to get out and canvass for petition signers for my father. Second and last was the factor of the Ladies' Republican Clubs. Especially in the Owego area, these fine women Republicans had been early out circulating designating petitions for the September primary battle for the GOP nomination for the county treasurership. Although their stance should have been neutral, my bedridden mother would later learn and inform me that the good ladies—even though she, my mother, was one of their charter members—had been beating the bushes going all out for E. Burt, thus having been a major factor in the giving to him, at the GOP designating petition filing stage, such a thirty-five percent advantage.

A Nice Little Upswing on the Psychological Roller Coaster

Had your Virginian gotten a job at home, where part-time he'd have been able to canvass for petition signatures for his father, to say the least, we'd have seen to it that E. Burt's substantial margin of signers of designating petitions for the contesting of the county treasurership would have been given a first-rate shrinking. Instead, hanging tight at Ann Arbor, I was being updated from home by mail and was commencing to worry about another old family bugaboo—my father's health. As a result of the tensions of his ongoing political campaign as well as my temporarily bedridden mother's not being able to cook for him, his stomach was acting up.

From late 1919 until early fall 1927 (with a short time out for a stomach operation in 1925), your unaware George Washington V as senior partner had successfully operated Owego's most important feed-milling business. Since your Virginian, say from age four to nine, had spent considerable time meeting the customers, talking to the salesmen, and otherwise observing operations there, having liked the after-school-hours life, he had been much disappointed when his father had sold out. So now, twelve years after the transfer from Dean & Dutcher to Holmes and Watkins, ingrained in your unaware George Washington VI was this desire to become a miller.

But then there was the drought! By early summer, the Lake Street weekly had headlined it as, "Worst Since 1900, Susquehanna [River] Lowest in Years."

By the end of July: "Drought Devastates Tioga County Crops. Victor Strong's farm off the Montrose Turnpike has to Draw 260 Gallons Daily from an Isolated Pool in Pumpelly Creek."

Next update from father in Owego to son in Ann Arbor: "You can forget getting into the feed business this season. The crop losses that the farmers are having this year are certain to have an adverse effect on next year's operations."

The time had come for your Virginian to forget the failure of his parents to encourage him to study medicine or law. The situation called for him to cook up a good morale booster for Mother and Dad. So now, you all . . . hear this! When I couldn't get a Saturday afternoon off to catch an early train eastbound, I could latch on to one after work around nine in the evening that would put me in Owego around twelve hours later, at nine A.M. Because I could take advantage of such a fine connection over the Michigan Central and the Lackawanna, by August 18, I had just about decided to make a quick trip home over the upcoming Labor Day weekend. But that's not the real point. When I so advised the folks at home about my possible homing for a quick trip by rail, your young man in business, with some words that Howard Lee Davis would have been quick to endorse, summed up the recent turns taken by his trainee's feelings, hopes and aspirations like this: "Incidentally, I am getting so that I like my job very well . . . so well that I have forgotten all about quitting."

Even though they knew that had I studied to become a doctor, I'd be halfway through medical school, my parents, my father in particular, must have loved seeing me follow in the footsteps of his father's uncle and two brothers and commit myself to Michigan. At this juncture, I thought that sticking to my hundred a month trainee's post was a duty owed to some higher authority such as Sewell the Great and Monkey Ward's shareholders. Who said so? Momentarily, it didn't matter. In short, since this was what I thought I ought to do, I was doing it. Forgotten temporarily, since I hadn't heard from them, was the traveling salesman's job with the fountain pen people. Also pigeonholed, but not for good, were my previous dreams of studying medicine or law. Without my now realizing it, the swim of events was moving me right back on this nice little upswing on the psychological roller coaster.

That's Money You Can Spend on Blondes!

When summer school at the university let out and the fraternity house where I was staying shut down between semesters, I moved to the other side of town and rented a room with an industrious German family. Soon, Junior Hurd delivered my trunk and I was comfortably ensconced much closer to my work station with Ward's. It was Friday, August 18, and gone were all thoughts of quitting Ward's by latching on to one of the rides home available with students motoring back to the Yankee Tier.

Keeping the pot boiling, an old pal from the Yankee Tier sent me a recommend to go pay a visit to a lady friend now vacationing from Ohio at a nearby Michigan lake. The bus soon dropped me off into this situation—lots of cuties sharing a camp—where, for a pleasant Sunday afternoon, your Virginian could hardly restrain himself from stepping into the shoes of the proverbial fox in the chicken yard. By midevening, to save a buck, at the behest of this cute brunette, I was hitching back down along the valley of the Huron River when a couple of nice local ladies stopped their sedan and gave me a ride. When I told them about my father's campaign for the treasurership, they were all ears. One brand-new first-rate social contact had thus led to another, this latter one being of a much more convenient sort thus generating visitations when I'd be back from the warehouse temporarily and at my salesman's stand at Monkey's. Amongst clients there, all mother and daughter combos were shifted so that your Virginian could do the selling of the paint while the other clerks, were they to find a spare moment, would be able to listen in on the line.

Then came some winds of further change. At the end of the same week that summer school had wound up, Bosso McCarty said: "Now, Dean, for the time being you have learned all that you need to know about our warehouse operation. Lyle Hurd, our retail store's delivery contractor, needs an assistant. His son Junior is going on vacation and I have arranged with Lyle for you to be his helper."

Soon, having gladly kissed goodbye to that warehouse life with all of its heavy lifting, I confronted a similar type of the same old stuff. With Lyle Hurd at the wheel, I was riding copilot while we honchoed into various homes all kinds of heavy items, furniture, stoves, refrigerators, big, bulky mattresses, etc. In doing so, we hit just about all of the satellite towns serviced by Ward's Ann Arbor retail store. Included were spots such as Saline, Milan, Oakville, Whittaker, Stony Creek, Willis, Belleville, Denton, Cherry Hill, Wayne, Ypsilanti, Dixboro, Plymouth, Whitmore Lake, Dexter, Chelsea, Lima Center, and Bridgewater. You name them and your Virginian had helped unload all kinds of stuff there, always, of course, giving all merchandise, fine wood finishes in particular, tender loving care to avoid damage. Already, on top of my fourth year of rowing, handling all of that heavy stuff previously at the warehouse had toughened me up some more. So before long, I was showing the regulars who helped out on the delivery truck my abilities to boost from the foot of the stairs stuff such as sofas overhead to clear upper railings, and with no scratches to the goods being delivered into place, so that various ladies presiding over their respective households wouldn't have to strain themselves readjusting the room position of such heavy furnishings.

, My pinch-hitting for Junior on his daddy's truck gave me the opportunity to observe a new dimension of Michigan life. One day, returning to Ann Arbor from the eastern perimeter of our marketing area, Lyle Hurd pointed out some acreage and said: "That land belongs to Ford. You see those plants flopping in the breeze?"

Whatever they were, to your Virginian they didn't look any too impressive. "What are they?" I asked.

"Soybeans," proclaimed Mr. Hurd.

"What's Ford doing monkeying around with soybeans?" I asked.

"Plastics, all sorts of things are coming out of Ford laboratories. They're experimenting with bean oil to make plastic fittings for automobiles," Lyle Hurd clued me in.

Nevertheless those soybeans, just then, didn't look like much to your Virginian, even though he was an unaware great-great-great-grandson of one of America's greatest farmers, to wit: George Washington. But several years later I would learn first-hand all about how fortunes could be made and lost speculating in soybeans futures contracts on the Chicago Board of Trade.

Late one Saturday night twenty miles or so from home base, when, displaying my stuff as a trainee with no squawks, even though Lyle Hurd and your Virginian were dog tired, an assembly problem that usually turned out tough, this time, snapped together like magic. "What a beautiful way to get done with our last furniture delivery chore of the late evening!" I couldn't help but exclaim to Lyle Hurd.

He agreed.

By then night had fallen and by the time Hurd pulled up in front of my new digs to let me off, he pulled out some green and offered it to me for working overtime—a most rare occasion when you worked, directly or indirectly, for Ward's. But, being the serious young man in business—as Howard Lee Davis in his book had said . . . money wasn't the thing, but it was the experience that counted; I turned down the extra overtime pay from Lyle. Whether or not that eventually garnered for me any Brownie points with Bosso McCarty, I never did find out. The moral of the story though, for you young 'uns just starting out, is this: You earned it (helping an independent contractor overtime), so take it, provided you then do something constructive with it . . . it's money you can spend on blondes!

The Cleveland Air Races Usher in Hitler's War

Still in Ann Arbor, your Virginian now commenced to sweat out the upcoming Yankee Tier GOP primary race for the treasurership. Yet, my copilot's position on Lyle Hurd's delivery truck was so interesting that first thing I knew Labor Day weekend was almost at hand and the running out of time was forcing me to make a quick decision on the question of whether or not to make my first quick trip back to the Yankee Tier. Adolph Hitler helped me decide. On Friday night, September 1, Germany declared war on Poland. At once (we all expected that the United States would quickly get dragged into it), I reviewed my options. My first move would be to give the old college try at getting into the Army Air Corps as a fighter pilot. To get updated on what was going on in the wide blue yonder, I decided to simultaneously renew some of my collegiate contacts at Cleveland.

Saturday night, the customary evening hours at the store seemed to stretch out endlessly. After a fitful night's sleep, instead of making the Labor Day weekend round trip to the Yankee Tier, early Sunday morning I went down to the Ann Arbor terminal and caught a bus to Cleveland to see the prototypes of what I expected to become the brand-new war's cutting-edge fighter aircraft.

Earlier in the summer, Si Glann and I had talked of meeting halfway between Ann Arbor and Marion, Ohio, to compare notes on Monkey's. But now that Si had so recently pulled up stakes as a trainee, and already was back East readying to commence his second year of law school, I was heading instead on a much more colorful mission to Cleveland. En route, at the bus station in Toledo, newspaper headlines were emblazoned with: "England Declares War on Germany!" What a shock! Even though the United States seemed to be left out of it, I couldn't help but ponder the effect of the new war in Europe on my career with Ward's. I thought: "What now, Howard Lee Davis for the young man in business? Are you going to send us a supplement to your book?" But that idea lasted for only a moment. Time rushed by and by late afternoon, my bus rolled into Cleveland.

When John Davol Williams, who'd been a college classmate, met me at the hotel, after I'd finished bending his ear about what a great place Ward's was to get started up the ladder to captain of industry, he, in his role of a Cleveland local, pointed out: "See those pictures on display of the various aircraft that will be participating in tomorrow's upcoming air races? You should take careful note. There are no pictures of any German aircraft. Last year they were here. This year they are absent. Right now the German pilots who were here last year are probably strafing Polish ground forces on Germany's eastern front."

The next day John had a golfing engagement so when the time came, I joined another Cornell classmate, Bud Davis, in his insurance firm's box amidst a sea of big-name industrialists and good-looking dames. Then we sat back and got ready to watch 'em fly.

When a seemingly ordinary little delay took place, I took a short walk. High at the back of the grandstand, an Owegoan who'd opted earlier on to achieve executive status in the light aircraft industry—Dick Washburn, accompanied by his beautiful wife—showed up while I was passing through the crowd. The star salesman had recently stopped off to visit his parents at Owego and get in a couple of sets of tennis with the Owego Eagle and Ken Brister. From home I was presented with the latest inside dope: Although Owego was first-rate, what better way to spend the holiday than to be right here to watch'em fly.

While Dick got ready to further his career selling light aircraft (in contrast to your Virginian's much less colorful assignment to merchandising), I returned to my seat in the box reserved for Bud's company. All of a sudden I got the news: high winds have forced the cancellation of the races. Did I feel disappointed? My trip was the thing. Now to get on with it.

Were the air races to come off instead on the morrow, the event would see your Virginian answering Monkey's bugle call. Labor Day evening my college friends dropped me off at the Cleveland bus terminal. As we headed west, the driver kept me posted on the dangers ahead. Criss-crossed headlights signaled close calls by the dozen involving big trucks on turnarounds. Then came a necessary switcheroo at Toledo. To get a few hours sleep I hit the hay in a nearby hotel until the attendant rang my room at some ungodly yet designated hour, around four-thirty A.M. But this meant that I was able to catch a different bus that put me back at work on time at Ward's Ann Arbor retail store, all bright-eyed and bushy tailed on the morning after Labor Day. Were the races finally held? If I bothered to find out, all that I remembered was that they had enhanced my interest in aviation. The scheduling of that major aerial-speed event at Cleveland had ushered in Hitler's war!

Some Michigan Cousins Show Up at the Store

Thanks to Hitler's move against Poland followed by Britain's declaration of war on Germany, it was a whole new ball game. Yet

Ward's merchandising operation proceeded on schedule. At the Ann Arbor link in the chain, it was business as usual.

Since there was a lull in warehouse activities and Junior Hurd had returned from vacation, Bosso McCarty had reassigned me to the post of sales clerk, principally in the sporting goods and paint departments. Stetler, by now, had left and the realization had finally dawned on me that neither of these departments would be assigned to me as manager until, as Art Pennala had outlined it, your unaware George Washington VI had racked up a lot more time with Ward's. Replacing Stetler was another very experienced merchandizer—Alan Parsley—and assisting him was your relatively inexperienced Virginian. I needed a shot in the arm. It was time for some of my Michigan first cousins once removed—three of the various and sundry unaware great-great-granddaughters of George Washington—to show up.

On this one nice, early September day Ward's sales clerks up front on the main floor looked out and saw a nice shiny Cadillac pull into a parking space before the storefront. Out stepped three fine ladies who walked through the principal portal and immediately inquired of Helena Babette in charge of Ward's catalog-order desk, and she pointed down one flight, "You see that tall chap selling that farmer a fish pole?"

"Yes."

"That's him!"

As mentioned, I had just been switched out of my latest blue-collar role (as copilot on Hurd's delivery truck), and I was all spick and span, dressed in slacks, saddle shoes, clean white shirt and tie, and wearing the customary sales clerk's jacket. So I was sufficiently presentable when these three fine ladies from such northwesterly points as Lansing and Dansville descended the flight of stairs to the paint and sporting goods department to look me up. We'd all met at various times during the 'twenties and early 'thirties when they'd come East to visit my father (their first cousin) at our home in Owego. Same as your Virginian, all three of these ladies were unaware descendants of George Washington by his secret son Israel Dean, whose younger son Pierce Dean had migrated from Canaan, Connecticut, in 1847 to New Milford, Pennsylvania. My visitors, Jessie, Sylvia, and Marjorie, were granddaughters of Pierce Dean by his son Franklin Pierce Dean, who was one of the older brothers of my grandfather, Frederick Wellington Dean.

About this George Washington line of descent, it would take your Virginian twenty-eight years before the light would get turned on. Only then would he first realize and become aware that his great-great-grandfather, Israel Dean was the secret son of George Washington, our First President.

A generation older than your Virginian, this welcoming committee suddenly made me commence to feel a lot more at home in Michigan. Jessie was the wife of Ead Mullen, the Dansville husbandman. Sylvia was the wife of Paul Cross, the Lansing salesman, while Marjorie was the wife of Bill Sessions, a leading Lansing trial lawyer. Since these natives of Mason had traveled a considerable distance from home, and since my only free time was my lunch hour, we made a good time of it at the first-rate German restaurant nearby. What a fine family reunion! Leaving with me invites to come and see them soon, my three cousins further impressed my peers at Monkey's when they stepped aboard their Cadillac and headed homeward, while I returned to work feeling like a bigger Michigander than Junior Hurd. Suddenly I found myself giving up a little bit more ground on the idea of going to law school. Here I was, settling down a bit more with the idea of making it big right here in Michigan with Monkey's.

Surfranc's Bold Stroke

Now, for a moment, here's a late political development that arose just now way back home in the Yankee Tier. Judge Boilerplate, as previously mentioned, in the left-footer segment of the Lodge was the kingpin. But in the right-footer segment, he had a peer—Surfranc, one of the Yankee Tier's decade-younger legal eagles. He was a big-shot politico residing in the village of Waverly in the town of Barton that was expected to play a key role in the upcoming GOP primary elections.

During the recent filing of designating petitions, Surfranc (who had waited until the end of June to announce) had come up with 738 signatures to 700 for Senior Rep. Last to announce (just before the Fourth of July) had been the previously retired DA, George Andrews. Although he had 800 signatures, he wrote a letter of withdrawal to Old Dingle in his capacity of county GOP chairman, copies to the other two candidates. This withdrawal just before the filing date acted out Owego's gift to Waverly of the DAship, as it created a major county-level contest, the one for DA, between two Waverlites (with Surfranc as incumbent believed to have the upper hand) as though the gift were now being accented and highlighted by inference to detract the focus from CPD's customary strength there.

But of the four county-level races (for sheriff, DA, county treasurer and county clerk), which contest was most likely to be the closest? Two Owegoans were much more likely to stage the tightest race. Yet, normal commentaries were missing from the print media, and CPD, having been hoaxed into waiting until 1939 to run a second time, saw contests such as Surfranc's (against Senior Rep), plus two more races for county clerk and sheriff, attracting the publicity focus from an otherwise very possible PR resurrection (that would be favorable to your unaware George Washington V) of the freak recount of 1930.

Now back to the question of the DAship and the incumbent— Surfranc, now finishing his first term as Tioga County DA. In the town of Barton, that was in all practicality of equal political importance with the town of Owego, the village of Waverly, located in such town of Barton, served as its focal point for the huddles over the cracker barrels. And for Waverly, before he'd been first elected DA (in 1936), Surfranc had served successfully for twelve years in the sensitive political post of village attorney.

Barton and Waverly were situated on the northerly side of the state line. Contiguous to Waverly, on the southerly side of the line was the borough of Sayre with its influential daily, *The Evening Times*. Its ads and editorials reached northerly across the state line to service Waverly, ensconced in its town of Barton area that, politically, was soon expected to play a key role in the upcoming GOP primary contests, particularly for the treasurership. But, as previously mentioned, in order to avoid reviewing in print the hornswoggling by the freak recount that had victimized my father close to nine years earlier (in October 1930), the horse-race aspect of the 1939 contest, was being muted by an editorial wet blanket.

Back to the DAship, the fortyish Surfranc, on the last day of August, came up with a bold stroke that enhanced his political image just over a fortnight before the GOP primaries. Headlines blazoned: the Waverly politico was named to the office of supreme prelate of the Loyal Order of Moose at the national convention in Philadelphia. Surfranc was The Man to be watched. This Waverly native as a kingpin in the town of Barton always had lived there except during his collegiate career and during the seventeen months he had served stateside with the Armed Forces during the Kaiser's war. He was a Notre Dame product who at one time had served as a newspaper reporter, becoming the county's foremost public relations (PR) wizard. In 1920, at age twenty-five, he'd been admitted to the bar, and especially thanks to his recent bold stroke based on well-publicized lodge-room politics, Surfranc was considered by pundits to have the inside track against Senior Rep for the DAship.

The Limited National Emergency

On Thursday, September 7, Owego's Democratic weekly provided an interesting highlight on the outbreak of war in Europe. "Owegoans Return from War Zone on *Samaria*. Sailed from Liverpool August 25."

"After a two-month visit to Ireland, Mr. and Mrs. Thomas Rogers, son George and daughter Jane arrived in New York, where Mr. Rogers' brother Joseph picked them up for the automobile trip arriving in Owego, Wednesday, September 6."

Two days later—Friday, September 8, Germany's attack on Poland was just a week old. FDR proclaimed a limited national emergency. In such a case, as previously mentioned, Howard Lee Davis hadn't told us, as a young man in business, just what we should be doing about it. So we kept right on working hard at our hundred-a-month trainee's position. At this point, try as we did, it was impossible for us'uns in Ann Arbor (where isolationist opinions came out of the woodwork) to see the United States getting involved in another of Europe's wars. We thought that Hitler as he chewed his way into the East would soon have all that he could easily digest . . . . that as they pertained to us Americans, the war clouds would go away and that we'd be able to continue to pursue our career. In fact, World War II had commenced. Although it was a whole new ball game, we all took it in stride . . . . like ostriches.

Chapter 2

A Four-Race GOP Go Orbits An Unaware George Washington V

Two-Job Sacrifice to Waverly of No Avail: CPD Still Leads

During CPD's 1930 campaign for the treasurership, one of the principal planks in his platform had been equitable distribution of deposits in countywide banks of county monies. In contrast, E. Burt's objective had been to give a monopoly on such public monies to his employer bank on Main Street, on the board of which the Senator was kingpin.

Now, nine years later in the 1939 campaign, this issue over which depository and how much, was being ignored by the print media. Such suppression was benefiting E. Burt.

By the same token, Cecil Berry, president of Waverly's principal financial institution, had taken a high-level position with a larger bank in New Jersey. The departure for a metropolitan position of such countywide banking leadership of the equitable distributionists was also CPD's loss, especially in the Waverly area.

Also during the 1930 campaign, Waverly politicians had complained vehemently that Owego was monopolizing all of the county-level jobs. For this and equitable distributionist reasons, Waverly voters saw CPD (although he was an Owego resident) as being non-aligned with Owego's Old Guard monopolists, and thus had provided him with the voting edge that had seen him win the 1930 GOP primary (tantamount to defeating the Democrat in the following general election in November) . . . . only to have been horn-swoggled out of his six-vote victory (when the Senator, as then detailed, had successfully masterminded the limiting of the recount substantially to districts where E. Burt had picked up votes).

Afterwards, the important Owego politicans who had CPD's ear had commenced successfully hoaxing him to wait three terms of three years each (for a total of nine years extending to the current year of 1939) before he would again run.

Once CPD had announced, in May, 1939 (E. Burt's entry coming a week later), pundits saw the unaware George Washington V as the eventual winner. Commencing three years earlier (in 1936), to cut down on CPD's odds of again carrying the village of Waverly and the town of Barton, as mentioned in the previous volume, the Owego Old Guard, by running the Senator in 1936 against the incumbent county judge, Boilerplate, had taken away enough votes from the Springdale resident (who drove ten miles weekdays to sit on the woolsack in Tioga County Courthouse at Owego), thus having made a gift of the county judgeship to a Waverly man (whose term wouldn't expire until the end of 1942, when current GOP county chairman, Old Dingle, not only now secretly aspired but also was highly confident that he would then bring the post home to Owego).

Also as mentioned in the preceding volume, when the Senator-led segment of the Owego Old Guard was busy dislodging Boilerplate from the woolsack, another Waverly man, Surfranc, waited until the last minute, then hopped on the back of Waverly's candidate for county judge, and won the DAship handily from the incumbent Owegoan, who thus had become a one-termer.

Of these two county-level elective posts that the Owego Old Guard had allowed Waverly to have (in an attempt to destroy CPD's vote-getting ability there), now in 1939, only the DAship was being contested. And the Senator, who was currently Owego's oldest active lawyer in politics (he'd gained his moniker when he'd served two terms in the state senate during the mid-twenties), now in

1939 had been the kingpin on the vacancy committee of George Andrews (the DA of yesteryear who had opted during the early 'thirties, and thus before the Surfranc-dislodged incumbent of 1936, not to stand for reelection) when such former officeholder had opted in the middle of August 1939 (as mentioned) to withdraw his candidacy, (instead of filing his most weighty designating petitions—800 signers to 738 for Surfranc, and 700 for Senior Rep). As though the Senator were a movie producer, by coaching Andrews to thus enter last then withdraw (instead of filing his designating petitions), the engineer of the freak recount of 1930 was seeing to it that the Owego Old Guard was now acting out in 1939 its gift of the DAship (on the heels of the 1936 hand-over of the county judgeship) to Waverly (now that either Surfranc or Senior Rep must win).

Once such a previously undreamed of, double-barreled political gift from Owego to Waverly had been made operational, the Senator's team for the reelection of E. Burt took some more secret soundings. Owego's gift of a county judgeship and a DAship to Waverly was still of no avail. So E. Burt did a door-to-door in Waverly and the town of Barton . . . . no help: CPD was still going to win the treasurership. At the Senator's law office, a frantic powwow was held by the gang orbiting Owego's Main Street Bank, where E. Burt was an officer-employee under a board led by the Senator. The conclusion: In order for E. Burt to have a chance to win, pull out all of the stops! With the actual election nearly at hand, there was just enough time left for the Senator-inspired cohorts to pull off a couple of major dirty political tricks.

Some Certified Expenditures for the Primary Campaign

Election eve was rapidly approaching. While the unpublicized horse race heated up, a word on expenditures surfaced in the news. With the hard money of the day it appeared that for a GOP primary campaign, a little would go a long way. Just over a fortnight before the primary slated for September 19, at the county board of elections, certified expenditures showed CPD's outgo for the county treasurership as $138.00 against E. Burt's $84.80. For the DAship, certified expenditures showed that Surfranc had spent only $49.75 against Senior Rep's $90.00. And for the county clerkship, as we hit the high spots of the campaigners, certified expenditures showed that Charles M. Haywood, with $75.76, had underspent his opponent Frank Beck's $109.70, with the four-way sheriff's race showing respectively modest outgoes. Otherwise, when the fourth estate let loose details such as these, they had a strong tendency to distract the voters from identifying the real horse race.

Who's In On The Know?

Were we all to say that the four-race, 1939 GOP primary was orbiting the second try for the county treasurership of an unaware George Washington V, who, amongst the various and sundry notables, might have been a great enough man to be trusted (by the nation's top-level political occultists representing interests that had exploited George Washington's vast estates) with so great a secret?

Take Boilerplate. In coming decades, under a different name he'd be included amongst the featured politicos of Springdale, the town adjoining the northwesterly sector of the town of Owego, in *Small Town in Mass Society,* by Vidich and Bensman.

After having been elected just before the armistice that had ended hostilities in the Kaiser's war, Boilerplate had served as district attorney until he had been voted county judge. Simultaneously, the prominent Owegoan, George Andrews, had become DA successfully presenting cases in Boilerplate's court. Before that, Andrews had trained as a fighter pilot with Jones of *Small Town,* the armistice having ended their chances to travel overseas to the Western Front for some combat. During the early thirties, when Andrews had retired to concentrate on his law practice, J. Laning Taylor, also of Owego had become DA, being subjected, at the end of his first two-year term, to the surprise 1936 supplanting by Surfranc.

Now back to Boilerplate. As DA he traveled to Owego every day (his last name being Young, as mentioned in *Small Town*), and thus in the minds and hearts of the Owegoans, was often thought of as being one of them, and the village's twin weeklies showed it. By virtue of his treatment by both the Democratic and GOP weeklies, Boilerplate, soon after he'd become an officeholder, had gained the unofficial title: Owego's PR God No. 1.

Then, after Boilerplate's two five-year terms as county judge, the Senator (who had successfully engineered at CPD'S expense, the freak recount of 1930), had unsuccessfully run for county judge, siphoning off enough Owego votes so that Boilerplate was dislodged and sacrificed. The county judgeship thus was switched to Ed Eaton of Waverly. Thus by 1939, Owego's Old Guard, could thus make the pitch in its sister village for E. Burt votes (at the expense of CPD's traditional preponderance there).

And Boilerplate, once knocked off the elective woolsack, continued to keep his cutting edge sharp substituting for judges on Long Island while opening up a law office in the heart of downtown Owego, commencing January 1937.

By 1939, although Owego's PR God No. 1 wasn't quite as prominent in the local print media, he was an important factor in the Lodge, and more lately with one of Owego's very popular service clubs. While the candidates for the treasurership had already announced and the aspirants to become DA were in the process of joining issue in late spring and early summer, Boilerplate was principal speaker at "All Kiwanis Night." His topic: "We Build."

Across our county line in western Broome county, before two hundred members at Hotel Frederick in Endicott, the former Tioga County judge said, "The fundamental rights of American citizens are taught so that these rights can be maintained.

"One of the best methods of assuming that realization of the Kiwanis motto, 'We Build,' would be to disseminate education in fundamental American principles.

"Kiwanis has a real part in maintaining the country's status as a democracy. We must exercise our voting rights to ensure the election of men whom we can trust with our democracy, men who will be honest with us after their election."

Back to the currently developing four-election GOP primary: As it orbited the political-genealogical motive, was Boilerplate one of those men great enough to be trusted with so great a secret?

If not just yet in the know, while maybe even now . . . . more specially in upcoming years it would appear, since you'd all like to know . . . . yes. Between devoted service to the Lodge, and to the service club Kiwanis, and on the bench in Long Island, most likely the burgeoning guru had been sworn in to hold the secret: The current challenger of the incumbent for the county treasurership, was unaware that he was the great-great-grandson of George Washington, and on the male line.

Next warranting discussion as to their possibilities of nurturing some follow-up greatness, are Surfranc and Senior Rep. The former was just commencing to be recognized as the leader amongst the new generation of fortyish, and Senior Rep as a comer amongst the thirtyish Tioga County legally oriented politicos. Just now, in the same GOP primary as the one for the treasurership, they were locking horns for the office of DA, giving the political newshawks just the fodder they wanted for the purpose of keeping the PR spotlight off the real horse race, the one between CPD and E. Burt.

Surfranc, the incumbent, was the older. As a native of Waverly and the *town* of Barton, the big shot of the Moose Lodge also had going for him his seventeen months with the Army during World War I. In addition he was an experienced newspaperman. Currently crowding out Owego's traditionally controlling Cornell coalition, he had earned his undergraduate and law degrees at Notre Dame and had been admitted to the bar for almost twenty years. He had served twelve years as Waverly official village attorney (as distinguished from the unofficial post of "attorney for the village") and he was currently in the process of completing successfully one term—his first—as county DA.

Was this participant in the DA sector of the four-race GOP primary, a great enough man to have been trusted with so great a secret? that CPD was an unaware George Washington V.

Who might have entrusted it to Surfranc? King Coal's Rep. A few years earlier, the Pittsburgh coal executive (where George Washington landtitles in the Saudi Arabia of coal were very hush-hush) and close friend J. Edgar's, had purchased some real estate from Surfranc in Waverly. Before King Coal's Rep had passed away unexpectedly in 1938, there was some chance that he'd sworn Surfranc to secrecy and then passed along to him the motivating factor for the currently being suppressed horse race, between E. Burt and CPD.

Next in pecking order, we present Senior Rep. Although he

would never become a Mr. Republican, he was a sufficiently important cog in the GOP machine. Thus his moniker would stick.

In this year's campaign he had been first to announce. As mentioned, his aspiring to dislodge the incumbent DA, was also put to good use by the edititorialists to muffle the horse race over the treasurership as the newshawks kept putting the spotlight on the contest for DA, while also loudly ringing in the contest for county sheriff and county clerk. Senior Rep, about eleven years younger than Surfranc, was born in Syracuse in 1906. The thirtyish challenger obtained his law degree in 1930. He was the product of a bureaucratic family in Albany where his father had been a well-entrenched, first-rate lawyer for the Empire State.

While playing his saxophone in orchestras from resorts in the Adirondacks to cruise ships on North Cape junkets and to social events along the Binghamton-Elmira axis, Senior Rep had stumbled across the Yankee Tier. One good look at its scenic river valley lined with lovely hills had been enough. In 1935, Senior Rep once he'd settled in the Yankee Tier's little paradise of Waverly, quit dreaming (at least while he was engaged in raising his family), of following in his father's footsteps at Albany.

In the early days of September 1939, Senior Rep for the DA-ship, had the backing of the musicians' union along with a strong following of satisfied law clients. From the political standpoint of my father—CPD, the only hitch about Senior Rep was this: Politically, he slept in the same stable with the Senator-led, E. Burt. The Senator had sparked the freak recount of 1930. Thus, predictably, in the soon upcoming all-important GOP primary, Senior Rep would in Waverly and the town of Barton area—from which some extra special political trickery, as previously suggested, could be expected to emanate against my father—tell his friends to support E. Burt.

Now back our question: Was Senior Rep a great enough man to be trusted with the big political-genealogical secret. Almost thirty years hence, after the light would get turned on and your Virginian would ask, Senior Rep (a good friend by then) would deny ever having been clued in. But what with his connections at high bureaucratic levels in Albany? Were I to learn that Senior Rep, especially in late years, had been let in on the know, it would be no surprise.

And going back, commencing with Boilerplate, from your Virginian's viewpoint, as to knowledgeability of the secret genealogy, he would be a certainty, George Andrews a possibility (he might have heard about it from the Kentuckians when he'd been flying for the army during the Kaiser's war), and Surfranc, with his King Coal contacts, a likely shareholder in the big political-genealogical secret, Senior Rep being a late arrival, if at all, in the know.

The Daylight-Saving Kettle of Fish

At the last minute, the political scribes highlighted a nice kettle of fish stewing over daylight saving time that may have been cooked to order.

Was this mess heated up and served as a clever distraction . . . . . a sort of mental sidetrack . . . . to keep the voters from becoming aware, before the election, and thus identifying that one contest in it, the treasurership, and keeping them from first seeing that the contest between E. Burt and CPD was the real horse race?

During the finalizing of arrangements for the primaries, state authorities had ruled that opening and closing hours of the polls should conform to the time in the individual voting districts. Now, a week before the day of the primary, the board of elections in Owego passed along such information. Residents of the county were asked to study the announced primary election voting hours carefully to determine the type of time their particular voting district would be observing, and it was pointed out that the applicable time standards did not always conform with the boundaries of the subject election districts. Nevertheless, the time was set by districts. That's why voters were reminded to pay extra close attention to their voting-day hours, in other words the type of time to be observed in their respective districts. Some districts would be operating on daylight saving time, while other districts would be announcing their voting schedule in terms of standard time! For instance, in the town of Barton—my father's 1930 vote-getting stronghold where in 1939 some sort of repeat was to be expected of the sixteen-unmarked-ballot ploy (that had taken place during the freak recount)—districts one through five would be open from twelve noon to nine P.M. on daylight time while districts six, seven and eight in the rural areas would operate during the same hours but on standard time! All districts in the towns of Berkshire, Beegildale, Tioga, Newark Valley, and Nichols would be open on standard time. But the town of Springdale (monikered from *Small Town in Mass Society*) and the 1930 E. Burt vote-getting stronghold of Owego (that had freakishly been treated as a sacred cow in 1930 and thus had escaped recount that would have been favorable to CPD) would be operating their voting districts divided between standard and daylight times. Districts two, three and ten in the town of Owego and districts two, three and four in Springdale would also observe standard time. In bizarre contrast, districts one, four, five, six, seven, eight and nine in the town of Owego, along with districts one and five in Springdale, would observe daylight time. In the far northwest corner of the county, the town of Spencer would also observe daylight time.

How would this confusion over time affect my father's campaign for the treasurership? Our best guess is this. Were anyone to figure out how to benefit from all of this confusion that might well arise over time and boundaries, it would more likely be E. Burt's side, as the Senator-led GOP clique could use the time confusion to distract any on-the-fence voters who might be commencing to take note that for the treasurership, a horse race under the wraps was flowering. Such a distraction over standard and daylight time would also help voters who remembered the freak recount of 1930 to forget the whys and the wherefores that would otherwise have reminded them that they had then been victimized, now leading them back to casting very certain votes for the unaware George Washington V. But the presence of this daylight-saving kettle of fish meant that some sure votes for CPD, thanks to the confuddlement, might get swept up by E. Burt's last-minute, door-to-door push, especially in Waverly.

A Clambake by Rotarians Looks Like an E. Burt Play for Waverly

During the last full week before the September 1939 GOP primary election, E. Burt was still striving to erase my father's 1930 lead that he'd then—nine years earlier—displayed in most of the *town* of Barton. In its GHQ, the *village* of Waverly, the incumbent, who was also a past president of the Owego Rotarians, was attempting to get the jump on my father by tying in his door-to-door with a clambake. It was held by around eighty Rotarians and guests from clubs whose coverage included the *town* of Barton area, in turn taking in, as previously mentioned, the *village* of Waverly. Although the bake took place westerly of Waverly across the line in Chemung County at Spring Water Park, the successful event's timing was perfect for some politicking that may have influenced the horse race suppressed in the print media, yet still unfolding, for the treasurer's post in Tioga County.

A program of softball and quoits was featured. Following the sports events, the clambake was served under the direction of Tunney Meade. Floyd Beers of the Waverly Rotary Club was chairman of the arrangements, and was assisted by Stan Harris and Jim Davenport, both of Sayre, where the out-of-state daily was soon to provide some critical last-minute political advertising skulduggery by which E. Burt would attempt to gain winning votes just as the covered-up horse race would then be approaching the finish line.

At this most significant outing staged by Rotarians, was E. Burt of the Owego club a featured and oft-pointed-out guest? While the print media didn't say so, his presence was an inferred certainty. Moral of the story: If you want to attempt to pick up some extra added county-level votes from Waverly, get the Rotarians going for you, especially if you're a past prexy of the Owego club.

The Proposed Rural Fire District: More Canvassers Galavant

Sayre's daily, although it was located southerly and just outside of the Waverly area in the southwesterly corner of Tioga County, nevertheless, just before the GOP primary, seemed to be taking an extra special interest in political affairs just north of the border in the Empire State.

A public hearing was slated on Monday (six days after the upcoming GOP primary) at the town hall at Tioga Center.

The issue: Whether to establish a rural fire district in the town of Tioga. It was located on the north side of the Susquehanna River, and spread out between the town of Owego on the east and the town of Barton on the west. This latter town (with its important village of Waverly) adjoined Pennsylvania's highly populated Sayre-Athens area and it was the Sayre daily that provided pre-primary coverage concerning the town of Tioga's seemingly unrelated proposed fire district. "Petitions representing $384,200 in property assessments have been presented to the Tioga town board. If the petitions are found to be in order and resident taxpayers vote in favor of the formation of the district, the town board will take steps towards its formation."

On the surface this looked like another relatively minor municipal development. But beneath the surface the implied issue relating to the otherwise unmentionable horse race for the treasurership was probably this: Who were the canvassers galavanting to get such petitions signed? The Senator had been born on a farm there. Thus were most of the people soliciting signatures partisans of Senator-backed E. Burt, you could expect him to carry the town of Tioga. Conversely, CPD had duly impressed the locals during more recent years when he had engineered the changeover of a creamery to an operating feed mill there. Were most of the petition circulators on my father's side, the unaware George Washington V would probably triumph in the town of Tioga. This surfacing of a seemingly unrelated issue—whether to create a rural fire district—brought up another mystery which, for its possibly planned side effects, would have to await Tuesday's election returns.

The Whispering Campaign

As the last weekend before the election approached, a new note surfaced that seemed to signify desperation in the Senator-led GOP clique that was supporting E. Burt. Timed to peak on election Eve (Monday, September 18) was this, of all things . . . . a whispering campaign. As it spread rumors like wildfire, although E. Burt himself lived in a glass house—one, needless to say, that my father and his friends never chose to attack—it was all to the advantage of E. Burt and his Senator-led backers to let the whispering campaign gain momentum.

This last-minute whispering campaign was based on the surprise haymaker that had boomeranged (detailed in the preceding volume) at Sheldon Court in College Town in Ithaca more than two and a half years earlier. At that time, during some horseplay, Deke, a classmate who also hailed from Owego, and your Virginian, along with a chap named Jockey Joe from Jersey, were all supposed to be watching a skit being put on by one Mercer as he brandished an ancient musket in imitation of Barney Google. Deke, although he was wearing glasses, when I had been looking the other way, had hauled off and socked me (just as I was turning to ask him how he liked the show), giving me a black eye. Instantly, although Deke and I were good friends from high school and Sunday school days, I'd been unable to stop myself from turning into an instant boomerang and delivering, as it had thus been so surprisingly triggered, the return haymaker that had inflicted, most accidentally and unfortunately on Deke (who just happened to have his glasses on), a much greater injury—the loss of an eye.

How come Deke had socked me when I wasn't looking? As a later analysis would indicate, some anonymous political occultist in Owego had influenced Deke's father to so advise Deke to look for and then exploit such an opening should more horseplay (by which all of us except Mercer had been targeted at one time or another) ensue. And to further illustrate the closeness of our relationship with the heart and soul of our home town of Owego, upstairs over the Main Street Bank (where E. Burt was cashier) were the good offices (rented from the bank) of Owego's leading life insurance sales agency where one of that nationwide company's foremost and best-known life insurance salesmen was Deke's father.

Now, just over two and a half years after the surprise haymaker that boomeranged, the last-minute whispering campaign against my father (and thus for the political benefit of E. Burt) noised it around that your unaware George Washington VI had struck the first blow.

The truth was that Deke had landed the first haymaker, laying the mouse on my mug when I wasn't looking. Besides reversing the sequence of the twin haymakers, the last-minute whispering campaign grossly puffed up what little means there were of my father's small-town wealth (when its relative insignificance was illustrated by his feelings that he couldn't afford to send his only son to medical school or to law school), making those who'd believe such bandied-about falsifications think that my father was some sort of a small-town millionaire. Once The Big Lie had laid the basis, the diffusion implemented the making of political hay for E. Burt by clouding up the settlement of Deke's hospital bill that had grown out of the return blow when his opener had boomeranged.

Although the whispering campaign implemented a door-to-door sale of pots and pans, and was deliberately timed at the last minute to prevent rebuttal by my father's side, the truth about the hospital bill was this: contrary to the whispers my father did pay it, but, on advice of counsel, had paid it as part of a later transaction during which settlement papers were signed and exchanged. But the family story that never outed was this. Just a few months before the surprise haymaker that had boomeranged, my father had confiscated my $500 chicken-money nest egg that had included monies inherited from my grandfather. Such exchange of settlement papers was thereafter used by my father as his prime excuse for not returning to me such seed money, the lack of which was now preventing me from buying a car to opt for the traveling salesman's job with the Sheaffer Pen Company. What had been tough on Deke physically was also tough on your Virginian, but economically and, even more importantly, psychologically. Although the boomerang end of the exchange was a *fait accompli*, I had always felt that fate had trapped me into being part of such an unwanted reaction. And when these current goings-on would likely effect a withholding by my father of any future encouragement for my going to med school or law school, I realized that the only way out was to grin and bear the damage.

Now, back to the whispering campaign. It had compartments. The final one even dragged in my mother. The whispers attacked her for having only sent Deke's mother—after Deke had been injured by the boomerang his first blow had triggered—a card of sympathy when my mother, the whisperers claimed, should have done more (no specific suggestions being allowed to surface). The truth was that my mother had wanted to do more but had had nobody to advise her on just what would have been acceptable. Deke's mother and my mother were both very fine ladies and members of the same Baptist Sunday school class. But during the weeks before the disaster of the swapped haymakers had struck—just when I'd been

trying to induce Deke's father to go along with the idea, and had
been urging my father to bring Deke's father up to Ithaca so that
the four of us, the two fathers and the two sons, could attend together a Cornell varsity intercollegiate basketball game at the Drill
Hall—normal lines of communication had been broken down by
the accident. Deeply disturbed by the misleading rumors even then,
my mother was afraid to send flowers lest they be returned. So
that's how come she had mailed Deke's mother a card of sympathy. It had been, of course, one of the best and nicest cards available and it had been sent in a sealed envelope.

Now, more than two a half years after the incident orbiting
Deke's boomeranged haymaker, the whispering campaign to help
E. Burt was denigrating this sympathy card, by which my mother
had then attempted to keep open the lines of communication between her ladies' Sunday school friend and herself.

Since such a whispering campaign had been mounted at the
last minute, my father had no time to counter it. Otherwise, if he'd
had time, he could have seen to it that in the news columns or else
in a political advertisement, the whispering campaign was identified and explained away. Furthermore (had there been time), my
father could have called on both E. Burt and his mentor, the Senator, to refute publicly the contents of the whispers, and to deny
their presumed part, if any, in them. Finally, my father could have
answered and explained away the whispers point by point. But with
time running out, E. Burt picked up votes.

E. Burt's Final Sting: Surprise Political Ads in the Sayre Daily

On the eve of the primary election came some pettifoggery by
E. Burt. Instead of sticking to Tioga County's available Tuesday
and Thursday weeklies, he took a cue from Waverly's two contestants for DA. Since they resided in the circulation area, both Surfranc and Senior Rep ran political ads in the Sayre daily. From just
south of the state line, it covered Waverly as well as the contiguous
Pennsylvania area. While their respective ads were honest and

forthright or timed sufficiently in advance to allow a fair rebuttal, not so with E. Burt's.

Nine years earlier, although E. Burt had won the freak recount at CPD's expense, E. Burt had been glad to benefit from my father's "No Hard Feelings" letter that had been published on the front page of Owego's GOP weekly. Without it, the Democrat would have defeated E. Burt in the 1930 November general election.

Would E. Burt show this appreciation? No. Already, after his friendly GOP notables in the Owego Old Guard had hoaxed CPD to wait nine years to run again, E. Burt, contrary to the planted misleading rumors, had failed to take his three terms of three years each and call it quits. Not long after he had announced for his fourth three-year term, he had pulled out all of the stops when surreptitious soundings indicated that CPD was going to win. Now for E. Burt's final sting.

Incidentally, this out-of-state political advertising ploy was surfacing in the same Pennsylvania Congressional district which in November 1914 had seen the Washington "Spoiler" Party curiously usurp the anti-Republican banner from my father's father—Fred W. Dean as Democrat—to thereby ease Louis McFadden, the Republican, into Congress. So now, almost twenty-five years later, a daily in that same Pennsylvania area was helping pull off a slightly different political trick on my father. For openers, it ran a political ad by E. Burt. There was a good picture of E. Burt's very acceptable Anglo-Saxon mug. The ad itself asked voters to mark line nine for him on upcoming Tuesday's ballot.

For some background, we first explain: were the unaware George Washington V to win, the county would have to furnish him with an office. Bandying this new-expense factor about had been another of E. Burt's political ploys. E. Burt, though, had been operating out of Owego's other bank, where he was employed as cashier. Stressing that he, E. Burt, was thus saving the taxpayers' money, some of this out-of-state advertising copy that his mentor—the Senator—had perhaps helped inspire went like this:

First: E. Burt, referring to his having been honchoing the treasurership out of Owego's other bank, addressed the poor, overburdened, put-upon taxpayer. . . . . . "Overloaded with taxes, now, a hard winter coming on, the profiteers busy with sugar and foodstuffs, and war in the air, it is a poor time to increase county expenses,"—E. Burt. in the out-of-state daily, and with such last-minute timing so that my father had no time to rebut it, kicked it off.

Next: E. Burt, but without coming right out and saying so, stressed his operation of the treasurership out of free office space at his cashier's post in Owego's other bank. . . . . . "Why have to equip a new office and pay rent and upkeep? [With E. Burt's employer bank were placed the county deposits but, in contrast to the 1930 E. Burt-CPD campaign, this factor now continued to go unmentioned.] Stamps and stationery are your only expenses now. You have service, efficiency and convenience now. Why change?"

Thus did E. Burt use this political-propaganda springboard from the southerly environs, leaping into the area of the village of Waverly and town of Barton through the print media of the Sayre, Pennsylvania daily . . . . and on the Friday before election.

And how cleverly did my father's opponent put it, saying it in a way that kept the voters from the realization that for nine years E. Burt had worked in his treasurership, salting away his substantial per-annum salary while living off the pay provided by his cashier's post at Owego's other bank which, in turn, had the advantage of the county deposits.

After scoring such points on the weekend before Tuesday's election, E. Burt (who would eventually leave an estate substantially larger than CPD's), closing out his out-of-state ad, said: "Vote Row 9 for Continued Economy."

Keeping the mishmash perking, on Saturday in the same out-of-state daily, E. Burt repeated substantially the same message. He was joined with another mate from the Senator-led GOP political stable—Senior Rep (who'd worked his way through school playing the saxophone with bands in the Adirondacks and on cruise ships turning around at North Cape). For DA, the musicians association ran a political advertisement giving the laying on of hands to Senior Rep as opposed to Surfranc.

For a little sidelight on upcoming GOP events, in the same out of-state issue, it was announced that between Tuesday's upcoming primary and the November general election, there was slated to take place a big Republican dinner at the Iron Kettle Restaurant at Waverly. Key speakers would be Chauncey B. Hammond of Elmira as GOP state senatorial candidate, accompanied by Martin Deyo of Binghamton, former state senator.

Now back to E. Burt's last-minute sting. As we finally arrive at the eve of Tuesday's GOP primary election, here come the out-of-state political ads to their climax. While my father, who was based twenty miles or so easterly at Owego (and who was normally accessing the voters through the weekly print media), had been taken by surprise and thus had been unable to counterattack in the Sayre out-of-state daily, not so with Surfranc. Based on Sayre's northerly environs but across the line in the state of New York in the village of Waverly, Surfranc, on election eve, ran an excellent political ad in the Sayre daily spelling out his rebuttal to voters that as incumbent he had not exceeded his salary budget as had been suggested in a political ad that Senior Rep had published in the Springdale weekly. Thus did Surfranc exhibit his skills as one of the Yankee Tier's leading PR wizards.

But what about E. Burt's final sting? The kicker that surfaced by secrecy and surprise in the election eve issue of the out-of-state daily was most cleverly timed by E. Burt. To this emotional issue now raised by his opponent, the unaware George Washington V would not have the time to respond. The final sting in the daily repeated E. Burt's picture along with his previous politically advertised points. But generating the final sting, E. Burt now added some first-rate pettifoggery that was liable to dig envious skulls for some critical votes. E. Burt's last-minute points interlocked with his wealth-stressing element of the ongoing whispering campaign against my father like this: "My opponent says he needs the job and it should be passed around. He has three jobs now and plenty of means. You can't deny the mortgage records and tax rolls. They are public records and authentic. Make E. Burt Number 9 on the Ballot Your Republican Candidate for County Treasurer."

Before the general election nine years earlier, in November 1930, my father, at the behest of the county GOP chairman, Old Dingle, had done E. Burt a great political favor. Thus by E. Burt's current PR skulduggery of the last-minute, out-of-state political ads did my father (whose three jobs were small and paid relatively low salaries) get paid back with such E. Burt pettifoggery. CPD didn't have time to answer.

It wasn't so much that this last out-of-state misleading political ad was the result of E. Burt's running scared silly; more at the heart of things were the secret feelings of the majority of the Owego Old Guard backing E. Burt. Were CPD to win, their having caused the sacrifices of the county judgeship and the DAship (from

Owego to Waverly) would go for naught. The members of the Owego Old Guard who had been so successfully manipulated by the E. Burt faction would look like fools!

Owego Ladies' Legion Auxiliary Works on Waverly Sisters

Gong back to CPD's 1930 election campaign, after the freak recount had done its damage, and after the whole thing was over, my father had learned that a large segment of E. Burt's votes in the village of Owego had come from the American Legion.

But for this election in 1939, the men of the Legion appeared to be keeping a low profile. After all, both E. Burt and CPD had never served with the Armed Forces. So this time the Legion's E. Burt partisans appeared to be working through the ladies. Objective: target CPD's traditional vote-getting strength in Waverly.

On the same election eve that the whispering campaign against my father was reaching its high point, a dinner at the Marble Bar in the village of Owego was being held jointly by the ladies of the American Legion auxiliary from Waverly and Owego.

Curiously, the announcement, gleaned during research for this saga, came from south of the border. This meant that the significance of the ladies' powwow passed relatively unnoticed in Owego. It was *The Evening Times* of Sayre, Pennsylvania, that announced on Friday, September 15, "Members of [Waverly's] Betowski Van De Mark American Legion Auxiliary have been invited to attend a dinner and installation of the Owego Auxiliary on Monday night [election eve!] at the Marble Bar at 6:30 P.M.

"Installation follows in the Owego auxiliary's rooms. Mrs. Ella Saphar [a contingent county-level political plum-holder] of Waverly, Tioga County American Legion Auxiliary president, will be in charge of installation. [In later years, she would exclaim, 'Oh, E. Burt. He did a door-to-door in Waverly!']

"All local [Waverly-area] members wishing to attend are asked to contact Mrs. Fred Pittsley."

To the uninitiated, its timing (with E. Burt's misleading political ad in the same out-of-state issue) looked like a happenstance. Hardly. While one of the Waverly lady leaders was probably on E. Burt's side, there was a slim chance that another lady of political substance from Waverly might have been on CPD's side. But going back to 1930, were our findings then of CPD preponderance there in Waverly to have carried over until now, the Owego ladies' mission at the Marble Bar would more likely have been to work on their Waverly sisters with some quiet campaigning for E. Burt, in particular, to build up his previously lagging political strength in the Town of Barton. So went another of the various and sundry gatherings of the mixed bag of seeming nonpolitical groups, yet much more likely timed to be factored in with the crescendo of the whispering campaign to the detriment of CPD and to the benefit of E. Burt.

The Results: Media Plays the Horse Race, But Only in Passing

Because it would have generated vote-getting sympathies for an unaware George Washington V during the campaign, the print media had balked at giving newspaper readers any substantial review of the freak recount of 1930. And this even though CPD's initial six-vote victory in the 1930 primary was best illustrative of the closest horse race in recent years. In a comparative sense, what better to talk about? The sacrifice by the Owego Old Guard of a county judgeship to Waverly in 1936.

Now, back to CPD's second try for the treasurership. It was Wednesday, September 20, one day after the GOP's four-race primary. On the preceding evening, a "Hear ye. Hear ye. The polls are now closed," had put the tally-takers to work in the big room on the main floor at the southeasterly corner of Owego's tall Georgian courthouse. The first publication of results in a weekly would have to wait until Thursday, September 21. Thus did *The Evening Times,* because it was a daily, first deliver the scoop, but from south of the border.

The Sayre, Pennsylvania, daily that had helped keep the estimates of the real horse race (between E. Burt and CPD) covered up, now that the returns showed the actuality, buried it. On the daily's *last* page, the headline read: "Surfranc and E. Burt Both Carry [the town of] Barton." (Because historically, it was the source of CPD's principal strength this was the more critical of the county's two major towns, Owego being the other.)

Subhead No. 1 read: "Town Republican Primary Vote is Second Largest on Record. . . ." Then subhead No. 2 named a couple of candidates for posts other than for county treasurer and DA who'd taken small but clear-cut advantages.

Under a Waverly dateline, the political yarn in the Sayre daily, still holding back information that would focus on the real horse race, said: "Surfranc and E. Burt were the chief gainers in a near record breaking *town* of Barton Republican primary vote yesterday.

"More than thirteen hundred Republicans cast ballots, the second highest primary total in the *town's* history.

"In the contest for Tioga County DA nomination between two *village* of Waverly men, Attorney Surfranc [against Attorney Senior Rep] carried *all* eight districts to gain a margin of 383 votes. For the *town* of Barton, Surfranc had a total of 864 votes to Senor Rep's 481."

(Thus did the Waverly home town boy, the personable Irishman—Surfranc—show the relative newcomer—Senior Rep—just exactly who was The Boss.)

Next for a big first, there appeared some details on the GOP primary race for the county treasurership. Continued the Sayre daily. . . ."Carrying seven out of eight districts (in the *town* of Barton) E. Burt rolled up a total of 736 to 532 for Clifford P. Dean. . . . [the differential being 204]."

It was thus thanks to what carryover there may have been from the *town* and *village* of Owego—where the whispering campaign had been launched—to Barton *town* with its *village* of Waverly, together with the trickery of E. Burt's misleading political advertisements in the out-of-state daily just before the election and circulated into Barton town from just south of the state line, that these devious moves together with other previously mentioned ploys, had well done their work. Partly as a result, E. Burt now in 1939 had won crucial votes in the *town* of Barton even though nine years earlier, the pro-Dean turnout in such Waverly area had turned the tide, generating my father's then six-vote initial (pre-freak recount) GOP primary victory.

For an editorial crutch (that kept the voting public from getting its recollection refreshed about the slick details of the freak recount of 1930, the Sayre daily, for its last paragraph of its last-page yarn concluded: "Yesterday's *town* of Barton Republican vote was exceeded *only* in the 1936 primary vote when Edward W. Eaton of Waverly was seeking nomination for county judge and Attorney Surfranc was seeking, for the first time, his present post of DA." (No mention was made that the Senator, E. Burt's mentor and one of Owego's political bigwigs, had made the 1936 contest over the woolsack a three-way, thus siphoning off enough votes to let Eaton in.)

While any resurrection in the print media of the freak recount of October 1930 was still taboo, the out-of-state daily, in a first-rate diversionary tactic, had thus reminded its readers of that curious primary race, not for the treasurership in 1930 but rather for a somewhat later GOP nomination for the county judgeship, a 1936 contest that had seen Boilerplate supplanted for the benefit of Waverly.

The suggestive picture of the give-up by Owego for the political fleshing out of Waverly, effectively scrubbed any remembrances of the six-year-earlier freak recount.

Now—on the day *after* the September 1939 GOP primaries—it came time for the out-of-state daily to get around to "discovering" that, for the county treasurership, there'd just been a horse race. On the *last* page, for the Sayre daily's second political yarn, the subhead gave the first hint that the media was playing the horse race . . . but only in passing: "Surfranc And E. Burt Both Win, But The Latter's Margin Is Narrow Over Dean For GOP Fall Ticket."

With that, the unaware George Washington V, to wit: the otherwise played-down Clifford P. Dean (CPD), finally, for a moment, broke into a subhead.

Until now, the print media, ignoring the existence of the horse race, had featured other contests. But now, on the day *after* the primaries, the cat was out of the bag. For DA, as previously mentioned, Surfranc, Waverly's native son, had carried all eight districts in the town of Barton to receive almost double the votes of a more recent settler—Senior Rep. Surfranc then had gone on to handily win the countywide GOP primary election. Very definitely this had been no horse race. For sheriff, Douglas Grant, although he had run third in the *town* of Barton, had won by a substantial margin the countywide election. Likewise, there had been no horse race here. Same with Charles Haywood (who incidentally, early on, had requested unsuccessfully that my father join political forces with him), who had won by a substantial enough margin so that there'd been no horse race there. Horse races were hard to find . . . except . . .

In the daily's second political yarn (on the same page) that followed the aforesaid subhead, but still without mentioning it as such, the out-of-state daily, while doing everything but spell it out, "discovered" the existence of the horse race. After the Waverly dateline, the Sayre daily was the first to out with it: *"Closest contest of the day* was between Clifford P. Dean and E. Burt, incumbent, both of Owego, for the county treasurer's nomination with E. Burt finally winning by a plurality of about one hundred."

From your Virginian's current Midwestern viewpoint, this was the first publication of the bad news. It would take some time for me to first read of it in a letter from home. But for you all to ruminate on: there in the Sayre, Pennsylvania, out-of-state daily, the buried-yet-big admission of tight narrowness grudgingly and sadly appeared.

In 1930, before the freak recount, my father had won his countywide six-vote GOP primary victory with 1,192 votes to E. Burt's 1,186. This time, thanks to his door-to-door in the *village* of Waverly, bolstered with the whispering campaign and the chicanery of his last-minute, out-of-state political advertisements, and other artifices and stratagems as mentioned, E. Burt as winner had 2,348 votes to 2,239 for my father in thirty-one election districts. "Votes in the one absent district in the town of Tioga will not be great enough to make any difference in the winner of this contest," said the out-of-state daily.

It then explained: "In his close battle with Dean, E. Burt owed his victory to the margin given him by the *town* of Barton where he had 736 [pre-1930 freak recount: 281] votes to Dean's 532 [pre-1930 freak recount: 391]." (The 204-vote differential was crucial in current 1939 favoring E. Burt, based as it was, in part, on the skulduggery evidenced in E. Burt's out-of-state, last-minute political advertisements and other stratagems.)

In contrast to 1930 when E. Burt received seventy percent, now, in 1939, and in spite of the whispering campaign that had been centered in Owego, the Sayre daily, continuing to ignore the 1930 horse race for the treasurership, went on: "In Owego the vote favored E. Burt *only narrowly* with a total of 851 to 812. [Out of Tioga County's nine *towns*] Dean carried five towns [Springdale—Boilerplate's home base, where Jones of *Small Town* was one of CPD's good friends—then, Newark Valley, Beegildale, Spencer and Nichols] to the winner's four [Owego, Barton, Tioga—where the 'rural fire district' canvassing as mentioned, must have worked—and Berkshire] but they [those towns won by my father] were those where the vote was much smaller than in Barton or Owego," explained the Sayre daily.

From the standpoint of growing good will, a big plus surfaced for CPD. In the face of the Senator-led segment of the Owego Old Guard, my father's Owego area political strength had increased in our home town. For instance, in 1930 (when E. Burt's people had harped that CPD's ten years as a resident wasn't enough) my father had received around thirty percent of the Owego vote. Now, in 1939, this percentage had soared to almost fifty. Had effective public relations steps (skills or access to which we all then simply didn't possess) been taken to give a 1939 airing to the 1930 freak recount, my father would have won Owego and then would have gone on to win the countywide election.

Two days *after* the GOP primary election of September 1939, Owego's Democratic Thursday weekly got its first chance to report on the results of Tuesday's GOP primary. Here's how the Lake Street sheet made the "discovery" that there'd been a horse race. Helping keep the attentions of the voting public focused away from the potential resurrection of the freak recount of October 1930 had been the outbreak of World War II. Making much of it, Owego's weekly on Lake Street said: "A week ago the cloud of the European war was believed to have overshadowed the Republican primary contests in Tioga County because not much excitement was in evidence.

"No one [not much!] expected the battle of ballots on Tuesday [September 19, 1939] to be much of an engagement."

Then, perhaps alluding in part to the chicanery of the out-of-state political advertisements by E. Burt and the people selling pots and pans door to door by whose political misstatements the

winner had also benefited, Owego's Lake Street weekly went on:
"A few days before the election, this [no-excitement] belief was
rudely brushed aside. Political advertisements [no details mentioned as my father's ads had been according to Hoyle while E.
Burt's had frothed up with skulduggery aimed at creating envy]
screamed the merits of each of the candidates in the four contests
[DA, sheriff, county treasurer and county clerk]. Mail carriers groaned
under the barrage of political letters suddenly unleashed. *At the last
minute, a whispering campaign was let loose against one of the candidates.*"

With that punch line, the 1939 campaign over GOP nomination
for the treasurership was buried by the Owego weeklies. Successfully handling the wet-blanket for the GOP, this Thursday Democratic weekly had omitted mention of some crucial issues. Why
hadn't the freak recount of 1930 been resurrected? Why hadn't the
real horse race been featured?

Once again, in such a way that the handling of the post-elec-
tion PR could be attributed to the Democratic weekly, the Owego
Old Guard, whose Tuesday GOP weekly, by having kept clammed
up on what could have been my father's winning points, left out
details of the nine-year-old freak recount.

But in any event, by the time the print media got around to
"discovering" that there had been a horse race larruped by a whispering campaign, it was too late! Primarily because the story of the
freak recount of 1930 had thusly been suppressed, nine years later,
but with a different kind of twist, the Senator-backed E. Burt did
it again!

For your Virginian in Michigan, this fatherly loss back in the
Yankee Tier of the Empire State not only put the quietus (at least
for the time being) on law school, but it also hiked my sense of
urgency to make good with Monkey's.

Unnoticed at the time, the perpetrators of all of these political
injustices on the unaware George Washington V were getting a good
but unseen dose of poetic justice. In order to cause all of this trouble, the Senator-led faction of the Owego Old Guard had had to
give up Owego's traditional grip on the county judgeship and the
DAship, relinquishing both posts to Waverly.

When would Owegoans exercise their historic county-seat power
to get these jobs back? Decades longer than they dreamed!

Chapter 3

Back Burner For Law School; Monkey's Up Front

Election Repercussions and Contrasts of Family Backing

Summer had just turned into autumn. At Monkey's Ann Arbor retail store, I was sweating out the result of my father's second try in nine years for the county treasurership. Finally, on Saturday evening after dinner, four days after the belatedly discovered horse race (that the newshawks had played on, but only in passing), I got behind my typewriter and petitioned my parents: "I would at least like to know who won the election. I have been expecting a letter from you concerning it. Since I've received no message, I assume that Dad lost. Anyway I want you to tell me about it."

From Mother's viewpoint, other matters of greater importance seemed to have intervened. She had told the Ann Arbor Baptist minister to drop in at the store. Responding one Sunday to his invite, I made my appearance. As I later clued in my mother by mail: "The congregation here has a fine gentleman for a preacher. He's about thirty years of age and has been here for only a few weeks and hails from Seattle, Washington."

"It's time for lots of harvest suppers back here at home," my mother reminded me. "Don't forget. They're usually at churches. You'll get good dinners there. So be sure to go to some there in Michigan."

"They don't have any church suppers here *that I know about* and my job with Ward's is keeping me so busy with such long hours that even if I did discover some such dinners, I wouldn't have time for them anyway," I wrote in reply.

But what about the treasurership? After I'd made my urgent request for news about the GOP primary, my parents left me on the anxious seat just long enough so that I sensed that the result of the election hadn't been good. Then a letter arrived in which my mother, but only in passing, mentioned that misleading and unfair last-minute political chicanery in the out-of-state daily had swung a very narrow victory for the Senator-sparked incumbent. To your unaware George Washington VI, what a tremendous letdown was this political loss by my father, and in particular I felt a lot of pain over CPD's opponent's having unabashedly gone about winning by use of crucial dirty tricks. Reverberating from the Yankee Tier to the Midwest, such of the opposition's artifices meant: Forget law school. Concentrate on your career with Monkey's.

The misleading out-of-state political advertisements, coming as they did nine years after the freak recount, left one salient point etched in my mind. A mystery remained to be solved. I knew that there must be some secret motive behind the treachery. How to figure it out? One thing was clear. Any possible dismasking of the forces behind the puppeteers would require a lot more observations and studies on the part of your unaware George Washington VI, but only the passing of decades would let me know that the setting down for you all on paper of this saga would provide the finishing touches.

At this time, five years has passed since Jimmy Patton, when home on vacation from Centre College, had declared Israel Dean to be George Washington's son. And about five months had passed since my good rowing friend True Davis had confirmed it. Yet it would take me twenty-eight years to realize that our family's ancestor was the real Israel.

Had my father won, it was likely that he would have changed his attitude and encouraged me to go to law school. But now that I was also victimized, but only indirectly, all that I now could do

for my father (when he lost on the second time around to E. Burt—
Dad also being victimized) was to feel sorry for him. Although I
had a strong hunch that I would eventually get to the bottom of
the opposition's skulduggery, never did I realize the decades that
it would take me to first dig up and review the salient details and
then write up the political hornswoggling in the light of a secret
political-genealogical motive.

This 1939 primary, as mentioned, was tantamount to winning
the general election in November. Once E. Burt would soon be
returned by dirty tricks to the treasurership, in spite of all of that
skulduggery, my father, as always, as he got on with "minding his
own business," would simply roll with the low blows. But these
psychological wallops, whomps, cuts, slices, and chops kept me out
of current professional school.

What if my father had won the election? Thanks to the added
source of salary, CPD might well have shucked his policy of discouraging his only son from going to professional school. But now
that the possibility of his election had been steered down the tube
to the tune of political artifices and fakements, as I looked to my
father for some sort of encouragement to take up legal studies, it
was an obvious case of: "Forget it." Furthermore, there was little
chance that my father would ever return my $500 chicken-money
nest egg with which I could buy a car and then still go after the
traveling salesman's job with the fountain pen company. But on a
more serious vein, back to the subject of graduate school: had I
pursued plans previously disregarded, already I was losing out on
what otherwise might have been my first year of law school or
a nice retry for medical school. But that election had put the icing
on the cake. The bugle call sounded. Face reality. So I was left
with no choice but to conclude: Law school was relegated to the
back burner.

What a contrast when it came to E. Burt and his only son who'd
given Cornell a two-year go right after the Kaiser's war. Would E.
Burt ever have loved it had his only son asked for and received
backing for any undergraduate degree. Further support for graduate work would have been an obvious yes-yes. Instead, E. Burt's
only son concentrated on living up the best of the available social
life. What better place than Owego!

But getting back to the contrast with my contemporary peers

such as Si Glann, Abacanocus and Young Dingle, in that order. On their fox farm, Si's folks were scraping the bottom of the barrel to see to it that he kept on with his legal studies, simultaneously supporting a wife and child. Since Abacanocus' father was already an established lawyer, the boy magician had always had unquestionable backing. As an undergraduate, he had been elected president of his fraternity. Recently he had graduated from Cornell Law School, then had passed the reputedly tough New York State bar examination. Already his father's one-man office had blossomed with the new name: Abacanocus and Abacanocus. And now succeeding in his final year of law school was Young Dingle. He hadn't wanted to be a lawyer. But his father, although he wasn't considered to be a man of wealth, had seen to it that his younger son didn't have any choice. Tossed in to this illustration for good measure, Old Dingle's older son, Junior Dingle, now a Cornell graduate employed by Heetreet's local engineering firm, was on a commercial sales junket demonstrating rail anchors and track oilers for lines carrying the important choo-choos of Central America.

While my contemporaries such as Si, Young Dingle, and Ab were getting to be lawyers, in contrast, your Virginian saw his father who actually was a man of substance, keeping right on acting out a thumbs-down attitude toward his only son. If CPD silently blamed me for the whispering campaign, he still would have to acknowledge, that in spite of it, he had picked up votes very substantially percentagewise over 1930, right in our home town of Owego, one of the primary targets of the whispering campaign. This meant that many people had recognized the misfortune emanating from the college horseplay as being pretty well put to bed. Yet, if my father continued to lay his loss on me (and I could only guess), just as silently I blamed him for conning me out of my seed money (that con, without either of us realizing it, having grown out of my father's having been victimized by the political occultists' sneak bill of early 1935). But I didn't let such lack of encouragement and departure of my seed money get me down. To compensate for this feeling of great loss, I commenced to glow with enthusiasm over my chances to make it with Monkey's. It was time to try to meet the expectations that had been laid down and spelled out orally during the initial successful job interview. To see about making myself more like the hypothetical trainee depicted by our regional manager, George Moore, I let the shock waves emanating from the Yankee Tier set me up behind my typewriter, where I knocked out a serious letter to my favorite brunette.

A Nice Try to Match George Moore's Ideal Trainee

That nice spring day at the Onondaga Hotel in Syracuse, when George Moore, our regional manager, had hired Si Glann and me, he had outlined his ideal trainee: "You'll get married, settle down, and we'll try you out in various positions in our region." That bit about marriage was rich. It tied in with Howard Lee Davis' perfect young man in business, who had to at least have a girl. And these two particular trainees that visiting lecturer Davis had helped pre-condition for Monkey's (when we'd still been on campus) had provided George Moore with a mixed bag.

Si Glann, who was then married, by now not only had become a father but also had quit Ward's to return to law school. Si's double-barreled example was now implementing the prods from Howard Lee Davis and George Moore. The time had arrived for your Virginian to at least make a nice try at playing some catch-up in the matrimonial department.

Figuring on doing it Ward's way, as though to commit myself economically to the hands of the higher authorities, setting up a potential demonstration of my will to dedicate my life to merchandising for Monkey's, without my yet getting tipped off that during my absence one of her compatriots had taken over my hot spot on the inside track, I sent a Pullman ticket to the Indian Princess to come out and join me.

This letter I addressed to her desk in a prominent finishing school where she'd been consigned some two hundred miles farther east from the Yankee Tier (as the evidence would eventually surface), to break up a romance, not with your Virginian, but rather to shut her off, at least temporarily, from her compatriot.

To set up the split, for some coolant, her parents had been quick to raise the do-re-mi by selling a family heirloom (an expensive Impressionist painting, as we'd learn some decades later) and had bundled her off. Her reply that came in the mail soon laid the obvious on the wood: because she was so enrolled, she couldn't just simply pull up stakes to become a Michigander.

Although I had to face up to the practicalities, helping me ease the pain, Ken Boyer, one of Ward's department heads downstairs in housewares, would soon be giving me a clue as to how lucky I'd been that she'd hung tight.

To let the brass hats know that I'd taken a positive step toward fitting myself into the role model of the perfect trainee that I surmised they had etched in their noggins, I'd been in hopes that I would be able to send a positive matrimonial-type message to some of the big shots with whom I'd been corresponding at GHQ in Chicago. Besides George Moore, who managed operations in a wide area including Michigan, there was Bob Harrison, vice-president in charge of Ward's retail division. Then there was Mr. Robinson (who'd rowed on a winning Syracuse freshman crew at Poughkeepsie during the mid-twenties), now in charge of personnel. He and Moore, as I'd learned, had hired me. When I would drop them a line, but without mentioning my nice try that had flopped, from GHQ always came back the consensus: "Keep showing Ward's that you mean business and you will be sure to get opportunities."

So your Virginian, while falling short of factoring himself into the form of Monkey's sterotyped trainee, continued to buy their line . . . still sleeping single.

Some Inside Dope from the Delivery Clerk

Just after mid-September, Bosso McCarty announced: "Dean, you've completed your tour of duty at the warehouse and on the delivery truck. At this time, our fall merchandise has already commenced to pile in. On your first few days with us last July you worked in the receiving room. You started off by helping check in that big load of paint. But now I'm assigning you there to help Louie Sinelli, our receiving clerk, check in the rush of merchandise throughout the fall and until Christmas. And remember this: on everything that passes through your hands, you will mark the price.

With your active participation in the checking-in process, you will be getting some of the best training in your career with Ward's. Your work in the receiving room will etch in your mind the values of our complete line."

(It would do more than that. Years and years later, this confidence that I was now gaining at handling merchandise would enable me to succeed at a temporary sideline of self-employed purchasing agent, role-playing as my own contractor, rebuilding my own place in the country.)

Thanking Bosso for my new assignment, I entered the portals of the receiving room, where I saluted the gate-keeping delivery clerk in his stall. Then I got right to work with Sinelli. As receiving clerk, he was also assisted by a fine young lady. Mrs. D. was quick to let me know that she'd already earned a couple of year's credits at the university and was shooting for her degree in political economy. What a nifty trio we made as we kept the merchandise flowing expeditiously into the hands of the respective department heads. Getting in on the act, our gate-keeping delivery clerk, after lending his ears to my overexaggerated sense of duty to Monkey's, spoke up from his stall.

From behind the thin five-foot walls of the compartment that provided some small bit of privacy to his mini-bureau, once, during a lull, Wes Eisley (who saw to it that goods sold for delivery were properly recorded in his ledger, then loaded up, up, and away on Lyle Hurd's truck) let some inside dope come out from his few years of observations:

"Ben, I'll tell you the way you've got to do it . . ."

"Do what?" I asked.

"Get ahead with Ward's," said Eisley.

"You mean work your tail off?" I asked.

"Not that," said Eisley.

"How then?" I asked.

"About three years ago," explained Eisley, "we had this chap who'd occasionally make suggestions to the store's management. When the suggestion would be rejected, he'd catch the next train for Monkey's Chicago GHQ. In most cases, when he'd return, he'd have the authority to override the store's management and put his suggestion into operation."

"Where's he now? I want to meet him," I said.

"Off some place . . . he's an assistant manager or a store manager," said Eisley. "But I just wanted you to know about how he operated to make it with Monkey's," the delivery clerk clued me in.

"Fat chance for me to conjure up such angles now," I said.

"I mean, after you've been with Ward's a few years and have been moved around from store to store and have picked up so much expertise that bubbles of suggestions froth to the surface," said Eisley, "by then an aristocrat like you [Eisley liked to pull this one, particularly when I was doing old-clothes work.] will probably be having insights to hand them like there's no tomorrow."

I found it difficult to tell whether or not the astute delivery clerk was putting me on. Would your Virginian ever develop the punch to apply such inside dope? To answer that one (as Sinelli yelled "Let's get back to work."), your trainee would first have to figure out the ways and the means to enhance the flow of his intuitive juices.

The Wilmark Shoppers Draw Blood!

Next, let me tell you about the Wilmark shoppers. Not long after I'd stepped off the Pullman and into the real world of merchandising just after the Fourth of July, Teeter—who'd since been promoted and transferred—had warned of such clandestine shoppers. Now, during the fall, when I was temporarily assigned by Bosso to the basement sales floor, looking very much like ordinary customers, these Wilmark people suddenly and simultaneously shopped, as a team, the salient sections of the store.

Their trick was to catch the trainee when he was out of his assigned department, their objective being to trip him up over less-familiar merchandise.

One of them locked on to your unaware George Washington VI, who this time was also unaware that he was being clandestinely rated on paper for GHQ by such a shopper. So slickly unseen was the role of this shopper that for the life of me, out of the various customers I'd waited on during what had been an extra busy day, I couldn't even remember the customer who'd scored on the secret mission. While I'd properly rung up the sale, had counted back the change correctly, and had handed the clandestine shopper the cash register receipt, I'd been given low marks on such points as failing to sell up from Ward's lower-priced product to some higher-priced product. And while caught off base in housewares, I'd failed to make suggestions of related products for sale, etc. By luring your trainee out of his customary paint and sporting goods department, the clandestine shopper had caught your Virginian with his pants at half-mast.

First notice that a Wilmark shopper had tasted blood came with a summons from Bosso McCarty, who had then gone over with me the various points that had been checked off on the written report. For a day or so, after resolving not to be caught by a clandestine shopper again, I had all that I could do psyching myself back up out of the dumps. Unfortunately, advice on how to best avoid getting your blood drawn clandestinely by these Wilmark shoppers was not covered in *The Young Man in Business*. And I never thought to drop a line to tell Howard Lee Davis all about it. To help our latter-day trainees, our campus lecturer of yesteryear might well have considered issuing a supplement. And what about that nice little bit of correspondence I had going with Chicago GHQ? With this tricky beginning of a gradual reshaping of my feelings toward Monkey's, I forgot it.

Foster Adams: "I Thought I Heard a Chicken Sneeze!"

In spite of the successful sneakiness of the clandestine Wilmark operative, I was still temporarily assigned to the sales floor. While the janitor kept within earshot, the time had come for a couple of Ward's older hands to deliver to your Virginian some choice angles on chain-store life. Letting some salient comments all come out were those two department heads, as mentioned, Boyer and Silloway, respectively. Boyer, who'd operated his own tire store until one of the financial panics of the thirties had pulled the rug, kicked it off.

The housewares merchandising expert (who was about five-feet, seven-inches tall) looked up at me and said: "Dean, to get ahead with Ward's you've got to learn to see things to be done."

This was a surprise. After all, I was working all of the time, restocking counters, straightening up, and doing housekeeping chores when I wasn't waiting on customers. But, maybe, there was more. While I was caught at a loss for words, Boyer (now that it was much too late for me to commence my first year of law school) continued: "Did you ever think, Dean, that maybe this retail store merchandising life isn't what you're cut out for. Maybe you should be doing something for which you're better fitted?"

Boyer, although he failed to suggest, "For what?" perhaps had something there. But to me, by now, Ward's presented a challenge to succeed. Was I ever glowing with hustle and bustle and enthusiasm. As part of my program of keeping myself psyched up, at every opportunity I was putting in a big plug for Ward's future, meaning the careers under Pres. Sewell Avery of such other basement hustlers as Art Pennala and George Silloway. . . . any employee within earshot. But, perhaps, seeing through it, Boyer continued to press: "Maybe here's something else you ought to be working at. . . . law. . . . medicine . . . Did you ever consider any of these?"

I should have insisted that the housewares head spell out just what he meant, for instance, did he want me to go to work for the State Department? But I was so committed to Monkey's that I couldn't bring myself around to grill him. Nevertheless, it did come my turn. "Suppose that 'something else' *is* the case with me? What about you? Maybe you too are better fitted for something else," I made my point while Boyer seemed to acquiesce to my surmise. "If so, why don't you go do something else?" I asked the department manager of housewares. But, on that one, Boyer was primed: "You can but I can't," said Boyer, and with some little air of plaintiveness.

"What do you mean?" I found myself perplexed, but only for the moment.

Seeming to be counseling me in such a manner that it would stick, not to let myself get too pinned down too early, enlightening me, Boyer stressed: "You should consider yourself lucky not to have any.

"Any what?"

"I've got little mouths to feed."

Came the aperçu! Your Virginian got it: What Monkey's wanted—a trainee with little mouths to feed!

From a wing of the stage came a chuckle. It was our all-around handyman, Foster Adams. He was taking home his broom-pushing pay to help raise several children. Just now, missing nothing, he had kept working while staying tuned in.

Moments after Boyer's punch line and Foster's little laugh, the head of next-counter hardware, who'd had an ear cocked, took over the act. "You're not the first trainee to hit this store," busted in George Silloway, who, shorter than Boyer, could breathe the lower, cooler levels of basement air while your six-foot, four-inch Virginian continued to stay mentally alert in the layer of hotter air closest to the ceiling.

"So. . . . . what about it?" I asked. "How'd this other chap do? I suppose he's a store manager by now," I took a stab in the dark.

"Like heck," said Silloway. "He's doing better than that."

"You mean he's been elevated to Chicago?"

"He beat that. He's been elevated right out of Monkey's," said Silloway.

In passing, how'd we all get this chance for such a confab? In the normally busy basement, just then there was an interlude, meaning that all customers had been timely waited on and the next batch was yet to arrive. Silloway, keeping busy as he talked (there was always a chance that Bosso McCarty might pop in on the scene), was straightening up one of his counters. So about this preceding trainee, I exclaimed: "Wow! How did that great opportunity happen to come about?"

"His uncle owned some money-making company farther out in the Midwest and summoned him to take over some management position."

"Wasn't that lucky for him?" I asked, as I thought I detected Silloway to be evincing some sort of an air of disenchantment. "You must have been sorry to see him leave the store?" I said.

"Me and my wife, both of us, but not right away. . . . only eventually we got sorry. . . . but not for him but for us," replied Silloway.

"What do you mean?" I asked.

"The wife and I and this trainee got to be real good friends. We'd have him and his lady friend over to the house for dinner frequently. When he resigned from Ward's and his uncle first made him a manager and then arranged it so he could eventually own the firm, my wife and I expected that he'd send for me, that I'd get some sort of a better-paying supervisory position."

"Obviously, you're still here. He never sent for you," I surmised. "But surely he must have sent you some sort of a fair bid for your expertise as one of Ward's best young department managers?" I said.

"Never heard from him once he left," said Silloway.

"So that means that I don't get any free dinners at your house?" I queried.

Then, same as Boyer had delivered what seemed to be his pet punch line, now from Silloway came this follow-up: "That's right; with you trainees, that once was enough."

Pushing a broom, Foster Adams, the colored building superintendent, closed in. As mentioned, he'd been working the vicinity and his ears hadn't missed much. Seeming to be signaling me that to him, Foster Adams, all of this spontaneous advice that your unaware George Washington VI had just been handed from first Boyer, then Silloway, was old hat, he was chanting a poem's openers: "As I was crawling on my knees,/I thought I heard a chicken sneeze. . . . . ."

The Delayed Proffering of a Tom Harmon Ducat

Besides poker parties that rotated the homes of the local store officials, currently, Ward's had another policy of enlightenment. "Dean," said Bosso McCarty. "There's a big homecoming game in the cards between Michigan and Minnesota. If you want to attend, we will give you the time off with pay and then, after the game, you return to work the rest of Saturday afternoon. But if you want to see Tom Harmon run with the ball, you must soon tell me so that I can plan for someone to take your place."

Since my arrival on scene the day after the Fourth of July, I'd been evincing a dedicated attitude and bowing to some higher duty assumed owed to Ward's, I gave little or no thought to the slimness of the pay. For instance, in the back alley I'd be going to a lot of extra trouble tying a big mattress in a carton on top of some lady's sedan. When I'd have secured it, she'd offer a tip. But in such cases I'd tell Ward's fine customers: "Thanks anyway, but I can't take it. I'm here to learn the business, so kindly accept such little extra services rendered as part of my training." A similar attitude now surfaced in response to Bosso McCarty's kind advance offer to us 'uns of time off to see the big home game. Reiterating, Bosso clearly conditioned it: "But you'll have to let me know by morning if you want to go."

Remembering that the big shots at Chicago GHQ had written: "You show Ward's that you mean business and there will be opportunities," to show Bosso that with Ward's I meant business, I now said: "It seems to me that my job here as trainee with Ward's is more important than the big game. If business is slow on account of the major football event, I'll study the store manuals. So thanks anyway, but I'll forgo this opportunity to see Tom Harmon perform."

A fortnight passed, then came the eve of the game. On the morrow I was slated to switch out of the receiving room (from which Sinelli, the receiving clerk, would be off for the game) and work on the sales floor, relieving the clerks such as Boyer and Parsley (both of whom were included in those much more hep to this annual customary outing to which all of Monkey's seasoned employees looked forward) who'd be part of the gigantic crowd of football fans at the nearby stadium. Then came the delayed proffering of the ducat.

As pregame hysteria was rising to a fever pitch, Junior Hurd appeared just inside the back door of the stock room where I was currently assisting Louis Sinelli as we checked in lots and lots of merchandise. Waving a ticket for a reserved seat on the fifty-yard line under my nose, Junior Hurd said "Here. If you can get time off for the game this ticket is all yours. It's on my father for helping him out on the delivery truck late Saturday evenings last month when I was on vacation."

At this surprising suddenness of the availability of this Tom Harmon ducat my eyes went boing. Up half a flight of stairs to Bosso McCarty's office I took them two at a time. Soon, to Bosso, I was explaining the great opportunity. But right back to your Virginian, Bosso was explaining *his* problem, to wit: arrangements had already been made. . . . . there was no one available other than me to cover my assigned sector on the sales floor on the morrow. "This I realize," I respectfully submitted to Bosso, "but with Junior's wafting that ticket, all I could do was try."

Bosso nodded not only with sympathy but also with some restrained mirth at Junior Hurd's having delayed the proffering of the Tom Harmon ducat until I was committed to help mind the shop. So back to see Junior I took the bad news, while he, most happily, took off with the ticket. When game time arrived, I settled for patrolling my sector of the sales floor. So went the life of the postcollegiate retail merchandiser while the big game over the Tom Harmon ducat was being played by the store's old hands with Monkey's star trainee.

Of Football Pools and Points

By midfall I was writing home, "The more I find out about this company, the better I like it." Just then some trucks arrived and commenced disgorging some more Christmas merchandise. Summoned by Bosso McCarty, I quickly switched my role from temporary sales clerk back to the post of assistant receiving clerk. Inside the portals of the all-important stock room, Louie Sinelli and his lady aide were awaiting their line backer. In some small but well-remembered part, we checked in barrels full of colorful imported dishes, marked the prices, and turned over the processed goods to the eager waiting hands of the department head who'd placed the order.

Although the store hours were long, back in the receiving room, Sinelli-inspired banter about sporting activities lightened the atmospherics. Ann Arbor was a football town and we had our fun. Sinelli was such an astute expert that he could predict winning scores within a tight margin but needed a front man. Many of the store clerks, along with the men who worked for Hurd on the delivery truck, bought into the pool at two bits a throw. Twice in a row, once with an exact score, the front man won the pool. Ten bucks was my net, as the other ten went to Sinelli, my silent partner, who'd called the shots. From behind the scenes, he won his own pool twice in a row. It was a perfectly honest operation in which anyone was free to win by outguessing Sinelli. But to make it look good the receiving clerk called on his assistant to play the straw man.

Although Cornell didn't play Michigan, Ohio State was usually on the schedule and this fall was also playing Cornell. Connecting up your unaware George Washington VI with this latter situation, Junior Hurd demanded that I bet on Cornell four dollars even money, while Junior thought he had sure thing on Ohio State. Because my stellar classmates such as Brud Holland, Sid Roth, Bill McKeever, George Peck, Carl Spang, Al Van Ranst, etc. had graduated, I had many misgivings. But being a good Cornellian, without hesitation, I took Junior up and we both planked down the money while Louie Sinelli served as stakeholder.

The big game came and went. Although Cornell had lost some stars, the team was, without my realizing it, still red-hot and carrying on with such unfamiliar newcomers as Ken Brown and Fred West. Thanks in part to their performance, down to defeat went Ohio State, and Junior Hurd had a tough time getting over his loss. But, quickly attempting to recoup, he was insisting that I give him points on the upcoming Cornell-Columbia game. To keep him happy I let him con me into spotting him ten points as I bet on Cornell. This time Cornell also won, but only by six points, so in spite of the victory, I lost my bet but fortunately, I'd reduced my bet from four dollars—as it had been laid on Cornell against Ohio State—to four bits!

Transmuted From Rowing to Pigskin-Snatching

Foster Adams, hep on football, couldn't help but take note that Cornell under Carl Snavely was having a great season. Heeding my six-feet, four-inches, "You must have played end for them when you were still there last year," said Foster as though his surmise immediately made it a fact.

"No. No. No. It was the crew. . . . the varsity crew. . . . I rowed on the crew for four years, was in practically every race. So I didn't play football," I tried to straighten out our colored janitor.

"Don't try to kid me," he chuckled as he gave his broom another push.

Not many days later, I could see that while to Foster Adams, eight-oared rowing—in other words crew—was a lot of Greek, nevertheless he was hep to football. So one day, I met his expectations: "It was like this. The quarterback called for a pass. From left end I raced down the sideline, cut in along the ten yard line, pivoted and beelined for the end zone. Just as I was crossing the goal line, the quarterback spotted a pass into my outstretched hands. It was a cinch to hang onto it. The stadium's Cornell fans went wild. We got ahead of Dartmouth by two points, and moments later during a great uproar the finish gun went off and the game was over! I'd made the winning score against Dartmouth!"

"I knew it. I knew it all the time. That rowing on the crew was a lot of baloney. You did play football then." Foster Adams made his pronouncement ring with truth by being positive in a loud voice as he transmuted my image from rowing to pigskin-snatching.

"Hey. . . . wait a minute," I told Foster Adams. "I was just kidding. I didn't play football. That pass-catching account was just fiction. . . . . . tailor-made to suit your personality. I rowed full-time on the crew, every race for four years." I attempted to set the record straight.

"Don't try to string me. I don't believe it. You're just being modest," chuckled our colored janitor. "That business about the crew is for the birds. You were a football player. I guess I've got that straight now," he snickered as he commenced to recite the rest of. . . . . "As I was crawling on my knees,/I thought I heard of chicken sneeze. . . . ."

Unfortunately, your scribe forgot to make a note of the body of that nice little poem that must have come out of the woodwork when, a decade earlier, Herbert Hoover had been promising a chicken in every pot, but the bird had backfired, sneezing itself into the poem.

Turning to Louie Sinelli, who knew that during my preceding four years on the Frank Merriwell road, the extracurricular sideline had produced the rowing degree, I said: "You know that I was only an oarsman. Now that Foster Adams has got me transmuted into a football star, we've got to undo it. We've got to convince our colored janitor that I never played football."

But Sinelli, pointing to a stack of freshly arrived boxes of merchandise that needed to be attacked, said: "Let's go on this newly arrived shipment. We've got to get that stuff unpacked, tagged, and delivered inside to the respective department heads on the sales floor in time for Ward Week."

Marsh

For this big midfall merchandising promotion, from one of Ward's new big Detroit stores there arrived well in time at Ann Arbor a brand-new assistant manager. Replacing the preceding assistant, who'd been the man of few words, the new man—one Marsh—in his portly thirties or early forties, was the big personality, to wit: an operatic singer. "Yes, in Scranton, where I managed a dime store, I used to sing duets with Teddy Allan Jones."

Did your know the singers in my mother's family?"

"Yes, I knew your uncle, Haydn Evans, who used to sing baritone in Welsh recitals, and I heard of your Aunt Margaret. As a young lady, she won the contralto prize at the World's Fair in St. Louis." Marsh's knowledgeability saw him putting his best foot forward with Monkey's star trainee.

After our new assistant manager left on a mission patrolling the store's most important department, Foster Adams, as he soon came pushing his broom back through the swinging door into the stock room, was chuckling: "Out on the sales floor, Marsh, who was singing some operatic tune, broke it off when he came by me. . . . . . . He stopped and said: 'Say there, Adams. Just pushing that stuff ahead of your broom isn't good enough. I know darn well just from looking at you that you're a good singer. From now on, occasionally, to let me know that everything is going OK, I'll expect to hear you break out into a song.' "

From behind his low partition, Wes Eisley popped up on his two hind legs. "Marsh doesn't know that Foster's a poet, not a singer." Then Eisley the delivery clerk told Foster the janitor this: "But maybe Marsh will write you the tune so that you can sing your chicken-sneezer of a poem to it."

"Our new assistant manager is a popular guy with the help," said Foster Adams.

Louie Sinelli had just finished telling me about local matrimonial prospects. "If you get your eye on one and her dowry or other share of the family pot is ten thousand dollars, then they'll expect you too to have ten thousand dollars," the perceptive Italian had explained. Then he'd broken it off to complete a tedious job of attaching price tickets to a new batch of goods. But distracted now by this yarn-spinning that had suddenly developed between Foster Adams and Wes Eisley, Sinelli, as bosso of the backroom, looked up from his work bench and said: "Enough for now. We've got a lot of stuff to get checked in for the Christmas rush. Look at all of those cardboard boxes right up to the ceiling. Let's go."

"OK," said Wes Eisley. "But first let me tell you. Down at our new big Detroit store where they recruited Marsh, they told him they'd pay him X dollars to run the Y department. Marsh told Monkey's: 'OK. But I'll take two-X dollars and I'll promise to double Y department's profits.' "

"What happened?" I asked.

"Grudgingly, very grudgingly," the way it was told to me, "Monkey's manager of the big Detroit store contracted to pay Marsh the two-X dollars but only provided he'd double the Y department's profits," said Eisley.

"So how did Marsh do?" I asked.

"He *tripled* Y department's profits," said Eisley, as he made us think that maybe we had on our hands some sort of merchandising wizard whose brain we could soon pick for some pointers on how, as a young man in business, to make it with Monkey's.

"So then, why didn't they keep him in that particular one of our big Detroit stores? If he's such a whirling ball of flame, what's this recently assigned heavyweight with a metropolitan opera-type of personality doing here in this old Ann Arbor store?" I asked.

"I don't know," said Eisley. "I heard that the manager of the big Detroit store got jealous."

The afternoon was wearing on and Sinelli again interrupted: "That's enough for now. We're all going to a store party at Boyer's tonight. Marsh will be there. You can get him to tell us all about it then."

But the party when it came about that evening had a new twist. Customarily these were run-of-the-mill poker parties with everyone chipping in for the drinks that were served. Momentarily, it was the same old drill, with your Virginian keeping out of the play but helping serve the drinks while taking in a scene that soon sparkled with some extra special atmospherics. Marsh, as the brand-new assistant manager, was setting the pace, dramatizing the play, fattening the pot with unusual speed, calling bluffs as though the bright lights and movie cameras were trained on him. The various department heads were orbiting Marsh. In short, Marsh was beating the boredom not only for himself but also for the rest of us, enlivening and injecting extracurricular chain-store life with a lot of extra added color. The cookouts that I'd envisioned with Monkey's management when on the Fourth of July last past, I'd stepped off the Pullman into the real world at Ann Arbor, had turned out to be these round-robin poker parties that commencing with the fall season rotated from the home of first one department head to another. Maybe it was a good place to get some clues on merchandising. If so, we weren't about to use these parties as another kind of school, one where you learned to play poker. It was as good as a movie. Then came an even better scene.

Before long, weekday mornings when we'd get to work at eight (with a view of dressing up our counters, etc. in good time for the 8:30 A.M. door opening for the public), we'd have to join a curious line of held-back employees. Normally, the assistant manager would be inside looking out, turning the key as the store personnel met the eight A.M. deadline. Not so during these new mornings under Marsh. Jack Frost nipped the heels of the help huddled outside the store's principal front portal. Everybody was waiting for the new assistant manager to get to work on time and unlock the door.

Illustrating the newly developed procedure, just then a big Lincoln sedan rolled up with Marsh behind the wheel. He stepped out on the pavement, but only for the moment it took for him to give his keys a toss. Making the catch was Foster Adams.

"Say there, Foster, let the help in. I've got to go get my car gassed up and parked. If Bosso McCarty gets in first, tell him that I'll be back in a jiffy," the new assistant manager instructed the colored janitor.

"Yes, sir," said Foster as he turned, unlocked the door, then took up the usual position of the assistant manager and commenced allowing entry for the help arriving, as mentioned, timed to get the place spruced up before the eight-thirty gong would signal the in-rush of paying customers.

Occasionally Bosso McCarty would arrive before Marsh! With the odds rising that the 8:30 opening for the public might soon get delayed, up would go Bosso's blood pressure. His wordlessness soon left us 'uns wondering just what would be the timing of the seeming programmed explosion between local store management's top two personalities. Then came a feeler for a promotion in grade, a development that made it look as though your Virginian might not be around to see the fireworks.

Mysteriously Sounded Out For a Promotion to Port Huron

It was early November. Bosso McCarty approached. "Dean. Our store at Port Huron needs a receiving clerk. I've recommended you for the post. But it has to be approved by Chicago."

Did your unaware George Washington VI follow up by writing his contacts in the top brass? Now that the Wilmark shoppers had drawn blood, I wasn't about to initiate any further correspondence with Moore and Robinson at GHQ. Yet the message from Bosso contained a positive factor. They were asking me. I wasn't petitioning them. If orders, presumably with a raise in pay, were soon to come through from headquarters, off to Port Huron I'd play the eager beaver. And this in spite of my becoming attached to Ann Arbor. After all, thanks to four years at Cornell, I'd learned to like college towns. Another factor that pleased me about my current location was that, waiting for me to find some time to make them some quick visits, were my many cousins throughout Michigan—many of them still undiscovered—all of whom knew that they were descendants of Israel Dean, who, almost three decades later, we'd wake up to realize was George Washington's secret son. From conveniently located Ann Arbor, already I'd been out to the Mason area to visit some of my father's first cousins. But, as mentioned, some of his second cousins, the Parr boys (descendants of Israel

Dean's older son, Julius), were farther away in places such as Big Rapids, Ithaca, and Flint. While waiting for the travel breaks, I stuck to my current slot as aide to Sinelli in the receiving room.

Maybe that bit about Port Huron was just to test my confidence and Bosso McCarty was merely fishing for this: One day after Sinelli had seen me in action for a good month, he sprung a surprise. "Every year, Dean, I take a ten-day vacation during the last half of November. I go down to South Bend to watch Notre Dame play football. This year when I go, during my absence you're going to be the receiving clerk. Bosso McCarty has already approved it."

So did the stockroom picture develop—Sinelli to South Bend, your Virginian to pinch-hitting as receiving clerk, the big feature being your Virginian's ability, though an Anglo-Saxon type, to put on the act of the industrious gesticulating Italian, making the truckers hold back deliveries until the frustrated drivers would successfully go over our head to Bosso McCarty, who'd then assign temporary help to put out the brush fire by partly clearing out the stock room. As soon as a batch of stuff would be processed out, out, and away, and into the hands of the respective department heads, we'd let the respective trucks quickly fill the freshly created space.

So it went. Your Virginian's pinch-hitting was a success. Bosso McCarty, as well as Sinelli when he returned, was pleased. It looked as though your Virginian, having passed the test by successfully spelling the Ann Arbor store's star receiving clerk, soon would be reassigned to Port Huron but, as previously mentioned, this time not as trainee, but as receiving clerk with some interesting salary hike. Maybe soon I'd be kissing goodbye the hundred-a-month aspect of this chain-store life. Around Thanksgiving, Bosso McCarty, returning from a meeting of regional store managers at Grand Rapids, at once reiterated to me: "Dean, I recommended you very highly for a receiving clerk's job at Port Huron. But it has to be passed by Chicago."

So, in one mirror, this Port Huron thing was still up in the air. In another reflection, I commenced to sweat out the possible transfer. But nothing happened! A mystery was left to dangle.

In Chicago new, unexpected factors may have been larruping the plans for trainees that had been laid out by Ward's big boss— Sewell Avery and his staff. Their policies were highly secret. Would I ever get around to smoking any of them out? Whether or not I knew it, that's what I was intuitively doing right now, day in and day out. But getting even inferential answers would take time. But expressly speaking, a pattern may have already crystallized indicating that your unaware George Washington VI would never be given any seemingly warranted explanations as to just what, in the way of progress with Ward's, he could expect. Perhaps it was the lack of little mouths for the Ann Arbor trainee to feed? Or maybe it was the war in Europe that was screwing up management's noggins and disrupting their plans?

Pennala's Not-So-Wishful Thinking

Since the German invasion of Poland had triggered Hitler's war, with us headline-readers at the store it had been business as usual as we'd ignored that quickly settled action that had seen the Red Army occupy eastern Poland on the Eastern Front. When hostilities had quickly frittered away to a level that had gained for what was left of the fireworks the moniker of a phoney war, we got right back down to brass tacks for Monkey's.

Then, at the end of November, the Red Army attacked Finland. When the Finns put up a terrific holding action, Art Pennala, a Finn from Michigan's Upper Peninsula, became an instant hero in the chain store. As a customer would exclaim: "So you're a Finn! Your side is putting up a great defense against overwhelming odds. Wouldn't you like to be there?"

"I'm happy to be right here where I am," Art would tell them. Then, as though the United States were already at war, Art, who must have taken a bit of a fright, turned to foist it on me and said: "Dean, what would you do if you got orders to go to the front? I'll bet you'd be scared," he announced for the benefit of the big retail store's basement sales crew, most of whom were older and married, and with little mouths to feed or otherwise above or just crossing (such as Art) the upper limits of the first potential draft that would be likely to exempt them from any potential wartime service with the Armed Forces.

Although there was no way in which I could very well answer Pennala's real speculative one, I was nonetheless curious. Since I was unaware that I was part of a British military family from way back, the scare tactic didn't bother me a bit. Even though I spent a lot of time reading up on the Kaiser's war and predictions by the experts of developments in this current war, what was there to say? For Pennala's benefit, I just shrugged. Yet the testing had started.

Although at Ward's we still pulled it off as a business-as-usual situation, the trainee's life was never quite the same. The headlines over the action by the Red Army against Finland, taken with Pennala's ongoing not-so-wishful "Boy. Oh, boy. Would I ever like to see Dean get ordered to go to the front," were gradually creating atmospherics making it seem as though the enlistment, as distinguished from the conscription, bugle might blow at just about any old time. But by concentrating on business as usual, maybe we could make the whole thing go away. That was the general ongoing attitude. Actually, our nation's war machine was being revved up in stages. By the time it would have a slot ready for us, hopefully any such new life with the military would be a lot more colorful than Monkey's.

First Trip Home

Christmas 1939 fell on Monday. Trying to live down that black mark that the clandestine Wilmark shoppers had lately slipped into my record, but with notice to me *after* they'd drawn blood, so well did I do my job on my recent switch back to the sales floor that Bosso McCarty, as Christmas approached, gave me the fixings of a long weekend. This included Friday afternoon off coupled with Saturday without pay, so that wearing a brand-new extra-long topcoat (a special order by a local haberdasher arranged for by one of Monkey's department heads) and equipped with a special gift for the Indian Princess, I boarded the eastbound Michigan Central passenger train home.

A bunch of university students piled aboard. One student, accenting the preponderance of young hearties in the coach bound for Detroit, moaned and groaned all the way home. His father owned a burgeoning tool and die works. There, he, the son, was going to be pinned, working like a beaver, all during his Christmas vacation. There was, for this crown prince of industry, no discharge from such chores. . . . . tough!

At Buffalo came the customary switch to the Lackawanna. I found myself sharing a seat with a prestigious member of the older generation—one Colonel Pistell (en route from Chicago to New York City), who'd been in charge of the American bridgehead at Cologne after the Kaiser's war. By the time I debarked at Owego during the wee small hours of Sunday morning, from Colonel Pistell I'd picked up a few clues as to what to expect in that way of Army life should we get involved in Hitler's current war. When the taxicab dropped me off at home, my parents were waiting up and, before hitting the hay, I spent an hour briefing them on goings-on at the retail store back in Michigan. After I had told my father that I was able to save around ten dollars a week, he downplayed it like this:

"That means in one year you can save just over five hundred dollars. . . . in two years just over a thousand dollars. . . . . . . And that's not getting ahead very fast financially," he slipped the realities to me in his nice-and-easy yet most discouraging way. Subconsciously he must have been spliced in on the thinking of our prexy, Sewell Avery. He was in the process of letting Sears and Roebuck successfully out-expand Monkey's, relegating my esteemed employer to the role of catch-up.

But I didn't let Father's taking such a downhearted view throw me. Glowing with enthusiasm about the opportunities that I foresaw with Ward's, I said: "There's a good chance that the chain will expand. New managers will be needed. I'm preparing myself now so that if the summons comes to be an assistant manager and then a manager, I'll be able to step right in and take over."

But my father quickly countered: "Ward's might be just as liable to contract. Then you'll have to stay put at some job for years at lower levels."

All of this didn't exactly encourage your Virginian to rush right out and see about creating some little mouths to feed (just to fulfill one element of Monkey's composite picture of the perfect trainee). Yet, playing around the fringes of such a possibility, just before leaving Ann Arbor, while deciding not to have it engraved with initials, I'd invested a third of a week's pay in a fine, exquisitely carved, gold-plated bracelet for the Indian Princess. But when— taking her, of course, by surprise—I knocked on the door of her folks' old Victorian mansion, my correspondent opened up with this always-much-appreciated signal, "What are you doing here?"

Playing it by ear, I surmised from her tone that her compatriot still had the inside track. Now, as I was quickly invited in from the bite of the cold early winter evening, we settled down temporarily in a warm living room furnished with antiques and decorated with colorful mementos. At once we commenced having a nice little yarn on a sofa that was slightly too wide to make a good love seat. After the fashion of the Princess (by now displaying the veneer recently added by her fall term at finishing school), I too (keeping Boyer's preachment in mind) played my cards close to my vest. Still it was an enjoyable occasion, and this, our first little reunion since the preceding June, aside from its being a nice, good, honest, and friendly chat, all too soon came to an end. Tough. But I knew that back in Michigan, Ken Boyer would soon be telling me that I'd lucked up because there hadn't been any constructive developments. Reversing all progress that had been made during my preceding visitations (right after I'd garnered my A.B. and rowing degrees), when hot June breezes had swayed the background colorations, by now, the current Canadian high outdoors seemed to have iced things up. . . . . or was it her compatriot waiting in the wings who'd played the wet blanket?

When, rolling with the punch, I got back to my parents' house, since the next day was Christmas, the younger of my two younger sisters, the twelve-year-old, who'd been keeping me posted, for her trouble was presented with the nicely carved, gold-plated bracelet. And during the evening of Christmas day, had the Indian Princess been waving goodbye from a snowy bluff, darkness would have faded the scene when I wound up my first trip home by climbing aboard the through Pullman car for Ann Arbor.

Siberia

When I debarked in Ann Arbor I felt like a horse that had had too many oats to eat. Helping me digest the raiseless portion of the first six of my hundred-a-month push for Monkey's had been this left-behind, small-town curbstone coloquy with a couple of my peers.

It had been a brisk early winter day on the avenue when the sheriff's son, curious about my position with Ward's, came right out with it and asked: "How much are you getting paid?"

Recently, with Clark Fitts', Lindley's picture had made the front page of Owego's Main Street weekly. The two football players were shining in the reflective glory of Coach Larry Kelly, famed Yale end of yesteryear, who was introducing these other two Owegoans to the Frank Merriwell-type life at Peddie. And since Lindley was an old friend as well as an important cog amongst the county seat's younger generation, a chap who dearly loved to play water polo, and since I was four hundred miles easterly of the merchandising mill in which I was playing out my role as trainee, feeling reasonably safe that the information spilled in the Yankee Tier wouldn't leak all the way back to GHQ at Chicago or to my co-workers in Michigan, I told my earstwhile water polo opponent: "A hundred a month."

"I wouldn't work for Monkey's for so small a salary," scoffed the plucky Lindley.

So I turned to the other member of our important little curbstone confab. He was Harry V. Taylor, Jr., one of tennis town's first-rate players and the son of a prominent merchant. "What about you, Harry? Would you take the trainee's job like mine at a hundred a month?"

"Certainly I'd take that job for that money." In contrast to Lindley's scoffing, Harry's words had the weightiness that emanated from right out of the horse's mouth. "If you don't make it with Monkey's," Harry added, "they're such a good training ground that you'll wind up at least as a vice-president of some other smaller but more rapidly growing chain in the Midwest."

Keeping Harry's crystal ball in mind, when I debarked, all bright-eyed and bushy tailed at the Michigan Central's Ann Arbor depot, I was ready to pull out all of the stops. Having had breakfast in the dining car, I legged it to my room, stashed my suitcase, donned old clothes and then stepped lively right back to timely punch in at the Ann Arbor outlet of Ward's great merchandising world.

Back in the cheesebox of a stockroom, the pace had cooled, giving Louie Sinelli, the receiving clerk, room to turn around. Curiously, any word on my proposed transfer to Port Huron had faded out. Silence reigned. Since the Wilmark shoppers by now had tasted blood, my stance had gravitated to, "I've shown them by successfully spelling Sinelli (for his long Notre Dame football week), so let GHQ contact me." No more letters of inquiry went to Chicago. Curiously, this was not a deliberate withholding on my part. It was just the unconscious way no more mail contacts were initiated by your unaware George Washington VI. And while the top dogs must have missed the missives, I took no notice at the time. For the young man in business, post-Wilmark, there'd been a subtle psychological change of sentiments.

As though for a fortuitous palliative, Monkey's management came up with a new angle. "Dean," said Bosso McCarty as soon as he came through on his morning inspection tour and saw me, "when you come back here tomorrow, you can wear your good clothes. You've finished your apprenticeships in the warehouse, on the delivery truck, and in the stock room. Tomorrow you're going to go upstairs and commence work in the furniture department under Mr. Faber. He'll show you the ropes," Bosso promised.

Whether this was what Bosso really wanted or whether he and Faber had programmed some rather slick playacting to test a trainee, maybe our regional manager, George Moore, was in on the move. Although I didn't know it, his overview included apparel and my new destination—furniture. At any rate, I took Bosso McCarty at his word, thanked him, and the next day went to work on the store's most prestigious upper deck.

Came my first chance to sell a big-ticket item. A lady from one of the minority groups was browsing among the full-size gas stoves in the area between the counter of the credit department and the second floor's rug department. Although she spotted the sales assistance that was all cranked up and ready to go, she seemed to be desirous of merely browsing. So I hesitated momentarily, to give her a chance. But Bosso McCarty just then popped through the tall portal from the upper floor's furniture section. Turning from the swinging gate that led into the store's credit department (where he had been called to do some decision-making), to your Virginian, Bosso McCarty sent a signal. Promptly taking the cue, I went to work on the customer. My only clue that something might be wrong was this: the sale of the sizeable gas stove was too easy. It didn't take long and I had written up the contract and the lady customer had signed it. Contrasted to selling run-of-the-mill sporting goods, paint, and housewares in the basement, Art Pennala, Allen Parsley and Ken Boyer down there would have to sell a lot of such smaller items to catch up to this big-ticket item, my first substantial sale on the top deck.

But alas! No sooner had I buttoned it all up, and not too many hours after the lady had left than I got word from Bosso McCarty. The sale hadn't gone through because it hadn't been approved by the store's credit department. But this wasn't the real lesson of these openers in the prestigious furniture department.

Came one of the granddaddies of 'em all. As I said, maybe Bosso and this one of his most important and highly skilled department heads, with whom he could huddle in confidence, were play-acting to have some fun? In contrast to the bang-bang selling but of smaller items in the basement, life among the big-ticket items on the second floor turned dull. How did the older Joe's handle it? Take Jory, Vogel and Crosby, along with Faber, they all were experienced hands who knew how to score very successfully at sales production, but with the slower pace. Your unaware George Washington VI, without realizing his knacks, would have better fitted into some ongoing military operation. Becoming impatient (as it may have been anticipated by Monkey's management), I mistook this standing around part-time as an awful drag. To perk things up I turned to Faber, king of the furniture department. During the pre-New Year's Day lull, he'd been busying himself at a cubbyhole desk with paper work, and paying little if any attention to training your Virginian—that was, until there surfaced this nice little lesson:

"Let's get with it. Can't I handle some of that paper work for you?" I submitted to the big, heavy fortyish star salesman and manager of the all-important furniture department that I'd already learned a similar handling of order forms for paint and sporting goods. "You must have some reports that I can help with, taking inventory, getting ready for the January sale and so forth?" I said as I attempted to grill some tidbits of merchandising skills out of the big impressive redheaded German who was raising a fine family. When he balked, then later on vanished, I wondered what had happened.

After work that evening, Art Pennala was asking me: "What happened with you and Faber?"

"I don't know. You tell me," I replied.

"When he went to see Bosso McCarty, whatever was said, they're going to take you back off furniture," said Pennala.

"I got tired of standing around. Maybe I ruffled Faber's feathers," I explained.

As it turned out, Faber, when I'd tried to get him to open up, had done more than that. Off the scene he'd exploded! He had dropped everything and had zipped right down to see Bosso McCarty. So in the morning, all smiles, the store manager handed me a ticket to take to the haberdashery department head, who graciously presented me with his biggest and longest pair of all-wool long johns (the legs, as you'd expect, falling well short of my ankles). "Dean," explained Bosso McCarty, "we need you in the warehouse again. It's going to be cold down there. This time of the year it's a veritable icebox. But with these long woolens that the store is presenting to you, taken together with your hustling around moving heavy stuff with Bill Wilkens, who, as usual, will be in charge, I'm sure you'll keep warm."

So went the switcheroo from the summer warehouse to the delivery truck to the stock room to basement paint and sporting goods, then most recently to the furniture department for the springboard back to the warehouse (now, on account of winter, also known as the icebox), where I'd be hacking it under conditions much more adverse than the dog days that had introduced my mid-July baptism into Monkey's world of merchandising.

However rough Siberia turned out to be, Saturday night socials made up for it. Kindred spirits came out of Ann Arbor woodwork, guys heading westerly for Jackson to play checkers. After the fashion of the end of boot camp for our soldiers in Panama, Louie Sinelli saw to it that as one of a party, your Virginian didn't miss this facet of extracurricular merchandising. When one beautiful blonde came out of a hallway and into the nice warm comfortable lobby where we all were lounging, someone cried out: "I saw her first," and a fine checker game was soon in progress. Simultaneously, for the others, there was another, another, and another. Thus, on the following Monday, Siberia or not, freshly stirred juices chased away the ever-present effects of Jack Frost and we all felt like a million. Putting us on the one-up side, when the local merchandising experts (with every set of ears cocked including the kitchen sink), otherwise wintering, thus unable to get out of the house even for a game of golf, got the details of the Saturday-night checker-playing operations from Louie, they too looked as though they'd have liked to be along to sample life with the bachelors' night forty miles farther west in Michigan. So incredible was the painting by Sinelli of the real picture that even Bosso McCarty rose to successfully request some verification. Then it was back to Siberia.

After a few seemingly short weeks of redeploying heavy crated items—the objective being to move out January clearance specials and to open up space for incoming stoves, refrigerators, sofas, and other house furnishings, to meet demands of the coming spring upswing—your Virginian's presence boosting the sofas and studio couches from one end of the icebox to the other spelled out a fine assist for the warehouse manager. My work in the long johns also pleasured Bosso McCarty to the extent that by mid-February I found myself reassigned from Siberia back to the retail store.

Upon my return, although no pay hike went with it (and I wasn't about to ask), Bosso McCarty, giving the impression that he'd received orders from Chicago GHQ, made your Virginian a department head. Technically it was the real thing. Otherwise it was just a bone or some sort of a palliative that Bosso McCarty was instructed to toss my way.

Once more: Back to what I didn't know about the big-business background of the executive who'd hired me. George Moore had come to Monkey's from Eastman Kodak, where he'd been an authority on paper. And what a department was now handed to Monkey's star trainee: wallpaper!

Chapter 4

Post-Siberia: A Life Rededicated to Monkey's

The Pep Talks at Grand Rapids

Very early on a cold mid-February Sunday morning, Bosso McCarty picked us up at our respective digs. In his big maroon Packard sedan, we rolled northerly, then northwesterly to Grand Rapids for some pep talks at the Pantlind Hotel. Why Grand Rapids? Monkey's didn't have a store there. So there'd be no uninvited drop-ins. Furthermore it was an easy run by rail from Chicago. In charge of the meeting was the regional manager, George Moore.

Standout amongst the sales promoters who took the podium on paint was the scenario of the movie depicting Ward's factory. Plugged in such a way that it would be etched in our minds forever were the points scored by Monkey's top-drawer, titanium dioxide white paint vis-a-vis the old-fashioned white lead product. And when it came to selling Ward's best paint brushes, the orchestrated speaker explained: "In China when the boars get itchy, they rub their sides against the shaggy bark that catches the bristles. The locals tag along and bag for us the disgarded bristles off the trees. Thus only these genuine boar bristles that better hold the paint find their way into Ward's best brushes."

Came an intermission. As I would soon write home, "I talked to George Moore for the first time since he hired me last spring. He says for me to keep doing just like I'm doing and that there will be opportunities.

"I am convinced that I will get ahead if I stick it out long enough and take a right attitude toward my work.

"Thus if I am to work for a corporation all of my life, I might just as well stick with Monkey's."

As the reader will note, the foregoing evinced that for the great devotionalist of merchandising, it was a post-Siberia life rededicated. Then there crept in a note of the spirit of independence, "If I change, it's going to be to a business that I can eventually own."

But in passing, up came the subject of the Federal Land Bank. I had already passed muster with key members of the Springfield administration who knew of my interest in the military and that I was impressed by the role that they had played on the front in France during the World War. Because of such contacts, my father in a recent letter had suggested that I bypass Siberia by switching to the Bank. Yet there still prevailed my sense of a higher duty, my ongoing rededication to Monkey's. So I said, "Thus I do not see the sense of changing to another institution [such as the Bank]. But when I get home on my vacation next summer, I will take some action then."

Now back to the pep talks at Grand Rapids. In addition to the regional manager, also present were a number of store managers. Here was your Virginian's chance to engage them in conversation. What about? My life in the warehouse, on the delivery truck, in the receiving room, on the sales floor, in Siberia, Cook's tour of Jackson? Most likely they all had had such experiences. Why bore them? And I couldn't very well tell George Moore to make me an instant assistant store manager.

So when the brass hats left to catch a train for the Windy City, and the rest of us fanned out in respective automobiles, our Ann Arbor contingent heard the dinner bell ring for the best restaurant en route in Lansing. Ward's had an important retail store there. Its delegates arrived in accompanying vehicles and once we sat down inside and commenced to peruse the menu, the local store manager spoke up, "This is on the company. I'm having a T-bone steak."

What an effective display of leadership! Everybody followed suit. For your Virginian, it was a rare but very well-received add-on to the hundred-a-month life.

Back on location Monday with Monkey's, I commenced to expand my new department. Previously in the wallpaper and paint department only one display panel had been alloted to paper. Suddenly the sales space was tripled. To back it up, Bosso McCarty handed me a set of plans and I built some bins in the storeroom behind the sliding fire door. Much to the amazement of the older and more experienced hands, not only were the new inventory facilities readily completed, but the receiving clerk, in response to my orders, was soon turning over to me large bundles of wallpaper to fill them. And when it came to percentage sales increases, wallpaper was setting store records.

Of course we (primarily including Parsley and Pennala) also presented customers with our new sales pitch promoting titanium dioxide paint and boar-bristle brushes, but when it came to wallpaper, what a thrill! Although the pep talks at Grand Rapids hadn't covered it, nobody could beat your Virginian's percentage-sales increases, all to the effect that Bosso McCarty, on the next staff meeting, after covering plumbing, housewares, automobile supplies, etc, eventually had to mention the big percentagewise winner. But as he announced Dean's new numbers, he did so in a real low and gradually fading voice. This translated: no raise was coming through from Chicago.

The Sun Valley Bubble

A year earlier, at Cornell, we'd been working out on the rowing machines indoors pending the ice going out of the inlet. Now, back on the real side of the magic mirror, to make up for my having run that gantlet through Siberia, I read a newspaper ad and sent for a brochure on Sun Valley. While I was waiting for it, the situation orbiting the new operatic-type, Figaro-chanting assistant manager finally exploded into some investigative work on the part of Chicago GHQ to break the big chain's contract with the popular singer from Scranton.

From the Windy City a lawyer for the occasion was parachuted into the store manager's private office, where he held court. Actually his stenographer was taking down statements. On behalf of the brass hats at GHQ the visiting legal eagle quizzed and cross-examined our retail store's entire staff but with two exceptions. One was Foster Adams, our colored janitor. And the other was your Virginian, the store's solo trainee.

When it was all over and GHQ broke the contract and made it stick, Wes Eisley, our delivery clerk, chuckled: "They brought Marsh down here when they should have kept him at the big store in Detroit and promoted him there. Now I hear that already he's obtained a new situation off down in Indiana with another chain at around twice the salary."

On the surface, Marsh the singing extrovert of an experienced chain store merchandiser, was a little bit too popular with the help. What was the inside story? Both Monkey's and Marsh clammed up.

Because we were the only employees who hadn't been called as witnesses, Foster Adams, I assume, along with your Virginian, must have felt slightly slighted. Since the brass hats had guessed correctly that I didn't have any negative testimony on Marsh, naturally I wondered what sort of an image I had with GHQ. But chasing away any misgivings, this Sun Valley brochure that finally arrived had registered like a good sharp bite from an exposed electrical wire.

When I'd recently been working in Monkey's Siberia, helping me survive had been that Sun Valley advertisement. Now, as I presided over my brand-new wallpaper assignment, the caller responding to my having mailed the clipping was the Detroit travel agent for Union Pacific. "You got the Sun Valley brochure we sent you?" he asked.

"I sure did."

"When do you want to leave? I can put you on the Michigan Central express next Monday afternoon. It connects out of Chicago, getting you into Sun Valley late Tuesday," the agent proposed.

I was on the spot. Assuming Bosso McCarty would be able to spare me, the question was whether to throw conservatism to the winds and blow my savings while chasing chippies on the slopes in the Rockies. On the other hand, should I keep accumulating do-re-mi for a new car, or better yet, a studied speculation that I had in mind—the stock market? It took me a moment. Then I said: "Sure, I'd like to make the trip. But now that you've called my hand, I must admit that I was only dreaming. I'm a first-time department head in a chain store. Sure I'd like to go, but it's got to wait."

What a temptation! But, fortunately, yet with diplomatic reluctance, the agent gave up. My loyalty to the big retail chain had won out as the Sun Valley bubble went bust!

Prussing's Book Left Out Chicago!

By late winter I'd been knocking myself out for almost eight months as a freshly minted careerist doing my part at helping make the merchandising mishmash perk for Monkey's. As mentioned, I was (and would be for more than twenty-six years) unaware that I was a great-great-great-grandson, on the male line, of George Washington. In addition, I was unaware that land titles descended (without a will and without a deed) by the laws of descent and distribution, meaning that I was a contingent *per stirpes* titleholder to George Washington's vast estates.

Had I realized that my great-great-grandfather Israel Dean was George Washington's heir, it would take me *more than* twenty-six years to discover that there was one heck of a lot of strategically located land involved to the tune of something like a hundred square miles, perhaps even more. And it is this "even more" part that may have by now titillated maybe at least just one or two extra special noggins at Ward's Chicago GHQ.

Men great enough to be trusted with so great a secret were few and far between. A couple of prime candidates were headquartered in the Windy City. Such great Chicagoans may have been clued in by their forebears in the hinterlands or by Windy City land-title professionals whose business it was to know family trees. Thusly, by February 1940, with furtherance of spring merchandising training just around the corner, after your Virginian had put in around eight months with Monkey's, our chain's prexy, Sewell Avery, and one of our chain's directors, a man such as Silas Strawn, both great enough men to have been so entrusted, may well have been sworn to secrecy, and by now perhaps had been told that their chain's long lean wiry trainee at Ward's Ann Arbor retail store was an unaware George Washington VI. If so, it may have been a case of Ward's having been in possession of or otherwise associated with occupants of Chicago lands to which the real legal title was held unaware by the descendants of Israel Dean. If so, this would mean that in addition to holding unaware a *per stirpes* title to the better-known vast estates of George Washington such as those on the Potomac in Virginia and in the erstwhile *Virginia* portion (that may have been illegally cancelled) of the District of Columbia, my father might also own a *per stirpes* title to valuable tracts of land in Chicago's metropolitan area. If so, it might well be that Ward's top brass hat would silently view your unaware George Washington VI as a potential rug-puller on Monkey's. So how to handle the eager beaver? How to play him down? Bandy it about behind top-echelon doors. Charge him *in absentia*. He's not willing to take himself or his career with Ward's seriously. Treat age twenty-two under the gun of an impending war as though non-existent (such insight to be fatefully provided in later decades by a soon-upcoming coworker who would stick tight to make it reasonably big with Monkey's).

Now back to your Virginian's current role: being unaware of my involvement possibilities in such a possible covered-up title, to my freshly minted career as a trainee, because of such surmised secret political-genealogical motivations, anything could happen.

But just how do we figure that Chicago lands might have been included in the tracts with which George Washington had died seized?

As mentioned, onwards from this point—early 1940—it would take me twenty-seven years to arrive at the realization that my great-great-grandfather, Israel Dean, was George Washington's secret son. By such time, the many, many extra clever costly political ploys—those already recounted and those still to come—would have turned on the light. When I would commence making inquiries with a view of verifying my findings, a kind official of the state of Virginia would recommend during the late 'sixties that I go to the extra trouble of obtaining and reading *The Estate of George Washington, Deceased*, by Eugene E. Prussing. He just happened to be a Chicago lawyer, who would thus presumably be knowledgeable about the Chicago land title situation that we will soon mention. But his book that's otherwise a remarkable work, as it focuses the spotlight on places other than the Windy City, may be, in part, a red herring.

While Mr. Prussing seems to be unaware that George Washington had a secret son and heir—Israel Dean, the Chicago lawyer does somewhat enlighten the reader by means of the preface of his book. The italics and parenthetical remarks are mine as I quote: "More than one thousand books have been written and printed about George Washington. They usually treat of his personal affairs *only* to the time of his death. The *subsequent* history of *his family* [most likely Prussing refers to the descendants of George Washington's sister and brothers] and his belongings, except Mount Vernon, has received practically *no* attention.

"Yet the subject is so large *so obvious* [excepting the conspiracy of silence in the media] and so interesting a study [as though Prussing may have subsconsciously smelled the rat], that it should have received earnest and competent attention long ago. It had to be begun now, [this preface was dated July 4, 1927, and the book was published by Little, Brown, and Company, in November 1927], to avoid the complete loss of records and monuments [east of Falls Village, Connecticut, during mid-summer 1987, the tombstone of Israel Dean in the Barrack (a/k/a Music) Mountain Cemetery, would be mysteriously knocked over] which are its witnesses.

[Hear! Hear!]

"After repeated casual readings of his will [actually a paper writing purporting to be a will] and schedule of estate and a number of visits to Mount Vernon, the subject was suddenly suggested to a mind [Prussing's] familiar with legal and probate history. A little examination of the estate and the recorded proceedings concerning it in the fifty-one years required to administer it sufficed to produce the conviction that here was an opportunity not to be neglected or lightly dealt with.

"Not to forestall criticism, but as an honest confession, it should be said that this book [Prussing's] is not an attempt at professional historical work or literary composition. It is the effort of one who is an amateur in both, yet saw a need and an opportunity which seemed to be going to waste.

"The *fact* that *no one* has hitherto even approached the subject has been a constant stimulant and also a source of fear; a stimulant to the desire to add something to the stock of useful knowledge concerning one of the greatest of mankind, a fear that this desire might mislead ambition to overdo and weary the reader with the writer's prolixity.

"In respect to the latter, I have found comfort in the knowledge that many of the facts which I shall give, often in great detail, are *not* to be found in print elsewhere, and so at least an accessible record is here given for such use as others may hereafter make of them. In respect to the desire to add something worthwhile to our stock of knowledge, I leave the public to judge. It has been well said that 'posterity loves details.' "

Then Prussing, referring to Virginia, Maryland, Pennsylvania, New York, West Virginia, Kentucky and Ohio, winds up his preface. Its last paragraph reads as follows:

"Washington's holdings in Virginia and *six* other states were manifold, so that the subject of this book offers variety enough. The administration of the estate [which your George Washington VI claims was hurdled over the unknowing heads of Washington's unaware secret son, Israel Dean, and his descendants—thus leaving his descendants as beneficiaries by the laws of descent and distribution of a potential constructive trust] was unusually long, its vicissitudes and experiences, legal and practical, were many and peculiar [Prussing may here be alluding to various most-curious 'title-making' proceedings on which he reports, the very bizarreness of which fingers the otherwise unseen presence of the unaware heir, Israel Dean, at first, then, later on, of his two sons and five daughters, and their respective descendants—ghosts that even Prussing couldn't shake], and the lessons in law [such as how by pettifogging expertise—apparently unrealized by Prussing—to 'make title'] and wisdom which it teaches are interesting and valuable. The effort made to trace the origins of his [George Washington's] holdings has compelled the writing of much of Washington's business and private life and resulted in *new matter*. It discloses him in the capacity of an engineer and captain of industry [America's *first* millionaire], which perhaps was his true career and character, with the purest of ethics and ideals and continental vision and purposes."

For his punch line, Prussing wrote: "If my readers derive a fraction of the pleasure, instruction and satisfaction which have been mine in the preparation of the book now submitted, I shall have been more than glad."

Ten years after Prussing's book was published, your unaware George Washington VI found himself rowing bow for Cornell in the varsity four-miler June 1937 at Poughkeepsie. A little more than two years thereafter your scribe found himself hooked up as a trainee for Wards. Now, after eight months of playing the role of a freshly minted merchandising careerist, the point on which we now focus orbits the locale to which I'd been assigned. On my job application I'd asked to be placed with one of Ward's many retail stores in New York State. In spite of such request, the brass hats at Ward's Chicago GHQ had first called me to Ann Arbor, Michigan. Curiously, this was in a state that had been settled at Mason by three of my Grandfather Dean's brothers (John, William and Franklin) and at Pontiac by my Great-grandfather Pierce Dean's older brother Julius (thus the older son of Israel Dean)—all unaware descendants of George Washington.

Michigan also was one of the states that had been carved out of the Northwest Territory. By the Treaty of Paris at the close of the Revolutionary War, it became part of the United States (with certain problems awaiting settlement by the Treaty of Ghent, 1814). By 1786 all of it but the Western Reserve (held by Connecticut) was ceded to the federal government. By the Ordinance of 1787, the Northwest Territory was all of the United States west of the Allegheny Mountains (eventually meaning west of Pennsylvania) and north of the Ohio. It included Ohio, Indiana, Illinois, Wisconsin, Michigan and part of Minnesota. At least one biography of General Anthony Wayne would indicate that by the time of the Battle of Fallen Timbers, land-hungry Americans, usually the more knowledgeable political heavyweights, commenced taking out valid patents for tracts of land in what was to become the Chicago area of the Northwest Territory. But Prussing, although he was a Chicagoan, while failing to mention in his book the possibility that George Washington may well have been numbered among the early birds who secured strategic land tracts in what was to become the Chicago area, does tell of another holding by George Washington in the Northwest Territory.

As detailed commencing on page 311 in Prussing, this was the 3,051-acre site just east of the City of Cincinnati and on the Little Miami River. After George Washington's death in 1799, on this tract was based a bizarre tale of a title sidetracked by pettifoggery from George Washinton's unaware heir—Israel Dean. Without opposition from George Washington's so-called executors, such strategic location of 3,051-acres just north of the Ohio River was jumped around 1806 by Joseph Kerr, a U.S. deputy surveyor (subsequently a senator from Ohio), in the name of General John Nevill, who had died July 20, 1803, at Pittsburgh, which locations as so jumped by Kerr were upon the identical lines and field notes of Washington's surveys and patents! Later on, the Nevill heirs (Presly Nevill and Amelia Craig) deeded the jumped land to Kerr.

Aside from such fascinating details concerning the cover-up of the true title to a large land tract on the east side of Cincinnati, Prussing appears to fail to take note that George Washington may have obtained patents on land in other parts of the Northwest Territory. For so farsighted and so astute a First President to have overlooked latching onto other tracts of the Northwest Territory, at such promising areas as Detroit and/or in the area that was to become the City of Chicago, would be unbelievable.

Now back to the work life at Monkey's in Ann Arbor. With the approach of 1940 spring training, and with your Virginian having rededicated himself to merchandising at Ward's Ann Arbor retail store, general headquarters being a a good train ride southwesterly in such salient Chicago land area, what if at the time of his death, George Washington owned some ponderous city-type tracts, other than the Clermont and Hamilton County land at Cincinnati, of the Northwest Territory in what had by now, the spring of 1940, become metropolitan Chicago. If so, we take note that Washington's so-called executors after his sudden demise seemed to have some special ability in the state of Virginia to make their dealings with his lands stick. Even were we to allow the homemade will that should otherwise have been denied probate even in Virginia, it is to be pointed out that the paper writing purporting to be George Washington's will was not duly executed with two witnesses. Already we know that, due to this deficiency, it was not effective in the Maryland portion of the District of Columbia, where it couldn't be used to pass title to tracts such as Square 21. Likewise, let us assume that it was invalid for transferring George Washington lands, titles to which were soon therefore covered up in Chicago. In such a case, no one except the descendants of George Washington's secret son, Israel Dean, had the power by the laws of descent and distribution to execute a deed to give good title. But George Washington's descendants by Israel Dean were unaware of their Washington ancestery, thus were unaware that they held the *per stirpes* title and that their rights were being kept in deepfreeze as one of America's great national secrets.

Helping remedy the situation (from the viewpoint of occupants holding unfounded titles, and to the detriment of Israel Dean's descendants, who remained unaware that they held the *per stirpes* title by the laws of descent and distribution) came the great fire in Chicago of October 1871. It's your Virginian's information that all of the historic deed books—from the beginning of the Northwest Territory up to the great fire—whisked out of the recorder's office ahead of the flames were buried in the shores of Lake Michigan. Afterwards they were dug up, only to disappear. My information is that while they were saved, they were not truly resurrected. The public recorder's office failed to get back these public records, but rather, somehow or the other, these historic deed books wound up in private vaults safe from rightfully prying public eyes (except through the good offices of such a non-public politically fortuitous holder). Thus did there expediently develop among the Windy City's legal fraternity, in the form of some rarely questioned dogma, this punch line: "All land titles in Chicago commence from the time of the great fire of 1871."

Oops! Pardon me! But we don't think that you all are supposed to hear about such matters as what happened to Chicago's deed books from the beginning of the Northwest Territory up to the great fire when, as I've been informed, they "disappeared." Fortunately, in spite of the cover-up, we got wind of the disposition of such historic records as they were privately squirreled in the Windy City. An esteemed lawyer from the Midwest clued us in. This fine gentleman served in both wars, as an officer in combat in the first and as a staff officer in the second. He hailed from one of the several states carved out of the Northwest Territory. Naturally we hope that you all do not suffer from stimulus overload—too much information—but here and now we have seen fit to insert all of these historical details, surmises, etc. in our story of your unaware George Washington VI as he hacks it as the young man in business.

Should such men as Sewell Avery, great enough to be trusted with so great a secret (that Israel Dean was George Washington's secret son and heir), ever realize now in early 1940 that the trainee at Monkey's mighty chain's Ann Arbor store would eventually succeed to some substantial *per stirpes* share of the true legal title of some very valuable lands on which Ward's Chicago GHQ area might be sitting, you've got a dramatic situation in which your unaware George Washington VI, as a potential target for some political ploys, will find life always tinted with that slight touch of danger that will make seeming ordinary goings-on better for the going than a good movie. And to reiterate: What about Prussing? Although he hailed from the Windy City, when it came to discussing George Washington's possible interests west of the state of Ohio, the lawyer-author left out Chicago!

A Waterloo Feeler Upstages Port Huron

While your Virginian was knocking himself out for Monkey's, I can only surmise that from the viewpoint of the top brass, they thought of him as not totally committed in the sense that had been suggested by George Moore almost a year earlier, upon our hiring. Then, as a key element for advancement with Ward's, Mr. Moore had envisioned the trainee's early embarkment upon the great sea of matrimony.

It wasn't that Ward's were wowsers. It was just that Monkey's probably knew from experience that their married men striving for upward mobility opted more rapidly into the harness of various management posts, and, being hungrier, displayed more eagerness in their questions than did the bachelors of the great chain's vast stable. And were it not for the presence of an oncoming war, and were a Monkey Ward trainee to join the club, whom best to select for a mate? The daughter of one of Monkey's successful department heads. Chicago may have had a secret policy to imitate the Salvation Army with the workers intertwined by fortuitous marriages into one big happy family.

Actually, in just over two years, instead of my now going for getting myself all burned out by my mid-forties, I'd be doing quite some bit of yearning for a dangerous voyage on a great sea. But when it would come to opportunities of making such a sea one of matrimony, these heroic voyages in the cards would decrease the available logistics for feeding little mouths while enjoying their company, providing instead life's great adventure that would supplant the sterotype route that would otherwise see any possible savings switched off into life insurance when your Virginian had a much stronger urge to become the owner of some common stocks.

Perhaps one of the great failings of Ward's administration was its lack of foresight to initiate an employee stock-purchase plan. That meant: If you want to own some shares, save your own money and pay the going price (a policy that would most likely conflict with family economics for starter-outers). While I was a risk-seeker intending to eventually buy some stock listed on Wall Street, I would be looking for a spot where one dollar would do the work of ten, and that wouldn't be Monkey's. In short, under obvious difficulties of getting an investment program off the ground, I wasn't about to bollix it up by running right out and, to please Monkey's brass hats, taking the big matrimonial risk when the accumulation of a stock portfolio came first on the principle that one good buy would be worth a lifetime of toil.

It may well be that some wowser-inclined official in GHQ ran a contrasty chart. How long did it take Ward's bachelor trainees, on the average, to forget stocks and get hitched? Was six months Monkey's deadline? If so, I didn't ever suspect that my hanging tight at sleeping single, or my solo receiving-clerk escorted Cook's tour to say how-di-do-di to Judy at Jackson (now that it presumably had been reported to The Top), might effectively nullify a crucial amount of the punch that I was otherwise putting into my trainee's job. Yet, had Monkey's brass hats taken a gander, they'd have seen that I was at least whittling away at eventually maybe getting around to doing it their way. More than one beautiful maiden and your Virginian enjoyed each other's company, attending the local movies, etc. In one location double features were twenty cents, in another two-bits. All flicks were first-rate for entertainment. From the lower-priced flicks, age had weeded out the bad ones. On the lighter side we saw *We Shall Have Music*. At the college town's major theater—the only one to which I squired the dolls—Don Bestor and his orchestra (last seen at the Criterion on Times Square, Thanksgiving 1934) made a fine personal appearance. But the heavier, yet most entertaining side, concentrating on reruns such as *Hell's Angels* and *All Quiet on the Western Front*, engraved in our noggin the brutal potentialities of American involvement that we all hoped would just go away before it got started in Hitler's war.

During heavy weather, cars would be creeping along snowy streets when we'd be waiting in line at the box office to get movie tickets. You could hear passenger transports droning overhead in the murk. They were letting down for Detroit Airport. When one moviegoer asked a lad how come he looked so worried, "That's my father up there piloting one of those planes on top of of those low clouds," the boy explained, without realizing that he was growing up in an atmosphere that would soon see him piloting bigger and better planes under even tougher conditions in the Army Air Corps, should the European war expand to include the United States.

In letters from the Yankee Tier, just past midwinter my father was stressing that at home business activities were very depressed. In reply, describing the Ann Arbor situation, I wrote: "All indications point to a boom here just as soon as winter shows first signs of running out. Right now for spring merchandising we're loading our shelves."

Then, to my father (even though not the scantiest of words of potential promotion or raises had filtered down to me from any of Ward's brass hats), I sent this astounding prediction: "If I don't succeed in finding a way to get started soon in my own business, I'll make up for it by sticking right here with the chain store. Probably, *at least* by next fall, I will get to be assistant manager. Even though I won't get to making any real dough until I get to be a full-fledged store manager, just watch my smoke!"

Were this eventuality (assistant in line to become manager) ever to take place, most likely I'd have to have a wife who'd drive down to the store after work and pick me up, thus shaping up the required image. And if GHQ had a six-month deadline for its trainees to comply, perhaps the administration had given up on Ann Arbor, figuring instead that the knot would get tied sooner were your unaware George Washington VI to get reassigned, this next time to the heart of the corn belt for a cornfed mate.

In contrast to the Port Huron feeler that had been delivered in person by Bosso McCarty (then left to fade into limbo), it was fair to infer that he suspected that he had lost credibility and so had instructed his oldest faithful basement department head to handle this next upcoming probe.

One bright and cheery winter morning, when I descended the stairs to my wallpaper sector, Mr. Foster (to be distinguished from our building superintendent, Foster Adams), master retailer of

Monkey's plumbing and heating supplies, let it all come out. "Dean. I hear that you're going to be transferred."

"Where to?" I bit.

"To Waterloo, Iowa," said Mr. Foster.

"That's interesting. My former colleague from the Cornell crew, Jovial John, is out there as a trainee for the oil company at Clinton on the Mississippi. Just got a card. He thinks Iowa's wonderful," I replied, but without otherwise giving away any of my pro-or-con feelings by quizzing the plumbing department manager, or running right upstairs to sound out Bosso McCarty, or renewing my correspondence with the big shots Robinson and Moore in Chicago.

"Well, from Clinton, Waterloo's well over a hundred miles northwesterly."

I said, "Oh." Yet, straightaway, I hied on the following Sunday afternoon to the library at the university. Off the shelf I picked the particular volume of the appropriate American information series and read up on Waterloo. Recently at Grand Rapids, George Moore (as mentioned) had pepped me up. "Keep plugging and there will be opportunities." Maybe our Chicago regional director had Waterloo in mind. With all due respects, it looked like a good place way out in the middle of nowhere.

What was the hitch, if any, this time? Same as during the preceding fall, then Bosso McCarty had told me that he'd highly recomended me for a receiving clerk's position at Port Huron, nothing had happened. Now, since Mr. Foster presumably had been instructed by Bosso McCarty to extend the feeler, and after the head of the plumbing and heating department (that I occasionally served as sales clerk) never pressed, when Bosso himself never saw fit to raise the hare, I ignored the whole thing. Same as with Port Huron, nothing came of it. Never did I learn whether Mr. Foster, as manager of the plumbing and heating department, was putting me on or whether Ward's even actually had a Waterloo retail store, and if so, what would be the position? And would there be a raise? Yet, Bosso McCarty never peeped. After the fashion of Port Huron, the Waterloo feeler was fated to remain a mystery as it upstaged Port Huron.

A Village-Level Palliative for CPD

Back in the Yankee Tier, where the unaware George Washington V had aspired to become county treasurer, he found himself in the process of being manipulated into a village-level post that was also a treasurership. Here's how the Tuesday, March 5 issue of the GOP weekly on Main Street disposed of the previous officeholder.

"Resigns Post as Village Treasurer, Effective Last Night."

A picture of Darwin E. Krum was followed by his statement: "Due to an existing opportunity to better myself in a business way which will need all of my attention, I hereby tender my resignation."

Actually, the outgoing treasurer was taking over a throwaway-type of advertising sheet and reputed moneymaker known as the *Pennysaver*, located upriver a number of miles at Sidney, New York. Currently that village (due to crop up several months hence in our saga) was the residence of Byron Dutcher, who had been my father's business partner in the Owego milling firm that had been known as Dean & Dutcher from late 1919 until the fall of 1927. Furthermore, Sidney was the home of Scintilla, the well-known magneto factory, such relatively unthought-of but precision items currently being of great interest to the manufacturers of fighter aircraft, motor torpedo boats, etc., handy for operations in the ongoing European hostilities.

Now, back to the ending of the announcement of Darwin E. Krum's resignation. It closed out with, "The appointment of a successor was deferred to the next village board meeting."

Concerning CPD, the special meeting was covered in the Tuesday, March 12 issue of the same Main Street sheet. The headline blazoned it: "Former Village Supervisor Unanimously Appointed Village Treasurer." Featured was the same picture that my father had used in political ads during his 1939 campaign for *county* treasurer. In later years, some Swedish industrialists would tell me that the George Washington V looked like Prince Wilhelm, brother of the king of Sweden. Maybe it had something to do with a Norman connection?

Back to the publicized details of the appointment: "Mr. Dean will serve out Mr. Krum's term which expires next January.

"All but two members of the board of trustees were present. Absentees: Trustees William Gay and T. Henry Cook."

Because of a lock-in-type of political ploy slated several months hence, the reader should take careful note: *No other* candidate for the position was placed in nomination.

"Mr. Dean held the post of village supervisor until that position was abolished by the famous 'sneak bill' in the state legislature in 1933. [Wrong: the bill that eliminated my father's few-hundred-a-year post was developed during March and April of 1935].

"He twice ran for county treasurer, once in 1930, again in 1939, being defeated both times by E. Burt [no mention being made of the freak recount of 1930, followed by the whispering campaign and dirty-trick political ads of 1939].

"Mr. Dean now holds the post of secretary-treasurer of Tioga County Patrons Fire Relief Association [a cooperative that covered many farms in all four corners of the county]."

What were some of the surmised objectives of the political occultists behind this move? Manipulate an unaware George Washington V into giving up his aspirations for the county-level post in 1942. Try to wear down my fifty-year-old father at a lower level, giving his health a chance to slip some more. For his having been twice defeated for the county treasurership—but both times, only by the opposition's having resorted to dirty political tricks, provide the unaware George Washington V with a palliative, but at village level.

Arnold Rich Steams into Ann Arbor, the *QE* into New York Harbor

By late winter Arnold Rich steamed into Monkey's Ann Arbor store. He was several years older than your Virginian and upon graduation from Dartmouth in 1931, had dedicated himself to the retail trade. After a stint with Jordan Marsh in Boston, he'd switched to Dennison's in Chicago. After a fall-out there, he'd applied to Monkey's. When George Moore had asked him, "What does Ward's want with your specialty retailing background?" Rich (as he'd tell me all of this decades later) had replied, "Mr. Moore, When you switched from Kodak, what did you know about furniture and apparel? Can't you give me the same chance that Ward's gave you?"

Rich's pitch worked. He was taken on as Monkey's highest-paid trainee, to deposit his check—three times your Virginian's—in a designated Grand Rapids bank (where, as mentioned, Ward's had no retail store).

Whereas your unaware George Washington VI, upon his post-Fourth of July arrival, had expected to soon take over the sporting goods department, Rich was now instantly assigned to run it. Did this arouse any consternation? No. I recognized not only the value of Arnie's experience, but also the expertise of Monkey's chiefs in making the assessment. While I was seeing what I could learn from my brand-new colleague, a steady flow of signals, the adversity of which seemed to be easily disregarded, kept coming along in the headlines blazoning the hostilities in Europe.

Shocking the West, Germany and Russia had entered into a trade agreement, making it look as though the United States and Great Britain might eventually have to fight the combined strength of the Nazi and Red Armies. German machinery and metals were going to Russia in return for foodstuffs, oil and tobacco. News from Finland put a sad look on the face of our coworker Art Pennala who, unofficially, represented from the curbstone the PR interests of Finns locally as well as from Michigan's upper peninsula. After beating off for thirteen days the renewed try by the Red Army to break through the Mannerheim Line, the Finnish high command announced that Finland was relying upon civilized nations for help. Several days later, the Red Army claimed the capture of the town and fortress of Koivisto during the twenty-first day of the assault. Fortunately, so it seemed, such hostilities were so relatively small and so far away that as we carried on like ostriches, we hoped that any threat that the United States might be dragged into the war would simply dry up and blow away. In my letters home, the war was a forgotten item.

Not so when we all were introduced to a new assistant manager, replacing the deposed Marsh. I told the home folks about Mr. McComber, a thirtyish Notre Dame product. Decades later he would be pictured in my rattrap memory as he hustled on long legs from cash register to cash register toting up the take, bagging the do-re-mi and then delivering it to Bosso McCarty's cashiers. This latest of your Virginian's positive role models had the image preferred by George Moore. His wife arrived in time to chauffeur him home after work.

But contrasty war news commenced giving us our first inkling. Perhaps an assistant's job might get to be an awful drag. Was the war on the Western Front phoney? Although one of my home-town correspondents, Mr. Moneybags, Jr., thought so, maybe not. In the Mersig sector of the French frontier, what was described as the first British-German infantry engagement of World War II took place. Twenty British soldiers were killed and sixteen taken prisoner. Prophetically, the Nazis had gotten the better of this little injection of reality into the war that the media had been characterizing as phoney.

But Britain held the upper hand on the Atlantic. For an extra special unnoticed accent on all of the various harbingers, when it came to a major element quietly applying to eventually service the kickoff of some yearned-for heroic voyages awaiting in the wings for your unaware George Washington VI, during mid-March the unfinished 85,000-ton British passenger ship *Queen Elizabeth* steamed into New York harbor.

The Cornell-Dartmouth Densification

But little notice was taken of the potential significance of such *QE*-type foreshadowers of wartime involvements that currently, astounding as they might seem, might well be in the cards that could put your Virginian into a one-up, first-overseas spot, should the United States get into the war. And by the time Rich arrived to be presented immediately with sporting goods, I had under my belt around a month's experience running my own department on Monkey's merchandising front. Thus by early March, I was honchoing successfully my new wallpaper department. Relatively speaking, it was a two-bit operation. But giving it the old college try made it a success from the start. After the first week, I was keeping sales well ahead of the preceding year's. Percentagewise, as mentioned, wallpaper was outstripping the store's other departments. As a result, I sensed that for the first time I had a foot in the door. Perhaps I would get my rightful place in Monkey's sun.

Suddenly I was an expert. When wallpaper customers approached our sporting goods, paint and wallpaper corner of Ward's basement, the other much more experienced clerks, old hands that they were, in deference stepped aside and waved the business on for your Virginian to handle. And it was just as the brass hats had planned it. I was significantly distracted by my success when the sporting goods department (that I'd expected to commence running shortly after my July 1939 arrival) was assigned instead to the newcomer.

This Dartmouth product who'd prepped at Tabor was a native of Back Bay Boston. He'd already racked up eight years experience at retail merchandising. Although he'd started off with a big-name Beantown department store, most of Arnie's postcollege work had been with a single-product retail company in Chicago. Rich and your Virginian had both been hired by George Moore. But Rich had been hired at Ward's GHQ in Chicago, while your Virginian had been employed by the former Kodak executive when he'd stopped off at Syracuse toward the end of my senior year at Cornell. Now on to a warranted inquiry. How come shortchanging one corner of Ward's basement that included automotive supplies, hardware, housewares, hardware, and plumbing and heating, over in this different northwesterly sector concentrating on sporting goods, paint and wallpaper were positioned by Chicago brass hats two Ivy Leaguers—this Cornell-Dartmouth densification—Arnold Rich and your unaware George Washington VI?

Aside from the new assistant manager and one of the older generation straight-commission salesmen two floors up in furniture, Rich and your Virginian, both trainees, were the store's only two college men. Did the presence of Rich as the future head of catalog order indicate that I was a candidate for eventually becoming one of Monkey's merchandising superstars? Was top management getting ready to move me through a series of managerial jobs to broaden my experience? Or was it this: when I'd opted to work for Ward's, one factor moving me had been Ward's merchandising men who'd given me and my friends, such as Dick Smith or Charley Bedell, a lift during precollege hitchhiking days in upstate New York. Always they'd been traveling in pairs and usually were going through the transfer process from one retail store to another. Always they'd indicated that they'd been to college, had opted to work for Ward's, that they'd frequently been moved from post to post and, most important, that they liked the life as career merchandisers with Ward's. They'd not only paved the way for my favoring initially the idea of hooking up with Wards, but they'd also displayed a possible secret policy of the big chain. This may have been the use of a team concept. Was this the objective of this Cornell-Dartmouth densification? Did the brass hats in Chicago have in mind turning Rich and me into a pair of trouble-shooters to be moved around Michigan to put out merchandising brush fires that might spring up in Ward's various retail stores? Or were the brass hats trying to discern how high your Virginian had the capability of rising with Ward's, and had they asked Rich for a guesstimate?

Some decades later, Rich himself would let his assessment come out. "When I knew you, Deanie, you didn't take yourself or your job seriously. But who would at age twenty-two with a gigantic war coming on!"

Rich's initial contact with the company had come through a good friend, the aide of Sewell Avery who eventually would write a recommend that would accompany Rich's successful application for a commission in the Navy, where he would go on to become assistant to Admiral Nimitz' top personnel officer in the Pacific. But now, while we all were waiting, your unaware George Washington VI commenced to shine in the light of the reflected glory.

Now that I myself was on Ward's firing line, giving prompt and efficient service to customers took up most of my time not being spent housekeeping, restocking display counters, assisting the heads of the other departments setting up new displays. During lulls of business, it was good to have an older brother-type of Ivy Leaguer with me on deck. Rich turned out to be a first-rate conversationalist.

"Did you like Dartmouth?" I asked Rich.

"I had no choice, Deanie," was the reply.

"What do you mean?"

"Both my father and my grandfather went to Dartmouth," came the explanation.

"Wow!"

Helping Rich sell sporting goods, tents, luggage, guns, etc., was a great pleasure. I soon discovered that in the bottom of a small rectangular cardboard box containing a casting plug-type of lure there was snuggled a paper which, when unfolded, turned out to be a fancy fish-catching policy. Using it for a prop, I devised my own personal sales spiel. After I'd wound it up, a fisherman would ask: "You say that if I don't catch fish with it, I get my money back?"

"That's what the fish-catching policy says; shall I wrap it up for you?" I'd ask the customer as Foster Adams, with a broad smile on his face, would glide by, pushing a big wide broom and reciting, as mentioned: "As I was crawling on my knees, /I thought I heard a chicken sneeze. . . ." Customers always bought. Rich kept restocking by means of rush orders.

One purpose of the dramatization was to keep the other personnel in our corner of the basement, such as Rich, Parsley, Boyer and Pennala, from getting bored to death with their jobs. Before long, they and other clerks temporarily working our side of the tracks were indirectly praising me as their successful imitations of my spiel almost outdid mine. Needless to say, all plug sales based on the fish-catching policy stuck!

Then there was paint. My prompter was unnoticed by the customer. To refresh my recollection, I read the pertinent data off the back of the can that I held up on display as though I were appearing in what would one day be an expensive TV commercial. Included was my spieling off of a heavy recommend for Ward's titanium-based paint as contrasted with white lead-based paint now, for various reasons, gradually falling into disrepute. Before long my co-workers, especially Rich, Pennala, and Parsley, were feverishly working up equivalents of enthusiasm, and contributing to the entertainment of the other clerks. Thus my three or four closest co-workers were pulling off equally good and effective spiels as we sent customers away loaded to their comfortable limits with lots of Monkey's best merchandise, such as paint, wallpaper, sporting goods, with some occasional automotive supplies from Epperson's neighboring displays. Then there was the case of the Chinese boar bristles.

Rich, Pennala, Parsley, and even Boyer from housewares soon picked it up from me as I'd previously learned it at Grand Rapids, and now relayed it from Ward's Chicago paint-department expert, who'd included—besides his pitch on titanium—this bit on Chinese boar bristles. This fascinating tale now, as my Ann Arbor basement co-workers adopted it . . . making it theirs, would be told to a customer something like this.

Holding up a paint brush, we'd ruffle a finger through its bristles. Tracking our wigwagging finger would be the customer's eye as we'd continue: "These bristles that you're viewing are genuine boar's. They've got mini-indentations—gashes, notches and serrations—that can be seen only with a strong magnifying glass. It's these mini-notches and mini-serrations that hold the paint," we'd point out to the customer. "Now about our keeping our supply of these boar bristles replenished, so that you can buy these brushes when you'll be needing them, there's going to be a problem," we'd point out.

"What's that?" the customer would ask.

"These boar bristles come from China. There the boars as they scratch away the itchiness from their sides leave behind them lots of boar bristles on tree bark. The Chinese workers then go around and from the bark of the trees, pluck and collect up these bristles. They're then packed and sent to the United States, where our paint brush factory's manufacturing process works them into these first-class paint brushes." Again we'd run a finger through those boar bristles while the customer would also try out the nice feel.

"So there's lots of bristles in China? I can get all of these boar-bristle paint brushes here that I need?" the customer would ask.

"Maybe there was. But . . . it's not going to be that way much longer," we'd warn the customer.

"How come?"

"It's the expansion of hostilities in East Asia. Wang Ching-wei, premier of China under Sun Yat-sen, has just set up a puppet government in Nanking under the protection of the Japanese Army and he's called on the soldiers of Chiang Kai-shek to lay down their arms."

"That means peace and lots of boar bristles!"

"But Chiang's men are keeping right on fighting. As the scope of war operations between the Japs and the Chinese widens, our headquarters just got a flash from the front and Ward's purchasing agents there in the Orient are already having a tougher and tougher time getting boar bristles."

"Wrap me up six of the larger brushes," would say the panicked customer who'd come in to buy just one. "I've heard all about those new-fangled, upcoming artificial bristles that are going to get foisted on us. I don't like any I've tried. The heck with synthetic bristles. As long as possible I want to stick with slapping on paint with boar bristles. They do a better job," the customer would reiterate as we'd wrap it up, ring up the sale and count back to the customer his change, then hand him his sales slip.

Like a flotation of a new hot stock on Wall Street, lots of Ward's fine boar-bristle paint brushes thus went out the window as our Pennala, Parsley, Rich, and Dean group, orbiting the Cornell-Dartmouth densification, impressed with rising sales figures the brass hats keeping tabs in Chicago. What a life . . . . . . expounding on boar bristles, paint, wallpaper and sporting goods, but more especially on boar bristles . . . . when I seemed to have forgotten that I should have been in professional school studying either medicine or law! The most enjoyable part of all of this spring training in the merchandising game was delivering successfully these sales spiels and seeing other more experienced hands pick up the style while adopting the act.

Pennala Injects the War Scare into Merchandising

Just before mid-March 1940 it looked as though World War II, at least the so-called phony part of it, might go away. But putting the damper on Pennala's spirits was this one signal, so easy to misinterpret. Russia signed a peace treaty with Finland.

Ceded to Russia was Viborg, all the territory around Lake Lagoda, and leased to Russia were the Hango and Ribachi Peninsulas. Before long from the ceded lands, a half-million Finns were leaving for Finnish territory. But in our retail store, these salient pointers generally passed over our heads. Yet everybody, especially our intrepid Finn from Michigan's upper peninsula, was still feeling the disquieting aftermath from Europe.

It came time for Pennala to inject some of the aftershock into Monkey's little local world of merchandising.

As though his objective were to get our minds off little Finland's loss to mighty Russia, Art Pennala came hurrying from a preceding and still-ongoing most curious canvassing job. And the seriousness of his demeanor stopped me in my tracks. "Dean. Are you scared of your job?"

"Certainly not. Are you?" I asked. (This was the first time I'd heard the idiom meaning: Are you afraid you're going to get laid off?)

"You bet I'm scared of my job," said the astute Finn.

"Well, you do good work so you shouldn't be."

"But you should be," said Pennala. "Good work or no, I'm nevertheless scared of my job. You're the only one here who isn't scared of his job. Everyone else is scared of theirs."

"You mean Parsley, Boyer, and even Rich?"

"Yes, they're all scared of their jobs. If you don't believe it just ask them."

I stopped and took a gander. Parsley nodded. Rich nodded. And Boyer next door in housewares, from whom you might expect it because he had so many little mouths to feed, even he too nodded. What the heck was going on? Never did exactly find out, but the upshot was this: before long, even your Virginian commenced feeling scared of his hundred-a-month job. Maybe it was a good thing. Pennala had psyched us out so that we now didn't feel quite so scared of the European dictators, were there anything about them of which to feel fright. We would soon see.

Just after mid-March, Hitler and Mussolini conferred for more than two hours at Brennero in the Brenner Pass. Maybe some of the expert dictator-watchers knew that something was up. But after Pennala's little brainwashing job, we forgot any fears of the dictators. Of our respective jobs, with your Virginian as the most recent man to jump on the bandwagon, we were a lot more scared. By the time Easter rolled around, I took off an extra day or two without pay and made my second trip home. My father was quite pleased. He had recently been appointed village treasurer. Otherwise, what was the holiday like? My rattrap memory fails me except to let you know that leaving Ann Arbor on the train, I shared a seat with one of Michigan's great beauties. Thus, once home, I found myself eager to get back to my secondary college town to see about seeing her again. But alas, although I managed a couple of brief interludes with her, it developed at once that she was committed to an older trainee—one, of all things, with a company that manufactured chain.

It seemed that my sales spiel more successfully sold casting plugs accompanied by fish-catching policies. And I had my wallpaper department to keep me warm. While still sleeping single I digested and then applied the contents of Ward's training material, *How To Be a Good Department Head*. All wrapped up in such a process, your unaware George Washington VI got on with his spring training, not rowing—as it had been a year earlier—but merchandising accompanied by the aftershock of Pennala's injection of war fear into merchandising. After making some astute observations of our on-going trainee-type chain-store operations during the first few days after my return, Arnold Rich detected a change. Making his customary big brotherly approach, he quipped, "Deanie. You've got a hunted look!"

Chapter 5

Hitler Muffles Monkey's

A Feeler From Monkey's GHQ

Once my unpaid Easter vacation had ended, from my re-charged battery some of that extra, overflowing energy was taken up by some unpaid night work at Ward's. In addition to two regular extra evenings, on this particular week I worked a third. My job was to assist a construction expert from Chicago GHQ as he mea-sured up the warehouse for some repairs. Since I'd been hired through GHQ and not by the local retail branch, from this emissary out of Chicago I was anxious to hear any pertinent tidings, com-ments or cues concerning my future as a trainee.

"You say that George Moore, operations manager for this entire region, hired you?" said the scout as we measured off the various areas of the warehouse to be fixed up.

"That's right," I confirmed it.

"If that's the case," said the inside man, "you don't have too much to worry about if you stick to business."

This, of course, coppered Pennala, who'd indicated that we all should be scared of our jobs. But, just now, curiously, with this emissary from Chicago GHQ, the subject came up concerning Ward's operations in my home area, back in the Yankee Tier.

"And you say that you come from the Binghamton area of New York State?" said the spotter.

"That's right," I again confirmed, as the spirit moved me to add: "On my original application with Ward's, to the question of to what region did I want to be assigned, I put down New York State. But Ward's Chicago office nevertheless assigned me to Michigan. Now that I've been here going on ten months and have had a chance to make contact with some of my many cousins whose parents and grandparents settled here starting a hundred years ago from Pennsylvania and Connecticut, it's not so bad."

Ignoring my connections with the settlers of early Michigan, the scout from GHQ raised a new hare: "Plans have just been completed for a new, large store in Binghamton. They'll have their warehouse on the third floor. We plan to give Sears a real run for their money there." The focus of the inside man's remarks seemed to indicate that the brass hats were more interested in making your Virginian a warehouse manager than a store manager.

If I'd been sounded out . . . . if my contacts at Chicago GHQ expected me to write them a letter envincing a great desire to aspire to run the Binghamton warehouse, they soon would be surmising that they had another think coming.

Actually I wasn't sophisticated enough to realize that chances were that I'd been offered a switch back to the Empire State. Since I never realized what had happened, I didn't bite. My ability to ignore the feeler may have been my first inkling that were I ever to pull up stakes in Michigan and return to the Yankee Tier, never again would I apply for a job with Monkey's, even if I could live at home and drive twenty miles one way to work there in Binghamton every day.

Still, here was my chance to apply for a couple of days off without pay and catch the next train for Chicago to sell the brass hats on coming up with a promotion-type of improved position. One big plus for this visiting official: at least he had triggered me into better analyzing my feelings. This other thought kept assailing me. Suppose that such an onslaught on headquarters worked! It may well have been that since, by now, I had just happened to have arrived at the process of seeking the truth that would make me free, I didn't want to thus entrap myself into a lifetime at merchandising. Admittedly, from the viewpoint of Ward's more experienced hands, I hadn't yet had enough experience to be given one of the big chain's more substantial departments to manage. It was probably against Ward's secret policy to turn a bachelor at age twenty-two into an assistant manager or even to give him a more substantial department to run. Yet, suppose that I made a pitch such as: "I've been here nearly a year, I like the work and I've been handling successfully all assigned chores, so what's next on the upside in terms of position and salary?" and suppose that Monkey's super-moguls of merchandising at GHQ did so come up with a new and better-paying slot for me and that I made good? It might be like my senior year of rowing when I'd opted to see what it was like inside KangarooGate. Even though a kangaroo court had made excellent use of secrecy and surprise to prevent the squad from voting me in as commodore, and in spite of the annual squad election's having thus been supplanted by a selection-type political ambush at my expense, were I to catch the next train for Chicago and make a successful pitch, I'd be committed and recommitted to merchandising, thus in all practical effect—locked in!

Flashes From the Front Shower Contrasty Cover on Plain Jane

Step by step, the rapidly unfolding operations on the European front were beginning to make the molasses-in-January life (as to advancement) at Monkey's look like a molehill.

On April 8, Great Britain and France planted mines in Norwegian territorial waters to prevent the free movement of German freight ships. On the next day German troops entered Denmark and Norway, professedly to protect those countries from France and Great Britain, and announced that all means would be used to break resistance. As the Germans seized Oslo, Norway moved its capital and declared war on Germany. Off the coast of Norway the British fleet was engaging the Nazis. On land the Norwegian Army was resisting the Nazi drive. Back in Ann Arbor, Michigan, against seemingly considerable resistance, your young man in business, with no supplement from Howard Lee Davis on how to cope with the clouds of war, after having been promoted to wallpaper, was seeking to climb the ladder one more rung toward his captaincy of industry. But for any further signs of advancement, it was still slow going with Monkey's when Plain Jane moved in under this contrasty cover.

As the spring season warmed up, so did business. We sales clerks in Ward's basement would be deluged with customers, such busy sessions being followed by short respites, especially during early afternoon. After a particularly busy morning, I had put away a substantial lunch at the nearby German restaurant. Back on the basement sales floor I was relieving Arnold Rich, who was taking a late lunch with Ken Boyer. Just outside of my usual bailiwick of paint, wallpaper and sporting goods was the momentarily very quiet automotive department. Just inside it I took note of this plain Jane who'd assumed a come-hither stance. Loginess left over from lunch and the downbeat of my early afternoon letdown tied in with a slight dose of spring fever, causing me to momentarily let down my guard. Such unsensed factors, just for some critical moments, dulled my usual rah-rah-Ward's spirit. With perfect timing, as though I'd been monitored and studied psychologically for this daily low, this plain Jane professionally launched her spear with all of the precision that it took to best make the kill. All of these factors led to the muffling of my customary energetic projection of a sales pitch. Without my realizing it, my usual fine tuning was tuned off. Also, by her having taken up a position at the foot of the stairs, just inside the automotive department, this plain Jane, presumably as planned, had shortstopped your unaware George Washington VI. She was cutting me off from the opportunity to show my usual stuff as she failed to indicate any interest in any of my specialties such as paint, wallpaper or sporting goods. Paint. Yes. But it was a gizmo in Epperson's automotive department. Where was the department head? He too was out to lunch.

In short, because of plain Jane's timing, and without my realizing it, I was being intercepted at a point where I wasn't nearly as gung-ho when it came to selling automotive gizmos and doodads. And she wasn't about to give me a chance to come alive on boar bristles, wallpaper, titanium-dioxide paint or the fancy little certificate for the fish-catching policy.

As it were, the plain Jane pointed out some seeming doodad, with a, "Do you recommend this?," thereby indicating some interest, in all of which I saw the opportunity to make the sale in the economy line, giving this plain Jane, who was about ten years older than your Virginian, the helpfulness of my presence but, taken off-guard, I missed her cue. When she asked, "What about that one up there? Is it better?" I missed my chance to meet Monkey's mandate and *sell up* to a better line of automobile touch-up enamel, a little gizmo involving paint, but for fender finish that was suggested to Monkey's clerk from the lady's cleverly selected monitoring stance barely outside of my real paint department.

Saying something like a halfhearted "that's first-rate too," I stepped up from economy doodad to regular gizmo, yet stopped short of going on to suggest the luxury hickey.

Again. Where was Epperson? Although I had never missed him, the head of this automotive department was temporarily a misser.

Plain Jane must have planned the scenario. In short, instead of my having wholeheartedly executed Monkey's mandate—selling up at least to the intermediate trifle, I let her buy the economy gimmick in which she had first feigned interest and the sale was soon completed with the customary wrapping, the counting back of change, and the handing over of the cash register receipt. Everything was according to Hoyle with the exception of my failure to turn on the sales personality and then to properly sell up to the luxury contrivance.

The plain Jane secured her change in a little purse, accepted her relatively small wrapped item and then vanished into limbo, that was . . . . . . until the next morning. Then, although she'd never again appear, awareness reached me as to what had actually happened.

Bosso McCarty called me into his office and waved a written report under my nose. For a second time, a Wilmark shopper had tasted blood! And whatever Bosso's advice, I treated it as heavyweight stuff. Not letting this seemingly picayune stuff get me down, I kept plugging in the face of the flashes that had provided such contrasty cover for the clandestine operative's trap.

Taking the spotlight was Admiral Stark's call for the U.S.A. to have the most powerful navy in the world. FDR said that the Democrats could win in November only by nominating a liberal pair of party leaders. A flash from the front indicated that in Norway, the Nazis, by capturing Roros, had a leg up on the British. By early May the British were leaving Norway south of Trondhjem. Soon it was revealed that the Allies had also evacuated Namsos on the night of May 2. As a result, the commander of the Norwegian Army in the Trondhjem sector, asked the Germans for an armistice.

On the home front, the American Pacific fleet was ordered to base its operations indefinitely on Hawaii. And in spite of the seemingly slow track that I was on with Monkey's, and in spite of the actual war in Europe and the seeming but still-played-down road to war by the U.S.A., more than ever and in spite of my having accepted a second stab from the Wilmark operatives, I was very much primed to become a captain of industry or bust. Yet, an off-again mood wasn't caused so much by the war developments as by my aim to gain some financial independence. Indicating an eagerness to become captain of my own ship and that, for a starter, it could be a nice little tub, I wrote home:

"The cigar store man was here at the store this noon. He takes winter vacations to Nassau in the Bahamas and says that he hasn't worked for 'the other guy' since he was twenty-two. He is sixty-four and wants to sell. He gives the impression that in his strategically located business he's made a small fortune. He says that most of the young fellows who want to buy him out don't have any money to do it with and that he doesn't intend to just give his business away. He says that it would take ten thousand dollars to talk turkey. My impression is that with some cash it could be bought for a bargain, as the individual proprietor wants to be free to spend his time in Nassau and Miami but no one can come up with any do-re-mi."

But upstaging my dreams of running my own little world, there came in the news another historic straw in the wind. Prime Minister Chamberlain, after defending himself from severe criticism because of the failure of the Norwegian campaign, announced that Winston Churchill had been put in charge of the operations of the British forces.

Again, thanks to *Britannica Book of the Year,* closing out this chapter with a final flash from the front dated May 10: German forces during the night invaded Holland, Belgium, and Luxembourg without warning; Hitler announced that the action had been taken to protect these countries from the French and the British;

Holland and Belgium immediately declared war on Germany and called on the French and the British for help.

The British landed troops in Iceland.

Chamberlain resigned as prime minister and Winston Churchill was commissioned as his successor, all of which finalized the limbo to which your unaware George Washington VI consigned the plain Jane and the Wilmark shoppers.

Monkey's Procedure Manual Gets the Midnight Oil

Back at Ward's in Ann Arbor, we weren't too worried. In 1914 Germany, before the start of that war, was already in possession of Alsace-Lorraine. This time with the French having repossessed, thanks to the outcome of World War I, such potential springboard region, the Germans should have that much more difficulty forwarding their line in France. We all foresaw the Germans' again bogging down in Northern France with a solid front holding there until the Western Allies could eventually push the Boche back into Germany.

Were the U.S.A. eventually to enter it, the same as in World War I, we looked into our crystal ball and guessed that the lines would be holding in Northern France with plenty of time for the U.S. Army to get rearmed, and to then again play an important role in helping win the war. So went our surmise as, ostrich-like, to get ahead with Ward's, I dug in to burn the midnight oil on a series of studies while learning backwards and forwards salient factors of merchandising from Monkey's big fat procedure manual.

Rich Enlivens the Merchandising Merry-Go-Round

From her post in charge of the catalog-order desk, Babette got a bird's-eye view down one flight into the sporting goods department. She liked what she saw, words of wisdom to Homer and Migi as the new department head developed the lighter side of the life of the Cornell-Dartmouth densification aided and assisted by a couple of Ward's long-term locals.

With the arrival of good spring weather, customers commenced snapping up bicycles. Lyle Hurd's truck would drop them off from the warehouse. The hitch was that the bikes came sealed in big, fat, individual cardboard cartons. Sinelli would bring them down the elevator or slide them down the stairs. Either way they'd get underfoot of Epperson, the star manager of automotive products.

To get rid of the obstructions at the rear, Rich, as head of the sporting goods department, had the job of getting the two-wheeled vehicles set up and integrated into his displays, otherwise filling spring demand, fixing up eager purchasers so that they could proudly ride their new wheels home.

But how to increase the pace of the setting-up process? A ruse that Rich had adapted from Tom Sawyer helped. The graduate of department store and specialty retailing, respectively, from Jordan-Marsh and Dennison's challenged: "I'll bet that you can't beat my time and set up one of these bikes in better than twenty minutes."

He soon had a race against the clock going among Art Pennala, Ken Boyer, Allan Parsley and your Virginian. Although, as a brother Ivy Leaguer, I sensed the ruse, and although the fun was a far cry from checker-playing in Jackson, it was all a first-rate production. Helping Rich develop his ruse, I strung along. The Dartmouth product was displaying executive potential.

' In Ward's stuffy basement, another facet of Rich's powers of observation surfaced. From time to time various beauteous mother and daughter combinations as they descended the stairs would make their dramatic entry into our paint and wallpaper department. At a signal from Rich, Pennala and Parsley would fade back, leaving center stage occupied by a trio made up of the new arrivals and Monkey's junior aspirant to become a store manager. Maybe it was because I was half-Welsh. Repeated successful handling of these marvelous assignments was the result of some inherent know-how, some gift of the gab, choice of just the right words, all of which turned these mothers and daughters into such great conversationalists that, as your Virginian sold them some paint or wallpaper, old hands such as Ken Boyer and Allan Parsley and, needless to say, Arnold Rich and Art Pennala, dusted and otherwise refurbished nearby counters, anything to get within earshot to hear the successful sales pitch and observe my mother-and-daughter customers perk up as the presence of their estimable personalities also made the lives of all clerks, especially that of your junior trainee, much more liveable, thanks to some invites to dinner.

At the same time, Rich supplemented the merry-go-round activities, ably providing his own share of the constructive entertainment. When a Chinese scholar from the university stepped up to one of our counters that displayed some spools of lightweight rope, one of our smoother salesmen (the one with the Dartmouth and Beacon Street polish) greeted him and, on the spot, devised one of the basement's more colorful sales spiels. Helping the Chinese eliminate several options, gravitating to his just having to choose between two, retailing's nine-year veteran, after describing and discussing the first, now pointed to the second and last option and to the Chinese said: "Sir, you may well like this lightweight rope on the spool to the right. But this other type of rope on the spool to the left that also seems to interest you is superior in my opinion, much better in that it has a special fuzette twist!"

"All right then," said the Chinese scholar. "I'll take ten feet of that one with the special fuzette twist."

An unexpected boomerang about all of that mishmash about the fuzette twist was this furthering of the footsteps of Mercer back at Cornell. There he'd introduced special nicknames from Mercersburg such as Softball, Big-U, Ninety Days, One Muscle, the Ox, Satch, and for your Virginian, "Benny Sent Me."

Likewise, Tabor Prep, through the good offices of Rich, now passed along some nicknames such as Migi and Homer. Pennala, after hearing the Tabor-Dartmouth product sell the Chinese some rope, reminded Rich. "You call me 'Migi' because I worked for a number of months on the Mexican border. You call Dean 'Homer' because you think he's a farmer. So now we've got a moniker to hang on to you."

"What's that?"

"Mr. Fuzette."

"How do you figure?"

"When your fraternity back at Dartmouth sang 'Alouette,' you said that 'a la fuzette' was your punch line. Remember?"

"Oh." Our senior trainee lapsed into deep thought. Yet before long a secret pal emerged to stand up for this notability.

What we all didn't realize was that during his few weeks in Ann Arbor, the senior trainee had been targeted by a devotionalist. Putting a damper on the fun, Babette, who had been keeping tabs while looking down from her catalog order desk at the head of the basement stairs, now stood up for the enricher of Monkey's merchandising merry-go-round.

Promptly, she scolded the downstairs staff, "You can call him Mr. Fuzette all you want so long as you don't call him that in front of me!"

Hitler Sets Europe on Fire, Triggers Winds of Conscription

When it came to specialty monikers, all told in our basement department, we stuck to first names, excepting the older generation where Mr. Foster, that resolute bossman of plumbing and heating, was always Mr. Foster.

Relatively unnoticed by our group of sales clerks, potential recruits for the military as the spotlight sought out and found the youngest, to your unaware George Washington VI at age twenty-two, came the news as previously mentioned. Hitler was setting the Western Front on fire. And Winston Churchill was Britain's new prime minister.

If only Howard Lee Davis had sent us a supplement for his book, making some specific suggestions as to how our chain's administration in Chicago could keep Hitler from muffling Monkey's as green fields for a career in the esteem of the young man in business. Why couldn't Davis have put out some suggestions as to what to do, when so nearly under the gun, while still trying to aim at becoming a captain of industry when this very real kind of a shooting war threatened to suck up such an aspirant! Very lately, Hitler's aggressiveness had triggered some winds of change in favor of a draft.

For a score of years conscription as an eventuality had seemed impossible to us Americans. Soon after the Munich Conference of September 1938, only thirty-seven percent of voters in Gallup polls favored universal military training. But leave it to Hitler! Just a year and a half after Munich, as the Nazi blitzkrieg opened up in the West, while there was still no alarming "What to do in a hurry at Monkey's," the straw vote quickly increased to fifty percent!

The Nazis Dominate the Flashes from the Front

Taking issue with the Nazis, FDR denounced their invasion of the Low Countries. Allied troops landed on the Dutch islands in the West Indies. The Nazis advanced beyond Liege and occupied about all of northern Holland, soon seizing Moerdijk bridge south of Rotterdam, cutting Holland in two as Queen Wilhelmina and her family reached England. Came another item of unrecognized portent. Through the Ardennes came a Nazi drive that captured the French city of Sedan. This raised a serious question: just where and when would the World War I-type of front crystallize and bog down the fighting into a long line in northern France?

As Churchill received a unanimous vote of confidence from the British parliament, the Dutch Army surrendered except in Zeeland. But the Allies, painting a bright stroke, claimed that they had successfully met a German attack along a sixty-mile front from Namur to the Sedan "bulge." Hearing such news in Michigan, all that we could do was to hope—that the Western Allies would soon reduce that "bulge." Prophetic was some news growing out of the blitz. One-fourth of the Dutch Army, or 100,000 men, were reportedly killed in battle. FDR asked Congress for more than a billion dollars for national defense and stressed that the Army and the Navy should be equipped with 50,000 planes.

When Berlin announced the fall of Brussels, Namur, and Louvain, gaps in French defenses around Sedan and at other points farther north along the border were already showing up. So FDR ordered the recommissioning of thirty-five more destroyers laid up since World War I. Perking up Arnold Rich at Monkey's (who frequently asked, "You want to become a fighter pilot?"), Col. Frank Knox of Chicago, with a nod from FDR, initiated plans for training at private expense ten thousand college students as aviators.

Antwerp was captured by the Nazis. In Northern France, by

mid-May, one prong of the German Army was driving westerly toward the English Channel. As their armored columns continued to dominate the flashes from the front, Hitler commenced to announce revisions of the Versailles Treaty unilaterally. The German government proclaimed reincorporation into the Reich of Eupen, Malmedy, and Moresnet, which had been ceded by such treaty to Belgium.

A Trainee Touches a Nerve

Back at Ward's retail store in Ann Arbor, while the import of all of the shocking developments from military operations on the Western Front was ever so slowly sinking in, we continued to hack it as a trainee for a merchandising career. Well-doing our homework, burning the midnight oil over Monkey's big, fat retail-store operations manual, we boiled it all down to one question for Bosso McCarty to answer. But by asking the question, without realizing it, we would be leapfrogging this other much more advisable approach.

At the time, your scribe somehow or other missed the better way by not paying close enough attention to Howard Lee Davis' preachments in this one of my bibles, *The Young Man in Business*. And there was a good chance that I had registered with the better approach but was too much concerned about Ann Arbor-bound shock waves that would obviously be emerging from the hostilities in Europe.

Also, it simply may have been that I was too proud to acknowledge Davis' suggestion's usefulness. If so, I should have swallowed my complacency, and made an appointment with Bosso McCarty, and then (even though I would have felt as though I were reciting lines on stage), I should have made my approach by saying to Bosso something out of Davis like this: "Naturally I want to do my work well and probably there are things that I could do better; also, there may be some things that I could do on the side, over and above studying, as I've been doing nights, the store's big procedure manual—certain reading or studying that would better fit me, not only for the work I do now, but also for the work I should be able to do after I gain more experience. I shall appreciate it, Mr. McCarty, if you will tell me frankly, based on your many years of experience in the retail chain-store business, just how you feel I am getting along, whether my work is as you think it should be, and in what ways I can improve. I do not want to drift, so please tell me, straight from the shoulder, where you believe I should put more pressure and where you feel it would be well for me to check myself."

Had I taken this approach, I could have better tapped into Mr. McCarty's great wealth of knowledge and could have procured all sorts of beneficial opinions from the great practical field of merchandising wisdom that had been generated from practical chain store experience by Bosso.

Included would have been the possibility of giving our store manager the chance of taking the lead in obtaining for me a pay hike (thus keeping intact my policy of not asking for a raise). Instead, while evincing no dissatisfaction, I kept right on plugging but without going to the well-warranted trouble of developing as aforesaid any cues from Bosso. Finally, but without realizing that I was taking the bull by the horns, I went to our store manager with this salient question that I had fingered as the most important point in the store's big fat operating manual. Catching Bosso in his office when he had a moment to spare, I told him that I had studied the formula and asked him to tell me all about the store's operating ratio, how it applied to our retail store here in Ann Arbor. (Such ratio was a number by which one establishment in Ward's big chain could be rated against the rest).

Although I thought that I knew *The Young Man in Business* backwards and forwards, unfortunately, I broke one of Albert Lee Davis' important rules. I put the store manager on the defensive.

Bosso reddened as he came up out of his executive's armchair saying: "Dean. It will be a long time before you get to know about our store's operating ratio. In the meanwhile just keep doing like you've been doing and you'll get there soon enough."

Although your unaware George Washington VI may have tried too quick a step up the ladder, he knew a nerve when he touched one. As diplomatically as possible, he beat a quick retreat.

Calamity Fans Urgency for Conscription

Feeling as though I had identified a very important secret portal into the guts of the great chain of stores, although still outside and unable to get a gander inside, I saw my inability to get at this invisible store-operating-ratio number as some sort of a blocker that stood in my path of advancement.

From my time of joining Monkey's, Bosso had encouraged me to ask questions. So now that this first real big one had gone unsatisfied, back to the sales floor I went with just as much enthusiasm as ever; but I was wondering not only just how long, how many years, it was going to take your twenty-two-year-old unaware George Washington VI to become a great enough merchandiser to be trusted with knowledgeability of a store's operating ratio; in addition I puzzled over just what sorts of factors were orbiting such operating ratio that made it such a big mystery. In short, although I didn't let it come out, I was just a little bit swamped by the growing contrast of my quest for a commercial captaincy with the war news. Same as the blood-thirsty Wilmark shoppers' two-in-a-row scores, this bit about the operating ratio was soon settled into the realms of the picayune by radio reports from the Western Front.

Shock waves from France and Belgium kept coming in. Your Virginian not only was of draft age but also was the store's leading candidate, were the United States to go for conscription. The nagging question: Which was preferable? Monkey's or the military?

Since your Virginian had a deep interest in the army though unaware that he came from a generations-old military family out of England, were the country to enter the war, he knew that he was going to enlist, as distinguished from waiting to be tagged by Uncle Sam. Would Congress get around to passing a conscription law? The recent change in sentiment by the Gallup polls was reflected in a resolution by the Military Training Camps Association. Out of it had grown the Plattsburg complex that had turned out lots of first-rate American fighting men in time for World War I. Now that this current shocking phase of World War II was turning into a sweep by the Germans into France, as calamity fanned sentiments, this association urged immediate compulsory military training in the United States.

No wonder! Already, by May 23, part of the Allied Armies were trapped in Flanders as the Germans advanced to Boulogne on the English Channel. A day later the Nazis reached Calais and were in the process of taking the city. In contrast, during World War I, the British had always successfully defended the French channel ports closest to England (although, as Frank Love of Syracuse would later point out, he'd then led his men through Calais to the tune of some German shellfire). Where was the stable front that we expected to crystallize this time in Northern France? It was nonexistent!

Near the end of May, as the British Expeditionary Force commenced to debark from Dunkirk, came this shockeroo. King Leopold of Belgium unconditionally surrendered his army to the Germans over the protests of his cabinet and of the French command. In minor contrast came a very faint glimmer through the dark clouds: the Allies captured Narvik and two adjoining towns in Norway. But on the Western Front, Lille fell before the German advance, as the Allies fighting to escape from the Flanders pocket flooded the Yser valley region and continued evacuating troops to England from Dunkirk. By May 31, London announced that three-fourths of the British Expeditionary Force in Flanders had been repatriated from Dunkirk.

Reacting on our side of the Atlantic, FDR told Congress: "It's imperative, because of the recent successful use of tanks and planes in war, that at least a billion dollars more should be spent for U.S. national defense," and the President asked for authority to call out the National Guard and *all* reserve forces if necessary.

And when it came to any remembrances of your Virginian's unsuccessful probe for an explanation of applications of Monkey's operating ratio to the Ann Arbor store, wire-service details of Hitler's planes-plus-tanks blitzkrieg made any concerns (over the little-known, held-back magic store-analysis number) do a fade-out!

Rich Raises the Hare: "How Much Are We Worth to Monkey's?"

Ongoing aftershocks from all of the bloody embroilments overseas created a silent undercurrent of ferment at our retail store. All of the proposed federal spending for rearmament didn't exactly fall on deaf ears. We'd all heard stories of the big money that had been made by wartime shipyard workers togged out during recreational hours in silk shirts. It looked as though there would soon be some even better money to be made during World War II, whether or not the United States entered the fray. Maybe some of it would rub off on Monkey's?

Presumably we all were keeping our lips buttoned and not complaining, although you could feel that we all thought that we were underpaid. Our senior trainee sensed our sentiments. Dredging back into his several years of retailing with Jordan Marsh and Dennison's, he raised the hare. "How much salary are we worth to Ward's?"

Participating in this unusual powwow (that took place at the junction of the aisles between housewares, paint and sporting goods) were Pennala, Parsley, Rich, and your Virginian. While any mention of specific numbers was taboo, and while Rich (who'd raised the hare) listened attentively, all of the sales clerks who managed to get in on the act started beating around the bush. "As much as I can get." Or, "More than I'm getting now." Plus various and sundry shots in the dark.

Thanks to a little lull, our huddle was enabled to be factored into the thick density of the daylong merchandising mishmash. But overhead, a sudden increase in the pace of footsteps indicated a pickup in the flow of customers as they headed one flight down for the popular and successful sales spiels that they so liked linked with their purchases.

On the basement sales floor, we clerks still had a free minute left. Sensing that the time had come to present the truth, Rich (who for several years before coming to Ann Arbor had developed into a senior merchandising trainee with lasting colorations from both Beantown and the Windy City) reiterated, "Just exactly how does a man tell just how much he's worth to Ward's?"

"There's no real way," ventured Pennala.

"What about you, Parsley?"

He shrugged.

"And what say you? Ben."

Turning it around, I asked Rich, "How much are *you* worth to Ward's? You tell us."

This seemed like a difficult question for anyone to answer. What were the tests? Studying pertinent parts of *The Young Man In Busi-*

ness, by Howard Lee Davis, might have helped. But there wasn't time to thumb the index. Seeking the right answer, our most closely associated clerks had been brightly taking some seeming pot shots in the dark.

Keeping it turned around, I again asked Rich, "How much are you worth? You tell us."

But before Rich could reply, a couple of other clerks, overhearing us, stepped right up and put in their two cents by submitting various and sundry self-valuations.

While somewhat perplexed over my still most secret hundred a month, I wondered just what point Rich was trying to make.

After the late arrivals had gotten in on the act, but had quickly shot their bolt, it came time for Rich to help us out. For consumption by the rest of our powwow, he answered my question: "I can't tell you just how much the rest of you are worth to Ward's, but I can tell you how much I'm worth to the company."

"How much is that?" asked Pennala as we all bent eager ears.

Only moments before a trio of customers rushed down the stairs, now that Rich had set the stage, for his moment of chain-store glory he proclaimed, "Just exactly what I'm getting paid."

Spelling the Delivery Clerk

Just as Rich touched the spot on the subject of salaries, three young cuties arrived to buy some colorful jockey caps. It was our turn to help wait on them and soon, with the fair locks on their respective noggins colorfully highlighted with the sporting goods department's best racecourse chapeaus, the Dartmouth product delivered a send-off speech as the vibrant dolls checked out for the Kentucky Derby. While we all were wishing that we could have joined them, we dutifully kept our nose to Monkey's retail grindstone.

The time had also come to commence writing up pink tickets for our annual inventory. If we sold something, we'd then have to adjust the appropriate inventory ticket. After soaking up lots of such very important experience, it also came time for me to switch to spelling Wes Eisley, our delivery clerk, when he left on his annual vacation.

Back in Eisley's previously described stall, yet in the same receiving room with Sinelli, my new duties encompassed writing up a manifest, a line for each separate item being delivered. Then we'd track down the goods to go and make sure that they got put aboard on time to depart with Lyle Hurd's big red truck. There were some interesting scenes. For instance, when I would arrive at the rug department upstairs, usually the item to go would be at or near the bottom of the pile and we'd have to wait for one of Ward's Ann Arbor stars, Louis Bycraft—who later on would become a big linoleum and rug man on his own account—to wind up another of many successful sales with some of his most important customers. Then, while the truckers, worried over the delay, stirred about us nervously, Bycraft (while still holding his customer) would flip back big carpets and tag the sold item so that we could get it going down the freight elevator, and then on the road to the home of the particular rug's eagerly waiting purchaser. In the meanwhile, more and more with each passing day, events in Europe got a foot in the door, making us feel all the more as though we at Monkey's might well be just marking time, and that any promotion in rank and salary would only be beguiling.

FDR Declares a National Emergency

By early June, the Germans were continuing their air raids against the south of France for the purpose, in a French guesstimate, of influencing an Italian decision to enter the war. Some of our nation's big ocean liners were leaving Europe with thousands of American refugees. On the continent, some aerial blows were swapped. The *Luftwaffe* dumped more than a thousand bombs on Paris while French planes, in retaliation, bombed some German cities. In the Empire State, Governor Lehman called out five hundred members of the National Guard to protect the seventy-four state armories. On the English Channel, in Dunkirk, the Nazis took over on the heels of the Allied evacuation. Belgium now was completely occupied by the Nazis. With the British Expeditionary Force homing successfully to England were 338,226 Allied soldiers, including 26,226 members of the French Army.

With the British forces out of it, Hitler renewed his blitzkrieg. Focusing on the French, the *Wehrmacht* began an attack on a battle line extending one hundred-twenty miles east from Abbeville on the English Channel with a reported force of a million men, a thousand bombers, twenty-two hundred tanks and fifteen thousand motor vehicles. For another rare glimmer of light, a press release from the French Army claimed wholesale destruction of German tanks but conceded enemy advances below Abbeville and Laon. Then it appeared that something was cooking with Italy. Over the radio in Louie Sinelli's receiving department at Ward's came the oratory of Mussolini outdoing Hitler. As we all took in with wonderment the emanations from the squawk box, Arnold Rich announced: "The Moose is at it again. Hear! Hear! That's the Moose speaking."

Maybe it sounded funny, but something *was* cooking with the Moose. Italian merchant ships at sea were ordered to take refuge in the nearest neutral port, just as the French Army's left wing was retreating along a line extending from Neufchatel to the vicinity of Soissons. Soon the battle line was extended to the Swiss frontier with approximately two million Germans engaged, their point men back towards the English Channel reaching Rouen.

When Wes Eisley returned from his vacation, thus releasing your unaware George Washington VI for return to his regular job as a sales clerk (heading Ward's local wallpaper department), to the tune of Italy's declaring war on the Western Allies, the returnee sagely posed the question: "If Italy now attacks France in its southeasterly quarter, do you think that Greece will help the underdog?"

With no time for us to ponder over it, FDR, in an address at the University of Virginia, referred to Italy's joinder: ". . . . the hand that held the dagger plunged it into the back of its neighbor." In addition, by FDR "all possible material assistance" was pledged to the Allies.

In France, the government moved from Paris to Tours and other towns of the Loire Valley. London announced that the British aircraft carrier *Glorious* had been lost during the evacuation of Narvik. In the City of Washington FDR signed a naval appropriations bill for well over a billion dollars. At once the Navy completed contracts for twenty-two new warships, including two new battle-wagons. Hopefully they wouldn't come on line too late.

In Paris, *The Paris Herald* folded on June 12. Evarts and Ken Koyen, who'd been part of the staff, set out for Bordeaux, joining an incredible exodus. *(OPC BULLETIN)* By June 14 (just about a year after my graduation from Cornell), in the east, the Red Army was in the process of taking Lithuania while, in the west, Paris was being occupied by the Germans. Another phase of the attack commenced on the northern flank of the Maginot Line. Le Havre fell as the French government left Tours for Bourdeaux. In Germany, Hitler ordered a three-day celebration of the capture of Paris.

Such Allied losses in Europe lit a fire under conscription proponents here at home. What an effect the shock waves were having on your Virginian's life as a trainee with Ward's. Came the result of the current Gallup poll. It was up to sixty-four percent in favor of a draft!

Overseas, French Premier Reynaud resigned, to be succeeded by Marshal Petain. By June 17 France sued for peace. The next day the *Luftwaffe*, for a nice little harbinger, in its first concerted cross-channel attack raided the east coast of England.

Two days later, on Thursday, June 20, E. R. Burke of Nebraska introduced into the Senate a bill for conscription. And on the next day the bill was presented to the House by James Wadsworth of New York. For such merchandising kingpins as Sewell Lee Avery, together with his many aides such as Robinson, Harrison, Moore, and even Bosso McCarty, a good question now applied. How could the merchandising chieftains at Chicago continue to inculcate draft-age trainees with rah-rah Ward's when Hitler's historic surges muffled Monkey's?

By June 25, when fighting between France and Germany and Italy ceased, the Germans had taken over the entire Atlantic coast of France. Nine months earlier (September 1939) FDR had declared a limited emergency. On June 27, 1940, it came time for FDR to take the spotlight. Making any grasp by Monkey's on your Virginian's aspirations of a merchandising career for a captaincy of industry look like a molehill, the President of the United States declared a national emergency.

Chapter 6

Openers Under the National Emergency

They'll Get Their Noses Burnt!

By June 25, fighting between France and Germany and Italy ceased. Incredibly, the Germans had taken over the entire Atlantic coast of France. Whether the Allies could ever drive the Germans out was the question that came up when I met one of my former landlords.

Before World War I, as a peacetime conscript in the German Army, he'd participated in training marches in which the grenadiers had kept going for a number of days, all in preparation (as it turned out) for Germany's then upcoming 1914 march through Belgium. But after my older-generation friend had paid his dues to the Fatherland, he'd gotten out in good time to stay alive. Thus by now he'd become a productive American citizen. Nevertheless he found himself numbered among the large body of German-Americans who couldn't help feeling proud of the accomplishments of the Reich's tank columns assisted by air strikes.

Sounding him out, I commented, "It looks as though the Allies will have a heck of a time driving the Germans back from the Atlantic coast of France."

"If they try it they'll get their noses burnt." Presumably the German-American didn't take into account that the United States might eventually get dragged into the war and that his own folks, unless they enlisted, might get drafted and have to fight their German cousins. Were the U.S.A. to get involved in plans to invade the Continent, such an attitude as evidenced by the German American would stay pervasive to the extent that when the time would come, any and all U.S. Army officers who evinced a belief that it couldn't be done would be sent home.

Now, back to the positive side: instead of recognizing the French government that, as of June 22, had just signed an armistice and agreed to surrender all sea forces and demobilize its land and air forces, Great Britain allied itself with the French National Committee in London as the leader of all "free" Frenchmen.

Making it look as though your young man in business had no choice other than to merely mark time with Monkey's, the war department ordered the creation of a corps of two divisions in the U.S. Army to be equipped with 1,400 tanks, 600 pieces of artillery and 13,000 automatic and semi-automatic rifles. From the viewpoint of a fellow Owegoan, Pat Vona, how serving with the Armed Forces in Panama, everything was hunky-dory. If Pat and his fellow soldiers got their hoped-for chance, just whose nose would get burnt? Hitler's!

The Fish Between Two Cats

By late June, counting my savings as a waiter back at Cornell, I had accumulated a fund of several hundred dollars. Johnson, formerly an ace baseball player in the Tioga County league at Spencer, New York, had finished up at the University of Michigan and now popped into Monkey's retail store. "Bosso McCarty says that you have some money that's burning a hole in your pocket. What about letting me sell you a brand-new Chevrolet?"

"How much for what?"

He named his price.

"That's too much for too many extras."

"There's nothing to it. You've got a good down payment. We'll finance the rest."

"Oh, no." I explained the background. My father had confiscated my chicken-money nest egg, not only stopping me from having previously bought a new car, but also having admonished me not to go into hock for one.

Temporarily, Johnson gave up. While I was kicking around this idea of a new car, I tried out a used one. My good friend Red, who ran a nearby gas station, put it on a hoist. When the underpinnings looked awful, Red counseled, "Don't monkey with a used one."

"You mean stick to a new one?"

"Yes."

"They cost too much."

"I'll show you where you can get one without a lot of extras for maybe six hundred bucks."

"Wow!"

"You interested?"

"Definitely."

Then came a seesawing. When France fell to the Nazis, Wall Street fell out of bed. Out of Monkey's backdoor and across the alleyway, I could duck into the rear of the local brokerage office. What looked to be an excellent chance to buy some common shares in International Tel. and Tel. (ITT) brought out my unrealized propensity as a risk-seeker and titillated it. But competing for my savings was my desire to buy a new car. Quickly my fund of a several hundred dollars turned out like a fish between two cats.

First in my thinking was the first pitch fielded for a new wagon. Even though it looked too expensive, the older-generation salesman who'd migrated a decade earlier from the Yankee Tier, had provided a great revelation. Long before your Virginian, the car salesman had once dwelt in Sheldon Court—that great collegiate palace of capers—while attending Cornell. At that decade-earlier date, a fellow student, during some horseplay, had fallen out of a window. To me, news of such an earlier debacle made the estimated decade-later surprise haymaker by Deke that had boomeranged (as detailed in Volume II) look like some misbehavin' at Sunday school. It was too bad that upon your Virginian's arrival at Sheldon Court, no one had tipped us off in time as to college-town horseplay's potential for the much more serious consequences now first illustrated by the tumble from a window. And it was also just tough that the story of the man over the side during the Roaring 'Twenties had been so well suppressed. Otherwise, the earlier disaster could well have taught us 'uns making the same scene during the latter 'thirties a lesson in preventive maintenance of the peace, as it would have most certainly squelched some otherwise hilarious capers out of which had grown another but lesser debacle (detailed in Volume II). Now back to the June 1940 question of using credit to buy a car.

Thanks to some inherited puritanical ethic whetted by my parents, I told Bosso McCarty's salesman friend that borrowing to buy wheels was out. And while the fish was still getting ripped at by the two cats, the next time I saw Red he reminded me, "Well, we looked underneath that used one. It was a mess of rusty worn-out junk. Why inherit someone else's headaches?"

I thought of the open-air taxicab with the shaky kingbolts, poor brakes, no horn, weak battery, and non-working windshield wipers that Jovial John had sold me for a hundred bucks just over three years earlier, and in which I'd been lucky to make it through its year-and-a-half existence alive.

Red continued, "Take advantage of our motor industry next door. Get yourself a brand-new car. If you haven't got enough cash to get the fancy extras down the street, I'll show you where to get a good deal."

"OK," I said to Red. "But first I've got to decide whether to latch on instead to some ITT stock. In 1929 it was a highflier—more than a hundred bucks a share. But now, with the Nazis running roughshod over a very substantial part of western Europe, where they can menace with potential confiscation some of this American company's very substantial overseas assets, that stock might be a steal. The plug's already been pulled on it. Right now it looks impossible for the Allies to win the war. So maybe the worst news is out. Maybe Hitler won't dare to invade Spain, where ITT has a unit. And maybe at a couple of dollars or even less, the share price of ITT common stock is on bottom, while the investing public thinks that its next downtick is going to be zero. Gambling that the Allies are going to do the impossible and win, all I need now is the guts to buy some ITT. If I put my allotted six hundred bucks in it and go without a car, over the upcoming years, if we do get into the war and help win it, the Nazis won't be able to confiscate any of ITT's valuable European properties, and I'll turn the six hundred bucks into thousands of dollars," I predicted.

"But suppose the Nazis wipe out ITT? And don't forget, even if the Nazis lose, what good is all of that money going to do you if we get into the war and you get knocked off in it?" asked Red. "Maybe the worst news *isn't* yet out? Maybe you can get ITT even lower when even more bad news comes out? Suppose it does go down to zero? Just in case, you'd better hurry up and get the new car and enjoy it while you're still around to enjoy it! If you survive, then you can buy some stock," came Red's pro-automobile advice from right out of the woodwork near the heart of America's motor world.

"OK. But first I make one last trip to the broker's office to decide," I told Red.

Taking another break from Monkey's, on the main-drag side of the alley, I scooted through the rear portal of the board room and focused on the ticker tape. Without realizing that by intuition, I was following the current thinking of Bernard Baruch, right crack off the bat I made a classic mistake. Many of the oldsters present had also focused on ITT. But were they ever scared! Instead of my quietly putting in my buy order, getting a cashier's check from my nearby bank, then taking delivery later on of my stock certificate and stashing it away, while keeping my mouth shut, I voiced my proposed move to latch on to a few hundred shares of ITT. Of the mixed bag of retirees hanging out, huddling with mesmerized eyes glued on a ticker tape shocked by Hitler, a tape that thus spewed mostly falling quotations, a pair of nearby ears pricked up. A retired traveling salesman of schoolbooks stepped forward and volunteered: "My boy, you don't want to buy any stock in ITT until the end of the war is in sight! Not until the end is in sight," he reiterated.

Such words, eventually, would be labeled by a perceptive Manhattan slicker (as he would one day attempt to steer me into buying some shares of Red Bank Oil that would later flop) like this: "That's why the schoolbook salesman stayed a schoolbook salesman." Since the eventual insight from the Manhattan slicker was yet to be revealed, such wait-and-see advice from the erstwhile book salesman now helped Red's good words get the upper hand.

It wasn't that my risk-taking courage had faltered. Priorities were the issue. Had my father not confiscated my chicken-money nest egg, I'd have already had my new car. Had such been the case, right now I would have made a Baruchian purchase of several hundred dollars worth of ITT. Now back to the real world.

From the way the Nazis had just run roughshod over France, Belgium, Holland, and Luxembourg, Red's words of wisdom had become king. You just had to consider that ominous possibility— the Germans might invade England. The U.S.A. might soon join the fray, meaning that in the possible war involvement your un-aware George Washington VI might get knocked off! When such atmospherics larruped me, "enjoy a brand-new buggy while you can" was the theme song of the new-car cat that got the fish away from the unsuccessful ITT yowler.

Displacing dreams of becoming a shareholder in ITT, the pro-posed automobile took over first claim on my cash. I knew what I wanted. Red phoned in the order. Within a week Red dropped me off at New Hudson. When I handed C. D. Shear a bank draft, for this cash on the barrelhead, this good dealer turned over title cer-tificate and possession to me of my factory-fresh, brand-new, light blue Chevrolet business coupe. Without knee-action and equipped with a baggage platform instead of a back seat, it cost just over six hundred simoleons, the finance company-in-waiting being left out of the picture.

Immediately I got to work arranging for my well-earned first annual paid vacation. I was just about to complete my first year with Ward's. The brass hats would have been well-advised, after I had given it a go for a year, to invite me at company expense to spend at least a day making a first-time visit touring Monkey's Chi-cago GHQ. But some sort of an inherent psychological strength growing out of this yearlong lack of a raise, helped along by inter-mittent news flashes from the war in Europe, was making me more hesitant about letting myself get hooked for a career in the Mid-west with Ward's.

When I motored through the northerly portals of Ann Arbor in my new car, almost immediately I huddled with Bosso McCarty and arranged for my entitlement—a week's vacation with pay. To comfortably handle my proposed round trip to the East Coast, to the one week with pay I arranged to add a week without. "Think Big," was my motto. So with an objective of breaking loose from

Monkey's fetters, there began my fortnight-long quest. Implementing the successful world of Dick Washburn, who sold small private planes, I dreamed of getting a position selling the biggies.

An Aerial Inspiration Out of Owego: Dick Washburn

Last mentioned, in attendance with the big crowd at the Cleveland Air Races, canceled on account of high winds, just as Hitler had been marching into Poland, was Dick Washburn.

Now, a year later, and during the summer of 1940, the local product was pointed out in Owego's Main Street weekly as having been written up in *Future*, published by the United States Junior Chamber of Commerce.

The young sales manager of Luscombe Airplane Corporation was a graduate of the School of Aeronautics. Although he was primarily interested in selling, *Future* described an all-around aircraft promoter. "He makes up contracts, keeps after the distributers with frequent visits. The New York City showroom at 247 Park Avenue is the first permanent airplane store in the big city. More than thirty planes have been sold from the floor in five months."

After getting the feel of over-the-waves waltzing with his outboard motorboat on the Susquehanna River, Dick Washburn was now a whirling ball of flame in Manhattan. Your unaware George Washington VI took notice: Another Owego boy was making good, and in a much more colorful way than having to run the gamut as a trainee for a coast-to-coast chain store operation.

Homing First Time on Own Wheels

Getting ready to home for the first time on my own wheels, I made my first year whole with Monkey's by rounding it with a full day's work on Wednesday, the day before the Fourth. Unless I otherwise informed him Bosso McCarty could rely on my return in two weeks; in other words, I'd next punch in on the time clock on the morning of Friday, July 19. Nevertheless, to keep my options open, I had checked out with my current landlady, packed all of my gear in the trunk of my new Chevrolet, and at Monkey's closing gong, easterly down the vacation road I rolled.

In the palmy twilight of the eve of the Fourth of July, I was soon motoring past Detroit Beach on the left, then observing General Custer's home town on the right. This was Monroe, Michigan. And of almost equal importance to me, it had produced Rustikins, one of Owego's great gains at the expense of such Michigan municipality.

Rustikins, after graduating from Culver Academy, where he'd chummed with Harry Lord (who'd come to Owego from New England to practice law with the Senator), was an astute student of the stock market. In Florida, he'd met one of Owego's most popular heiresses. As they rolled round town in a light gray Packard convertible, their marriage added a bright new facet to the Yankee Tier's social life and Rustikins, as a newcomer, promptly made a name for himself as the leading social lion of Owego's silk-stocking district. To us younger chaps including Hawk and Kayo, Rustikins played the role of a reliable and admirable big brother, a Clark Gable-type figure to imitate, and even more especially, we frequently paused to hear from Rustikins thumbnail sketches on stocks such as North American Aviation. The war news wasn't getting any better. So Rustikins saw it as an investment that would take off any old day now.

As I concluded that Owego's gain was Monroe's loss, off starboard, a nostalgic scene drifted up. When I caught the glints of bright lights reflecting off polished brass, having been a high school bandsman specializing in the sousaphone, and, during summer vacations, a town bandsman specializing in some oompah on the tuba at such tunes as "The National Emblem," as much in tribute to Rustikins as to General Custer, while I didn't exactly stop and take the time to enjoy the marches and overtures being played by the Monroe brass band, I did double-park, get out, and run over, vowing to at least touch the bandstand.

In their fancy uniforms, these musicians breathing life into the municipality made come alive a cover on the *Saturday Evening Post*. On the green, a substantial crowd, sympathetic with my urgency (as I muttered my motive), opened a pathway. As they continued to enjoy the renditions on the eve of the Fourth, I let it all come out: Too bad, but for your unaware George Washington VI, his mission being a fortnight-long quest for something new to pitch into, it was onward over some big bay bridges past Toledo, Sandusky, and Lorain to Cleveland.

There, spending the night with some former college classmates I soon learned that most of them were making a minimum of twenty-five dollars a week. And those who'd jumped the gun in the business world by dropping out of college, for the extra time spent garnering their extra added expertise, were being paid as much as forty dollars a week. One of my more brilliant classmates, who'd opted for the engineering school, had been snapped up by a recruiter for some perky manufacturing company. His starting salary was out of this world: ten thousand a year—an unheard-of rate for a trainee. But once in a such a harness, he would find that he'd been fitted robot-like into a highly organized, first-rate management team. After a year or so at the high-paying position, he would give it up. What would he switch to? Of all things—retail merchandising! But, by then he would have saved up enough capital so that he would be able to honcho successfully his own department store.

During my overnight garnering of the latest reactions of my former Cornell classmates to the war in Europe, some applicable straws turned up in the wind. John Davol Williams expected that his cavalry unit of the National Guard would soon be called up and that he'd be leaving. Albert Rees Davis II, on his own account, was taking some extra added flying training just in case. Then, should the U.S.A. get into the war, he'd have a leg up at becoming a B-17 pilot. Even though during lulls between headlines of Hitler's various boasts, it occasionally seemed as though the war in Europe might just dry up and blow away, these Cornell products and other chaps from the Cleveland Heights and Shaker Heights area were not only getting prepared, but also were itching to go.

Without realizing that before we'd again meet, we were all fated to get into uniform, then back into mufti, after an early breakfast, I hit the road for the Yankee Tier. East of Kingsville, Ohio, I cut off from the main drag and crossed by secondary road into my native Pennsylvania. Between the state line and Albion, when I stopped for gas and flashed a twenty-dollar bill, the lady hied with it to the house. When she soon returned and counted back my change, she explained away the added bother: "We just don't see money like that around here!" Just then, so it seemed, western Pennsylvania's oil patch was in the doldrums. But farther east, after a goodly and tiresome haul through the Alleghenies, dotting the Bradford oil patch, lots of squeaking pumps were lifting buckaroos out of mother earth. Pressing homeward, I crossed into the Empire State near Westons Mills. This settlement was the home town of F. Van Wormer Walsh, who'd served so ably as pace-setter in our Exigency Rabbit—as mentioned in a previous volume—during the Cornell varsity crew race lost by just a deck length to Navy on the 1938 spring opener on the Severn.

Next on the cross-country trip was Wellsville, New York. There I threaded my way through heavy traffic that was slowly shaping itself into long parked rows of cars from which passengers were viewing the Fourth of July air show. Almost twelve hours after leaving Cleveland and just in time to home for supper, I drove into the westerly portals of Owego. It was a beautiful Thursday evening and, needless to say, after such a long haul, I learned that I was not as tough as I thought I was. That dark streak indicated that my tail was dragging the ground.

While the older of my two younger sisters, Sylvia, was by now working for the Land Title and Trust Company in Philadelphia, and the other was about to leave for Girl Scout camp, it was just great to be greeted by my two parents and Peggy. After I'd enjoyed the latest of the always first-rate good home cooking, I took all needed time for satisfying my mother, Father and Peggy with the details of my trip home. Then, to show off my first brand-new car to the Sugar Bowl crowd downtown, bushed or not I sallied forth to see some old acquaintances such as the Hawk and the Eagle and then to do some night prowling.

After a curbstone update from some old buddies, I said so-long and then, with my fingers crossed, I checked up on the Indian Princess, only to miss having her come to the door and ask, "What are you doing here?" She'd flown the coop. But it hadn't been with her favorite compatriot. As she would later explain, I hadn't told her (for good reasons) that I was homing. So she'd spent the evening with a neighborhood crowd at a delightful rodeo twenty miles downriver at Waverly.

Then came this surprising new factor . . . . the brown-eyed brunette had heard about your Virginian's new Chevrolet. Not about to be one-upped, she'd had her parents fix her up with a brand-new Mercury. When your unaware George Washington VI commenced playing motorized catch-up, the Princess played wheel-spinning hard to catch just long enough to make your Virginian realize that back in Michigan, he'd already much more than caught up and, as currently being enlightened, might just happen to go back. Homing on wheels hadn't turned out to be all that it was cracked up to be. With a crowd of interesting locals, a good week-end swim in bright, hot weather at Cole's Grove saw your Virginian getting it right out of the horse's mouth from Stanley Wolslegel, a former high school classmate and now a chief petty officer with the Pacific Fleet based at Pearl Harbor. Most convincingly, he assured me, "The Japs are never going to attack us. And we're never going to attack them."

Thinking that perhaps the threat of war actually would dry up and blow away, I put all of my best dreams of the Indian Princess on the back burner. Envisioning my chances as being excellent at latching on to some brand-new peacetime commercial career, I got ready to tackle the East Coast megalopolis.

An Obit Focuses on an Influential Dream-Maker

While the exploits of Hitler were generating conscription, the imminence of which was slowly making mush out of the dreams of a young man in business for a great future with Monkey's, another Cornell lad, but of an older generation who'd made it big on his own hooks, topped the obits in Owego's Main Street weekly.

When your Virginian kept touching base in the Yankee Tier during his fortnight-long quest, the Tuesday, July 16 issue of Owego's GOP sheet announced the passing of Willis Sharpe Kilmer. What had he done to make your young man in business at least get his hopes up that there were avenues of success other than those expounded by Howard Lee Davis for primary application to great, nationwide firms such as Monkey's?

A number of decades earlier, Willis, after graduating from Cornell, instead of becoming a trainee for some big-name company of his day, had taken over the leadership of his father's small patent medicine business in Binghamton. His major move, as featured in his obit, saw his staff inserting small ads describing the merits of Swamproot in newspapers from coast to coast. At first it was thought that the bills from ads were going to ruin the upstate firm. Then orders exceeded bills in quantity. The plant on the railroad in Binghamton ran at capacity. Loaded boxcar after boxcar rolled into the Midwest and West. The formula was a trade secret. Yet a privileged friend had found the occasion to ask the area's leading entrepreneur, "What's in Swamproot?"

Drily, Mr. Kilmer had replied, "Five Hundred Thousand Dollars a Year!"

The Swamproot story turned out to be a forty-million-dollar fortune.

As a lad, your unaware George Washington VI, in the company of his father, had marveled at the paintings of famed horses such as Sun Briar decorating the lobby of the tall Press Building that helped evidence this one of the great success stories of Binghamton. There the standout amongst the mansions that vied for public attention along Riverside Drive was the big stone Persian Palace where the great entrepreneur resided.

Inspiration yes. Envy no. Had your Virginian's father held on to his Owego feed-milling and grain business that he had sold in 1927, by now your unaware George Washington VI might well have had a similar stepping stone from which to give outfits such as Purina a good run for their money. In contrast to Willis Sharpe, no such early building block was available from Father (now contentedly servicing his own niche—secretary-treasurer for the small cooperative fire insurance company together with village treasurer). Even were there home-town opportunities for your Virginian (And what firm was going to waste any time on a potential conscript?), the step-by-step moving of your Virginian closer and closer to a beckoning stint with the Armed Forces was going to keep your unaware George Washington VI off balance sufficiently so that the odds would be stacked against his finding anything better than merely working at a job, whether as a trainee or as some contrasty blue-collar moneymaker.

And when it came to help from above, what your Virginian didn't know wouldn't be about to hurt him. Far in advance of Willis Sharpe, your scribe's great-great-great-grandfather was America's first millionaire. And while the laws of descent and distribution were a linchpin of our national legal system, the abnormal workings of the trickle-down theory had seen *per stirpes* inheritance interests and other monies normally due to your Virginian's father (and eventually to your Virginian) clandestinely shunted off to untitled third parties exploiting on the Q.T. George Washington's vast estates. Yet the inspirational yarn on Willis Sharpe was a good and positive influence. As I continued my fortnight-long quest, I kept right on conjuring up ideas, say, for starting a small manufacturing operation for aluminum items such as cookie cutters that I could then peddle to the five-and-dime stores, all thanks to the ripple effect from the story about the older generation's influential dream-maker.

Down "Think Big" Road

It was Monday, July 8, and I was rolling down Route 17 towards the George Washington Bridge and Sheaffer's sales headquarters in midtown Manhattan. A parking lift there soon whisked my new Chevrolet up and out of sight while I bravely marched a short distance down the street; then, after taking an elevator up a number of flights, I walked in and the receptionist promptly escorted me into the office of Mr. Evans, whom, a year and a half earlier, I'd informed that I had wanted to accept the offer of becoming a fountain pen salesman but lacked the required car.

And about my previous shortage of wheels, in the process of thinking it my duty to take my fated medicine, I had never thought to tell him that some high-level politicians had played sneak-bill dirty tricks on my father, to the effect that he had balanced it off by unilaterally confiscating my seed money that I otherwise could have used. So here was your unaware George Washington VI for his first face-to-face interview. "You said that I had to provide my own car. Now I've not only got a year's experience with Ward's meeting the public as a trainee, but I've saved the money and now own my own car. Do you still want me to go hit the road as a traveling salesman for your company? If so, I'm ready to roll."

After being taken slightly unawares, Mr. Evans looked up from his big executive-type desk and said: "Right now all of our sales spots are filled. But we have been keeping on file your application from a year ago last spring, together with our intervening correspondence. Keep us posted on your whereabouts and, as soon as an opening occurs, we'll contact you."

By now it was going on midafternoon. Had I thought to have left Owego Sunday afternoon instead of Monday morning and then to have stayed all night in close for a midmorning arrival in Manhattan, and then had I known enough to have suggested lunch, I would have had some chance of then walking away with a brand-new traveling salesman's job to go with my new car. But my fortnight-long quest was tempered by the overhanging European war that by now, with conscription developing step by step, must also have been worrying the heck out of Sheaffer's. Yet this personal contact was otherwise gratifying. Mr. Evans looked like a countryman for whom I'd like to rack up some sales. But once I'd touched base, instead of hanging around and pressing overeagerly for an immediate job on the road selling fountain pens, thinking big, I got back into my car and beat it across the nearest East River bridge for Long Island.

At the World's Fair, I quickly found the knowledge-machine pavilion. Concluding a demonstration of a thinkumthinkum was one of my favorite former coeds—Columbine. A couple of summers earlier she had kicked over the traces for a competitor because he'd had, in Columbine's estimate, a brilliant sister. But by the time that little bit of tenderness had gone poof, I had become enamored of the Indian Princess. But with the Princess on her own motion currently on the back burner, it was primarily at the behest of my sister Sylvia that I was now paying some short court to her very good friend.

Columbine seemed to be footloose and fancy free, except that it was your Virginian's hunch (usually correct) from her present stance that she had some much better catch—with qualifications far above those of your unaware George Washington VI—in waiting. While I could have hung around, taken her out to dinner and then stayed a scoreless night in the area, with only that which (in a relative sense) would seem to be a hemorrhage of green induced by the more inflationary metropolitan economy to show for it, I proceeded instead to get out of her what I wanted fast . . . . some advice.

To pick the Columbinian brains, for openers, I said: "I've given

Monkey Ward's both barrels on the trainee's job, but they've given me no raise in pay and no promotion except the dubious yet most successful percentagewise command of a mini wallpaper department, to the effect that I feel like I'm rowing in a varsity eight that's dragging a lobster pot laced with clandestine boathouse politics." Then I further explained my quandry. "When I first went out to Michigan, my father told me, 'You made your bed, now lie in it.' But since the fall of France he hasn't had the nerve to reverse himself. But my little sister tipped me off. My father thinks that if I'm going to enlist or get drafted in the Army, that I should do it not in Michigan but back at home in the Empire State under the jurisdiction of the home county draft board. And yet he acts as though he expects me to keep plugging with Monkey's in Michigan because his great uncle Julius went out there a hundred years ago, followed by his uncles John, Franklin, and William. So I get the idea that so long as I come home to respond to any new draft law, my father likes my staying in Michigan while I'm sweating out the oncoming war, even though I don't get a raise or any promotion of consequence. So what do you think?" I asked Columbine.

"Then you've kept on working for Ward's just out of loyalty, just because you feel you owe them some higher duty?" asked this one of my favorite former coeds.

"That's right. I feel some sort of compulsion out of loyalty, and because that's what my father wants me to do—to keep plugging blindly with Ward's" I confessed. "Howard Lee Davis' book instructing me how to get ahead, has imbued me with some higher duty to Monkey's," I added.

"But your father once talked you out of pursuing a medical career," said Columbine, who was knowledgeable about the more salient points of your untimid Virginian's aspirations, ". . . . and he failed to encourage you when you wanted to go to law school; thus you didn't start in September after your graduation. Howard Lee Davis is OK. You've applied his principles to the point where Montgomery Ward and Company, even though you've completed a year with them as trainee, hasn't given you a raise and hasn't really hooked you up with a position in which you feel that your true capabilities are being used?" Columbine hit the nail on the head.

"That's right," I confirmed.

"Now that you've put in your rule-of-thumb year, I don't see any reason for your further toughing it out as a trainee with Ward's just because you think because your father thinks that that's what you should do. I don't think that you should stay with Ward's just out of some perhaps misguided sense of loyalty that's unwarranted. Loyalty works both ways. They've given you little or no encouragement, particularly of the more practical type . . . . a raise in salary. Obviously they just can't be very serious," concluded Columbine as the public relations bugle call blew. It summoned Columbine's early return to her glamorous post. A new group of sightseers had just piled into the pavilion and wanted to enjoy a demonstration performed on the thinkumthinkum by this great beauty. At a nod from the boss, Columbine went into action, putting one of her employer's latest knowledge machines through its paces. From the inquiring crowd, Columbine fielded the latest penetrating questions with answers that put the askers on the buy trail for some of the great knowledge machine company's latest and best stuff.

When our beautiful favorite former coed got another little break, a good steer from Columbine soon saw me saying so long, and then walking over to another exhibit and applying her recommend. This diplomatic out was the colorful simulated transcontinental air voyage sponsored by General Motors. Through cloudless skies, pulled along by four fans, I soared. The barker's detailed, description of our constant ground contact by way of a fantastic diorama, laid out by the motor industry's best artists, gave me a fated introduction to an upcoming actual possibility as the trans-American scene floated below. The realistic yet simulated flight saw us hurdle the Appalachians, the Mississippi River, the Great Plains and the Rockies. Night was falling as we landed on the West Coast. All of this, taken with my keeping posted on current wartime events, whetted my interest in the aircraft industry, with a new focus on military aviation in general commencing to grip me. As the war atmospherics continued to heighten, I was developing a new goal, to shoot for the aviation branch should I eventually join up.

Not long after romping so briefly through this remarkable World's Fair, I found myself getting a big kick out of wheeling my own buggy across the big suspension bridge over the East River and then along the coastal pike to Connecticut. Once I'd made this latest break from Columbine, whom I had reason to surmise had a potential sawbones up her sleeve (sighting on such a category for a nice catch then being the rage among ex-coeds), as fledgling slicers were more likely to develop into the desired big game, my thoughts on Monkey's were nevertheless well-tempered with Columbine's much-valued advice. So focused was I on making myself a success with the mighty chain that, even would I eventually switch to some other industry, my short-term thinking, as it commenced to crystallize, was that I'd continue in the East my fortnight-long quest, keeping it targeted on obtaining a selling job. Yet time would soon be commencing to run out. Were I to fail to soon latch on to something different—something new to pitch into—if only for the short term, I'd finally go back on time to Michigan and go for broke at giving Monkey's their last chance. But before I would do so, I would continue to focus my attention on sales while thinking big.

An Unexpected Distance Factor Beats an Aspiration

While Sheaffer's had left me to sweat them out, I looked forward eagerly to this possibility of becoming a traveling salesman. But Congress was getting closer to enacting a conscription law. Thus I was also sweating out my possible involvement in World War II, should the United States join in. While so sweating, and just in case peace should return, why shouldn't I attempt to think big about sales? I might just as well leapfrog for some distribution work in something more substantial than fountain pens, and a lot closer to the burgeoning defense preparedness effort than providing fountain pens for the hands of scribes . . . . say, the aircraft industry? By the time Hitler's war might encompass the U.S.A., aircraft would be a great part of it and I would be in on the ground floor. My approach worked like this:

After reaching the perimeter of Hartford and getting a good night's sleep at a tourist home, for a seven ayem breakfast reunion at a restaurant downtown, I met my contact with the inner sanctums of the eastern aviation industry—Robert Knickerbocker. This product of the University of North Carolina had been an Owego Sunday school classmate, now on a much faster track as an accounting trainee. Later on, well in time for work, I dropped him off at the front gate at Pratt and Whitney's Hamilton Propeller unit. Security there, thanks to the recent fall of France, was tight as a drum. When I couldn't get inside to make some inquiries from a big shot, this one of my former high school buddies and tennis-playing partners—who, decades later, would become a vice-president of various units of the parent company—served as intermediary. Outside of the tall fence I showed up far along one side of the big manufacturing plant. There the son of Owego's astute Lackawanna passenger agent soon reappeared, this time out of a door marked "private." Having much better luck than expected, he had just found the right Mr. No. 1 executive inside to whom to talk. How to open the dialogue? Through the chain link fence I told Knickerbocker: "Tell the chairman that I want to become a salesman of big transport planes, but that I'm willing to start with a job selling propellers."

Knickerbocker scampered back inside and huddled with Bosso. In due course he returned from the executive suite, and through the chain link fence security barrier told me: "The chairman says that he can't give you a job selling propellers. They're packaged with the motors and no salesmen are involved. He says to tell you that our sales and specification engineers, working back and forth with the airframe manufacturers, move our props out to market and that there's not much of a sales problem here."

"But it's the big, completed aircraft that I really want to sell," I stressed to Knickerbocker. This time, as soon as I'd made my ultimate objective clear, he quickly reentered the big plant's side door and put in the further query at the executive suite. Then he returned, giving me through the fence the chairman's final advice, "The big boss says that maybe you really can get a job selling airplanes. The airframe manufacturers do have salesmen. But it would normally take you a long time to work up to such a spot unless, on account of the current expansion accompanying the national defense effort, you can get lucky. But to try your expedience you've got to fly right out to the Pacific Northwest or to the West Coast of California and talk to Boeing and Lockheed, in person."

While such advice was most constructive, it was more a shockeroo! The lack of necessary funding to leapfrog a continent was beating my aspiration to a pulp. Could I get any help from my father? No point mentioning it to him. While he would have been glad to get me started as the biggest dairy farmer in the Yankee Tier, I knew that he wouldn't gamble on sending me by air to the West Coast. He'd think that I was trying to recoup my chicken-money nest egg (that he'd unilaterally confiscated). Although there would come a day when I'd think nothing of taking a four-month air trip around the world, just now, relative to my limited resources, I was at least giving a semblance of the old college try to my investigation. Although I was bravely attempting to think big, I just wasn't geared financially to go flying cross-continent on such a gamble. Bizarrely, that simulated trans-America trip that I'd taken at the World's Fair was going to have to make do.

Feeling that for the time being I'd given it my best shot, after thanking my good friend Robert Knickerbocker and asking him to convey my thanks for the advice to the chairman inside in the executive suite, and convinced that my aspiration to sell passenger transports was outdistanced, I hit the road to huddle with an old friend of father's in the Federal Land Bank, an easy run up the Connecticut River valley at Springfield.

Some Feasibilities

Soon Homer Odell, inside The Bank, was shoving an employment application my way across a billiards-sized executive desk. "As your father probably told you some time ago, we'd be glad to have you come to work for us," he said. "As you know, I'm administrative assistant to the president for the whole Northeast including New England, New Jersey, and New York. This means that I'm in charge of field personnel and that's where you'll be . . . . . out in the field appraising farms. The job pays twenty-five dollars a week to start plus expenses. Your appraisals will be the basis for Federal Land Bank mortgage loans."

This pay was better than Ward's. In case the reader might wonder how come your unaware George Washington VI was being offered a job before he'd filled out an employment application (as though they were first asking me instead of my having to first ask them), it had come about like this: The bank job, although I probably didn't mention it or played it down at the time, had been amongst those few for which I could have opted when I had graduated from college. Even after I'd put in my first six months with Monkey's, my father had written suggesting a switch to the Bank. This was because one of my father's various jobs entailed the handling of Federal Land Bank business at the local level through the bank's unit in the Tioga County sector of the Yankee Tier. The Springfield officials may have assumed that some of my father's financial expertise would have rubbed off on your Virginian.

Furthermore, we shared each other's views and interests concerning the American military. During the interval between my year-earlier graduation from Cornell and my embarking on the eve of the Fourth of July for Monkey's, on one fine occasion, some of the Federal Land Bank's officials from Springfield had come to dinner to our house. Quickly it had become apparent that your Virginian was a history buff on the United States Army's military operations in France during World War I. Our dinner guests turned out to be some new sources of historic information. Present were eyewitnesses and participants in the battles of the Argonne Forest and St. Mihiel salient. Included among those who'd served the United States Army in the various big-name infantry battles in northern France were the gentleman on whom I was now calling, Homer Odell, and his accompanying Land Bank friends. So why didn't I jump at this opportunity to quit Ward's and go to work at once for the Land Bank?

In contrast to the preliminary try that I'd just taken down the Connecticut River valley at becoming a salesman of big exciting stuff—aircraft being pulled by from two to four fans—an appraiser's post with the Federal Land Bank just didn't seem glamorous enough. Furthermore, the salaries of the bank's upper echelons, in contrast to the gnawing challenge of taking aim at the boxcar figures pulled down by the captains of industry such as Ward's Sewell Avery in the world of big business (or commissions from selling passenger transports), didn't seem like too exciting a target. In so assessing the situation, thanks to my having attained merely the age of twenty-two, I missed this point. Actually, going to work as an appraiser for the bank would have been a good opportunity to learn a new skill. But it would be one learning opportunity that would have to be fated to remain, for the time being, unrecognized by me. Had I known enough to latch on to the proffered post, I'd soon have been studying values of farm land not only for the benefit of my federal employer and citizen borrowers, but also to build up a store of knowledge on land values and locations to eventually invest in for my own account. At an early date, would I have managed to set aside savings for a goodly down payment, I might well have sensed the possibilities of buying my own farm or farms in spots on the outskirts of some growing city. After getting something installed on the land to generate just enough funds to pay the taxes and other carrying charges, I would have been able to sit back and wait for metropolitan expansion to gradually reach out and boom the equity of my acreage. Furthermore, even without eventually embarking on such a risk-seeking course, were I now to simply get interested in such federal banking business in and of itself, it wouldn't have been too bad a life—one with lower salaries but with a lot less ulcer-conducive pressure, to which I could expect to be subjected if I continued to zero in on becoming a captain of industry with a big chain like Ward's. Had I now switched to The Bank, it also should be noted that I would have had the opportunity of learning the ropes while working for so great a man as Homer Odell. Besides his World War I Army background, one of the sparkling facets of his varied executive talents was his writing ability. Periodically emanating from his typewriter came an internal newsletter to which the staff of employees serving under him and the various Federal Land Bank officials serving local units, such as my father, looked forward to reading for guidance and direction. As my visit to Springfield headquarters drew to a close, I thanked Mr. Odell and I tucked away the blank application in the inside pocket of my jacket. At the same time, instead of displaying any enthusiasm towards going to work for this branch of the federal bureaucracy, my erstwhile desires of going to medical school or to law school at this juncture being all but forgotten, I stressed to Mr. Odell my objective of attaining some high-level post in big business or else getting hold of a business of my own to operate. Having been indoctrinated as a rugged individualist, in no way could I see that there was a lot more than a Chinaman's chance of setting the world on fire working for a government that just happened to be in the expansion process. Also coming back like a broken record was this: were I to make the job switcheroo, military conscription already was in the wind and I'd just get nicely started, only to then have to leave to go to war! Were this to be the case, survival would warrant some sort of a new and perhaps more artistic postwar life that would be more satisfying in a psychic sense. Perhaps only subconsciously, I didn't want to be obligated to go back to a prewar job. Furthermore, had I now gone to work for the big, important federal agency, and had I eventually attained some post of significance, from the patterns of tracks being left in our saga by political occultists of whose existence we were unaware, it would only be a question of time before they'd catch up with some first-rate clever tricks of cloudy attribution. Yet, in all due respect to this good business connection with The Bank, because it involved my father, I promised Mr. Odell that when I'd soon return home, I'd talk over this feasibility with him. In the meanwhile, the consensus from various friends with whom I'd take counsel smothered my seeing just now this great opportunity to make it through federal portals into the realm of becoming an expert at the art of evaluating all sorts of farm land over the far-flung northeasterly corner of the United States.

By midafternoon, having turned westerly towards home, unaware that a pre-college pal, Dick Foster, was serving as a counselor in a nearby camp, I was driving my new car across the Berkshires, and never giving a thought to visiting the grave of Israel Dean, just a short drive southerly along the same range. By late afternoon, I arrived at Hudson, New York. There I stopped at the home of one of my former college friends from the boathouse world— Richard A. Dittmar, Jr. But Dick, according to his mother, was in the Pacific Northwest working as a trainee in the apple-packing business, his first job out of college. Serving as substitutes, Dick's younger brother Bob had the summer off from the university, and his father, who was the general manager of the local cement plant, soon came home to the highlands from his GHQ at the big kilns located far below on tidewater. Over dinner, as I still had in mind switching to selling bigger stuff boxcar-style than Ward's titanium dioxide paint gallon by gallon, I asked Dick's father for the lowdown on becoming a cement salesman.

"Right now," the local manager of one of the big cement plants of the East Coast area explained, "these jobs selling cement are all filled up. Furthermore, if we get into a war there will be shortages, and salesmen will become mere public relations agents, not really needed to actually sell until we get the war out of the way, get some new plants built and develop a surplus that will then need lots of selling. Our present crop of salesmen is going strong. All of them well know their job, and without experience you'll find it just about impossible to find yourself such a cement-selling opening."

Figuring that my aspiration to sell big airplanes would be over everybody's head, I didn't have the nerve to bring it up. So Dick's father stuck to the mentioned feasibilities: "If I were you, I'd keep my job with Montgomery Ward." Confirming my hunch that, to say the least, I should get back to Ann Arbor on schedule, if only to give Monkey's their last chance, Dick's father pointed out: "Maybe the hundred-a-month pay doesn't seem so hot, but when you stay with a company for a long time, that first year during which they forget to give you a raise won't seem like much when you make it big later on. In any event, even that hundred a month is a lot more than a lot of experienced hands are getting, and don't forget that working for Ward's at the retail level is considered to be very valuable experience that will open doors for you elsewhere if not in the upper echelons of Ward's." As your Virginian put all of this advice in his pipe and smoked it, this captain of the cement industry confirmed the old adage being bandied about the world of the young man in business: if Monkey's were nothing else, it was still one of the American chain store merchandising scene's top schools of practical training. So went some of the feasibilities.

The Boiling Down

In the morning, heading westerly toward home in the Yankee Tier, I crossed the high bridge over the Hudson estuary to Catskill. Ninety-three years earlier—as I now failed to take note of such an important event in our family history—my great-grandfather, migrating from Canaan, Connecticut, to New Milford in northeastern Pennsylvania, had made this crossing, but by ferryboat. As mentioned, such ancestor was Pierce Dean, an unaware grandson of our First President, George Washington.

From Catskill, Pierce Dean with his wife, two sons, and a daughter had then sailed a relatively short distance downriver along the Hudson's westerly shores. Transshipping at Kingston, they had voyaged southwesterly on the Delaware and Hudson Canal to

Honesdale, Pennsylvania, from whence they'd traveled overland by team to settle at New Milford, Pennsylvania, in September 1847.

In contrast to that lengthy trip by canalboat, now in my own automobile I drove westerly through the middle of the Catskills, passing a relatively short distance northerly of the same New Milford, to home on the same day through Binghamton to Owego.

Once I wound up this three-day-junket part of my fortnight-long quest, now that I just couldn't manage to think big enough to stretch my resources to the West Coast aviation industry, perhaps I should have rested at home a night, then taken off for the City of Washington, seeking a commission in the Army? On the minds of the deep thinkers was the possibility of war. But again at one of the Yankee Tier's old swimming holes I bumped into my former high school friend, Stan Wolslegel, who'd soon be en route to the Philippines. As he'd previously put it, "Just like World War I, Europe is our only worry."

"What about rumors that war might break out in the Pacific?" I asked.

"That's a lot of poppycock," said my friend. "Because we've got a good navy out there with lots of battleships, we've got too much strength." Then he reiterated, "The Japs aren't about to start anything with us and we're certainly not getting ready to attack them."

Famous last words. My erstwhile high school friend eventually would be one of the few to make an astounding escape from the Philippines. But his remarks, just now, made me think that the thing to do was to keep right on concentrating on my role, not as a potential member of the Armed Forces, but rather with a display of upward mobility as the ongoing young man in business.

Once back home, I made an investigation of some of the possibilities of getting into the feed business. (As detailed in Volume I, my father had been a successful miller, only to have sold out a splendid location where your young scribe-to-be, at a very early age, had spent lots of very impressionable off hours. Had my father hung on, such a business would have by now been making a great commercial springboard for your Virginian.) Between Binghamton and New Milford, on the south side of the Susquehanna, my Uncle Glenn was running a small feed and grain operation out of a partly remodeled creamery that my father had purchased on his older brother's account. With your unaware George Washington VI serving as the assistant of the unaware George Washington V, we spent some of our time making the rounds in a small feed truck, so that my uncle saw to it that I not only got acquainted with some of the Susquehanna Valley's leading feed dealers based at Binghamton, but also got the opportunity to observe first-hand conditions. My uncle would tell them: "Evans [your Virginian's middle name] here thinks that he'd like to get into the feed business, but I tell him that the hangover from the drouth leaves no present profit in it for this agricultural area, and it doesn't look as though there's going to be any money in it for some time to come."

During such visitations, one after another, the area's top feed men shared my uncle's view, to wit: the feed business, at least for the summer of 1940, was and was going to stay very much depressed. No risk capital was available for gambling that the industry would immediately turn around. Hearing it out of the horse's mouth from these various big-shot Yankee Tier feed dealers as they stood behind their respective counters—their command posts—soon clothed the Yankee Tier feed mill industry with a shroud of something at least temporarily forgettable.

Then there was my senior-year unfulfilled aspiration at college: the hope of becoming a double registrant in law school. By now—mid-July—all thoughts of commencing first-year law school during upcoming early September were out. Si Glann, my former senior-year roommate—who'd once sold me on trying to make it for law school—on the other hand was spending the summer supporting his family by slinging bags of cement, helping build a new stretch of state highway at Apalachin. In September he would be earning his three squares by hanging very tight to my former waiter's job at the fraternity house while commencing his third and last year of law school. In contrast, with a possible war coming on, still playing it by ear, when I, too, should have been studying to attain a profession, no more encouragement surfaced, and I was still groping in the dark. After reconnoitering the Elmira area for self-employment opportunities but getting no new leads, I got ready to head westerly to get back to my job on time at Ward's Ann Arbor, Michigan retail store. But, before I did so, my father raised an alternate feasibility: "What are you going to do about your application to the Federal Land Bank? Are you going to fill it out and send it in? They want to know whether you're going to go with them or not." Dad took a most rare interest in my desire to make good as a young man in business.

Boiling it all down, I replied: "I've got so much time and energy already invested in my trainee's job with Ward's that I've just got to find out more about them, whether they're going to give me a raise in pay and a promotion. To see whether they're serious, I've got to go back to give Monkey's a final fillip. So tell our friends at Springfield I've got to go back to Wards," I made it clear to my father. "I've got to give Monkey's their last chance."

And when I hit the trail for Michigan, it didn't seem much like openers for the national emergency that FDR had so recently declared.

Chapter 7
Monkey's Last Chance

First Drive Back to Michigan

Some passengers and a couple of friendly stopovers enlivened my trip from the Yankee Tier back to the Midwest. To pay a visit to his uncle, who was a Buffalo haberdasher, Phil Smith rode with me as far as the Niagara Frontier. Crossing to Canada, I paid short visits at Bay Beach to Jack Teach, then pumping gas for a conglomerate, and Fred Munschauer, then having a summertime go as trainee in his family's shearing machine works. Again I found out that for collegiate vacation-type jobs, twenty-five a week was a lucky run-of-the-mill sort of emolument.

On down the road crossing the southern-Ontario section of an Allied nation that had been at war for almost a year, I picked up a hitchhiking uniformed member of the RCAF. He was serving with the ground crew of a fighter squadron. After observing his enthusiasm over the life of an enlisted volunteer, I told myself that such a spot in our own air corps would make a good second best, provided I couldn't eventually pass the eye exams to become an aviation cadet.

Wondering about the constitutional right of the Canadian provinces to become states, I asked, "You think that someday maybe the United States and Canada will merge?"

"Never, not now anyway," he said.

After I dropped him off at the easterly portals of Windsor, I continued downtown, where I stopped for an hour's coffee break and told a haberdasher that I wanted to buy some suiting. Opening a big drawer, he pulled out a bolt of all-wool material from Burberry's, Ltd. "If you skip a vest and go for a double-breasted suit, this yardage is enough for your height."

The pattern was a narrow herringbone in gray. Quickly we made the dicker. By the time I crossed the Detroit River into Michigan, I had the makings for a tailor-made suit. Until now, I'd been wearing suits size 42 long (jackets of which had failed to cover the wrinkles in the seat of my trousers) when I required a generally unavailable 42 extra long. Of course, some of the haberdashers had tried to con me with an, "Oh, yes. We have an XL in your size." But the hitch was that they had been talking about a dog while I'd been talking about a cat. Their "XL" meant not "extra long" but rather "extra large," in which case I had known enough not to endeavor to learn to swim in it.

Thanks to my new yardage, now all I had to do was to budget the required green and then find the right tailor who would be able to correctly fit a six-foot, four-inch, 182-pound unaware George Washington VI.

An hour later I was entering Ann Arbor's easterly portals, I turned to a newspaper advertisement in the classifieds. Previously I had roomed with the parents of the head of our store's shoe department. But now I wanted a place closer in with some younger people. On my first try I found a room with a fortyish couple living on John Street. We'll call them Jerry and Jane, a business machine technician and registered nurse, respectively.

Afterwards, after a relatively short walk, I dropped in at the store. One of the popular lady clerks, Mary Kokenakis, greeted me with a: "You gave up your room before you left so, Dean, we didn't think that you were coming back."

"Where's Store Manager McCarty?" I asked.

"He's gone to Florida on vacation," was the reply.

"What about that chicken dinner? After the results of the June inventory would be tallied up, he said, 'We're all going to eat chicken.' "

"Bosso, just to be on the safe side, so they say, decided to take his already earned vacation at once. . . . . . He took his family to Florida . . . . and Florida in the summertime. . . . . They say that's the best time to go . . . . provided you go to the northeasterly coast where they say there's a nice offshore breeze this time of the year."

"But what about the June inventory? Did it turn out OK?" I asked.

"It turned out satisfactorily. But we don't think that it turned out as well as Bosso had expected. Whatever there was about it, all of us were disappointed, though. There was no chicken dinner . . . . except that one referred to by Foster Adams . . . ." my informant trailed off.

"As I was crawling on my knees,/I thought I heard a chicken sneeze . . . . . ." our colored janitor came a-pushing his big broom.

Taking the cue, Mary enlarged on the misser, "That's just what we got of the chicken dinner."

"You mean the 'sneeze' part of it?" I asked.

"You've got it right. It was something about the store's operating ratio; we heard that it had slipped . . . . . . something about some simple final number such as four point eight, or five point three."

Referring to Pennala's springtime attempt to inject some fear, I said, "Back then, when Art started insisting that all store employees were scared of their jobs, he was throwing in everything and everybody including the kitchen sink?"

"That's right," Pennala stepped up and developed his previous theme song. "Even Bosso's scared of his job."

It sounded like an odd refrain. Hopefully I hadn't jinxed Bosso when I'd queried him (but had been rebuffed) on that very point—the operating ratio—a month or so earlier.

Explaining that I had to get back to my room and get unpacked, I took my leave and in the morning—a nice Friday not long after mid-July—with a two-week vacation under my belt, I was back on the job selling primarily paint, wallpaper, and sporting goods.

During my fortnight-long quest, I'd gotten a bit rusty on some of the finer points of merchandising. Actually it wasn't nearly as bad as it might sound to you all. But, unaware that she was setting the tone for the kickoff of your Virginian's giving Monkey's their last chance, and more so just for laughs, Mary, the beautiful Greek maiden who clerked in nearby housewares, pointed out (while fellow employees such as Parsley, Rich, and Pennala nodded confirmation), "Dean must have had a marvelous vacation to the extent that he's having to learn his job all over again."

Needed: A Biblical Laying On of Hands

Not long after I had returned to the big merchandising location in Ann Arbor, a nice little old lady approached. Quickly she indicated an interest in a gallon of Ward's titanium dioxide white house paint.

So that the reader can assess whether this next incident was just some happenstance or whether it was possibly some programmed ploy being pulled off psychologically by some political occultists on your unaware George Washington VI, thus making it more difficult for Monkey's to evaluate your Virginian from their personnel chief's end of the trainee situation: This clouding process now took place just as your Virginian was giving Ward's openers for their last chance. So your scribe will now pass along the details of this little embranglement, even though I was unaware at the time of the possible political-genealogical motivations. This meant that to this incident, while I couldn't very well appreciate it, I now attached little or no significance, yet never forgot it.

Against an unaware target, this ongoing secret, civil war by the exploiters of George Washington's vast estates now focused into an attempt to lay it on your Virginian. Stuff like this just didn't happen to the other clerks. And its bizarreness eventually would make it surface amongst events deserving a temporary spotlight among the passing oddities that have warranted inclusion in our saga. So back to life would come this caper that interrupted the normal processing of the sale of a gallon of house paint. And as previously mentioned, the titanium dixoide variety was one of Ward's important offerings.

During late-July dog days, when we sales clerks were under plenty of pressure, out of a steady flow of customers the proverbial nice little old lady showed up. The gallon of paint, as mentioned, accompanied by a well-worded sales talk, was promptly sold to her. To illustrate the close-out, we'll round out the amount of the sale at $3.45 including sales tax so that the amount of the change came to $1.55. Following the required procedure of ring, then wrap, to ensure that the lady's paint wouldn't be sold inadvertently behind my back to a different customer by another clerk, I picked up the sold gallon from a shelf and placed it on the counter beside the register. Then I took the five-dollar bill proffered by the lady and said, "That will be three forty-five out of five."

As trained by Ward's, I followed the proper steps of operating the cash register, laying the five-dollar bill on the ledge above the register drawer, setting properly, then ringing the register, and checking the cash register receipt to see that I had rung the sale for the correct amount and in the correct merchandise division. Then I placed the receipt on the ledge. Next, I put the sales tax money in the tax box. Then, I built my change up to the amount the customer gave me, the customer's five-dollar bill until now having been properly left on the ledge. Finalizing the cash-handling part of the sales transaction, I commenced to count the $1.55 change back to the nice little old lady, *piece by piece*, as $3.45 - $3.50 - $4.00 - $5.00. But before I could finish, the nice little old lady forcefully interrupted. "I want that wrapped." She pointed to the waiting gallon of paint.

At this point, as I'd been indoctrinated, it is fair to infer that I completed counting the change and then that I'd explained to the nice little old lady that I had to give her the change at this particular time, that I'd then put the five-dollar bill in the register and closed the drawer, all of this in accordance with Ward's published training material for sales clerks. Furthermore, as we customarily did upon a customer's request, I now trimmed a piece of wrapping paper to the correct size, wrapped it around the cylindrical gallon of paint and sealed the wrapper with a piece of sticking tape also being used to stick onto the wrapped gallon the cash register receipt. Then, after pointing out the presence of her receipt to the customer, I mentioned that I had previously customarily fitted a small thin but tough notched fiber grip on the gallon's handle of heavy wire so that the thin strip of fiber would pad the little old lady's fingers when I now handed her the gallon with some pleasantry such as, "I enjoyed waiting on you."

After having put away her change, the nice little old lady nodded, then took hold of her purchase by its hoop-shaped bail and left. Thereafter I continued to concentrate in turn on stacked-up customers, to whom I made sale after sale. As I toted the numbers up on a card to eventually be submitted, closing out the day with the office, I really felt as though I were more than carrying my weight with Monkey's. Then, as much as a half-hour later, the nice little old lady returned. After she sought out the department head, the two of them came my way and she charged, "You didn't give me my change!"

At once I realized that by her having interrupted my normal process of counting back the change, she had engineered, whether by deliberation or by happenstance, a mental block. In all honesty, I couldn't actually remember counting back the change to the lady and thus wasn't up to taking a firm stand against her as she tried to lay it on me. Although I insisted that I had followed procedures, her having so singularly interrupted me loomed like a distractive psychological trick. Your Virginian was twenty-two. She was perhaps sixty. It was unlikely that senility was a factor. The interruption was a little bit too well timed.

Presumably the customer had received her $1.55 in change. I certainly didn't have it. It was unlikely that I would have placed it where some third party could have picked it up. It was time to call in the store manager and let him see first-hand the details of this freak thing.

Down came Bosso McCarty. I told him (as his spies, presumably, had already confirmed it) that during my several months as sales clerk I'd been following, in accordance with company training material, ring-then-wrap procedures religiously to the effect that I was certain that I'd automatically counted back to this nice little old lady her change, but that I suspected that by her well-timed interruption, she had deliberately and artfully psyched me out of my being able to visualize my having actually handed her the change, even though I'd actually done so. An inspection of the cash register showed that the sale had been rung up and that the $3.45 for the subject gallon of paint was in the till. Presumably none of my co-workers had intercepted the lady's change. Presumably the lady's change had properly been counted back piece by piece to the customer, and she was now shooting to get it again. Following ring-then-wrap procedures, I'd done my job acceptably and correctly. But this nice little old lady was back making a scene of this incident, the issue being not one of *short* change but rather one of *no* change at all.

Although Bosso McCarty didn't say so, I sensed that to him this possible good one by the nice little old lady was old hat, that he immediately understood the truth and was at once aware that the customer by a cleverly timed interruption had psyched me out. If so, he never told me. Furthermore, there was no indication that the complainant was one of some irregular internal company intelligence bureau, or of the clandestine Wilmark shoppers who'd previously drawn blood twice. After deliberating briefly on the unusual situation, Bosso McCarty ordered that the nice little old lady be *again* given her change. While that then settled it, this reviewing of the incident in the light of a possible ploy on an unaware George Washington VI raises some questions: was the lady customer traveling around psyching out run-of-the-mill salesclerks? On the other hand, did she pull this real good one on your unaware George Washington VI, and with some critical timing, because she or her clandestine principals, if any, were in on the great political-genealogical secret?

After my having recently completed my first year of hard work as a trainee for Ward's, I was now, more than ever, endeavoring to impress the administration to recognize my efforts by giving me for the first time, and without my having to ask, a hike in my hundred-a-month salary together with some promotion more meaningful than heading the wallpaper department. The issue remained: was the incident happenstance or a programmed ploy?

So the little old lady took the Bosso-authorized $1.55 in change and departed into limbo. Whether anything concerning the alleged "no-change" incident went into Monkey's personnel records at the expense of your unaware George Washington VI, I never would find out.

Since Howard Lee Davis (in his book that focused on the young man in business) didn't include any easily discernible cues, I never thought to ask Bosso, "In your long years of experience, have you ever seen anything like this happen before?"

Had such a needed explanation ever been forthcoming, such possible enlightenment from Bosso would have been warmly appreciated. While I was certain that I had counted back the change, the lady's interruption meant that I would never be able to swear to it. With the "I want that wrapped," distraction she had tried to lay it on your Virginian, actually, what the little old lady had really needed was a Biblical laying on of hands.

The International Turmoil Puts the Quietus on Sheaffer

More on my aspiration to become a traveling salesman for Sheaffer Pen Company: My ownership of a good automobile made me eligible. Thus as mentioned, during my fortnight-long quest, on the Manhattan part of my itinerary, I had stopped to see Mr. Evans, the eastern district sales manager, in his New York City headquarters and reported this qualifying factor by now enhanced by my year's experience, a lot of it in sales, working for Monkey's.

Although there had been no openings, Mr. Evans had listed me for the first vacancy. So what sort of a follow-up could your Virginian expect, now that evidence had additionally piled up that a war was coming on?

In the Midwest, I wasn't back on the job very long with Monkey's in Ann Arbor when Mr. Evans phoned my home base at 443 Main Street in Owego.

As my mother would relate the story. . . .

"Is Mr. Benjamin Dean there?"

"No. He's gone back to Michigan. May I tell him who called?"

"This is Mr. Evans, sales manager for Sheaffer Pen Company. Are you Mr. Dean's mother?"

"Yes."

"Very recently your son stopped by my headquarters in Manhattan and said he was interested in going with us as a salesman. So now I'm here in Owego between trains at the Lackawanna passenger station. I was hoping that I would be able to interview him?"

"Well, Evans [my mother, whose maiden name was also Evans, explained the use of the middle name] is a trainee for Montgomery Ward and went back to give them another try."

. . . . End of report as it would eventually come through in about one sentence in the mail. Whatever else was said, Mother, although a great teacher of the lower grades, didn't know how to develop this contact into a job-switch for your Virginian.

But look at the crazy international situation putting the finger on all concerned, making everybody hesitant. The mounting turmoil seen through windows of headlines boosting newspaper sales commenced to cause Sheaffer people and your unaware George Washington VI to put off pressing. Actually we liked each other. But the *Luftwaffe's* ongoing antics caused your Virginian's oft-mentioned backup career concept simply to get lost in the turmoil.

July Events Larrup Monkey's

Now, back to our giving Monkey's their last chance. News involving the war continued to be a major factor in our lives and July events kept larruping the grip of big business on the hearts and minds of its trainees, especially those, such as your Virginian, of prime draft age.

As Group Captain John E. Johnson would later point out in *Full Circle,* in England, the first American volunteers were joining the fighter command. Operation *Sealion,* the strategic plan for the invasion of Britain by Germany, awaited the write-off of the RAF, scheduled for early August, the panzers to be barged across the Channel during early September.

Currently, Arnold Rich returned from vacation bringing some scuttlebutt about the war in Europe, as it was now mirrored in the Midwest. Jumping the headlines by a few weeks, Arnie had picked it up from old friends who'd scouted Army and Navy headquarters in Chicago, "Deanie, they wanted to commission me right away in the Navy. It certainly looks like a chance to get in on the ground floor. Unofficial Washington sources are saying that we will be at war within four months. From the activity I saw in the Windy City, I can almost believe it."

"Then how come you don't flag for the nearest recruiting station?" I asked.

Shrugging, Arnie said: "Whether the U.S.A. is going to get

into the war, we don't really know, do we? So all that we can do is to keep plugging at our jobs."

All of us 'uns—even the thirtyish ones such as Arnie and Art—were too young and without advisors to tell us and make us believe it, to wit: that there really was going to be for the United States a shooting war, to get in the Armed Forces now, get some rank and be ready to get ahead should the the real thing occur. Instead, we kept right on keeping our heads buried in the sand while hoping that a peaceful solution would come out of the woodwork. Had I taken advanced ROTC at Cornell, such a background would have now been telling me to plan for war. Furthermore, the lull that followed the British evacuation of Dunkirk and the fall of France meant only one thing. The German Army was regrouping for a bigger and better mass attack somewhere else, at this time, England. While we thought that the lull might mean peace, all that remained for the German high command was to set a date . . . . to occupy England. As potential transferees from Monkey's to the military, momentarily we expected to hear that a cross-English Channel invasion was underway, with any success giving our government grounds for mandating that we all be called up.

As gleaned from *Britannica Book of the Year,* just after mid-July, FDR was nominated by the Democratic National Convention on the first ballot for a *third* term. He said that he accepted the nomination from a sense of duty to serve the country in a crisis.

By July 19, Hitler told the British to withdraw from the war or see their empire destroyed.

On July 20, FDR signed a bill appropriating $4,000,000,000 for a two-ocean navy. In conjunction therewith, a nice little invite soon arrived in your Virginian's mail.

Presumably my name had been obtained from the ROTC roster at Cornell. The letter pointed to officer candidate school (OCS) and made it sound as though all that I had to do was to go make application and I would be in. With four years of Cornell rowing under my belt, I felt that I would feel right at home in the U.S. Navy. War or not, what an interesting out this would make from Monkey's stuffy basement! Caught up in the fever, as soon as I arrived at the store the next morning I discussed the naval matter with Bosso McCarty. In the air there was a semblance of war hysteria. Surmising that the Navy must have lowered their eye-exam standards and believing that I had Bosso's consent, on the morning following the confab out of which I'd thought that I'd obtained a two-hour leave, I jumped into my car and on my own time, scrammed down the pike easterly during high summer.

At the Navy recruiting office on the shores of Detroit River overlooking Belle Isle, I was soon presenting the OCS notice of great opportunity to the officer in charge. While he must have realized that the mailing list from which my name had been obtained indicated that I was otherwise fully qualified, he wasted no time having an aide give me an eye exam. As previously indicated by the Ann Arbor campus recruiting officer, glasses were not acceptable as a crutch. The Navy's eye-exam standards remained just as tough as ever. Since I had nobody to coach me on memorizing charts, hiding my glasses, some negative news followed. If only I had at least used the occasion to get some practice for an eventual attempt to beat the same barrier. Next time maybe I might successfully achieve acceptance by the Aviation Cadets.

After this hundred-mile round trip, I parked my car back in Ann Arbor. About 10:30 A.M., I entered the store, where I was greeted at the time clock by Bosso McCarty, who unexpectedly was upset by my use of less than two hours of company time. There had been a misunderstanding. I had thought that I not only had Bosso's permission, but also that it was company policy to let an employee-applicant for the Armed Forces have a couple of hours off to go see about joining up. Not so. My previous discussion with Bosso hadn't generated such short leave. But just then from the basement, the wallpaper bugle blew. I had become the expert at estimating amounts needed and some customers were waiting to see me. Quickly, Bosso simmered down. So my two hours AWOL on such a patriotic mission turned out to be nothing more than a dry run.

On Monkey's sales floor I was soon busier than ever racking up sales of mostly paint, wallpaper, and sporting goods. Jazzing up the day, we'd occasionally successfully feature the previously mentioned fish-catching policy—a fancy paper certificate that accompanied a certain lure. When the Shakespeare salesman of fishing tackle and sporting goods would drop in to see how his company's stuff was meeting the competition, I'd ask him how often he got to try out some of that tackle and how often he managed to get out into the wide open spaces to test it? He stressed that in his line of work, he made it frequently into the great outdoors. It made me think that with such a sales job, and perhaps lesser pay than I could eventually aim for with Monkey's, I could sooner generate a better quality of life. The point was that even though by now I was still pitching in wholeheartedly selling stuff for Monkey's, doing the housekeeping, and helping revise counters for the upcoming fall merchandising season, I was looking forward to some raise in pay, some promotion that might get me out of this confining basement work, and into some other merchandising area where the air would be fresher, as I continued to give Monkey's their last chance.

But the odds kept growing that a different sort of wide open spaces were in the cards. Making it look as though in the relatively near future I'd be wearing some kind of a military uniform came jolting bits and pieces of war news that set a tenor of increasing operations.

By July 22, aviators attached to the French Army organized in England joined the British in bombing Germany. Prince Fumimaro Konoye, new Japanese premier, formed a cabinet (probably meaning one geared for expanding their war operations) which he said would enhance the spirit in which the empire was founded. The Canadian government was building a dozen munitions factories at the cost of $19 million. The U.S. Civil Aeronautics board reported that 50,000 students were training as air pilots. FDR asked Congress to call out the National Guard for a year's service. Britain extended its blockade to include all of continental Europe. The foreign secretary protested against the wholesale arrest of British citizens in Japan. Last but not least, as July ran out, the compulsory United States military service registration bill was revised by the Senate committee to include men between ages of twenty-one and thirty-one only. For such potential cannon fodder, your unaware George Washington VI, going on twenty-three, was thus included among the real ripe ones.

What a life for a peacetime merchandising trainee trying to hack it under such an ever-looming threat! Although Monkey Ward was getting its last chance, the July events kept tugging away at the big chain's underpinnings with its souped-up strata of college-grad help as war news kept larruping Monkey's as a career concept.

Quite A Guy! F. Dean Rundell of Sneak Bill Fame

In March and April of 1935, when legislation had been sneaked through at Albany eliminating my father's few-hundred-a-year county-level elective post, F. Dean Rundell, as Tioga County Democratic chairman, had announced in the print media, "Blame me."

Of course we didn't blame him. Especially after Governor Lehman had *uncustomarily* signed the sneak bill, we all knew that high-level interests had been behind the move that had destroyed villagers' right by state charter to elect a village representative on the Tioga County Board of Supervisors. Although such a right had been in effect for scores of years, the political occultists had waited until the unaware George Washington V was winding up his second two-year term. Then they clandestinely lowered the boom.

And what about F. Dean Rundell's given middle name of "Dean"? Was he a descendant of our ancestor Israel Dean? That unaware son of George Washington had left two sons and five daughters. One daughter had married a Beebe and one of their daughters had married a Dean. Where'd they all go? North Carolina, California, etc. And were perchance F. Dean Rundell one of them, the political occultists must have had quite a laugh at playing George Washington's unaware descendants off against each other. But as mentioned in an earlier volume, our respective families traveled in different social circles, Baptist as distinguished from Catholic, and thanks to the small-town situation, the opportunity never availed itself for any of us to ask either F. Dean or his two estimable sons the genealogical source of the possible link.

Just a few days after I had left the Yankee Tier and a few months more than five years after the sneak-bill gambit, I was back on my job as trainee for Monkey's when Owego's Tuesday weekly announced the passing of F. Dean on July 23. At age forty-nine, he just happened to have been a year younger than his avowed sneak-bill target, CPD. At that time there had been a relative shortage of details on the "quite a guy" background of the decedent. Some unrealized facets now surfaced.

F. Dean was born at Mack, Pennsylvania in 1891. He had moved to Athens as a small child. Later on he attended the Meeker Business School in Elmira. As mentioned previously, in this saga, when it would come to political gambits (such as the sneak bill and many, many others), your Virginian, once involved in doing research about them, would have reason to be on the lookout for the Cornell University connection. And here we first note: F. Dean Rundell went to work for Frank Ernest Gannett (who as a member of the board of trustees was a veritable Mr. Cornell University), widely known newspaper publisher and White House aspirant. As part of Gannett's big, burgeoning print-media operation, F. Dean Rundell became city editor of the *Ithaca Journal*.

After becoming expert in the realms of public relations, F. Dean envisioned a great future in the motion-picture theater business. After returning to Athens, he marked time in the grocery business with his father. Eventually following his flare, he purchased the Morley Theater in Athens about 1915. Later on, he joined forces with the late M. E. Comerford, Scranton movie magnate. Rundell then acted as district manager for the group's Sayre-Waverly area operations including the Tioga Theater at Owego. The group erected the Capitol Theater on Broad Street in Waverly.

In 1930, Rundell withdrew from the Comerford organization and purchased the C. F. Young & Son haberdashery business in Owego. He ran it for two years, then sold out. In 1933 he returned to the Comerford group until around New Year's Day, 1939, when ill health caught up.

As we all would look back, F. Dean was a major figure in the operations of the Tioga County Sportsmen's Association, his picture appearing frequently with other notabilities attending the annual summer outings. From the viewpoint of the youth of Owego, the well-known films at Tioga Theater, where his popular brother-in-law Ed Cangley often served as master of ceremonies for special Saturday programs for children, provided an unsurpassed outlet for the development of our dreams and imaginations into the later-year realities of success.

And whether the political occultists had set up one Dean relative to politically pull the sneak-bill rug from under another will have to remain as one of the unsolved mysteries of this saga.

CPD Reverses Himself

Now that I had commenced giving Monkey Ward its last chance, what did all of this about the war in Europe have to do with your unaware George Washington VI as he continued to give the big chain the old college try, hacking it as a trainee at a hundred a month in Michigan? It was this: Almost a year earlier, during August 1939, when your Virginian had sounded his father out about resigning from his trainee's post with Ward's and then returning to take his chances in the Yankee Tier, CPD, coming on unexpectedly like a wise guy handing out some sort of an un-thought-out, thus meaningless pronouncement, had written: "You made your bed, now lie in it!"

At that time CPD had been in the midst of a GOP campaign for the nomination for the *county* treasurership. And then the opposition was readying to lower the boom with some real slick dirty political tricks. Since then, as previously detailed, the unaware George Washington V had been tossed an early March palliative—the treasurership of the *village*.

But with Hitler's victory in France had come some winds of change. That bill for conscription that had just been introduced into Congress must have turned the trick. In the mail from my father came an instruction: "It looks as though sooner or later there's going to be a draft. If you are going to either enlist in the Army or get drafted, don't do it in Michigan. If you are going to join up, be sure to come back to your home town here in New York State and if that's what you're going to do, join up back there. If you want to come home and stay, you can."

What was my father's reasoning? As Boilerplate's law clerk, Splanaway would eventually explain, "During the Civil War, the New York politicians ran it." Would they also have great influence in any upcoming war? Normally the political occultists were engaged in adversely manipulating the unaware descendants of George Washington. Yet occasionally such clandestine warriors passed along some word that happened to be constructive. Presumably my father had sent me such an instruction based on a word from his counselors such as Boilerplate and Old Dingle, who'd likely heard through intermediaries from the Top. Were the Empire State your life-long domicile, maybe there was some unseen advantage to be gained by enlisting in the Yankee Tier.

But at age twenty-two and more than well over a score of years away from even suspecting that my father and I were being harassed clandestinely by political intrigues orbiting our unawareness that, on the male line, we were part of George Washington's secret line of descendants, I never thought to ascertain any why or wherefore. Aside from the foregoing, I have to guess at what may have been going on inside my father's head. Without my realizing it, he had been larruped by all of those flashes from the front. Also, I hardly even realized that, thanks to all of the war headlines, the meaningless old saw: "You made your bed, now lie in it" . . . . , had been junked, scrapped, and tossed over the side by CPD. By the end of July 1940, all of this obviously translated, "Come home when you see fit."

Unexpectedly, my father seemed to have stepped out of character. On his own motion, he had reversed himself!

More on My Michigan Cousins

To make up for being cooped up weekdays during high summer, about every other weekend I would head for a mini-family reunion at the home of one of my Michigan cousins, an easy drive northwesterly of Ann Arbor. There at Dansville, the three sisters who'd convene were first cousins of my father. One sister had a beautiful daughter, my second cousin, Lillian. All of us were unaware descendants of George Washington. The three ladies (four, counting my second cousin Lillian, who was the daughter of Sylvia), Jessie, Sylvia, and Marjorie, were daughters of Franklin Pierce Dean, who was the brother of my grandfather Frederick Wellington Dean. Franklin and Frederick were numbered among the sons of Pierce Dean, who was the younger son of Israel Dean, who was the secret son of George Washington. Thus did the big political-genealogical secret march on.

The men present included Ead Mullen, the husband of our hostess, Jessie; Paul Cross, the husband of Sylvia; and Bill Sessions, the husband of Marjorie. Bill's presence gave me the opportunity to observe the likes of a successful trial lawyer off hours. The Cadillac-driving Bill wasn't very tall. But in court he was a giant-killer, winning, in particular, substantial automobile negligence cases while cutting down to size the biggest and the toughest of the Lansing area lawyers specializing in negligence cases. But just now it would be tough for us to communicate. Success in that department would require at least a couple of intellectual links. While it would take some possible eventual legal studies by your Virginian to interface communications, Bill during the upcoming fracas would become a major in army intelligence. Were I to obtain some sort of experience about which we could then compare notes, communications would be much improved, provided I could expound on the basis of some great firsthand knowledgeability on the military. Just now the newspapers and radio broadcasts were signaling that, if only I'd be patient, I'd get my chance in a real shooting war. Because more and more political gossip in print and on the grapevine indicated that the United States might get dragged in, for me it was becoming more and more difficult to devote my heart and soul to some mighty chain store such as Monkey's.

Out on the Mullen farm at Dansville, the country-style dinners were tops. While the men played poker and the ladies enjoyed each other's company, in spite of my having achieved this nice reunion with this one of many islands of my various cousins that were spread out between the Atlantic and the Pacific, I couldn't help but think that I'd like to be back in the Yankee Tier.

The Phantom Pitch

A few weeks after the departure of the nice little old lady who had really needed a Biblical laying on of hands, a second and last similar incident took place. Instead of change, this time it orbited the small locked sales-tax box. It too would be in the nature of a possible ploy.

On Monkey's same busy basement sales floor, but over on the far side at the counter of a different cash register station, George Silloway's hardware department provided the props for the phantom pitch. The pint-size human dynamo was one of Ward's first-

rate merchandisers. Pinch-hitting for the vacationing Duke Duchinsky, head of housewares, who customarily helped out Silloway
in that sector, your Virginian was completing a sale of some of Silloway's wares while the department head concentrated on counting
out the Change Fund (the amount of money assigned to his register) and putting it in the Change Bag. He next counted out all
remaining money and checks and entered such amount in the Daily
Register Report as "Cash at Close." He put this money and all
"Over-ring" receipts, "No Sale" receipts, and other papers (completed Time Payment Delivery Receipts, Employees' Purchase
Records, etc.) in the white "Sales Cash" bag.

Next we come to the crux of this particular tale. Silloway put
the sales-tax money from the locked tax box in the green Tax Bag
and must have given it the "phantom pitch."

Simultaneously, your Virginian had arranged during Silloway's
close-out of the hardware register for change for his customer, had
counted back the change, piece by piece, then had wrapped up
the package of items such as a screwdriver, small hammer, pliers,
nails, etc., and handed it to the customer, who had then gone on
his merry way.

Now back to the esteemed department head of hardware, as
he was currently being assisted by Monkey's junior trainee. A series of long work-for-nothing evenings rearranging counters, reworking merchandise displays for the fall season, had kept Silloway
on edge. Charged with a duty of performing lots of glamorizing
puttering, the rest of us clerks naturally borrowed tools from the
beefing Silloway's hardware counters. "Don't forget where you got
that when you're through with it," he'd admonish us. There were
small hammers, tacks, push-screwdrivers, pliers, glass-cutters, etc.
Occasionally you'd be so tired after the long evening piled on the
long day, after performing Monkey's various assigned tasks, that
you'd have forgotten to return to Silloway a pair of pliers or a tape
measure, etc., some jigger or the other that had happened to have
remained in your pocket. Such inadvertent toting off must have
worked the same with the other rebuilders of counter-top displays.
What did they do with the excess tools thus inadvertently carried
off from Silloway's counters but gradually accumulated at home? I
wouldn't know. But any collection that might eventually accumu-
late in my room would be carefully bagged, then taken back to the
basement hardware department and dumped on the counter in front

of Silloway, the department head noted for running a tight ship. His eyes would pop as he would explode, "Where did you get this stuff?"

Quickly I'd explain item by item just how the bits and pieces of Silloway's hardware had been carried away inadvertently late evenings when we'd been too pooped to realize that we still had the stuff on us. "I don't want any of this stuff, so here it is; you've got it all back," I'd tell Silloway, as such restorations must have made him wonder whether he shouldn't be getting back an equivalent amount of hardware items from the other clerks whom his counter had been equipping with tools for their dutifully reworking the store displays during unpaid overtime.

On the occasion of all such returns, Silloway quickly snatched up the restored tools and quickly sorted them into their proper bins. And he well knew that he could count on me to return to him any hardware that had been borrowed for Ward's work. Rarely did Silloway lose his cool. Ordinarily he was all business and highly efficient. Then came this particular hot summer midafternoon. At the hardware department cash register station for which Silloway was accountable, as mentioned, I was pinch-hitting for Silloway's absent aide. Nearing closing time, the last customers of the day were commencing to trickle out of the store. And as the department head commenced closing out his register, he wanted to watch your Virginian's final sales operation, but his current duty as a money-counter demanded all of his attention. Your Virginian's last customer, what'd he look like? He was a six-footer of a middle-aged man with an ashen complexion. Could any of us identify him? No more than we would know the monikers of one out of a dozen of our customers.

While I had been dutifully following Ward's ring-then-wrap procedure, Silloway, as mentioned, had been in the process of closing down his register to the point where the emptied drawer would be left open. He got ready to turn in to the office the three bags: change, sales cash, and sales tax. Suddenly the little man let out a king-size roar. Where was the last bag, the one with the sales tax cash in it?

When he looked to your Virginian, since I'd been servicing one of his department's customers, I hadn't been able to take note of Silloway's particular money-counting and bagging procedures. They were his affair, not mine.

Other than the departed customer, there were no witnesses present. Had any other salesclerks been present, they too would have been just as mystified by the phantom pitch.

When my day's last customer had been gone for a matter of minutes, the relatively short Silloway, from his daily duty of counting cash register contents, looked up at your relatively tall Virginian and roared: "Where's that green tax bag? It's got the money in it from the sales tax!"

Shrugging, I replied, "You're counting the money. You're the department head who's accountable. Where is it? Ask yourself. Don't ask me."

The little green bag containing an estimated several dollars in tax monies had disappeared. But where?

Quickly, the astute and seasoned merchandiser of a five-foot, three-inch hardware department manager looked all around the counter next to the cash register. His eyes swept the area from which I'd just served the last hardware customer. Right on the beam, Silloway, peered down into the wastebasket and riffled through its contents with his fingers. Then, turning to your unaware George Washington VI, Silloway looked me up and down as though he suspected that I was playing some sort of a "trainee trick" on him. Injurious suspicions effervesced. Losing an unusual lot of his composure, he stepped forward and patted me down. Although he found nothing, no apology for his having taken such a liberty was ever forthcoming. In short, the green bag with the sales tax money in it had vanished, and Silloway, who'd had its official care, custody and control, thus wouldn't be able to account for the relatively small yet still very important amount of chicken feed in it.

"Either the customer with some sleight of hand snatched that green bag and made off with it or else, when I was completing the sale to the customer," I told Silloway, "or maybe *you* inadvertently pitched the green tax bag into that little pile of goods that I had assembled there on *your* counter for the customer. I couldn't watch you and count out change to the customer at the same time. So maybe by the time I later wrapped the package, you'd already, behind my back but inadvertently, made a phantom pitch that I wrapped up?"

Silloway was fit to be tied. Although this was the second, fortunately it was to be the last unsolved mystery at Monkey's both of which concerned some chicken feed involving cash register routine. With some insights that decades later I would garner, were the political occultists now operative, it's at least warranted that we consider this other motivational possibility. Coming a fortnight or so after the incident involving the little old lady, such perpetrators of little strategems might have sent in an agent to pinch the sales-tax bag with its several dollars, their objective being to create some ill feelings and to stir up some injurious suspicions. The potential misattribution thus left Silloway in a very temporary state of ill humor and, among the help, such potential for misattribution left Monkey's merchandising atmosphere, for the moment, miserable and cheesy.

But Bosso McCarty, when he got the report—although he was as mystified as Silloway and your Virginian—seemed to consider it as just one of those things. Kissing it off, Monkey's local merchandising world soon forgot any clandestinely manufactured ill feelings. And the store absorbed the pain-in-the-neck loss over the phantom pitch.

A Very Disquieting August

By the last day of July, as the Germans saw the best of high summer now in the past, four weeks of Channel fighting, time enough to have conquered half of Europe, saw their bombers ranging over England every night, causing lots of alarms and small loss of production. In contrast, as J. E. Johnson would eventually further explain, the daylight raids were not going to plan. The more maneuverable Spitfires and Hurricanes were knocking off too many twin-engined ME-110's. So the Germans, who'd used hardly a third of their available strength, now marshalled three air fleets *(Luftflotten)*, and planned to destroy the RAF (same as they'd done to the Polish and French air forces), this time by August 10.

And other developments heralded by the first of August saw Japan signaling its intent to dominate China, French Indo-China, and the Dutch East Indies. Premier Molotov, addressing the Supreme Soviet in Moscow, said that Europe's "imperialist war" might soon involve America; he reaffirmed Russian friendship with Germany. It looked as though against such a combination, we Americans, if Hitler and Stalin joined to pitch on us, would have a tough row to hoe.

By August 2, the Japanese ambassador in Washington protested against the U.S. embargo on the export of aviation gasoline.

General John J. Pershing said that the U.S.A. should make available to Great Britain, as a national defense measure, at least fifty destroyers left over from World War I. More than 300,000 officers and men of the U.S. Army, the National Guard and the organized reserves assembled for war games. The U.S. secretary of war put six U.S. arsenals on an operating program of twenty-four hours a day, six days a week.

By August 9, Great Britain recalled all troops from Shanghai and northern China and John Cudahy was rebuked by the department of state and summoned to Washington after reputedly declaring in an interview at London that there would be starvation in Belgium during the winter, that King Leopold was justified in surrendering, and that German soldiers in occupied areas were acting better than American soldiers would have acted under similar circumstances.

Then on August 11 came a possible signal for an invasion of England. Eagle Day had been scheduled on August 10 by the Germans, but on account of weather, the timing of the proposed wipeout of the RAF was then delayed from day to day while enemy moves viewed by the British as the *start* of massed attacks took place when the *Luftwaffe* increased the intensity of the bombing of the southeastern coast of England.

And what about those of my friends who were in law school (as your Virginian would have been had I won double registry my senior year, or had I commenced in September 1939 following graduation)?

By August 14, FDR urged young Americans to continue their studies instead of rushing for jobs in the shipyards or slots in the Armed Forces. This meant that my friends such as Si Glann and Ralph German would graduate from law school in June 1941 (as I would have been slated to do had I commenced at Myron Taylor Hall my senior year as an undergraduate). While my chance of becoming a legal eagle looked like a dead duck, whether I knew it or not, it was still stewing on the back burner while more very disquieting events transpired in Europe.

By mid-August the *Luftwaffe*, more than a thousand planes strong, dropped bombs on Scotland and England, attacking for the first time London Airport. Included in the *Luftwaffe*'s attacks on the Fighter Command's vital sector stations was Biggin Hill, now stressed because it will provide some colorful background for adventures coming up in the next volume of our saga.

Here at home, lessons learned from observations of the panzers in action led to an award to Chrysler Corporation of a contract for erecting a factory and building one thousand 25-ton tanks. On August 16, metropolitan London was heavily bombed. And on the next day, Germany proclaimed a complete blockade of the British Isles, covering a thousand-square-mile area. Great Britain, by 20 August, was in the process of placing its transatlantic possessions at the disposal of the United States. Prime Minister Churchill also announced that Britain would not relax its blockade to permit food to reach continental Europe.

General Marshall, U.S. chief of staff, told a Congressional committee that the U.S.A. would need an army of between three to four million men to defend the Western Hemisphere. In the Dover sector of England, an ongoing shelling from German artillery on the French coast was confirmed. Canada and the United States came up with a joint board of defense consisting of five members from each country. Britain announced that the RAF and the Royal Navy would go to the aid of Greece if she resisted invasion by Italian forces on the Albanian frontier. Showing that the military leaders of the United States weren't exactly asleep, a military plane with a speed of 500 mph plus was demonstrated. By August 23, FDR was saying that unless Congress passed the Army conscription bill within two weeks it might set the defense program back a year. At Bermuda, the Great Sound was proposed to be offered to the U.S.A. as an air base. On August 24, an almost continuous stream of bomber and fighter units assembled over Pas de Calais commenced attacks between which there were no distinct gaps. These blows were aimed largely at sector stations and fighter airfields in the southeast. But more German bombers commenced to be shot down on the withdrawal.

By August 25, London "City" was hit hard by the *Luftwaffe*. In retaliation, Berlin experienced the first sustained air raid by the RAF. By August 27, FDR signed the bill passed August 23 authorizing him to call out the National Guard and organized reserves for a year's service. The Nazis still weren't getting everything their own way with the French. By August 29, General de Gaulle announced that the greater part of French Equatorial Africa had decided to join the British in fighting Germany and Italy.

As August wound down, constant hammer blows by the *Luftwaffe* aimed at opening up the invasion route from the Kent coast to London. As the German pilots gave increasing attention to sector stations, Biggin Hill was included. There, one hundred accurate bombs hit and set fire to the operations block, destroyed hangers and other buildings, cratered the landing area, and shattered vital communications. Nine JU-88's, protected by ME-109's that strafed, detached themselves from other formations. Each JU-88 dropped two bombs so that eighteen bombs wrecked workshops, living quarters, and damaged most of the transport. Two Spitfires were burned up. Utilities were cut. Thirty-nine personnel were killed. Six Spitfires harassed the retiring JU-88's. In this most successful attack carried out against a Fighter Command station, four Spitfires fell while the cost to the Germans was one ME-109.

Also, thanks to J. E. Johnson in *Full Circle*, during the last four nights of August, an average of nearly one hundred and sixty bombers attacked Liverpool and Birkenhead, along with targets in various parts of England, and at a very small cost, British antiaircraft fire providing the primary opposition.

While Johnson's report wouldn't become available for a number of decades, guesses and speculations at Monkey's retail store in Ann Arbor filled the gap. Between Rich, Pennala, and your Virginian, we all read between headlines that kept inferring that for the United States, war was in the offing, and conscription was coming up. What a disquieting month!

A Sidetrack To Our Saga Goes Poof!

It was Monday, September 2, better known as Labor Day 1940. Eventually to be included in Group Captain Johnson's update of the *Luftwaffe*'s attacks on the sector stations vital to the defense of London, Biggin Hill was bombed for the second time in two days.

Four other sector stations, four fighter airfields, and a big Coastal Command airfield at Eastchurch were hit.

In the air, the battles were being fought on terms favorable to the German fighters. During a four-day peak of intensity, Fighter Command lost one hundred and one aircraft. *Luftwaffe* casualties numbered one hundred and six, of which only a small proportion were bombers. As the *Full Circle* would eventually conclude: at this time the battle was between two fighter forces.

Last year, Hitler's war had broken out just as I was leaving Ann Arbor for the Cleveland Air Races, where German pilots were bodefully absent. Immediately preceding Labor Day this year, I had written a reply to some of my parents' concerns. "I haven't joined the Navy and I am still working for Monkey Ward. But with the passing of these weeks since my first annual vacation, Monkey's last chance is starting to run out. Will they come up with a raise in pay and a promotion? If they do, then I'm going to stick with them for as long as they show that they're serious. In other words, before very much longer, they've got to get busy and play ball." Then, referring to the preceding letter from home, I wrote: "The reason that I didn't write sooner is that I wanted to wait until I could tell you that Monkey's had lost out and that I had a new and better job. While I don't have a different one yet, as things now stand, I have an appointment on Monday, Labor Day, with my new landlord's business associate. He is Mr. Kittredge, sales manager for the Jackson district of Burroughs adding machine company. If he makes me a good offer I think that I will take it."

But what happened to my aspiration to sell big air transports? And how come I didn't start thinking about making my way to the good offices of Lockheed and Boeing and Pacific shores first? For once, any of my latent abilities to think big were hibernating. So four P.M. Labor Day rolled around and Mr. Kittredge arrived at the home where I was rooming. Without my then realizing it, he did me a great favor. Before I filled out the sales-job application form, Mr. Kittredge handed me an innocent-looking paper. "This is a little examination," he explained the surprise. "It won't take you long. So go back to your room, sit down at your desk, and answer the questions."

Into my digs I promptly disappeared. Because arithmetic always had been one of my relatively easy subjects, I was confident that I could handle that which, at first glance, looked like some relatively easy test on which I was only too glad for the opportunity to prove myself. But it was too bad that I didn't have some uncle in the business who might have given me a cram course. Talk about my being rusty on handling trick questions. . . . . . trick fractions, trick decimals, trick divisions, trick multiplications, etc. When I wound up the nice little exam and handed my paper back to Mr. Kittredge, he just took it, glanced at it, then slipped it into the inside pocket of his jacket and the four of us—the couple with whom I roomed, Mr. Kittredge, and your unaware George Washington VI—continued to carry on a nice friendly chat.

A day later my landlady Jane gave me the news. "Mr. Kittredge says that there isn't a chance. His company knows from experience. If you can't manage those figures for a starter, you'll never succeed at their sales job."

Normally arithmetic was a snap. Had I had any inkling on how to prime myself, I'd have passed that exam. Suppose that immediately afterwards I'd written down the questions and had studied them to the effect that, if not later on for the same company, then for some other, I'd eventually have made myself look brilliant, effectively latching on to the supposedly desired type of sales post. Otherwise, it was probably a lucky day for me that I let that little arithmetic test throw me. Had I made good, I'd have been sidetracked from ever setting down on paper for you all this George Washington—then his secret son Israel Dean—lineage down through Pierce, Frederick Wellington, and Clifford Pierce Dean to your unaware George Washington VI, who has wound up as your faithful scribe—Benjamin Evans Dean, the Virginian in Yankeeland! I was lucky but didn't know it, lucky because the adding-machine sidetrack from our saga went poof!

Aerial Combat Over Britain Sets Tone For Draft In USA

By early September, my deadline with Monkey's had been set—the last day of the month. And while the proposals for conscription were making their way through Congress, what a distraction the step-by-step news items made against my continuing to tie my fate and fortune to the big chain that had left me in the lurch for well over a year without a raise.

And what a wet blanket did the war developments place on any thoughts of my still getting started with my first year of law school.

As gleaned from both *Britannica Book of the Year* and *Full Circle*, on September 1, FDR issued the first order calling out 60,000 members of the National Guard from twenty-six states for a year's service. He made speeches warning the country of the danger from abroad and urged unity in support of national defense. And on September 3, he informed Congress that he'd made an agreement under which the United States had obtained the right to lease sites and build air and naval bases in the Bahamas and other British islands and points on the Canadian eastern seaboard in return for fifty overage destroyers.

During the first few days of September, the numbers that we could feel between lines of dispatches in the print media showed that ninety *Luftwaffe* planes had cost the RAF eighty-five fighters. The total wastage of fighter pilots was about one hundred and twenty a week and, since inexperienced trainee replacements were coming in at sixty-five a week, Fighter Command was fighting a losing battle. Were the Germans to take out the radar stations and hug the terrain, it would end quickly. If they continued against sector stations it would be a photo finish. Between Ostend and Le Havre, the massing of barges for transporting panzers was increasing. Concentrations of Stukas were observed at Pas de Calais. Britain's hope: hold out during all of September. In October the chances would be very good that weather would prevent the daily assembly of the big gaggles.

On September 7, there was a switch. Bomber command had raided Berlin. Hitler's threatened reprisals commenced. Goring switched from RAF sector stations and other airfields to London and its world-renowned dock areas. The defenders destroyed forty-one for the loss of twenty-eight fighters. Yet it was a success for the German bombers. They left raging fires at East India and other big-name docks, and also at the oil farms at the mouth of the Thames.

Before night fell, another gaggle hit Hammersmith, Battersea, and Paddington. Thus began the Blitz, fated to continue unabated for two months.

On September 9, FDR signed a supplementary defense appropriation bill for more than $5 billion and immediately thereafter the

Navy Department awarded contracts for two hundred warships, including seven battleships.

But what news that same day from England! Twenty German aircraft destroyed *before* bombing, for the loss of four Hurricanes and two pilots.

Although for the next few days, bad weather curtailed the *Luftwaffe*'s daylight operations, not so at night when enemy bombs inflicted nearly two thousand casualties. But that didn't stop Hitler from postponing the invasion for three days. He blamed the weather for his failure to wipe out the RAF, and forecast that only a few more days would be required to do it.

By September 11, the Reichstag was damaged by the RAF during a raid on central Berlin. FDR, in contrast, was stressing that he had: "one supreme determination—to do all that I can to keep war away from these shores for all time."

Then came some news that had been delayed briefly. On one of the raids there had been some damage to Buckingham Palace by the delayed aerial bombs that had been dropped on September 10 by the *Luftwaffe*.

On September 14, a U.S. naval statement declared that the policy of maintaining an Atlantic Fleet that could be expanded into a two-ocean fleet had been superseded by a policy of maintaining both a Pacific and an Atlantic Fleet in peace as well as in war.

Back on the sales floor at Monkey's, news concerning the Pacific Fleet was smothered. We all were most concerned about the inroads the *Luftwaffe* was making against the RAF. Yet without our realizing it, on the morning of Sunday, September 15, a turn took place. Two fighter sweeps came inland. Thanks to a long interval between first warning and the *Luftwaffe*'s advance, the RAF controller scrambled ten squadrons and assembled them into wings, and brought in reinforcements from the adjacent groups *before* the first German bombers crossed the coast, when a further six defending squadrons were sent off. *Full Circle* would provide the details. Thirty *Luftwaffe* planes were downed at the cost of seven RAF pilots.

There came a two-hour break. In the second big attack, although the radar warnings were shorter, RAF pilots claimed fifty-nine bombers and twenty-one fighters at a cost of eleven.

Now back to earth—in the States. On September 14, came what appeared to me to be a clarion call to home to the Yankee Tier, unless Monkey's very soon took advantage of their last chance and gave me a promotion and a raise. By a two-to-one majority, Congress passed the selective service bill, providing for the registration of all men between the ages of 21 and 35 (this latter number including Rich and Pennala). FDR asked Congress for $1.6 billion to pay the cost of the first year's training of the draftees. All of this meant that your Virginian redoubled his efforts with Monkey's. . . . to make certain that as a trainee hired around a year and a half earlier at Syracuse by a big executive out of Monkey's Chicago GHQ, your Virginian, would now give Monkey's two more weeks— their very last chance.

On Monday, September 16, as it would later appear, German troops may have actually embarked for the invasion of England except for the activities of the RAF. And on the same Monday during those fateful days of mid-September 1940, FDR signed the draft bill and called on all men within the prescribed age limits to register on October 16. That clinched it. If encouragement from Ward's administration wouldn't materialize by the end of the month, your unaware George Washington VI would walk at the end of the day, Monday, September 30.

The Drooping of a Career-Concept Hook

Conscription cast a new shadow on the Howard Lee Davis advice to the young man in business: find out how you stand in the estimation of the leaders of the big chain. I would need all of the information that I could obtain as to my future prospects.

"Analyze the whole situation thoroughly, then go have a good talk with Bosso McCarty," Davis, as a personnel expert, author and lecturer, would have said. Such analysis I'd done, but just a little bit too well. Some time previously, as mentioned, I'd gone and asked Bosso about the store's operating ratio in such a way that he'd balked at explaining it, indicating that by my putting our trainee's quiz finger on such a ratio, I'd struck a nerve. Thus at age twenty-two, instead of making such a diplomatic approach as to have gone asked Bosso to point out my strong points that needed some more emphasis and those weak points that might warrant strengthening, my approach, after the rebuff on my having tickled a nerve over the store's operating ratio, had been to pitch in with greater fervor than ever to all assigned merchandising tasks to the effect that by now, I was still leaving it to Monkey's management to make the next move. The ball was in their hands. The longer they waited, the more their commercial world as a career concept drooped.

After all, hadn't I been knocking myself out for them at a hundred a month now going on a year and a quarter? Even though the administration was a bit tardy, the company's brass hats could easily breathe new life into your Virginian merely by jacking up his pay from the current little over twenty a week to say thirty or thirty-five a week, then giving him a new post at which his services, if successful, would warrant even higher pay. Do that, even at this late date, and they'd find that they had a ladder-climbing slave who'd have made them a lot of do-re-mi.

Whatever Ward's secret policies in dealing with trainees, maybe your Virginian, as mentioned, because of George Washington land titles, was the exception. And maybe it was fortunate that Monkey's remissness with its trainee maybe was now trending toward letting your unaware George Washington VI off the hook, to the effect that instead of getting all burned out, he might preserve a posture that eventually would enable him to study law—the key to figuring out (almost three decades later) his George Washington lineage!

The Actor

Four days after military conscription became law, I got behind my typewriter on Friday, September 20, and told my father this: "Unless GHQ comes through with a promotion, I intended to resign from Ward's by the end of the month. So you can expect me home soon after."

As September wore on, the frustrations of being cooped up selling sporting goods in Ward's basement had heightened my desire to get out into the great outdoors to do some actual hunting. So, to prepare for this possible upcoming semimilitary respite from the rat race, I glommed on to a couple of nice guns that had arrived in good time with the fall line of merchandise bolstering Arnold Rich's sporting goods department. For upland game, one was a Browning semiautomatic shotgun that had been beautifully made in Belgium. For deer hunting, the other was a Remington .45 semiautomatic rifle. When I typed a line to my father that I intended to buy these two guns, but was hesitant over spending the money, he wrote right back: "Hold up on those guns. Don't buy. Save your money. You can use the guns that we've got back here."

Rich, who'd been looking forward to making such a substantial sale, was crestfallen. In any event, I always regretted not having made the purchase. With my employee's discount the fine workmanship on such guns, to say the least, would have enhanced a first-rate, long-term investment. So I forgot buying the guns and commenced putting in my last few weeks as a trainee, expecting word of a promotion to come through at any moment. Were such to be the case, I'd cancel homing plans and hang tight for fame and fortune with the big chain.

The suspense, coupled with the arrival of the new fall line of sporting goods, brought out the actor. The Cornell-Dartmouth densification was going stronger than ever. Already we'd unpacked hunting coats and hats and had them on display in the Dartmouth Indian's sporting goods department. After my father had instructed me not to make the first-rate buy on guns, I had to do something to buck up Rich. Because the department head had lost the sale, he was down in the dumps. Some improvised entertainment was mandatory.

One morning before the doors opened, from a nearby coat rack Parsley helped me into one of Ward's best Woolrich-type red and black plaid hunting coats. Next, off a glass display shelf, I picked up a beautiful wool matching cap, jammed it on my noggin and pulled the earflaps down over my ears. Standing nearby was Art Pennala, the Finn who'd thrived on a boyhood of hunting the Upper Peninsula. Although Rich was the key member of the sales force being played to, also getting ready to watch the show were Silloway, Duchinsky, Parsley, Boyer, and Epperson as well as the beautiful Mary. As they continued with their pre-opening early morning housekeeping chores, they peeked around corners of displays of their respective departments, glass shelves that were loaded to the hilt with new fall merchandise. Playing to the tight-knit group, from Rich's display I picked up one of Ward's pump-action deer rifles and checked its chamber and magazine for emptiness. Pennala, standing nearby, double-checked it. Foster and Duchinsky, both expert merchandisers over in plumbing and housewares, made sure that the coast was clear. Pennala surveyed the landscape. "There goes one, Dean!" he yelled. "He's got a big rack!"

Crouching and aiming past loaded displays as though they were trees of the north woods, I set my sights and commenced tracking the big buck.

"Get 'im, Dean!" Pennala yelled.

Pumping off three bursts of imaginary fire, to the tune of which Pennala was calling out: "Bang! Bang! Bang!" after the third one, I yelled: "I got him!"

"Good show!" yelled Boyer.

From halfway down the stairs where he'd just taken up his lookout's post, Foster Adams had no time to call for a chicken sneeze. Instead, our affable janitor warned: "Watch it, fellows. The party's over. Bosso and the assistant manager are just opening up the front doors for the customers."

Overhead we heard footsteps on the main floor. Our clientele was heading towards the basement for paint, hardware, and sporting goods, etc. In one moment the Dartmouth half of the Cornell-Dartmouth densification was helping the Cornell half off with his coat and hat, while Pennala snatched the gun and locked it back in the display. In the next moment, I was helping a newly arrived and excited customer into the same coat. Then, he tried on the same hat. Finally, while big brother-type Rich looked on approvingly, Pennala handed me right back the deer rifle. This three-piece outfit—to wit: the same hat, coat, deer rifle and all. . . . . I proceeded to sell the customer, lock, stock, and barrel! Heightening my desires to also go hunting, I had to watch the customer, so freshly equipped, beat his quick retreat for Michigan's renowned deer-hunting country. Without mentioning the thought to my co-workers, I knew that to make up for all of this being closeted in Monkey's basement, if soon it were to be back to the Yankee Tier for your Virginian, once home, I was going to go hunting every day for a month straight.

When Jane and Jerry, with whom I roomed, got word of my acting ability, they pressed for some background and I let it come out. During the fall of my senior year in high school, I had successfully played the role of the Englishman in the senior play *Sally*

Lou. So my host and hostess soon lined me up with a coed from California, the niece of a movie magnate. Had it not been for my oncoming deadline to head home, what a combination we would have made! She was as pretty as they come. But everything had to be according to Hoyle. And by the time the young man in a hurry would figure it out, it would be way too late. The actor had been offered a job but without his realizing—it came with the territory.

Getting Out The Alternatives And Kicking Them Around

Although my September 30 deadline for resigning from Monkey's had crystallized, only a few locals were in on the big secret.

Take my tennis-playing pal who could take me every set. When Bosso McCarty intercepted me at the time clock, it meant that I couldn't do the vanishing act promptly at five P.M. (but rather would have to go below and spend the customary half-hour dusting and restocking counters); so when weather permitted, shortly after dawn, my pal and I got in a couple of sets. Between them, we got out the alternatives to Monkey's and kicked them around. "Why not go to law school?" The lady joined Si Glann and the Senator among the very few who'd attempted to inspire such a great intellectual effort. And had it not been for the crazy international situation presumably soon to call on my services in the Armed Forces, I would have taken her up, probably winding up at Ann Arbor instead of back at Cornell.

And who popped into the store one day but Lewis B. Daniel from Cincinnati. As classmates in the college of arts and sciences at Cornell, thanks to the proximity of our names, we'd frequently held down neighboring seats. By now he had taken a turn at medical school. "That wasn't my cup of tea," he enlightened your Virginian, whose first ambition had been to study medicine at Harvard.

"You weren't the first one to tell me that."

"Who else?"

"Si Glann's big brother, Fred. He tried med school for a year and got out."

"What's he doing now?"

"He's a big-shot furniture broker out of Baltimore."

"Oh."

"What are you doing here in Ann Arbor?"

"Law school."

"Don't tell me you're just starting?" My thinking, as mentioned, was that on account of the war, why try starting at this late date?

"That's right. If all goes OK, I'll get my law degree in June 1943. You've still got time to register."

Then I explained the contrast. Daniel had the backing of his father while mine had confiscated my seed money, so forget it.

Oh, yes. Who arrived with Lewis? None other than the beautiful coed Betty Nixon. And once school started, there was still time during your Virginian's last days in Ann Arbor. We attended a fine ball at the university.

Now back to my tennis-playing pal. She hailed from a brilliant and intellectual family. When we were kicking around the options (other than Monkey's), her mother got in on the act. "Consider becoming a CPA. There are a lot of small growing companies here in the Midwest. Some one of them is bound to put you on as treasurer. You'll be able to buy some stock."

What brilliant advice! Although accounting had been an easy subject in college, I was seeking a spot with more exposure to the public. Yet, not often in my travels would I find anybody able to paint such a constructive future.

In return, I might well have tipped off such nice people on the buy that I'd called for ITT. Percentagewise it would greatly outdistance some more-secure, thus more popular bonds, but wouldn't get started until something could done about putting Hitler on hold. So at this point, when most war news was negative, I was afraid of giving them the idea that I was some wild speculator (while it would turn out that even Bernard Baruch was sharing my current money-making idea). Yet my friend's mother's advice would have a positive effect. I'd borrow only part of it, and then I'd buy a spread of stocks in some specially selected small companies, even though it would take a while to line up the wherewithal.

And when it came to kicking around the alternatives, there was a lot to be said for Ann Arbor. You could always go for the extra point.

The RAF Starts To Hold

Opening the last half of September 1940, increasing defensive pressure from the RAF caused Goering to insist that his fighters provide close tactical support for the *Luftwaffe*'s bombers, whose crews, during the daylight raids, were growing increasingly nervous. But friction was growing. The commanders of the fighter wings wanted to cast off such fetters in order to carry out their natural mission—to fight.

While the foregoing was gleaned from *Full Circle*, here are some items from *Britannica Book of the Year*. On September 16, the Italians occupied Sidi Barrani on the Egyptian coast after a sharp engagement with the British. Previously, on September 12, had come the announcement: Italian forces had crossed the Libyan frontier to invade Egypt. Thus, on September 21, four members of the Egyptian cabinet resigned in protest of the refusal of the government to declare war and place the army at the disposal of Great Britain. At the same time, President Cardenas of Mexico issued a decree granting Mexicans exclusive rights of fishing off the west coast of the country, where Japanese under the guise of fishermen had been engaged in mysterious operations for several years.

September 22, the governor general of Indo-China agreed to permit the Japanese to establish three air bases in Tongking, to be garrisoned with a maximum of six thousand troops, and to maintain a small force at Hai-phong. Despite the agreement, the Japanese crossed the northern border and attacked the French defenders.

The next day, FDR called upon the state governors to set up boards to supervise the registration of men under the selective service law, beginning October 16. And Germany warned Egypt and Greece that they should renounce their ties with Great Britain. Egypt was placed under martial law.

By September 24, Berlin announced that Finland had consented to the transport of German supplies and soldiers through the northern part of the country to Norway. Until now we all at home with Monkey Ward had been rooting for the Finns. But the significance of this last item would be almost impossible to explain away. Art Pennala was down in the dumps.

At the same time French planes dropped bombs on Gibraltar

in retaliation for the British attack on Dakar, Senegal, on September 23.

Then, by September 25, the British abandoned the attempt begun two days earlier to land Free French troops under General de Gaulle at Dakar after French forces loyal to the Vichy government resisted the attack. And the German high commissioner for Norway set up a government with Vidkun Quisling, Norwegian Nazi, as its head. The U.S. Export-Import Bank loaned $25 million to China to be secured by $30 million in tungsten to be shipped to the United States (no mention being made of boar bristles).

Here at home, newsreels had been focusing on American scrap being loaded on ships for Japan. By September 26, complaints by Americans were rampant. Doing something meaningful about responding, FDR placed an embargo on the shipment of steel and iron scrap, effective October 26, to any point outside the western hemisphere with the exception of Great Britain.

On September 27, representatives of Germany, Italy, and Japan signed a treaty in Berlin under which Japan recognized German and Italian leadership in the creation of a New Order in Europe. In return, Germany and Italy recognized the leadership of Japan in the creation of a New Order in "the greater East Asia"; the three powers agreed on mutual assistance with military and other means if one of them were attacked by any power not involved in the European or the Sino-Japanese war.

At the same time came the part concerning which Howard Lee Davis in his book entitled *The Young Man In Business* might well have written another chapter. If opportunities for advancement didn't exist just now with Monkey's, they did exist with the military. But we failed to take a cue from FDR when he promoted eighty-four colonels to the rank of brigadier general and twenty-nine brigadier generals to the rank of major general.

In contrast, we redoubled our efforts as one of Ward's trainees. We were expecting momentarily that we'd get notice of promotion from Chicago as we commenced to round out our fifteenth month with the big chain. It was a little more than a year after the beginning of Hitler's war. And if I didn't get any good news from Ward's GHQ in the Windy City, making up for it, the last two weeks of September saw daylight attacks against Britain so strongly escorted by fighters that they outnumbered the bombers five to one. A new lesson was learned. As would later be mentioned by Group Captain

Johnson in *Full Circle*, the *Luftwaffe* occasionally launched heavy attacks against quiet and widespread areas. But RAF casualties were reduced by one-third to about eighty a week and the production of fighters was higher than the wastage. For Fighter Command the crisis was passing as the RAF started to hold.

Looking Up The Carburetor Kid

But I didn't yet give up on attempting to get around the frustrations generated by Monkey's failure to breathe new life into my trainee's post. The administration was long overdue on coming across with my first raise since I'd started with them at the hundred a month more than a year earlier. So I kept playing even more new contacts.

By now I had run across a new consultant. My contemporary was Frank Clickner—the nephew of my cousin Jessie's husband, Ead Mullen. Hailing from nearby Dearborn, my new-found friend knew my cousins Donald Elwood Dean and Wayne Pierce Dean from their boyhood days in Mason, Michigan, where their father, Grover (son of Franklin Pierce Dean), had operated a hardware store in partnership with his sister Sylvia's husband, Paul Cross. Later on Donald and Wayne, with their parents, had moved, first, to New Milford, Pennsylvania (where we'd see each other frequently), and then to Florida (where our contacts were still good but much more infrequent).

Now back to my new consultant, Frank Clickner. We each had our own cars. When we'd leave my cousin's (his uncle's) farm at Dansville, he led the way down the Huron River Valley, showing me how we could test his Mercury against my Chevrolet on the tighter turns, squealing our tires. It was a Mexican standoff. At Hell, a spot of great natural beauty just westerly of the Pinckney area, we stopped while I talked land speculation and risk-seeking in real estate with a couple of local operators. But from my first trips in my own car to Detroit from Ann Arbor, I thought that I had spotted a better and closer-in realty business idea—planting some roots on the burgeoning westerly side of Detroit. I made my pitch for such a location through Frank's father. He was an important factor in the administration of the Ford Motor Company and on his days off from his home in Dearborn, he frequently dropped into the paint, wallpaper, and sporting goods sector in the basement of Ward's, where he would make a purchase through your Virginian's good offices.

Although I was working on a job switcheroo, it never occurred to me to hit up this new family contact for a job with Ford. His son Frank took me down there on a holiday and showed me around. We saw his office as well as the area where the riots had taken place during the labor unrest of recent years. Consider this possibility: perhaps I had been offered a job with Ford but hadn't realized it? And if I had, I had nevertheless kept mum, because if life with Monkey's was tough, I'd heard that even though you'd make more money with Ford, you'd also get burned out at a much more rapid rate. That gets us around to my probe at the realty business. It was to a friend of Mr. Clickner's that I made my next pitch with an unmentioned view of escaping Monkey's fetters. Again a sales spot was my goal, and to Mr. Coe I explained my views. "I would like to work the westward expansion of Detroit. If I locate in this Dearborn area selling real estate, I should be able to do well, provided that I can manage to keep away from a fixed salary and to stick to straight commissions."

Then Mr. Coe explained that such a proposed out from Monkey's was not quite as easy as it seemed. His clincher was this: "What you say is true. If you do like you say, over a substantial period of time you could probably fix yourself. And true, it's a big plus that you own your own car. But to follow your proposed plan, you would have to have the capital on which to support yourself for *at least* six months." He made my idea of digging in on Detroit's westerly environs grow wings and fly away because, in contrast, back in the Yankee Tier, I could try out any such gambles while living at home, getting back indirectly some spinoff from my previously confiscated $500 chicken-money nest egg. But the question remained: did I really want to devote my life to selling real estate on that westerly fringe of Detroit, back in the Yankee Tier or, for the matter, anywhere else? I supposed that the real test was, "What occupation would you choose if you were a millionaire?"

Your Virginian wasn't the only one interested in switching jobs. As mentioned, friend Frank Clickner (Mr. Clickner's son) also worked for Ford. Yet, same as your Virginian, he was ever on the lookout for a good, new, personal contact. Thus, when I proposed that we drive over one evening to Grosse Pointe Farms and say hello to the Carburetor Kid, who'd ably (as detailed in Volume II) served as coxswain on our 1937 Cornell varsity crew, Frank was quick to second the motion. After supper at Frank's home in Dearborn, my Chevrolet rolled up to the millionaire's big, stone mansion where the Carburetor Kid was waiting and ushered us in to a comfortable living room. The three of us were about the same age and there, Frank and the Kid got acquainted. As a result, Frank would eventually come up with a new and better job, this one with the Kid's father's carburetor company. For your Virginian's part, the odds were that Monkey's wasn't serious and that he'd soon go home and stay there to make one last try for the favors of the Indian Princess before enlisting in the Armed Forces. But here in the motordom job market, while I was sweating out a still-possible promotion and raise from Monkey's merchandising kingdom, there was nothing like doing a favor in the automotive world for a Michigan friend.

The Resignation

With my end-of-month deadline already in effect, and a few days after military conscription became law, I got behind my typewriter on Friday, September 20, 1940. In part, I again told my father this: "Unless GHQ comes through with a promotion, I intend to resign from Ward's by the end of the month. So you can expect me home soon after."

Were Monkey's to sit tight, any last-minute reaching out my way by the brass would have to be by my paycheck that would arrive on Monday, September 30. Were no raise or other message included, that would be it.

Came my deadline. What was to be my final fortnight's pay (based on the hundred a month) arrived in the customary doubly sealed secret envelope before lunch. When to actually resign? All day long I had my hands full at a temporary assignment, spelling Wes Eisley as delivery clerk. Throughout the long afternoon, I never found time to go tell Bosso McCarty my decision. When time was running out, I was up on the second floor in the process of getting

Louis Bycraft to dig out, tie up, and tag a couple of his rugs for delivery. When I was putting them on the elevator for a quick trip to Lyle Hurd's delivery truck waiting in the alley below, Bosso McCarty came up the stairs from his regular command post between flights to confer with the department head inside the credit counter to the rear of the rug and stove departments. When he had a moment, I successfully called for a brief powwow and broke the news: "The time has come. I've thought this over for a long time. I want to resign. What's the procedure? You want two week's notice?"

Making it real easy for me, Bosso said, "That won't be necessary, Dean."

"Then we can agree on this day as my last?"

"That's right."

"So what do I do?"

"Just sit down at one of our typewriters here behind the counter in our credit office," Bosso pointed to an idle machine, "and then type out your resignation. When you've got it worded the way it suits you, sign it and hand it to me and that's all that's necessary," Bosso graciously explained the unexpectedly simple ropes for cutting my ties with Monkey's.

Was Ward's serious? As I commenced plinking away, this little writing job was in the process of making such a question moot.

Keeping it short, I mentioned neither Monkey's failure to up my salary, nor their not having followed through after they'd sounded me out on becoming receiving clerk at Port Huron. Since war atmospherics had become so implicit, I also felt it unnecessary to mention the disquieting tone that had arisen from Hitler's war.

Thus for resigning, my stated reason was simply to return home to the Yankee Tier. With no misgivings and with not the slightest hesitation I handed my completed letter to the waiting Bosso. From his demeanor it was easy to see that we all were still on good terms. While I was certain that I would never want to come back, I felt that should I change my mind, a job would be waiting. What a relief!

So Long, Dartmouth Indian

The post-resignation final hour of the day was almost over. How to get word to my colleagues? For a year and a quarter I'd been working with a bunch of first-rate merchandisers, all of whom, for relatively low pay, were dedicated to Ward's. Ordinarily there'd have been some sort of a going-away party. But on account of the suddeness generated by my having fairly given Monkey's their last chance right down to the wire, like an Arab, I was now in the process of folding my tent in the night and slipping away. How to let the staff know? I told Foster Adams that I'd resigned. At first he thought that I must be joking. But when I explained the war angle, at once this father of several children understood my desire to have some time at home before enlisting. To this superintendent of all of the store's niches, I entrusted the job of spreading the word that the Cornell-Dartmouth densification was breaking up.

Since I had been absent all day from paint and sporting goods in the basement, in order to substitute for Eisley, getting sold goods lined up for Hurd & Son to deliver, I didn't get the opportunity to clue in Rich. When I dropped in to his department, Rich was out of the store carrying out some duty for management—comparative price-shopping, etc. For the last visit, on that same Monday evening, at his digs in the university section, I dropped in as though it was just for another of our occasional brief off-hours yarns. Rich must have had his ear to the ground. "Deanie, I realize that this isn't just another ordinary little visit."

"What do you mean?"

"We're the only Ivy Leaguers around. We were both hired out of Chicago headquarters and we were assigned to the same departments in the same corner of the same store at Ann Arbor. Your visit seals the breaking up of our merchandising team that was put together by GHQ."

"Probably I should have resigned in July. But by coming back for an extra three months, I've given Ward's their last chance. The brass has failed to come through. Furthermore, for some time, we have all been agreeing. We expect to be at war by the end of the year. So home I go to get ready to enlist."

"You're twenty-two. Just the right age."

"And you're already a relatively safe thirtyish. The draft board won't be pressing you for a long time if at all. You can keep plugging while going right up with Monkey's." (Maybe that's what the densification was all about—the knowledgeable brass' sending the older Rich to a college town where the more eligible students would get lots and lots of priorities in the draft.)

Although the Cornell-Dartmouth densification angle went unmentioned, all that we knew about each other's pay was that we both received highly secret salary checks in respective double-sealed envelopes. Instantly old hat was this densification that had been given its operational birth in Monkey's Ann Arbor paint and sporting goods section eight months earlier. As mentioned, Rich—with several years more experience but with Dennison's and Jordan Marsh—had been moved into the Michigan college town to join your Virginian, who'd already been at Ward's Ann Arbor store for around eight months. Such a teaming up, if that's what had been intended, now came to an end. Maybe that's the way Monkey's had reacted to the ever-increasing clouds of war. The draft board wouldn't be pressing the older Rich the way they would be showing lots of interest in your younger Virginian. With Rich now being left to hold the fort, Monkey's would have more time to develop their Dartmouth Indian.

Breaking Camp at Ann Arbor

To the tunes from the campanile of the morning bells, it was with mixed emotions that I got ready to decamp from Ann Arbor. Had I stayed there much longer, I think that my host and hostess would have sold me on leveling my sights on the economic boom now going on in California. Had I gone out there, I would have had various options. From the top level such as selling air transports, opportunities would have ranged downward to the much less practical but more sporting side: settle at a tennis school where I would perfect my shots while never forgetting that should an emergency arise, I would have been able to reapply, probably successfully, for another go with Monkey's.

From my digs, it came time to make the final rounds. My gear was all packed in the trunk of my Chevrolet when I bade farewell to Jane and Jerry, with whom I'd roomed for more than two months. But their "California, here we come," wasn't the path for which your Virginian was fated.

This time, what difficulty I had making the break from Ann Arbor! Starting out early I made the rounds, catching coed friends between classes, hostesses at home for a cup of tea, and finally, saving the best for last, stopping at the most popular book store, where my tennis-playing pal took a short break to see me wrench myself away to head for Ann Arbor's easterly portals.

It was midafternoon. Behind my departure and coming up with the evening tunes from Burton Tower, I could sense a great wailing. So often had I heard it, that it made me think that the coeds on campus in the Midwest were a much happier lot than those far above Cayuga's waters. When the chime tower wasn't drowning it out, their chant filled every little set of breezes, as the words came from just about each and every one of the college town's lovely ladies in unison: "How can we ever leave our little paradise?" Realizing that I needed substantially more than a hundred a month to show them the way, as I rolled through Detroit and crossed into Canada, on my mind was a larger question. What did the supposed last few months before war hold in store for your Virginian?

Nearing Dunnville, steady driving at 55 mph brought me upon a couple of car-pushing chaps followed by an anxious driver. As they pushed their car, the in-a-hurry follower pulled around into the path of a speeding westbound vehicle that almost turned turtle. Only after I saw that the westbound vehicle had made a lucky recovery, I took advantage of a clear road and, continuing easterly, passed both the people-pushed car and the car that had almost caused the wreck. But without my realizing it, the victimized car had stopped, turned around and after it too had passed both the people-pushed car and their unrealized tormentor, commenced pursuing, not the instigator of the near accident, but your Virginian.

Came time for a short respite at a roadside restaurant. Just as I was finishing a bite, in came my pursuer insisting that my 55 mph had made me difficult to catch and that I'd given his passenger (who administered to Canadian creatures great and small) a good shaking up. On account of the shifts in position on the motorized totem pole, as described, my explanation wasn't accepted. But when

I asked, "You're so insistent in your refusal to believe the way I say it happened; is it that you expect me to pay you off?" This scared my pursuer, actually an informal sort of chauffeur. He introduced me to the famous horse doctor, who was more amenable to my recounting of the actual cause of their narrow escape. But they took off minutes too soon!

After their red taillight vanished westerly, the author of their miseries pulled into the parking lot. Too late! When I told him about the nuisance that he'd caused me to have to put up with, he dummied up.

After that tempest in a teapot, before midnight, your Virginian crossed the Niagara Frontier and commenced rolling along Route 20 toward the northerly approaches of Finger Lakes country. As my Chevrolet coupe purred east, then southeasterly through Geneva to the heart of the Empire State, helping me fight off sleep was the pain. Not only from leaving behind all of those lovelies, but also from cutting my ties with Monkey's, there was genuine sorrow. On the one hand a career with big business was getting larruped by two elements: Monkey's failure to recognize my efforts with a raise, their nonfeasance being capped by conscription. On the other hand, hoping that I'd at last struck upon some truth that would make me free, I was about to make the most of my last days in civvies.

It was well after midnight when I passed through my old college town of Ithaca, where I latched on to a cup of java, then continued southerly through Springdale and entered the northerly portals of Owego. Upon my last return to Monkey's, in July, when my father had sent the written instruction. "If there's a draft, come home to register for it," he had bought for my room my first tall man's bed. After attaining the height of six-feet, four-inches in 1934, now, six years later, it was around 3:30 A.M. when I flopped on my first pad of sufficient length.

In the dark of the morning, like the bird that flew around the world, then returned to its nest, about twelve hours after evacuating the trainee's little world in Michigan, your unaware George Washington VI completed his final leg home. The Virginian was back in the Yankee Tier.

Monkey's Epilogue

For those of you who have faithfully found yourselves wrapped up in the life of a trainee, it's only fair that I should now present Monkey's Epilogue.

While I'd now aim for new, better, and more interesting experiences in what was left of peace, then war (fully expecting that we'd be in it by Christmas 1940), we look back momentarily. As Howard Lee Davis had inferred in his book, for a young man in business, starting as a trainee and merchandising it with the objective of becoming a store manager didn't mean that such an aspirant would wind up later on, when higher up, still in the store-management sector of merchandising. For instance, I might well speculate that had I stuck it out, Monkey's internal headhunters might have discovered (as such a skill would eventually slowly surface) that your Virginian had been sharpened up by his father's having confiscated his $500 chicken-money nest egg. Thereafter he had learned to apply principles remembered from lectures by esteemed professors of economics, etc. at Cornell. Such applications would see him successfully putting money out at risk in contrasty equity-type investments. So what?

Eventually I might have been showing Monkey's how to formulate policies that would see them staying in touch with and perhaps setting the pace against Sears.

An actual but non-Virginian illustration of such a non-store manager success would eventually be generated by Rich. In later years, Rich would write. . . . "I was in a number of stores like Petoskey, Cadillac, Sturgis, etc., etc. Ended up in Lansing as 'assistant to be store manager,' under dear old John DeMerit, manager. Then I was summoned into Chicago to head up catalog order. DeMerit told my district manager, 'Arnold is the best assistant I have ever had in my years at Ward's.' Considering he opened Ward's *first* store in Plymouth, Indiana, years back, it was a moment I'll always fondly recall."

All of this progress was being made by Rich while your Virginian will next be winding up this current volume of our saga, ending with the coming of the war years, by which time the then-thirtyish product of Beantown and Dartmouth would write, "I drew the last number in the draft, registered in Ann Arbor, with all those students ahead of me. In 1942, I decided to apply for a commission in the Navy. My good friend Dick Leese, an aide to Sewell Avery, told me to stand by and expect a call. A few days later he asked, 'Can you come over now?' I flew across the street from the mail order building. Sewell was waiting in the huge office. Very nice to me. I'd talked with him maybe four or five times when he passed through [mail order]. The reason I wanted his recommend, apart from the prestigious impetus from the chairman, was that it was 1942 and dependable emoluments such as the GI Bill had yet to surface. So an approval from the Top would slightly assure my being rehired when I would come back some three, four, or five years hence, were I to be so lucky.

"The old guy was charming as only he could be when he wanted. He assured me that he would be glad to give me a fine sendoff. When I stood up to leave he said, 'Why in the hell do you want to go to war? The godamn Democrats got us into this thing. Let them get us out.'

"Enough for now."

As Rich would later brief it, his military career: "Commissioned a Lt. (j.g.) in 1942. Was No. 2 personnel officer on Admiral Nimitz' staff for the Pacific Fleet; got out in 1946 as a lieutenant commander; came back to Ward's, where they made me employment manager in the home office; retired twenty-six years later."

Thus did the Dartmouth product get to spend the better part of his merchandising career in a couple of those sectors other than store management, a positive switch to which Howard Lee Davis had alluded.

In other words, Rich got the type of training that your Virginian had been expecting to get started at before Hitler's war. Instead, and with no semblance of an explanation, Monkey's brass hats had kept me glued to Ann Arbor when I'd expected to get some transfers (such as Rich got after I left) to get some varied experience at various posts in different stores, and not necessarily limited to Michigan.

When Rich, who'd been concerned about getting his job back after Hitler's war, would make a career of Monkey's, although it would take a while, eventually, he'd go right up—all to the effect that the Dartmouth half of the densification would become one of Monkey's top dogs while the Cornell half would be seeking his fortune as a free agent on the economy at large (as will be detailed in upcoming volumes).

In comparson with the older, more seasoned Dartmouth Indian, from the viewpoint of Monkey's brass hats, how did your Virginian stand? In a letter of recommendation that I would have reason to eventually request, O. O. Lokken, Ward's regional personnel manager, would tell it, in part, like this: "On July 5, 1939, Mr. Dean was employed as a trainee in our Ann Arbor store. He came to us directly from Cornell University and was given this assignment as a trainee for store manager based on his record in college.

"He resigned on September 30, 1940 to return to his home. [If my reason for homing sounded a bit flat, that was because my resignation should have spelled it out that I expected that we'd be at war in four months and expected to enlist. . . . Mr. Lokken continues.]

"During the *short time* [one year plus an extra three months to give Monkey's their last chance] that he worked for us, he was a very willing worker and in spite of his lack of experience in our type of work, he made satisfactory progress. His first assignment was in the receiving room where he handled both incoming and outgoing merchandise. This part of our operation requires accuracy in the handling of detail and was handled satisfactorily by Mr. Dean.

"His record with our company is clear and his services were entirely satisfactory."

Now back to my side of the story: What did your unaware George Washington VI think of the way a Mr. Personnel out of Ward's hire-and-fire department handled your Virginian's previously detailed case? While having mentioned receiving room experience, Monkey's left out all mention of my sales-floor work where I'd spent more than twice as much time—eight-months—much of it as department head of a leader in percentage increases—wallpaper.

Also going unmentioned, assisting both Rich in sporting goods and Parsley in paint, I'd sold a raft of merchandise for Monkey's.

How to solve Monkey's reactions that from your Virginian's viewpoint were a bit mysterious? A pet guess is that they were having difficulty finding reliable receiving clerks. While I'd gladly have accommodated them, provided they had let me run a big enough situation to suit my talents, I wouldn't have wanted to make a career out of seeing to it that incoming goods were properly checked in.

Who else went on his own? Eventually I would hear that Louis Bycraft would open his own floor-covering store and make it big on his own account.

What about Bosso McCarty? He took a cue from your Virginian. Although Bosso, in contrast, would remain with Ward's, he would eventually be assigned a store in Indiana and return home.

Pennala was a somewhat different story. During Hitler's war, he would go back to his pre-Monkey's life in the manufacturing plants, garnering some good supervisory jobs. But when he would retire, it wouldn't be to the hunting and fishing paradise of his beloved upper peninsula of Michigan. Art would select a valley named "Paradise" out in California.

As for the rest of my various and sundry coworkers who elected to stick with Monkey's, they not only had their own personal reasons for so doing, but all of them whom I ever observed had learned their jobs very well, and all contributed to the tight-ship status of the Ann Arbor retail store from which all inefficiences seemed to have been flushed by the immediate aftermath of the great depression.

Chapter 8

A Respite From The Rat Race

Some Of CPD's Visitors: At Least We Knew Their Status!

As more and more signals surfaced enhancing the likelihood that the United States before long would be dragged into Hitler's war, FBI agents, reporting on the temper of the populace, etc., were quietly combing our county. Included among their sources, such as credit bureaus, banks, and brokerage offices, was my father's bureau in the back of the barn. With Hitler's ongoing bombing raids on Britain hiking our chances for war, Dad's office was becoming more and more a calling place of various members of the new generation of young men neatly and conservatively attired in dark suits, white shirts and ties, dark felt hats and shiny shoes. After all, the occupation of the unaware George Washington V included part-time jobs as village treasurer and as secretary-treasurer of a countywide fire insurance cooperative, this latter position frequently seeing him making contacts at farm buildings in all four corners of the area on which policies were written. He was thus very well acquainted in village, town, and county with current economic conditions as well as with data that might enable J. Edgar's finest to develop their various and sundry leads.

As my mother, Peggy, (the younger of my two younger sisters, who was still at home), and I would have the occasion to look out the window and see such important persons come and go, we figured from the heightening of a preparedness atmosphere that perhaps military secrets or other matters of national security were involved. Presumably we had no need to know. Thus, no members of our family ever inquired from Clifford P. Dean (CPD) about the FBI's business. And he never raised the hare.

But we did take note that the respective agents would park in the street, always lock their cars, then, heading out back, proceed the forty yards or so on the sidewalk alongside our driveway on foot, enter the spacious front portal of the barn, and proceed past my father's Chevrolet, to make contact in the built-in office that the carpenters had installed some years earlier at the rear of the garage section of the barn.

At least we knew who these visitors were!

In contrast, during 1926, a bit more than fourteen years before my current return from Michigan to the Yankee Tier, another fine-looking chap whom we would eventually surmise to have been some much higher sort of a federal agent had arrived in town with a glistering Buick touring car adorned with Pennsylvania license plates and had made arrangements with my father at the Dean & Dutcher feed mill to store some household goods in a then-available corner of this same barn behind our dwelling house. He was Bruce Martz. After then having had a good yarn with my father, Bruce's mission may have been to first get it out of CPD, then to advise the government, meaning J. Edgar himself, that my father was unaware that he was a George Washington V and thus unaware that he, my father, was holder of an important *per stirpes* title by the laws of descent and distribution of the vast estates of George Washington. Just then moves were underway in the City of Washington to decide on a location for a new airport. Federal eyes had then fallen on one of the most important of such tracts of the George Washington Estate—about 1,200 acres fronting on the Potomac and situate between Four Mile Run and Columbia Pike in the Virginia sector of the District of Columbia.

And to further ascertain the identity of Bruce Martz, during later years, when we'd have a friend ask some of his buddies who worked for J. Edgar the identity of Bruce Martz, my contact man would report back, "On my previous questions over the years, my friends always gave me a 'yes,' or a 'no.' But at the mention of the name Bruce Martz, they just got stoney-faced."

This significant contact by Martz in 1926 at our home wasn't the first by feds. Preceding him by as much as six years, but more indirectly, through the home of a business partner, came one Carothers. Not long after my father and his partner, Byron Dutcher, had moved to Owego from New Milford, Pennsylvania, Carothers rented an apartment in Dutcher's house. Since such tenant had retired from the United States foreign service in Mexico, his moving to Owego, although not then seen as anything significant, was more special than it had then seemed. Occasionally the State Department retiree served up Mexican dishes to Dutcher's son Duane and his friend Splanaway when they were in their early teens. Again, it was likely that Carothers had learned, then passed the word along to his principals: CPD was unaware that he was a great-great-grandson on the male line of George Washington and thus a *per stirpes* titleholder of his vast estates, including George Washington's tract on Four Mile Run.

A little more than eight years after Bruce Martz had sent a truck to pick up his stored goods, for a 1935 Easter holiday, a brilliant buddy, Dick Smith, and your unaware George Washington VI had hitchhiked to the City of Washington, basing sightseeing operations there at the home of Dick's Uncle Ray Smith, the well-known chiropractor. As detailed in a previous volume, one of our junkets had gravitated to Hoover Field. But by the time I resigned from Ward's on September 30, 1940, Hoover Field was being transmuted on the drawing boards shaping lands north of Columbia Pike (in the Virginia sector of the District of Columbia) for the Pentagon and its accompaning spacious parking lots, especially on its north side.

On that same Easter 1935 trip, south of Columbia Pike, the bus driver (referring to but without mentioning by name Four Mile Run) had pointed out to Dick Smith and your Virginian a spacious tract with a, "These are George Washington's lands."

Now, by early October 1940, it was frontage on the Potomac of such a 1,200-acre tract that had been filled in by the government for the so-called "new airport." And although my father was a *per stirpes* titleholder, the government (as well as exploiters of the rest of the 1,200-acre tract) could feel secure on the basis of reports from people whose identity we would never know for sure—Martz and Carothers. Again, from the viewpoint of the preemptive beneficiaries: what CPD and his family didn't know wouldn't hurt them.

The New Airport On The Potomac

On Saturday, September 28, on the last weekend before your unaware George Washington VI pulled up stakes in Michigan for Owego, while four hundred and eight (408) combat planes flew above the new airport in Washington, FDR laid the cornerstone of the airport's administration building and said that the planes were "symbolic of our determination to build up a defense. . . . . capable of overcoming any attack against us."

No mention was made in *Britannica Book of the Year* of the Potomac, or of George Washington's Four Mile Run tract. But undoubtedly, this was the unmentioned specific site. And since my father (as a great-grandson of George Washington's secret son—Israel Dean) now was one of the various unaware *per stirpes* holders of the true legal title of the George Washington Estate's Four Mile Run tract on the easterly river-front portion along which the new airport is believed to be stretched, some more angles of suppressed history of this colorful strip, we will submit in the following chapter to you all, details for posterity to love.

Implementing the current up-front squib, the same edition of *Britannica Book of The Year* (as the next year's book would customarily report this year's events. . . . at page thirty-one) would run a nice little feature, as follows:

"Washington National Airport.—Upon completion in early 1941, the Washington Airport may well serve as a model for all metropolitan terminals of air traffic. While not the largest in the world, its size is sufficient to provide with future developments for all foreseeable airline traffic. . . . . Runway lengths are: N. to S., 6,875 ft.; N.W. to S.E., 5,300 ft.; N. E. to S. W., 4,820 ft.; and E. to W. 4,200 ft.

"The terminal building lies almost in the center of the development and is connected by taxiways to the ends of each of the four runways. The building itself runs 540 feet along a curved line and is three stories high exclusive of the control tower from which every part of every runway is visible. The ground floor is almost exclusively working space; the main floor is devoted to the handling of passenger traffic and visitors; the upper floors are for airline and airport officials, except for the dining room in the north wing and for the operation of airway and airport traffic control, radio communications and weather bureau.

"The main dining room extends 120 feet by 40 feet, and its east wall is entirely of glass and faces a 20-foot dining terrace overlooking the flying field, the river and the city. The lessees of this space are expending some $300 thousand in decoration and equipment.

"Parking space will be provided for about 5,000 cars ordinarily, with emergency space for about 3,000 more. There likewise will be bleachers or a grandstand along the edge of a flying field and ten feet above it running north from the terminal building. These facilities were determined upon after careful studies of airports, both in the United States and in other countries. It was learned, for instance, that before the war which started in September 1939, a large part of the patronage of the Dutch airlines was secured from among the sightseers who came to Schipol Airport at Amsterdam, and that the patronage of the restaurants and observation terraces on the mile-long roof of the hangers at Tempelhof in Berlin paid a large share of the cost of the airport.

"With one hundred forty-four (144) scheduled landings and takeoffs every twenty-four hours," it was indicated that Washington was to become, for the entire year of 1940 "the third busiest airport in the United States." In addition, the item indicated that other airlines were now filing applications for service into Washington. It was predicted that the new airport would be devoted mainly to airline service. As finally gleaned from *Britannica*, the new airport would cost in the neighborhood of $12.5 million when completed.

Coming up next: the part that the newshawks liked to overlook—the *source* of the title, if any, for such occupants of the original river frontage on which this new airport was based.

From Whence the Title?

Keep in mind that, should you all decide to take a gander, at the time we set this down on paper, Four Mile Run is a relatively small stream that's hard to spot as it flows easterly and with much of it covered by the broad railroad yard on its way to the Potomac. The confluence, as we see it, is on the downriver corner of *the new airport.*

The Four Mile Run tract of the George Washington Estate sits in the Virginia area of the District of Columbia that at one time was known as the County of Alexandria, according to *Britannica*, (23:393). And it may well be that heretofore, the *re*ceding in 1846 of such County of Alexandria by the federal government to Virginia was illegal!

Now, turning to Four Mile Run itself, George Washington (according to Eugene E. Prussing, at page 227 in his book *The Estate of George Washington, Deceased*, published in 1927) acquired his Four Mile Run tract from George Mercer and others on December 2, 1774. This tract was on the *north* side of the stream (Four Mile Run) which, according to Prussing, empties into the Potomac midway between the Long Bridge and Alexandria, where the machine shop, power house and barns of the electric railway now (as of 1927 or during the prior period of time it had taken for the writing of Prussing's book) stand. Washington's Four Mile Run tract ran up the little Four Mile Run to the west and uphill to the north, fronting on the Potomac for a mile (making up the major if not all of the Potomac River frontage for the new airport by September 1940). (Said northerly end of such Potomac frontage, along with the Four Mile Run tract in general, according to our information, abutted on lands that, pre-Civil War, were known as the Custis-Lee Estate.) From the waterfront intersection of Washington's Four Mile Run tract with such Lee Estate, the northerly boundary of the Four Mile Run tract ran westerly, a very substantial distance, all or in some substantial part, along Lee's southerly boundary, as we surmise from Prussing. . . . . abutting on the Columbia Pike (as it existed in 1927) and what is now (as of 1927) Fort Barry. While it would make our yarn that much more interesting were the Pentagon to be located on George Washington's Four Mile Run tract, we believe at this writing that the Pentagon (that had been slated for completion in early 1943) sits just north of the northerly boundary of Washington's Four Mile Run tract.

Of this particular Four Mile Run tract belonging to the George Washington Estate, a seeming conspiracy of silence would eventually descend on its various monuments and distances as they likely were crystallized by George Washington. Popular road maps would color the area as though included in the Custis-Lee Estate of Arlington. In contrast, during the last year of his life, George Washington personally resurveyed Four Mile Run, according to Prussing (page 228). It is indicated that George Washington ran the lines and remarked the boundaries. "The notes Washington took of this (re)survey were written by him on the back of a letter of introduction given by Patrick Henry to an aspiring youth. This and Washington's transcript of the description in full are now in possession of the trustees of the Protestant Episcopal Theological Seminary." While Prussing calls them owners of a large portion of the property (such "property" meaning the Washington Estate's Four Mile Run tract), it would appear to your scribe that actual *per stirpes* legal title to Washington's Four Mile Run, as it includes such "occupants" as such seminary, various developments, and *the new airport,* now rests instead with the descendants of George Washington's secret son— Israel Dean—of whom your Virginian, as mentioned, is a great-great-grandson. In short, it's as *a party in interest* that we set this all down on paper for you all. And we thus claim that the seminary does not have title to its realty. . . . and. . . . that. . . . . neither does the government have title to *the new airport* as it derives from Four Mile Run acreage. At most, we surmise that occupants are trustees; and descendants of George Washington's secret son Israel Dean are beneficiaries of a potential constructive trust.

Thus it's also to be pointed out that on page 23 of the paper writing purporting to be the will of George Washington, mention of Four Mile Run is made. Had George Washington gone so far as to very unlikely ignore his personal local attorney—James Keith of Alexandria—possible custodian of a possible real but suppressed will—and had George Washington actually intended to make a homemade will (and such intent is very questionable because he presumably injected lots of confusion or some secretary who could write like him did it for him in part bollixed the date of the homemade job), were it his (likely as a stall until he could get to Attorney James Keith and get him as his local attorney to finalize what he, George Washington, may have planned to be his *real* will, in the customary formal manner for execution by the testator), any devise of Four Mile Run to the purported beneficiary Custis, therein at such page 23 named, would have been invalid in our opinion, because the page wasn't subscribed, as well as because Washington's secret son—Israel Dean—never had his day in court.

Furthermore, the possibility exists concerning the paper writing purporting to be George Washington's will that, if our First President was actually the writer, then he never intended to complete it to a point where it could be probated. In other words, he had intended that title to his vast estates pass in intestacy, by the laws of distribution and descent, to his secret son Israel Dean.

Now back to this further angle on Four Mile Run: According to Prussing (in a footnote at page 227), Four Mile Run also came to be know as Washington Forest and, during the Civil War, because of the involvement of General Lee on the losing side, some of the Lee Arlington lands (those north of George Washington's Four Mile Run tract), of which northerly lands the Lee people actually held true title, were confiscated by the federal government. But during such involvement, the government knew enough not to monkey with George Washington Estate lands. His Four Mile Run tract, also known as Washington Forest, was *not* confiscated. Thus if the government was basing its chain of title for the new airport on page 23 of such purported will of George Washington, the government, with its knowledge of that great national secret—political genealogy orbiting George Washington's secret son—Israel Dean—from whomever the government (the seminary too, and anyone else, for that matter, later locating on lands in the Washington Estate's Four Mile Run tract). . . . . from whomever such parties actually and eventually were to take a deed, such grantees took delivery at their peril—they may have taken possession; but it was a possession without proper title, as such grantees simply couldn't get good title from their actual grantors, ignoring the descendants of George Washington's secret son, who held the actual *per stirpes* title but were unaware of it! From whence the title? By virtue of the laws of descent and distribution, the actual true legal *per stirpes* title is still in the descendants of Israel Dean. And that's why FDR, in June 1938, had summoned our Cornell varsity eight to the Dutton Lumberyard in Poughkeepsie (as detailed in Volume

II) to watch him debark from a destroyer. He was treating his Secret Service entourage to a viewing of an unaware George Washington VI who just happened to be a contingent *per stirpes* title holder to the Four Mile Run portion of the then-upcoming new airport on the Potomac.

Greetings From Headlines Enhance The National Emergency

Home in the Yankee Tier, I awakened to the tune of headlines mirroring the feelings of Owegoans that the real thing was going to engulf the United States. In England, the daylight bomber attacks ceased and it was left to enemy fighters and fighter-bombers to tie down Fighter Command. Eventually, Capt. J. E. Johnson in *Full Circle* would indicate that the day battle had become a straight fight between the opposing forces. But from the viewpoint of Fighter Command, the interception rate was still far from satisfactory.

Next we glean some chronological events from *Britannica Book of the Year*. On October 2, the day of my return from Michigan, the Navy Department began the organization of a patrol force of 125 ships in the Atlantic supported by an undisclosed number of planes.

On the next day, Secretary of War Stimson announced the organization of an Army parachute corps. One of my local contemporaries in the Yankee Tier—Hugh Hogan—lent an ear to the bonus-enhanced eliteness through that newly opened door to some potential action fated for an extra special twist that would see his outfit help tip the scales of battle. In a number of months, our paths would would cross not only on the high seas but also on exotic foreign shores.

By October 5, Hitler and Mussolini conferred in Brenner Pass. And Premier Konoye of Japan said that if the United States would recognize Japanese leadership in East Asia, Japan would recognize a similar leadership of the U.S.A. in the Western Hemisphere.

At home the national emergency intensified. Secretary of the Navy Knox ordered into active service all organized naval and marine reserves, numbering 27,591 men.

While developments in Europe usually grabbed the spotlight, rising tensions in the Orient caused the State Department by October 8 to instruct U. S. consuls in the Far East to advise all Americans to leave Japan, Manchukuo, China, Indo-China, Chosen, Formosa, and Hong Kong.

On October 8, German troops moved into Rumania to guard the oil fields against sabotage.

Highlighting the remaining months of Stateside peace, in the World Series, Cincinnati defeated Detroit.

From London came word from Winston Churchill. He announced that the Burma Road, closed on July 17, would reopen on October 17 for the transit of military and other supplies to China.

On October 9, an article in Mussolini's newspaper offered to give the United States such British possessions as Canada, Australia and New Zealand if the United States would remain neutral in the establishment of a New Order in Europe.

In the United Kingdom, Churchill was unanimously elected head of the British Conservative party as successor to Chamberlain.

Although Germany had won the opener in June, General de Gaulle signaled that France intended to keep fighting. He landed at Duala, French Cameroons, to take charge of the Free French forces there.

A German bomb dropped through the roof of St. Paul's Cathedral in London, wrecking the high altar.

On October 10, FDR ordered the impounding of $100 million Rumanian funds in the U.S., bringing the total of impounded funds belonging to nations invaded by Germany to about $3 billion.

On October 11, Japanese Foreign Minister Matsuoka, modifying a previous statement by Premier Konoye, said that the treaty with Germany and Italy was a peace measure and was not directed against the United States.

An official broadcast from Ankara, Turkey, warned the Germans against a drive into the Near East and announced that the way there was guarded by two million bayonets.

On October 12, FDR said that no combination of dictator nations in Europe or Asia would stop United States aid to the British and that the United States would defend its right to peaceful commerce in the Atlantic and Pacific Oceans.

More evidence surfaced on Germany's great hunger for fuel for its war machine. On October 15, Germany took control of the production and distribution of Rumanian oil.

While such headlines in the media enhanced the tempo of the national emergency, such were the current events that dominated the question of war or peace for the U.S.A., while lots of potential conscripts relaxed over a beer evenings at the taproom of the Ahwaga Hotel—all of this during your Virginian's first fortnight of the respite from the rat race.

Registration is Followed by the Big Drawing

They called it selective service. Soon it was Wednesday, October 16. Just a month earlier, in September, Step No. 1 of conscription had been completed with the signature of FDR. Now came Step No. 2. Registration day had been proclaimed by FDR for the continental United States. Responding, 16,000,000 men between the ages of 21 and 35 registered for conscription. For all of us 'uns, we now had something to sweat out......the real thing! But there were still some good moments of relaxation.

On the last Saturday of the month came the Ohio State game at Ithaca. A year earlier I had won a bet from Junior Hurd. Would Cornell make it two in a row? If so, Junior, having been left behind in Ann Arbor, would save his money.

When I arrived a day ahead of time in Ithaca, the same law students with whom I would have been rooming had I become a September-1939 double registrant as planned not only put me up, but also took advantage of their captive audience and resurrected some old advice.

This extra special group of law students orbited Si Glann and Ralph German. What a constructive broken record! "Forget everything else and get started next term at law school." While such fine counsel may have appeared to them to be ignored, the right way to go was slotting itself into my sensorium's deepfreeze. Perhaps some future thaw would activate some serious law studies. But just now the football game in the Cornell Crescent was the thing. Ohio State sparkled in their Red and White uniforms. "Where do they get all the money?" I asked Ralph German, son of the president of a coal-carrying railroad, and destined to become a leading legal eagle in the Pittsburgh realm of King Coal.

"Oil," he replied tersely.

But the game was the thing. Once Snavely's men started throwing passes, Cornell came from behind to win 21 to 7.

Forgetting the go-back-to-school advice, but souped up over Cornell's victory over very tough opposition, soon I was right back in Owego. While marking time for the opening day of deer season, I went for small game. Occasionally, as I would be accompanied by the Indian Princess, we made it our business to hunt rabbits and ruffed grouse, eventually switching to migratory birds. Both of us were good shots. The competition was scintillating. But after I gave the hunt my best try, word came back from my spies, "She says, 'He's not going to get me.' "

Upstaging such pursuits, on October 29, for conscription it was step No. 3. Out of the same goldfish bowl that had been used for World War I, the first number—158—was drawn by a blindfolded Secretary of War Stimson. By the time the lottery had ended, seventeen hours had elapsed. Mother would write in her diary: "Evans' serial number is 1211. The order number sequence in which the number is drawn is 6458."

Was I high, or was I low? At this writing, I honestly can't remember. Whatever the significance, I wasn't much concerned. As soon as the real thing would come along, I was going to enlist.

From the local crop of patriots, the Thursday, October 31 issue of Owego's Democratic weekly headlined the names of the Big Seven—volunteers to take one year of military training. According to Senior Rover, chairman of the draft board, they would be called previous to the men with regular order numbers.

Said the weekly, "Ever since the posting of serial numbers on Monday, crowds gathered around the *Gazette's* office window in search of their sequence. Some of the faces of those studying the lists show anxiety. But most are taking the first conscription since the World War in stride and are enjoying the excitement. Most of the anxiety is shown by parents."

Did your unaware George Washington VI bother to take a gander? No. He ignored such a great opportunity.

Finally, I merely commenced sweating out receipt of the ducat coming up for all registrants who didn't sooner enlist: Step No. 4— a postcard in the mail with your personal draft notice on the back.

A Sterling Sister Displays Unrealized Prescience

While I was enjoying the respite from the rat race, I was also reviewing my options for a career. There was still time to get started on my first year of law school. But little did I realize that by my not now matriculating, I was missing the very course of studies that would, decades into the future, wise me up that I was a George Washington VI. Instead, I'd reverted to my original professional aspiration—medicine.

In 1934 I had allowed my father to talk me out of a premed course in September, when he had insisted that I would do better in business. But then he had pulled the rug on that by conning me out of my seed money. Recently, post-Monkey's, I realized that I should have stuck to my original goal—med school. Furthermore, I was inspired by the likes of Sam Dugan, who'd graduated from the college of arts and sciences with an economics major (the same as your Virginian), but then had turned around and had taken a premed course to the effect that he was on the verge of the early stages of medical school. So not long after my return, I announced to the home folks that, better late than never, I was going to resurrect my original aim and start a premedical course at the end of January 1941.

First flak came from my current favorite brunette. Even though I'd gladly have laid the eventual certificate at her feet, Nan, as we'll call her, just couldn't see my spending all of that time.

Curiously, my father didn't squawk. I sensed that maybe with a war coming on, that to keep me out of the trenches, he'd back me. Then a curious thing happened.

My sterling sister (who was the older of my two younger siblings), after having graduated with me from Cornell, had worked through June 1940 for a gargantuan land title company in Philly. In July she had switched to a better job, proofreader for a book manufacturer.

What's this got to do with your Virginian's aspirations to become a doctor of medicine? It was this: Paying her respects to the Yankee Tier for a nice weekend, especially to attend the Ohio State game at Cornell on October 26 with Johnny Meaden, the former track star, my sterling sister, as though by foreknowledge sensed the great importance of keeping me from being diverted into medicine. Such a career would have kept me from generating the right sort of legal insights that would be necessary before I would be able to eventually set down for you all this saga.

As soon as my sterling sister heard that I'd resurrected my original educational plan—to start premed studies in September 1934—she surprisingly announced: "If you are going to go to medical school, then I am going to go to Katharine Gibbs."

It was a test of my determination. And it turned out, just then, with a war coming on, to be weak.

This threat that actually was a fateful favor took the wind out of my sails, primarily because I was very concerned over the state of my father's health. A hide-and-go-seek accident when he was a lad before the turn of the century, falling down a hay shoot from the top of his father's three-story barn, had caused hidden complications. The adverse affects were implemented some years later when the measles had gone back on him. In 1925, I had peeked through the crack in the partly open door of the operating room and from the distance had observed my father undergoing some major stomach surgery. By now, 1940, how well-aware I was of his health problems. So, on hearing from the older of my two younger sisters this economically competitive challenge to my resurrected plan to go to medical school, I decided then and there that Dad's health came first. For him to put two children simultaneously back into school, post-Cornell, would be too much of a load. Suddenly, under the preparedness atmospherics, playing catch-up ball seemed like too much to go for. Although I may well have felt burned up at the time, the passing of decades would provide the answer. My sterling sister, by her having threatened to go to Katharine Gibbs, actually had fortuitously done your unaware George Washington VI and his whole family, herself included, a great favor. Had she not gotten a most weighty oar in at helping bollix the attempted revival of my aspiration for a medical career, I'd never have gotten started years hence at working up some contrasty studies of still unrecognized values that would eventually enable me to be setting down this saga on paper.

So, as mentioned, by the end of October 1940 the possibility of my resurrecting a medical career, to say the best for what was left of it, was being pigeonholed. It's thus thank you, thank you again, and again I say thank you, for the yet unrecognized benefits, that would head to a surely upcoming positive turn at a crossroad, leading to expanded intellectual blessings fated to grow out of a sterling sister's unrealized prescience.

Ambassador Cudahy Brings the War Home to Owegoans

A few days after I had returned to the Yankee Tier, my father practically led me by the hand to the neighborhood polling place. Personal registration wouldn't be required for another year. By then, the 1940 census would show that the population of Owego village was more than 5,000. But now, while my father didn't tell me how to register, I did it his way anyway, and marked the ballot as a Republican and stuffed it in the box, never dreaming that my stance might soon create a minor small-town furor.

On Saturday evening, November 2, Ambassador Cudahy, recently in residence in Belgium, appeared as featured speaker in the auditorium of Owego Free Academy. I anticipated that this would be the next best thing to reading a book by an author such as Negley Farson. The Ambassador had been in Belgium when King Leopold III had surrendered the Belgian Army. Your unaware George Washington VI wasn't about to miss hearing from such an "I Was There"-type of observer of Hitler's recent march through the Low Countries. Getting into my double-breasted gray-flannel suit with the chalk stripes, white shirt, silk foulard tie, and Florsheim cordovan shoes, I arrived early and occupied a good seat in the orchestra. Greeting me with smiles and hailing signs were just about all of the Democrats of importance in the community.

Coverage of the affair in Owego's Democratic weekly emblazoned it: "Hon. John Cudahy, Former Ambassador to Belgium, Speaks at Democratic Rally."

"This was the last large gathering to be held by Democrats in Tioga County previous to election day.

"A concert at 7:30 P.M. was presented by the South Side Center Choir, of Ithaca, directed by H. Hamilton Williams.

"Chairman of the Democratic county committee, David J. Relihan [an old friend of father], presided. He said, 'Tioga County is proud of Paul Smith [currently director of the state fair].' "

After Mr. Smith told us that the 1932 election of FDR may well have saved the country from a revolution, next, turning to sarcasm, the director read from a recent speech (gleaned from a daily such as *Bingo PM Bugle*) by Republican presidential candidate Wendell Willkie. Commented Smith, "Wendell Willkie is quick to change when he's made a misstatement."

The director then introduced his house guest, pointing out that from 1933 to 1937, he had been Ambassador to Poland. Later he had been in Ireland on a special mission. In January 1940 he had been sent to a Belgium threatened with seventy percent of the German Army including seventeen mechanical divisions, on its border.

The Ambassador carried on. "The Belgian people, although aware of such threat, did not believe that war would come. During the May 10 attack, a flock of birds turned out to be *Luftwaffe* bombers. A combination of a lightning storm and an earthquake followed. The people reacted in the worst possible way. Two million out of eight million took to the roads. Of the two million, two-thirds are unaccounted for—caught between two armies!

"When the truth is known, people will say that he [Leopold III] followed the only possible course. It was mass panic. In six days [off the start line] the Germans were in Brussels. Citizens got one-half pound of bread a day. No comforts, no phone service, no railroads."

Stumping for unity, the Ambassador concluded, "So I ask you to stand by FDR. Send him back to the White House."

After the Ambassador had finished and the group filling the high school auditorium was breaking up, again I found myself greeted with smiles of appreciation and warm handshakes from many important Democrats.

Back home, the reaction commenced to come in from the grapevine. Young GOP leaders such as Mike Major, (a Cornell aluminus the same as his father, *the* Major), and Junior Owego (son of another prestigious local lawyer) had been heard to squawk. Their beef soon got bolstered. To my father, some of his friends in the Old Guard were prompt to ask, "What was your son, Ben, doing down there at that rally with all of those Democrats?"

Although my father had then been quick to explain that Evans was much interested in foreign affairs and had taken the opportunity to get the latest word on the situation in Belgium, and hear it from right out of the horse's mouth, he felt that his peers among our Republican friends seemed to have had some little difficulty accepting the explanation (valid as it was).

As the Democratic Lake Street sheet further elaborated, "The rally was attended by *both* Democrats and Republicans who admire FDR from all sections of Tioga County."

But the way your unaware George Washington VI would recollect it, the minor furor arose because he was just about the only Republican there!

No War by Christmas: Otherwise, Plenty to Chew On

Making it easy for publishers to sell their newspapers, the print media provided a steady stream of war information for all of us to chew on evenings in the taproom of the Ahwaga Hotel.

By October 18, the British air ministry announced that German troops had embarked on ships for the occupation of England during mid-September, but the attempted invasion was prevented by the RAF. My hunch was this: had such an invasion been carried out successfully by the Germans, by now, the expectations that had larruped us back at Monkey Ward's in September would have come true. By now, the United States would already have been at war. Instead, we all found ourselves marking time for the draft. Our previous belief that we'd be in the war by Christmas vanished!

Another ray of light appeared when the Vichy government declared on October 23 that under no circumstances would France make war on Great Britain or permit the Axis powers to use the French Navy.

On October 28, Italy invaded Greece. Hitler and Mussolini met in Florence for reported consultation about peace terms with France.

To psych myself up on the semi-military sport—hunting—in which, almost daily, I was engaging, *Field and Stream* had become my temporary bible. Soon I'd developed quite a lingo for recounting the day's operations in the far blue hills. Kindred spirits soon surfaced in the taproom crowd at the Ahwaga Hotel, owned by Doc Decker, his son Dwight playing the successful role of genial inn-keeper.

Occasionally the war news was upstaged by politics. The No-vember general election rolled around and FDR was reelected (for a third term) by 449 electoral votes to 82 for Wendell L. Willkie; the Democrats retained control of Congress, losing four seats in the Senate and gaining nine in the House.

In foreign affairs, more developments followed and it looked as though, for some yet-undefined upcoming overseas war, my cur-rent semimilitary vacation—as though for the infantry—might be fine-tuning your unaware George Washington VI.

On November 5, the British established an air and naval base on the Greek island of Crete.

Then, on November 7, nothing to do with the war, but worthy of mention, the 2,800-foot span of the suspension bridge between Tacoma, Washington, and the Olympic peninsula was wrecked by a windstorm and plummeted into Puget Sound. (As Ensley M. Llewellyn would eventually assess the matter: "Anyone who knew anything about how the sails on a ship work knew that the wind eventually was going to take that bridge!")

Now, back to the update on the war overseas: the prime min-ister of Ireland announced that the British would not be allowed to use Ireland's ports. Bombs being intermittently rained down on London by the *Luftwaffe* caused Commons to meet outside its usual spot in the British Parliament, this time convening in an unnamed hall.

More chronological events thanks to *Britannica Book of the Year:* By November 8, FDR announced that about one-half of the planes and other war materials produced in the United States would be allotted to Great Britain. The RAF was en route to Munich while Hitler there was celebrating the anniversary of the beer hall *Putsch*. He rejected any compromise and declared that he would fight until there was a decision. He'd been gone from his forum for just an hour when the RAF, aiming at railroad lines in the city, landed some bombs on the hall in which Hitler had just made his appear-ance. On top of this red-hot poker up the Nazi chieftain came a blow against Mussolini—another British air strike. This one was scored by the Royal Navy's fleet air arm. A number of months later, the lesson that it now taught to the wrong people would be revealed. On the night of November 11–12, a British naval air force, in a surprise attack, disabled three Italian battleships, two cruisers and two fleet auxiliaries in the harbor of Taranto, Italy. How little did we all realize that such an incident had hiked the tempo. Almost instantly, the technical aspects of the British exploit was being mulled over by some of the brainiest leaders of the Combined Fleet in the Orient.

Also on November 12, Premier Molotov of Russia arrived in Berlin to confer with Chancellor Hitler.

As Group Captain J. E. Johnson would eventually record in *Full Circle,* as winter drew on, the fighter-bomber sweeps petered out. November saw the return to sporadic German attacks against coastal towns. Such pattern signaled that the daylight battle was won by the RAF. But much might bombing had to be endured.

On November 14, the *Luftwaffe,* in retaliation for the British bombing that had sent Hitler scampering for cover at Munich, dropped bombs on Coventry in the English Midlands, killing about two hundred persons, injuring eight hundred, and wrecking most of the buildings of the city, including a vital magneto works.

Here in the Yankee Tier, a relatively short trip up our Susquehanna watershed from Owego was the Scintilla Magneto Company. It commenced an expansion of production.

Heightening suspicions of potential aid from the East soon made the Nazis look more formidable. There was even some speculation that the Nazis and the Reds were sleeping in the same bed. Following a conference between Hitler and Molotov, it was announced on November 14 in Berlin that agreement had been reached on all questions of importance to Germany and Russia. But the United States was girding up for eventualities.

By November 18, a selection of sites for seven land, naval and air bases in British Atlantic possessions was announced by the United States navy department. With such headlines, it would be hard to recall that Thanksgiving soon came and went. But Mother's diary would indicate that all family members but Sylvia, now in Philly, dined at the Green Lantern Inn.

Benjamin Evans Dean   As an Unaware George Washington VI

BACHRACH

Another of the pictures taken of the author by Bachrach in 1975. At that time expectations were for completion in a year's time of the book. Instead, the day-to-day work turned *A Virginian in Yankeeland* into a saga of several volumes that took well over a decade to complete.

Pierce Dean, younger son of Israel Dean and great-grandfather of the author. In 1847 he moved from the Falls Village area of northwestern Connecticut to New Milford, Pennsylvania. Pierce was born July 21, 1807, and died January 11, 1890. He was 6 feet 4 inches tall and weighed 225 pounds.

Campaign photo used during the summer of 1939 by Clifford Pierce Dean (CPD) during his second try for the treasurership of Tioga County. In 1930, after he'd won the GOP primary nomination by six votes (tantamount to winning the general election in November), he was finessed out of his victory by the freak recount (detailed in Volume One). As mentioned in the story, he had then been sold on waiting three, three-year terms on the grounds that he might have no opposition. But for CPD's second try that's not what the Owego Old Guard had up its sleeve.

Decades later, some visiting dignitaries from Sweden would notify your Virginian that in this picture CPD looked like Prince Wilhelm, brother of the then-recent King of Sweden.

FOR COUNTY TREASURER

CLIFFORD P. DEAN

Candidate For The Republican Nomination For County Treasurer.

———

PRIMARY ELECTION
SEPT. 19, 1939

———

Your Vote Will Be APPRECIATED.

No. 8 ON THE BALLOT

Late summer 1939—Political advertisement clipped from Owego's GOP weekly. This straightforward announcement by Clifford P. Dean (as an unaware George Washington V) contrasts sharply with his opponent's damage-doing, last-minute ads embroidered with tricky political copy inserted just across the state line in *The Evening Times* of Sayre, Pennsylvania, (as detailed in this tome).

A larger version of the photo in this ad appears elsewhere in this picture section.

Just before the Fourth of July, 1939, when your unaware George Washington VI was about to respond to the call to Michigan by Monkey's, he spotted a swarm of bees and called it to the attention of the unaware George Washington V who promptly hived it. Prior to the final containment, Clifford P. Dean (CPD) proudly holds high the collected swarm.

Julius Dean, older son of Israel Dean, was born December 25, 1804. Leaving the Falls village area of Connecticut, he served in the New York State Militia at Albany then settled farther west. He died February 3, 1868 at Pontiac, Michigan, where he was the proprietor of a drug store.

Martha Youden from England became the second wife of Julius (older son of Israel Dean) and is pictured with the baby George H. Dean, father of Hattie (Dean) Stadlberger.

The name Julius is prominent with the first and second generation of the descendants of Israel Dean. Why such an interesting military name? No explanation has been handed down. As pictured in Volume One, Julius I was the older son of Israel Dean, Pierce (the author's great-grandfather) being Julius's younger brother. Pierce's oldest son was named Julius Irwin Dean, born in the Falls Village, Connecticut, area. In 1847 he migrated with his parents and siblings to New Milford, Pennsylvania. Later he operated a state-line hotel at Waverly, New York. Finally, he settled at Washington, New Jersey.

Now, back to Israel's older son named Julius. According to an old letter, he left the Falls Village area, Canaan, Connecticut, to serve with the New York State Militia. The person drafting his discharge certificate inexplicably inserted the middle initial "D". Julius attended school at Ann Arbor, Michigan, where he met and married Harriet Noble. His first wife died during the birth of his first son Sam. Julius then married Martha Youden who arrived from England. After moving from Ann Arbor, Julius continued to raise his family at Pontiac where he operated a pharmacy. Julius's second son (his first son by Martha) was named Julius Noble Dean, Julius II's middle name coming from his father's first wife and not from his own mother.

It's Julius Noble Dean who's pictured, his father Julius I (Israel Dean's older son) also appearing in this section.

Julius Noble Dean left Pontaic for Alaska. After a career as a fisherman, he died at Sitka, December 25, 1933, age 80. Persons acquainted with decedent during his lifetime: T. G. Hanford, and S. N. Harvie, both of Wrangell. His sister was Mrs. Hattie Parr of St. John, Michigan.

The lady with the ukulele is Hattie (Dean) Stadlberger, daughter of George H. Dean, one of the sons of Julius Dean. Julius, pictured on the preceding page, was the Pontiac pharmacy proprietor, and was the older son of Israel Dean, secret son of George Washington.

According to a notation (presumably by some family member) on the back of the original for the above picture, this is Charles Webster Dean, who was a grandson of Julius Dean, who was the older son of Israel Dean. However, the gentleman standing in this picture is more in stature of Julius Noble Dean (son of aforesaid Julius Dean who was the Pontiac pharmacist). Julius Noble Dean was just over 5 feet 5 inches tall. In contrast, his nephew Charles Webster Dean whom the author met in 1969 was more than 6 feet tall. Thus the author figures that the gentleman standing in this picture was probably photographed a number of years earlier and is thus the same Julius Noble Dean who is pictured at the top of the preceding page.

Looking ahead, during the later years of our saga, the New York Chapter (SAR) will swing an election in favor of your by-then-aware George Washington VI. April 17, 1971 at the Thayer Hotel, West Point, four patriots appear prior to the annual banquet of the Empire State Society, Sons of the American Revolution (SAR). (Left to right), the author, president of the Society; Major General William A. Knowlton, Superintendent of West Point Military Academy, guest of honor whom the author, on behalf of the Society, will introduce as principal speaker and to whom the author will also make a presentation of the Society's gold Good Citizenship medal; finally, Harry S. Schanck, vice president general of the National Society SAR, and J. Moreau Brown III, past president Empire State Society SAR, dinner chairman and master of ceremonies.

At the Thayer Hotel, West Point: Immediately after the annual banquet, April 15, 1972, Empire State Society, Sons of the American Revolution (SAR), General William Westmoreland, after serving as honored guest and principal speaker, signs authographs for well-wishers. Looking on from the General's right stands the author as President of the Society. Previously, he introduced the General. Also, on behalf of the Empire State Society the author made the presentation to the General of the Society's large, silver Chauncey Depew Medal.

THE YOUNG MAN IN BUSINESS

During deferment days before the U.S. involvement in Hitler's war, an itinerant photographer showed up at Sidney, New York, and took a number of pictures of your unaware George Washington VI. The word "Paramount" was handwritten on the folder presenting this particular shot. Otherwise, the only remembered clue: The photographer mentioned that he was part of the Holland family of Texas. It's hardly six months after "Monkey's Last Chance" (item detailed in Volume Two). The spirit displayed by the author in the photo exemplifies the gung-ho attitude engendered by the application of some of the tenets set forth by Howard Lee Davis in *The Young Man in Business*. Although Monkey's was now in the past, your unaware Geroge Washington VI kept right on applying points out of the bible by Davis while he continued to storm the portals of American big business, but only partly by Davis' book.

Benjamin Evans Dean: The rest of the angles photographed by the itinerant cameraman at Sidney, New
York, spring 1941.

Peggy in 1938, age 12, the younger of the author's two younger sisters.

At the headstone of Israel Dean whose parentage was traditionally a mystery to his children. In June 1936, little sister Peggy takes a gander at the burial place of her great-great-grandfather much unaware that he is George Washington's secret son. Because mere guesstimates led us to believe that Israel was the ostensible son of Oliver Dean, we all got carried away and mistakenly assumed that he was also the natural son. It would take the author almost thirty-one years to realize that this headstone marked the grave of George Washington's secret son. This is the same tombstone that during August 1987 hooligans using great force would knock over thus leaving such gravestone flat on the ground, the damage when discovered being promptly reported by the author to the First Selectman in charge at Falls Village, Connecticut.

Watching the ceremonies at Versailles. The author (seated on the right), accompanied by dignitaries representing the Bicentennial Congress of the Sons of the American Revolution, watches the trooping of the Colors by the Expedition Liberte in the Royal Courtyard of the Chateau. This visit took place on August 2, 1983. It was one of a memorable series of activities in late August and early September 1983, celebrating the Treaty of Paris, September 3, 1783, which concluded the Revolutionary War.

During the ceremonies conducted by the National Society SAR in northeastern England, on September 8, 1983 the author appears at the foot of the stone stairway leading up to Washington Old Hall.

A SPIRITUALISTIC CONTRIBUTION TO THIS SAGA FROM WALES

Rev. Thomas Daniel Evans was a native of Dowlais, Wales. In 1875 he graduated from the seminary at Pontypool. After migrating to northeastern Pennsylvania he was ordained June 26, 1878. In Pennsylvania he preached at Duffton Grove, Providence and Mayfield. He was pastor of the Welsh Baptist Church at Audenreid, and Mahony City. Later he had charge of the Baptist Church in Throop and Jermyn, his last calling being to the Welsh Baptist Church, Olyphant, Pennsylvania.

Margaret Parry (on the left) was a native of Abernant. She came to northeastern Pennsylvania from Wales with her mother who had been widowed when her husband Morgan Parry an ordinary coal miner was mistakenly done in at Hazleton by assailants thinking him to be Morgan Powell a mine boss. Since the killers never touched the money and steamer tickets in their victim's pockets, the wherewithal was forwarded to Wales to finance the widow's trip. The widow then married Daniel Davis. After his demise, the widow Margaret Davis sold the nearly 42-acre family farm fronting on the Pennsylvania Railroad at Scotch Valley, Beaver Township, Columbia County, Pennsylvania, to her son-in-law and daughter, the author's maternal grandparents Rev. Thomas Daniel Evans (above) and his wife Margaret Parry Evans (on the left). Over the years following the 1895 transfer of realty, some of the hunting by family members, of deer and upland game alluded to in this tome, took place on this family farm at Scotch Valley. While some nice tries at attempted pettifogging of the tract's boundaries appear to have taken place, it's the policy of the courts and title companies to stymie moves, if any, to place deviously drafted "top deeds" from untitled third parties on this nearly 42-acre tract that's been in the same family for almost a hundred years. Regardless of such nice tries, if any, the Evans family farm is still owned by the family, taxes always having been paid, currently by the author out of respect for his grandparents.

In later decades, the author had the occasion to visit Lloyd's of London. From the balcony, he has been taking in the view of the activities of the many underwriters on the floor.

In contrast to the picture in Volume One, here's what 443 Main Street looked like after receiving its pre-Hitler's war face lifting.

Relaxing in early spring (1941) sunshine before returning to our respective turret lathes on the night shift at Scintilla Magneto works at Sidney, New York. A fellow operator holding a bachelor's degree from Hamilton College rests over his bike's handlebars appears on the left, while your Virginian also all bright-eyed and bushy tailed, is eagerly looking forward to returning to work.

Sylvia Dean, great-granddaughter of Israel Dean, sister of Glenn Cobb Dean the author's uncle, and Clifford P. Dean the author's father. Sylvia Dean was the wife of Grover Dean who was also a descendant of Israel Dean but on another line. After moving to Florida, Aunt Sylvia would become one of the bearers of the title: Mrs. St. Petersburg.

A Deer Hunter Gets Hunted

It was early December 1940. The windup of the deer season was at hand, and your Virginian's semimilitary respite from the rat race was reaching for its peak. During one of the last days of our recent Indian summer, when I was actually on a deer hunt, a farmer in a vale along the inlet of the big reservoir scared a red fox away from the chicken coop. When it trotted up a side hill through some woods and entered the sights of my shotgun, thinking that I couldn't miss, from behind a big log, I let loose a deer slug. The smoke cleared and I started over to pick up my kill. But on hearing that big bang, that fox had thrown it into high gear and as though by magic, had done the vanishing act.....all because I hadn't bought that Browning semi-automatic shotgun through Rich's sporting goods department back with Monkey's.

After the fox episode had highlighted an otherwise deerless day, I complained about the lack of venison to Ken Duff (the University of Michigan graduate of the roaring twenties who'd tried out as a trainee Down East with Lincoln Stores before he'd gravitated to his home town in the Yankee Tier, where by now he was a successful gasoline retailer). The supplier of fuel for my Chevrolet sent me westerly into the boondocks of the town of Tioga to comb some tall knobs owned by his cousin Sam Harlin, whose instructions I was soon soaking up. In deep snow, bloody deer tracks led me higher and higher towards surrounding ridges. When the weather was just right, clouds billowing into the heavens would give you a backdrop equivalent of scenic Alpine peaks. But just now focusing on bloody tracks wasn't paying off. The current scenery was of no help. So I switched to a clean trail. It led through intersections and cross-tracks farther and farther into the snow-covered bush on a little plateau. In spite of all of this evidence, not even a doe came into sight.

When the frustrations of the situation were at their worst, there came some crust-crunching sounds. A big buck was about to show up, and I suspected that after he had commenced backtracking me, by some sort of prescience, I had taken up a position to the effect that he was now about to step right out and confront me.

In a beautiful snow-decked spruce and hemlock park, I had

dusted off a foot of freshly fallen snow, then had eased my tired tail down onto the round surface. Just sampling the great outdoors in the late-fall, wintery-looking scene made all of this tramping up steep hills in the snow worth it. Then, from behind a solid screen of snow-covered spruce and hemlock trees came this slow, sneaking, crunching sound.

As I pricked up my ears, my X-ray eyes suddenly told me with uncanniness that on the opposite side of the snowy evergreen wall, a buck was approaching. My heart commenced to pound. Momentarily I expected a big buck to tiptoe out into the open where I'd get my long-sweated-out good clear shot. Imagining that the wild beast towered to the sky, for the moment I found myself on the verge of panicking. Maybe I should jump to my feet and fire into the bushes? A lucky shot might then drop the buck before he suddenly charged out face to face and would have no choice in escaping but to give me the flip-flop with his big rack? Obviously, some self-protection was in order. I could do everything but envision, with an imagination suddenly running riot, a gigantic beast about to fill the open space fifteen feet in front of me. Then, when I'd done everything but jump up and fire into the snow-decked screen of evergreens, out stepped a buck .....but not of the expected sort.....Instead of being four-legged it was merely two-legged....It was Don Evelien, a classmate from grammar-school days. And the newcomer had no cause for concern. All that he saw was your Virginian enjoying the winter scene from his very relaxed and enjoyable spot on the stump.

Next, I present to my readers an epilogue: A good term of years would go by before I would get up the nerve to tell Don that I'd almost made a blind shot. Maybe my report would be belated, but it would be beneficial. It would be perfectly timed by fate to restrain Don's trigger finger when, in later years, he would draw a bead on a sleeping buck. When his recollection of my report would stay the shot, the effect would be that Don would then discern that the sleeper wasn't a buck, and that actually it was a sleeping hunter.

Now back to this early-December 1940 day on the snowy ridge laced with deer tracks. Had I made a blind shot and hit another hunter, such an accident would have been a disaster. As detailed in the preceding volume, with that escapade over Deke's surprise haymaker that had boomeranged just under four years in the background, and with the automobile wreck at Springdale that had almost caused serious personal injuries only two years in the past, I couldn't now afford a third such mishap.

Here in the local Yankee Tier wilderness, even though a mistaken shot might have missed my former grammar school classmate, it would be a long time before Don would know just how close I'd come to accidentally letting loose a deer slug. Instead we discussed our bad luck at hunting. By now our view was that all of the deer had been wounded, wised up or spooked.

With the deer season on its last legs, we slogged through medium snow down the side hill to the valley below, discussing old times—relay races in the late-twenties at the Farmers' Picnic at the county fairground. And as far as the deer season was now concerned, for different reasons, we'd both had it. Darkness was an hour away by the time we reached our respective parked cars. Don headed north for his farm and I started driving southeasterly towards the village. Suddenly I had my decision.

Perhaps, subconsciously, I had been pursuing this semimilitary sport just in case, a number of months from now, I was going to find myself in the infantry. But the other important reason I'd been going hunting at all, day after day for almost two months, had been to make up for the frustrations that had been generated when I'd been cooped up selling deer rifles, etc., in all of that stuffiness at Monkey's.

So here was the hot flash: No longer would I take the risk. Before I'd accidentally shoot some good old friend, I was quitting the woods. And now that the light was turned on, although no job was in sight, the United States wasn't going to be at war by Christmas and I was feeling no pressure from my conscription number. Winding up this respite from the rat race, I knew that I'd soon be going back to some regular position with big business.

Goings-on About Town

During the several weeks prior to my decampment from Ann Arbor, some of the goings-on about the village and town of Owego saw Dwight Decker participating in the Business and Professional Men's training camp at Plattsburgh.

Currently, Doctor Decker was the proprietor of Owego's famed Ahwaga Hotel, from the front porch of which the world's richest man, the late Senior Beegil, Sr., had once handed out brand-new dimes to the kiddies.

Of the same hotel, Doctor Decker's son Dwight held forth as manager, and while playing out his genial role of innkeeper, he let our younger generation become well aware: he'd served in the army as a lieutenant during the Kaiser's war.

During August, at Plattsburgh, Dwight was hobnobbing with such notabilities from Manhattan as Winston Guest.

While Dwight was vacationing near the Canadian border, a farewell party took place at the Baptist Church for Reverend York.

And Owego's GOP weekly in its August 27 issue announced that Ed Sargent, who'd been one of your Virginian's classmates at Cornell, had been appointed district director of the Willkie campaign.

By September 3, the same sheet announced that Fred Miller (son of Bill Miller, a leading automobile dealer who was a key factor of the county GOP committee) had been taken ill en route home from Socorro, New Mexico, where he was enrolled in the New Mexico School of Mines. Friends of the family would intercept Freddy in Chicago and see to his getting successful hospitalization.

Switching the scene to Ithaca: when I'd been rowing on the crew, for an evening's recreation, our varsity eight had occasionally bowled at the Eddy Street alleys. Greeting us there had been Everett Wait, the proprietor. By September 10, Owego's Main Street weekly announced that native son Ev had sold his business to a couple of other well-known Owego fellows, to wit: C. Herrick Johnson and William J. Thomas. When Ev would now return to his home town of Owego, he'd leave behind him a reputation as having been one of Ithaca's greatest promoters of the leagues. Together with Si Glann, Ev would become another of those voices out of the wilderness: "Forget everything else. Go to law school. Pass the bar. Practice law."

By September 17, the same GOP newspaper reported that Rev. Selby Swift, pastor at the Owego Baptist Church during the roaring twenties, had left Immanuel Baptist Church at Syracuse for Benson

Baptist Church in Omaha, Nebraska. The Midwesterner was thus touching down considerably closer to his old home town of Mexico, Missouri.

In official proceedings of the board of trustees....although CPD had been serving since early March as village treasurer, that's all that the newshawks would mention in the print media—the title only.

Big loss to Cornell University's all-important constituency of alumni at Owego! Walter Bridgeman and family moved to Racine, Wisconsin.

By the time your unaware George Washington VI had motored easterly from Monkey's to reenter the portals of Owego, Doctor Decker had just resumed charge of the Owego Hotel. While the more-renowned Ahwaga was on Front Street, the village's other very adequate hotel was on Main Street.

When your unaware George Washington VI (after having pulled up stakes in Michigan) was back in his home town for a fortnight, the GOP weekly announced that the Elks Club planned to initiate a large class on Thursday, December 5, to be named after General Pershing. What's that go to do with our saga? The immediate past exalted ruler was Dapper Dan, the local haberdasher. And current exalted ruler was Will Leahy, Cornell, Class of 1928. Included among the inductees was CPD. What about his son? They left out your Virginian.

By October 22, the first two draft numbers were pulled: Clayton Barnes, of the town of Berkshire, and Floyd Oscar Shirley, of the town of Owego.

New preacher at the Baptist Church....Ted Conklin was slated to start Sunday, December 1.

Now back to the attainments of professional rank by some of your Virginian's contemporaries: By the time I'd returned to the Yankee Tier, the efforts of the less well fixed but more discerning fathers of some of my contemporaries had paid off for their sons. Since this first batch was somewhat older than your Virginian, they had graduated from Cornell when I was winding up my sophomore year in the four-miler on the Hudson.

Becoming a double registrant during his senior year had eventually paid off for Abacanocus. He had graduated from law school when I was getting my A.B. degree from undergraduate school.

After passing his bar exam on his first try, he had gone into partnership with his father, Abacanocus & Abacanocus (as mentioned) being the official name of the new law firm.

But Young Dingle, having opted out on double registration, had commenced law school during the September after he'd copped his undergraduate degree. Thus he had recently graduated (while Hitler was romping through northern France) during June and was now clerking in the law office of his father while sweating out passing the bar exam.

Still another of these big brother types, but six years older, was Splanaway, with whom I'd dug ditches, otherwise manicuring the southerly approaches of the new bridge over the Susquehanna River, in June 1934, an opening scene of Volume I of this saga. At that time, Jimmy Patton, home from Centre College, had first let the cat out of the bag that Israel Dean was the son of George Washington. Now, back to Splanaway: after he had earned his law degree in 1937 from a college in the South, he had been taken under the wing of Owego's PR God No. 1 (as frequently sketched in Volume I). While the publicity had faded somewhat after Eaton of Waverly had supplanted Boilerplate as county judge in the GOP primary of 1936, Splanaway was still able to shine in the substantial remaining reflected glory as he served as law clerk for the former county judge. And while Splanaway was waiting word that he had passed his bar exam, the Owego Old Guard found a nice appointive plum for him— acting village police justice.

Now that military conscription had so recently become law, Splanaway, who'd drawn a springtime number, was sweating out an eventual call from the county draft board.

Up front chronologically amongst the county's legal-eagle aspirants was Flint, who would gain national fame in the realms of collegiate sociology courses featuring studies of *Small Town in Mass Society*, by Vidich and Bensman. Flint, one of the greatest scholars among the ranks of Yankee Tier lawyers, had graduated from Cornell in 1936. But instead of going for a well-qualified double registry in law school, he'd used his senior year customarily for the benefits of more background courses from the college of arts and sciences. Thus he had been latching on to his LL.B when your Virginian had been picking up the sheepskin for his A. B. in 1939.

Now, back to mid-October 1940. Owego's Republican weekly announced that Flint would open a law office in Springdale, where he'd serve his clientele on Tuesdays and Thursdays. The rest of the time he'd spend with an associate in Ithaca, a member of the infantry reserve who would need coverage should war erupt.

Last but not least was Si Glann, who would be coming along in June 1941 as a tail-end Charley in what could well have been the same law-school graduating class that also could have given a law diploma to your Virginian, had I been successful when I'd attempted to opt in June 1938 to become a double registrant with Si in September.

Each and every one of these chaps was a constant reminder to your Virginian, and not merely because all of us were subject to that great equalizer—conscription. They all were more in mind as examples of scholastic achievement. Had I not been busted by Becker in European History, several months from now I'd be getting my law degree. A year from now, if I passed the bar exam on the first try, I'd be getting admitted to the bar. But in contrast to these above-mentioned intellectual stalwarts, and yet to go off the starting mark, I was getting less than zero encouragement from my own family while Si Glann stood out as a sterling example of accomplishment. He came from a much larger family with lots less money, yet he was emerging well ahead of your unaware George Washington VI. But save this hidden kicker—years into the future, Si would keep encouraging me to study law. Perhaps the time would come when there'd be no more impending war, and I would find the ways and means to get down to brass tacks and go about generating knowledge leading to assessments of circumstantial evidence indicating that my great-great-grandfather was indeed the secret son of George Washington, our first president.

During mid-October an on-again, off-again dream of going to law school was interrupted when the phone rang at 443 Main Street. Keeping an appointment, a headhunter from a firm headquartered in Columbus, Ohio, drove up, parked in front of the house and was ushered into our living room. This recruiter wanted to hook me up with the Farm Bureau Insurance Company headquartered at Columbus, Ohio, situated on the headwaters of the Scioto River. Were there some unseen linkage with the 23.3 thousand-acre interest of the George Washington Estate in the Virginia Military District of Ohio (bounded on the east by the Scioto), it never came out that George Washington's Revolutionary War bonus had never been claimed by the descendants of his brothers and sisters. As mentioned, George Washington's actual descendants by his secret son Israel Dean had not filed any claims. In contrast, George's nieces and nephews knew who they were, but the General's actual descendants didn't know their Washington lineage and thus also lacked realization that by the laws of descent and distribution, they were *per stirpes* titleholders of his vast estates.

So what did become of the Military District? As detailed in Prussing, *The Estate of George Washington, Deceased,* and E. O. Randall, pages 304–319, Vol. XIX (1910), *Ohio Archeological and Historical Quarterly:* Ohio State University had become by now the beneficiary of the residue, royalties from oil and gas, if any, included.

Who referred this headhunter? I never thought to find out. What became of him? Months later I would try to restablish contact to renew my automobile insurance policy with his bureau. Nobody had ever heard of him.

Actually, he was for real, but I had neglected to ask for his business card. The offered post would have been a normally acceptable position, starting with better pay than Monkey's, and could have led to a high-salaried post over the years. But I turned it down.

At least my job as trainee with Monkey's had been embroidered (even without a pay hike) with a substantial amount of stimulation. This insurance company sales job that probably would have led to a fine administrative post lacked one necessary element (eventually to be confirmed by friends in the know), the missing link being....excitement!

What else made me hesitate? Besides my currently being buffeted by the progression of steps toward war, lack of encouragement by Monkey's meant that for the time being, I'd lost confidence in the otherwise undoubted opportunities in the world of big business.

Now, back to some more goings-on about town: On December 4, J. Laning Taylor, former DA, passed away at age forty-six. In 1917, he had enlisted in the medical branch of the aviation branch of the U.S. Army. After graduating from Cornell during June 1919 with a law degree, he had practiced law in Owego.

On Thursday, December 12, it came time for Owego's Lake Street sheet to announce the makeup of the week-earlier General Pershing class initiated at the Elks. Besides my father (CPD), the class included Bill Dunn, Jr., Heavy (who would eventually become an important factor in our saga), Charley Hills, Herbert Wilke,

Dan Devine, Junior Dingle (upcoming players of political substance), as well as the Hawk (also a substantial background member of this saga's cast). What was wrong with the Pershing class? Although they included my father, it bears reiteration, they left out your unaware George Washington VI.

Presiding was Exalted Ruler Willam P. Leahy (a fellow Cornell alumnus, as mentioned). Chief guest of honor among out-of-towners present was another Cornell graduate, Dr. Philip C. Sainburg of Ithaca, Class of 1912, district deputy grand exalted ruler, who paid his official visit.

But, switching gears of this column from fraternal organizations to wartime service, the Owego Eagle upstaged the lot of us. After unsuccessfully trying in 1934 to commute a sixty-mile round trip to classes at Cornell and then pass exams, he had completed a two-year course at the University of Miami. So we all had expected the Eagle, once he'd polished up his sideline by perfecting his mixed bag of tennis shots in all of that Florida sunshine, to come home and sweep everybody off the upstate courts. Instead he exploited experience gained working for his father's Yankee Tier bus line by taking a position as a junior executive with a Connecticut transportation company. When he did home to participate in goings-on about town, we'd spot him weekends in the taproom at the Ahwaga accompanied by his favorite blonde. But when it came to his vocation, he festooned his ground-level transport activities by earning his aviation pilot's license. Where to best get on with the flying? The Aviation Cadets? No. The Eagle hadn't learned the art of memorizing charts and hiding his specs. But such U.S. disinterest soon got flipflopped in Canada. When the Owego Eagle asked the RCAF for work, the recruiting officer perked right up. After taking one good gander at the Eagle's pilot's license, the Canadians booked him, then started training him at Victoriaville, P.Q., to become a fighter pilot. Thus representing the Yankee Tier (and perhaps a much wider upstate area), the Eagle became Owego's first man to enlist in the war.

Three days later, on December 6, 1940, a Canadian official, perhaps inspired by the Yankee Tier's contribution, announced that ten thousand citizens of the United States had volunteered for service in the RCAF since May 1940. But from out of your Virginian's Yankeeland neck of the woods, the Owego Eagle was the only such volunteer ever heard of to date.

Chapter 9

Hocus-Pocus Quinine-Syndrome Shindig Closes '40, Opens '41

A Time to Celebrate

With the end of the deer season, no sooner had your Virginian made up his mind to forget hunting and go back to work than he went right after his his next job after Monkey's.

Instead of following the stereotyped path that directed most locals to the portals of IBM, and not realizing that the punch-card industry would eventually go electronic, I fished around for some other field to provide some relief from merchandising. When I took advantage of my connections with the director of the Cornell University job counseling branch for alumni, Herb Williams, then in charge, presented two or three openings for my consideration. One of them was with Container Corporation out of state. One of the others was not only with the pharmaceutical industry, but also wasn't any too far from my Owego home base. As mentioned, should I eventually either enlist or get drafted, as previously instructed by my father, I wanted to be in a position to do so in home territory. So Herb phoned and set up an appointment.

Before long, it was just before mid-December 1940 and time to celebrate both conscription and the slating of the personal interview for a potential next job after Monkey's.

Flashes from the international scene embroidered the Owego home-town atmospherics at the taproom where Dwight Decker, who'd served in the Kaiser's war, presided at the Ahwaga. Even though it was now clear that for the time being Hitler had given up his plan to invade England, the threat of war was permeating the Yankee Tier atmosphere, keeping our draft-age generation all keyed up.

Earlier on, Germany had announced that Lorraine had been incorporated into the Reich and united with the Saar region under the name of Westmark. A treaty formally recognizing the puppet government of China under Wang Ching-wei was signed by Japan in Nanking. On the heels of such recognition, the United States announced that arrangements had been made to advance $100 million to the government of Chiang Kai-shek.

On December 1, Joseph P. Kennedy had announced his resignation as the United States Ambassador to Great Britain to take effect on the appointment of his successor. And the British House of Commons, by a vote of 341 to 4, had rejected a proposal to seek a negotiated peace.

That's just a little bit of how things were when I finished making preparations to take a trip on Monday to apply for my next job after Monkey's. Then I went downtown, where they struck up the band.

Here at this Saturday evening session at the Ahwaga, my local buddies present were all Sunday school boys. Yet the atmospherics that kept rubbing off from the hostilities in Europe were such that when one chap said: "There's a war coming on. We're all going to be killed in it. Ben. You've got a car. How about running us down the line ninety miles into Pennsylvania where for just this one long evening, to shape us up for the action into which we soon might well be tossed and never get back, we all do our thing?"

Passing Danceland at Kirkwood, we stopped just long enough to say hello to C. Robert Dean, III (he would never bother to look up his ancestry. Presumably we weren't related, though he always called me "Cousin"). Accompanied by our mutual friend Darlene, he was attending a gala affair in honor of a pal about to be drafted.

Scranton eased prewar tensions. But when I returned to retrieve a pair of my all-wool, Norwegian knit gloves, nobody had seen them.

Back in Owego in time for breakfast, after just a few hours of sleep, a phone call came in for a Sunday of skiing. Joining in the fun were Junior Dingle, Spike Lowry, Red Geller, Freddy Miller (on leave from New Mexico School of Mines), and your Virginian. How could those few of us who'd made the two-hundred-mile round trip stay out most of the night, then ski most of the next day? The extra-added hormonal energy was generated by the feeling that we had to make the most of any civilian life that remained.

My good friends were skipping both church and Sunday school, and making such a sacrifice for finding their own in the far blue hills.....skiing. A ski tow was lacking. Yet we all herringboned it upslope many times, bashing the knob while cutting turns down through medium powder, breaking out a trail that was lined with the contrasty greenness of snowy spruce trees. Putting the icing on the cake, who drove up in her Mercury and soon helped set the downhill pace? The most welcome Indian Princess.

Alas! All good celebrations have to come to an end. By sunset, it was time to get some sleep for the early morning drive north-easterly to apply for my next job after Monkey's.

A GOP Caucus Ambushes an Unaware George Washington V

After my father had been appointed in March to fill out the term of Darwin Krum (after he had resigned a week earlier as village treasurer), the new salary enabled the unaware George Washington V to hire a full-time secretary, Miss Jane Dunne, who previously had been in the employ of J. Laning Taylor, a practicing attorney who had served one term as district attorney before Surfranc of Waverly had won his first term to the post in 1936.

The bimonthly meetings of the village fathers were usually run-of-the-mill affairs and the Tuesday issue of Owego's GOP weekly usually reported Monday night's board proceedings. After my father's March appointment, when fiscal summaries were included as supplied by the new treasurer, his name was never mentioned—an important, yet then-unnoticed clue. This mention of the office only heralded some real fancy skullduggery. A faction of occultists was itching to show its hand in the ranks of the majority Republican Party.

It is important to note that CPD's appointment had come about when some important members of Owego's Old Guard had made the approach and had successfully suggested that he become the new village treasurer. As the months wore on, though, all concerned indicated that they were much pleasured by the manner in which the unaware George Washington V was providing the board with precise village accounts. Aside from the withholding mention of the treasurer by name, all straws in the wind accompanying words from the GOP kingpins indicated that my father would be on the ticket for the upcoming January election.

But with the approach of winter, an occult faction in the GOP got ready. Then it struck, and with secrecy and surprise.

In accordance with the charter to the village from the state legislature, an election was scheduled for January 7, from 6 A.M. to 5 P.M. at the Central Fire Station.

But first it was necessary for the GOP to hold a caucus (also referred to as a convention). It was planned to come off in the supervisors' room in the big, tall, orange-red brick Georgian county courthouse. Its purpose would be to designate the candidates whose names would then appear on the January ticket.

Normally such a Republican selection process would have been totally a perfunctory matter. But not when the slate of incumbents included an unaware George Washington V. In such case there just had to be a bizarre exception.

It was Monday evening, December 16, 1940. Our family (father, CPD; mother, NED; and sister, Peggy; along with your Virginian) was eating supper. My father was in his customary mahogany armchair finishing off his dessert when a ring reached our ears. Dad got up, turned, opened the door with the glass panes and picked up the phone from the marble-top table in the hall. On the wire was John Tobin, building superintendent, who kept an ear to the ground at the courthouse. When my father returned to supper, he told us that it was too late to take any counteraction, but that an ambush was planned to take place against his interest at the courthouse while he would soon be customarily tied up elsewhere, attending the Monday-evening village board meeting in the office of the village clerk, Fred J. Davis, up one flight on Lake Street.

On the next day, the GOP weekly, so it could emblazon the shock effect, skipped the customary Tuesday mention of Monday night's board minutes, leaving them for the regular Thursday issue of the Democratic weekly on Lake Street to cover. While no mention was made that the caucus had been slickly timed to take place while its target was tied up at a regular village board meeting, and while a soft-pedaling was given to the elements of secrecy and surprise, at the bottom of page one, left-hand corner, this is the way the editorialists on the GOP Main Street sheet handled the anti-CPD result gained by the tricksters:

"Republican Village Ticket Chosen"

"Junior Owego [as we'll call the older son of one of the village's prominent attorneys named Old Owego] Wins Treasurer's Designation."

The weekly next listed the nominees. For Mayor, Dr. S. Welles Thompson. (As mentioned in Volume I, CPD had then served under him as trustee. This time the incumbent mayor heard his name placed in nomination by an important member of the Old Guard. George Andrews, son of a county judge, had served as DA before the recently deceased J. Laning Taylor. But in 1939, it was George Andrews who had withdrawn his Owego candidacy from the GOP primary, enabling incumbent Surfranc to win his second term as DA....after Owego's Old Guard had allowed the county judgeship and the DAship to go to Waverly in order to undermine CPD's balance of power there in favor of E. Burt, who had thus won the 1939 county treasurership as detailed.)

Now back to the GOP Main Street sheet.

Next to be nominated was T. Henry Cook for trustee, first ward. (He was an important cog in the Main Street Bank, that had been on the side of E. Burt's campaigns against CPD in 1930 and in 1939 for the county treasureship.

Who had nominated that bank's official? A bit of background: In 1930, it had been the Major who'd approached CPD to handle the then-upcoming recount of his six-vote GOP primary victory for the county treasurership. And it had been the Major, as seen from the viewpoint of the cohorts of CPD, who had let the six-vote victory go down the tube in the freak recount.

Now back to who nominated T. Henry. It was Mike, the younger son of the same Major who'd handled the freak recount so unsuccessfully for my father.

So far, all nominations were perfunctory and more incumbents were next tapped. They included: trustee second ward, Ray W. Smith; and trustee third ward, Charles Hulslander. But when it came to tapping the incumbent for police justice, George Andrews stepped back into the picture and nominated Charles H. Barton.

Next....village treasurer. Up on his feet came Mike Major. The Cornell graduate nominated Junior Owego. Unless somebody nominated CPD, only the name of the surprise nominee would appear on the January ballot.

Following came some other nominations: for assessor, Lewis W. Smith; president, board of school commissioners, Dr. Howard M. Noteware, who got the prestigious laying on of hands from George Andrews; and finally for school commissioner, Hubert L. Smith.

Again it's time for another paragraph from the GOP sheet: "All of the foregoing candidates are incumbents with the exception of Junior Owego who, in the only contest marking the proceedings, defeated the present village treasurer, Clifford P. Dean, who is serving out the unexpired term of Darwin E. Krum, who resigned in March and who has since removed from town.

"All of the foregoing candidates are Republicans except school commissioner Hubert L. Smith, who is a Democrat.

"The candidacy of Mr. Junior Owego, who is president of the Owego unit of La Chambre, came as a complete surprise to the Dean forces few of whom, including Mr. Dean himself, attended the convention [CPD's having had to attend a conflicting village board meeting still being kept covered up by the print media]."

(Curiously, no mention was made: Junior Owego was bookkeeper at the Buick agency. While the media couldn't be expected to air this: in later years we'd learn that the proprietor swapped motor-car services for legal services with Old Dingle, GOP county chairman who happened to be CPD's lawyer.)

As the fourth estate muted the rug-pulling, now back to another paragraph from the GOP Tuesday sheet: "Mr. Junior Owego was placed in nomination by Mike Major.

"Mr. Dean's name was presented by Miss Jane E. Dunne [CPD's secretary had unsuccessfully attempted to counter the political ambush].

"The result of the ballot was Mr. Junior Owego 31, Mr. Dean 18.

"Tellers were Harry Lord [junior partner of the Senator, who'd masterminded E. Burt's side of the freak recount of 1930], and Donald G. Davis [a blacktop magnate who'd migrated to Owego from Utica, relatively unknown scene of George Washington Estate land holdings, Don now being host during summers of your Virginian's clay-court tennis crowd].

"The mayor and village treasurer are elected for one year; trustees, two years; school commissioners, president of board of school commissioners and assessors, all for three years.

"There were about fifty Republicans present when County Clerk Haywood, chairman of last year's village Republican committee, called the assembly to order shortly after 8 P.M. in the supervisors' room at the courthouse. Subsequently Mr. Haywood was elected chairman of the convention and Charles S. Hills [who would become a local political kingpin of later decades] was elected secretary."

The Tuesday sheet then went on to detail the names of those personages who did the nominating, and gave a final clue to the key figures who might have been reflected in the estimable vacancy committee: George Andrews (from the east end of the silk-stocking district); Mike Major (from the west end); and Bill Thomas (of the Flats).

By Thursday, the time had come for a briefer account of the political ambush. Burying it on page twelve, the Democratic weekly's headline writer came up with, "Republicans Nominate a Village Ticket. There Is Only One Contest."

Then a subhead: "The Exception was Village Treasurer Clifford P. Dean Who Was Beaten by Mr. Junior Owego in the Only Contest at the Convention."

While it was taboo to mention the political ambush elements of secrecy and surprise, they could be inferred from a key point made in the yarn itself: "Mr. Dean did not know, it is said, that there was to be any opposition to his nomination. He did not attend the convention."

Again, after the suppressive tone had been set by the GOP Main Street weekly, even the Democratic Lake Street sheet failed to report that the victim was tied up attending to his duties as treasurer at a regular village board meeting (for which the occultists at the convention had so obviously planned a conflict). Yet the Thursday weekly did point out separately on the following page that the regular meeting of the village was held on Monday at the office of the village clerk (as mentioned). But unmentioned, of course CPD was there. And slickly singled out for stress, the Democratic editorialist emphasized that the most notable transaction was payment of annual salaries of fifty dollars to the trustees.

The Next Job After Monkey's

It was Monday, just after mid-December. On this lead from Herb Williams, I drove northeasterly across Broome County, and soon arrived at Norwich, the county seat of Chenango County. There, and without my realizing it, for a position in the purchasing department of that area's leading industry, I would be vying with some other applicants, at least one of whom was equipped with a master's degree.

At the reception window of Norwich Pharmacal Company, a thirtyish but youngish-looking lady invited me into the inner sanctum for an interview by Edson Collins, the purchasing agent. We hit it off right away and this Harvard Business School product, who was about fifteen years or so older than your unaware George Washington VI, soon introduced me to his assistant, an older Mr. Mott, who was nearing retirement. His job was to be the carrot dangled at the end of the stick. But to break in for it, the recruit would replace the young lady who'd greeted us at the reception window, and for whom the maternity alarm clock was soon to ring.

After Edson Collins and your unaware George Washington VI had gotten sufficiently acquainted, he turned me over to the company personnel man—Mr. Clark. Previously he'd worked in Chicago. From luncheon sessions at the Black Hawk Restaurant he'd become acquainted with Arnold Rich, the Dartmouth half of the Cornell-Dartmouth densification situation back at Monkey's, as mentioned. With a brief swapping of yarns soon behind us, Mr. Clark proceeded to escort me around the plant, introducing me to the various heavyweights who made the pharmacal company tick. They included Mel Eaton, George Bengert, John Alden, etc.

Before long I realized that I was now operating in the bailiwick of the Hamilton College gang. For what it's worth to you all, in a few years, far across the sea and after some Kentuckians (to be portrayed early on in the next volume of our saga) would have jogged my sensorium's deepfreeze, I'd get the opportunity to ask a very astute Army intelligence officer: "Did George Washington have a son named Israel Dean?"

"I can't answer that question yes or no, because I don't know," back would come the reply. But then my respondent would volunteer: "But I do know that Alexander Hamilton was George Washington's son. And, for that reason, some substantial part of George Washington's very substantial estate was turned over, in the early days, to Hamilton College."

If this were the case, someone outside of the family of descendants had latched onto the opportunity to be charitable with property actually belonging, by the laws of descent and distribution, to Israel Dean and his descendants.

Now, back to that Hamilton College gang's bailiwick. Once the heavies in this Norwich stronghold had all approved, my job application boiled down, so it seemed, to the issue of table manners and whether I could touch-type, this latter test coming first. Our circle tour of the plant saw us back to the same interview room from which we'd started. Edson Collins, who'd previously vanished to take a long-distance phone call, soon rejoined us.

"Can you typewrite?" they asked as though expecting an answer in the negative.

When I told both Mr. Clark and Mr. Collins, "Yes," they commenced to act as though they had come from Missouri.

"Did they teach you to type in school? We didn't think that you took a commercial course?" they chimed.

Explaining how I'd acquired such a skill, I told them: "I taught myself."

"How?" they both wanted to know.

"Out of a book," I replied.

(As mentioned in Volume I, such self-instruction had taken place when I had served as my father's aide during part of 1934 and 1935, when he'd been getting started at home as secretary-treasurer of the countywide fire insurance cooperative.)

"Oh," one of them said. And they looked at each other with an air of slight puzzlement. Momentarily, the spirit of doubting

Thomas took charge, only to be immediately supplanted by a show-me.

On a signal from the purchasing agent, the personnel man walked over to the side of the room and pulled back a green curtain. There stood a typewriter on a mobile rolling typewriter table. At a further nod from Mr. Clark, a workman came through a side door, rolled the machine to center stage, fetched a chair, then turned and left the room.

Handing me a page of copy, Mr. Collins said: "Here, let's see you sit down in this empty chair and type this."

Whatever or how complicated that printed sheet was, it made little difference. With an inward chuckle, I knocked it out while the eyes of the two heavies "from Missouri" popped.

Not long after I'd passed the typing test by "showing them," I found myself taking the knife and fork examination. At lunch, Edson Collins, having an interest in getting informed about the state of solvency of a potential employee of his purchasing department, said: "I see that you have a brand-new car. Is it paid for?"

I said, "Yes."

Thirty years or so later the purchasing wizard would retire, and by then he'd be very well-fixed. But now, remnants of the depression still hassled us 'uns. So, with a plaintive air, he let a little of it come out: "But I don't see where you get the money?"

Of course, it would have been just a little too much for me to have attempted to brief the heavyweight purchasing agent about all of that sweat and self-denial, regularly banking bucks out of my hundred a month from Monkey's. I even forgot mentioning that old bugaboo—my currently trying to make up for my father's slick possessory action of my seed money on April Fools' Day 1935, followed by confiscation a year and a half later during the fall of my sophomore year at Cornell. Although my father still had my $500 chicken-money nest egg locked up, I never even dreamed of getting it out and dusting it off as part of my reply to the mournful inquiry about the funding of my Chevrolet. So with no mention of the prior taking away of the seed money, I tersely responded: "I saved it."

Although the purchasing agent seemed to have hardly heard my reply, his manner indicated that in spite of his surprise, he was taking me at my word. In short, once I'd passed the table manners test, followed up by a medical exam including a blood test, I was hired, but not before we'd mutually entered into a valid employment contract. It sounded innocent enough. Edson Collins said: "If we give you this job, we expect that you'll stay with us for at least six to nine months. [Presumably they'd checked estimates of when my draft number would come up.] Is that understood?"

"That's agreed," I told him.

As a result, were either party to break the agreement, the other would have a cause of action. But the hitch was this: the company doing the hiring knew it, but your unaware George Washington VI didn't. A good distraction followed—a list of places to room. It didn't take me long and I selected the most homelike spot—with the Donaldsons on the east end of the village.

Once again the young man in business, as inspired by Howard Lee Davis, was off on a nice try, this time in more acceptable home territory—Norwich, a non-commuting, but otherwise easy drive from Owego.

The Quinine Syndrome

At the scene of my brand-new job at Norwich with its big-time pharmacal company, my weekly take-home pay came to around sixteen dollars. Although the new job's hourly rate was higher, it paid less than the hundred a month formerly at Ward's, where you worked frequent evenings, an occasional Sunday, and always on Saturdays.

Thus the bottom line at Norwich was less, thanks to the Empire State's advanced social legislation where a forty-hour week was the buzzword.

What about the experience that I'd racked up with Monkey's? No credit at all. But, figuring that I'd eventually make mine in the stock market, where you could make one dollar do the work of ten, why bother to haggle? As Howard Lee Davis said, "Get the experience." So I'd give Norwich my best shot.

During time off, what about eats? Right after I found a fine room on the north end of town, I checked in at a boarding house on the east side. I didn't lodge there; I just ate there, joining a fine group of comers in Norwich's various industries. It was a sketch out of a newspaper cartoon. We sat around a big oval table spread with fine victuals provided by a greathearted Irish lady. While thoughts of Emily Post curbed your extra long reach, the lady in charge took care to dole out individually any extra cuts or chops.

In line with the tone of the day, war news was the chief dinner table topic.

Toward the end of December, twenty German divisions were reported passing through Hungary and Rumania to the Bulgarian frontier; Russia was reported massing troops on the Rumanian frontier. Contrary to our hopes, the war in Europe just simply refused to peter out.

Over Christmas, an unofficial two-day truce in the aerial war ended when a lone Nazi bomber raided British shipping at the mouth of the Thames. Making it look as though we might successfully sweat out the draft, FDR, in a broadcast address, said that his whole purpose was to keep the United States out of the war while supplying to Great Britain and its allies all possible help in the way of shipping, munitions, planes and food. Then, around forty-eight hours before New Year's Eve, the Germans subjected London to one of the severest bombings of the war, dropping incendiary bombs on the heart of the city and causing destruction said to be as great as that from the great fire of 1666. In *Full Circle*, Johnson would call it an incendiary classic by one hundred and thirty-six bombers against London. Pathfinders started the beacon fires. Then followed more incendiaries, high explosive bombs, and parachute mines. Hundreds of fires raged around warehouses, docks, railway stations and churches. Many water mains were burst. Adding to the firemen's difficulties, the Thames was at its lowest ebb when the attack reached its peak.

All of these things, or sufficient hints from which we could guess at the enormity of the damage, triggered no little conversation at the boarding house luncheons. Tony Heil, a junior executive with a local fireplace manufacturer, said: "My brother is a brain surgeon working in London eighteen hours a day."

"Wow," I said, as I accompanied it with a little nervous seeming but otherwise unintended chuckle.

Misinterpreting my reaction as an actual, intended laugh, this other chap complained about it. And I had a tough time explaining to him that it was just a nervous one, such as two long-parted friends would utter involuntarily when they would meet in a battle zone and compare their recent losses in action of mutually good friends. Actually, I'd intended to become a surgeon myself. Had I stuck to my original plan by getting started back in September 1934, a year and a half from now, I would be joining Tony's brother overseas. And I told Tony, "For your brother I've got nothing but admiration. He's risking his own life against the *Luftwaffe* in order to patch up numerous brains of Britons ripped by bomb fragments." But by the time I'd find the ways and the means to try to say hello personally to Tony's brother, the English lady on the phone at the hospital would say: "Now that the air raids have lessened, Dr. Heil has returned to the United States for a much-needed rest."

Just where was all of this sweating over war headlines leading us? On the job with the purchasing agent, the executive from the next office, in charge of moving out to markets huge shipments of bulk drugs, stepped in for a drink at the water fountain. After slaking his thirst, he clued us in like this: "I'm now handling the largest order for quinine tablets that this company has ever received. And the buyer is the United States Army."

At once, in my sensorium's deepfreeze I stashed such a tip. Should the United States get drawn into the war, before I'd heard that quinine clue, I had expected that I would be sent to Europe. But from now on as I watched the war news develop, I felt that I would eventually get from Uncle Sam the clarion call to leave for some place near the equator. But my best guess was Panama. It just didn't make sense.

Then the quinine syndrome got embellished with a civilian yarn. The patent medicine sales executive came into our office with a sample of the stuff I'd often heard advertised over the radio in Michigan. Back in the Midwest, the favorite station of the receiving clerk had also carried the intermittent advertising message by a gravelly voice. The words of the sales plea were big, comforting, and homey—a pitch for us'uns to drink more Purina.

I now discovered that the Michiganders' favorite elixir was being concocted right next door to our administrative office building—in the Norwich manufacturing plant. And to keep the staff well-educated on various company products, the Purina executive saw to it the members of the purchasing department were well aware of the contents. While the water fountain supplied the chaser, respective doses were soon sampled by Bosso Collins and his assistant Mr. Mott, as well as your Virginian. That Purina, for lunch now looming, made a good appetizer as it ran circles around Lydia's. As it hit the spot, it made sense....as a reincarnation of Swamproot. But when all was said and done, what really counted was that tip about where we were most liable to wake up and find ourselves fighting....were the U.S. to get drawn into the war....the quinine syndrome....tropical jungles!

Getting Hooked on Writing

Without realizing that I was commencing a process that would see me getting hooked on becoming a writer of my own stuff, I used some of my spare time at my room with my Norwich hosts on a literary matter. My mother was in the process of writing a novel about her mother, Margaret Parry, who hailed from Abernant in South Wales. The source of inspiration was the popular novel *How Green Was My Valley*. But instead of Wales, the setting for my mother's story was in the anthracite fields of northeastern Pennsylvania.

Mother's father, (my grandfather) Thomas Daniel Evans, a native of Dowlais, Wales, had graduated from the seminary at Pontypool in 1875. After migrating to America, he had last preached sermons in the Welsh language at the Baptist Church in Olyphant, his sons becoming soldiers and miners, his daughters schoolteachers.

After hours in Norwich, helping Mother (one of the daughters who'd become a teacher) get down on paper what it had been like for her mother, once she'd left Wales for northeastern Pennsylvania, where she'd become Mrs. Margaret Evans, my first objective was to type up the handwritten portions of Mother's manuscript entitled "The Greenhorn." As I did so, I fancied myself to be a copy editor. Before long the writing bug commenced to bite. For instance, my four years of rowing at Cornell kept prodding me to set some of my collegiate adventures down on paper. But a start-up on the real thing would have to wait. Nevertheless I would keep right on generating enough more of my own material to eventually write this saga.

Now, back to winding up the year of 1940: New Year's Day we responded to an invitation to the overseer's home at Lily Lake (officially Chenango Valley State Park). After-dinner entertainment was provided by cousin Robert Glenn Dean (also an unaware George Washington VI), his cousin Nelson Stark (whose father Arthur Stark, was park superintendent), and your Virginian, the skit being for the benefit of our respective sets of parents present. The three cousins took turns running through the manual of arms, Nelson, yet to receive his travel orders, having already been tapped by Uncle Sam.

After the fine holiday where the military overtones contrasted with the view through the big bay window of pheasants romping across a lawn lightly dusted with snow, my parting path was aimed back to Norwich, first work day being Thursday, January 2. While I buckled down at keeping up with the paper work on my new job, spare evenings were focused on my new editorial work.

When Friday evening rolled around, I headed home to Owego for the weekend and turned over to Mother the typed-up pages of her story. Building up my brand-new sideline, Mother then gave me the next part of her handwritten manuscript to be typed up.

Even though I hadn't gone for broke in my college English courses, the profs had always liked my write-ups of rowing life. But only now, while working on Mother's yarn, did I commence to realize that I had been constantly generating my own material. Before long I found myself caught up in an irreversible process—getting hooked on the idea of writing fiction. The realization that my ultimate goal would be setting down a fact saga based on life, would have to wait.

A Brief Job Description

Oh, yes, temporarily I forgot. Learning the intricacies of my new position itself was like learning a new tune on the piano. Once I got some classical pieces down pat, I soon could reel them off from memory. Like mastering another piece of sheet music, my new job impressed me. I had to type up lots of purchase orders, some few letters, handle invoices, etc. A rubber stamp came down as I'd seen it done in a movie. There, a Bolshevik commissar had brought it down for the firing squad that had been voted by a committee of the people. Intercepting it, the lover of the lady being so sentenced had stuck out his hand. When the lover's mitt thus got stamped instead, he took the lady's place.

Unconsciously imitating such theatrics, but only as to the vigor of the whacking, down came my rubber stamp with a nice comfortable punch. Up on his two feet and out of his executive chair came Bosso like a jack-in-the-box. He hastened kitty-corner across the office to my clerk-receptionist's desk. He picked up the rubber stamp, and with a gentlemanly, "Here, let me show you," he carefully, delicately and neatly impressed the rubber stamp at its designated spot. Not only did I thank Bosso Collins but also, forever afterwards, wherever and whenever I would be using any kind whatever of a rubber stamp, I would most carefully follow Bosso Collins' instruction, so good was his knack for teaching carefulness and gentleness at making it stick.

Another day, at the window from the lobby there appeared two businessmen. Through the glass porthole one of them asked to see the purchasing agent. Giving them prompt service, I turned and walked over to Bosso's desk and reported: "Mr. Collins, there are two guys outside in the lobby. They want to see you."

As he got up to go out to greet them, Bosso Collins meaningfully said: "Those *guys* are gentlemen."

That night your Virginian stopped off at the local library to commence refreshing his previous gleanings from Emily Post.

But the real hidden kicker, presumably, as I can only make a guesstimate, was this: it boiled up on top of the big pharmacal company's speculative mishmash, as I executed my job otherwise perfectly, excepting purchasing—processing proceedings that gyrated around a Cardex-type file. Of the daily paper work which it was my duty to handle, from the outset (after my predecessor had given me a few days of instruction and then, as programmed, had left), one stack of stuff would back up on me. The line-items in it I was additionally charged with the duty of recording in the file. But not long off my start line, the closing gong started catching me with my work half-finished. The lady whom I'd replaced had been able to do the job blindfolded and within the required time. But she'd been there on the job, an old faithful (although young-looking) for years. Now that she was gone, in the matter of a week or so, I was expected to achieve the standard pace that had been so set by my lady predecessor. When I failed to hack it fully early on, an executive secretary-type of middle-aged lady exuding expertise and office management skills from the bulk-sales executive's office would be brought out to pinch-hit some after hours catch-up in my absence. When Bosso Collins reminded me that such fine lady had had to be brought in to make my work whole, and that I therefore wasn't cutting the mustard, I still had plenty of confidence that any old time I'd get the hang of keeping up with the paper work time-wise. Was I scared of my job? No. The conscription notice might arrive most any time, setting me up for shipment a month or so hence. Furthermore, the pay was so low that I didn't worry.

But Bosso Collins was several inches shorter than your Virgin-ian, and I wondered whether he might not require instead an aide whom he didn't have to strain to look up to. If so, he could easily have hired a shorter chap. But as mentioned, Norwich had gone bananas over my typing abilities, while I had resolved to give the big pharmacal company my best shot and was very determined to successfully play catch-up. So I suggested to Bosso Collins: "I'll come in Saturday mornings. Then I'll not only get the paper work caught up, but also I'll more quickly get up to the standard pace."

"But you can't come in weekends and work."

"Why not?"

"We're on a forty-hour week. You can't go over the forty hours," Bosso Collins emphasized.

I explained, "OK, then. Within the forty-hour framework, I'll keep plugging until I shrink that pile of paper work down to zero."

Bosso nodded, but grudgingly.

After that nice little colloquy, since I was in such a relax-and-enjoy-it double bind, what more could I say? Actually, there was no point in giving Bosso any sort of an argument. And I took note that he must have also seen himself as being in a similar bind. Following my only alternative, I pitched in to give the paper work an even better go. Then came the closing gong. It was time for me to give some deep thought to this problem. How to otherwise use up more juice out of my only partly drained reservoir of working energies?

Some positive factors had stuck from Monkey's. For instance, I was used to working *more than* forty hours a week. As I kept plugging at my brand-new Norwich job, expecting any old time that in my noggin the light would get turned on and that I'd attain the standard pace that had been set by my lady predecessor, evenings when I didn't have a date I'd drop in at the taproom in the local version of Owego's Ahwaga. There I would forget this brief job description by talking over the good old days back at Cornell with that great sport, Utica native, and red-blooded member of our junior alumni, Marvin Langley, fearless leader of downhill skiers.

For Village Treasurer: An FDR-Type Landslide

It was New Year's Day, 1941, and one of the most important facets of the ongoing hocus-pocus focused on the unaware George Washington V. Going back about ten months, not long before his fiftieth birthday, in March 1940 one of the objectives of the political occultists had already emerged. This was to confine to *village* level the aspirations of the unaware descendants of George Washington, particularly those such as CPD who had displayed some political skills at fiscal affairs.

As mentioned, in my father's case, in 1930 he actually had won the county-level treasurership, only to then have been hornswoggled out of his six-vote margin. And more lately, in September 1939, he'd been KO'd narrowly when the other side had resorted to previously detailed dirty political tricks.

The move by the political occultists to lock CPD in at village level had commenced, as previously detailed, when the incumbent, because of some physical infirmity, had resigned and my father had been appointed to fill the vacancy. Lately, more details explaining away the political motivations had been published in one of the Owego weeklies. The village fathers had wanted a detailed statement of receipts and expenditures from each village fund. Once a month ordinarily would have sufficed. But since March 1940, when my father's predecessor had resigned and CPD had been appointed, he then had commenced to rebuild confidence by providing the much-wanted detailed statement at *each* regular meeting.

Regular meetings were slated twice monthly. As the situation required, special meetings were called by the mayor; i.e. CPD had been appointed at a special meeting.

Adding another facet to the hocus-pocus tone of the new year, the political impetus behind CPD's March 1940 appointment (emphasis your Virginian's) had recently been summed up in a December issue of Owego's Democratic Thursday weekly: There was just then *one man* who predictably could give the board the wanted fiscal statements. The board had thus appointed *him* to fill the vacancy. Afterwards, fiscal happiness prevailed in the village. The public, in general, considered the appointment to be most excellent. From the outset, order had been, in all practical effect, restored to village accounts. My father had submitted the desired reports like clockwork. But after the unaware George Washington V had thus earned the right to be placed on the ballot, he'd been subjected, as previously detailed, to the political ambush on December 16 last past, during the so-called village convention that had been set to conflict with his attendance at the village board meeting.

During the aftermath, the nature of the new surprise clique was quickly reputed by lots and lots of villagers to be a so-called cocktail crowd from the silk-stocking district. As CPD had later explained to his family, "Obviously they knew that I couldn't be present at the caucus to be held in the courthouse because they had been informed that I had pledged to attend all village board meetings at our usual meeting room, up one flight in the village clerk's law office on Lake Street."

So as we entered the new year, the actual village election was slated, as mentioned, for Tuesday, January 7. With no opposition, the name of the estimable young man, Junior Owego, was printed on the ballots-in-waiting.

The young Republicans hadn't yet heard of women's lib, but especially from the thirtyish ladies, signals now emanated. "Lib" was coming. While the automatic slate of all of the other incumbent candidates remained undisturbed and was duly approved, these young Republican ladies, perhaps unaware because they had been cleverly manipulated, focused on pulling the rug on the unaware George Washington V. The village post paid some relatively low salary for the high class of fiscal service that the taxpayers were getting from my father. Yet, for the village treasurership in which he was now the incumbent with many of the attributes of a lame duck, creating such a seeming impasse, these young Republican ladies had assumed the prerogative of lending their weight to Mike Major, who had placed in nomination the name of a candidate other than my father, to wit: thirtyish Junior Owego, in whom they had some particular interest. But other than coming up with the estimable-young-man moniker, the details of such an interest, the weeklies would fail to ever spell out.

The estimable young man looked the part of some English country gentry who took life fairly easy. During his earlier days, his plain yet interesting Anglo-Saxon face gave parishoners an ethnic thrill of being in the presence of a Yankee Tier blue blood when they observed this son of a prestigious local solicitor operating as crucifer of the procession at the Anglican branch on Christmas Eve and Easter Sunday. Currently, his allowing himself to be used as a blocker of CPD for the village treasurership was in and of itself a political curiosity. From the ranks of those very, very few of the villagers noted for their fiscal brains, this estimable young man, buried as a bookkeeper for the Buick agency, was relatively an unknown.

At the most recent village board meeting, my father was customarily commended for the fine midmonthly report that he'd just submitted voluntarily. It was an extra one because the only one required was the one that would be submitted to the board by my father at the end of each month. While my father had been demonstrating on paper that village fiscal matters were now in order, back at the court house, the cocktail crowd had pulled off the political ambush. Characterizing the aftermath, when the new year rolled around, the cocktail crowd, the ladies in particular, were elated with their coup. With the approach of the actual election, such an unopposed nomination would be tantamount to a shoo-in, so the crowd's members thought.

In recent years, there'd been no village-level contesting ticket put in play. There still wasn't. My father had been shoved out into the cold. At the end of the 1940 year, my father had completed his appointment (filling out the official year of the previous village treasurer, who had resigned in early March). With his name missing from the ballot, CPD's being out of office would soon become official.

Soon it was Tuesday, January 7, 1941. Came the village election in which the beneficiary of the mid-December political ambush at the caucus was twenty years younger than Dad, who, on the surface, seemed to be allowing the political occultists play their own game. Nevertheless, that real smart secrecy and surprise to the tune of which the ambush had been sprung by Mike Major when he'd proposed the name of Junior Owego had caused substantial grumbling amongst the backers of the loser—the unaware George Washington V. While behind the scenes the defeat could easily be presumed to have triggered lots of smoldering and must have given my father's followers a slow burn, their solid front was serene as it would have been noted by any of the silk-stocking district's cocktail crowd, had they taken the trouble before the upcoming January election to sound out my father's backers, who knew when they'd been victimized. On the other hand, the leaders of the cocktail crowd expected their estimable young man, a product of their own silk-stocking district, to become an unopposed shoo-in.

Hours of voting at the Central Fire Station ran from six A.M. to five P.M. From the east end of the village, my father and mother appeared early and rather unconcernedly at the polls and voted. My father's supporters seemed to have completely left the political picture. The sides of the estimable young man, on the other hand, commenced wheeling to the front of the Central Fire Station, their shiny sedans spewing out three or more estimable voters from the silk-stocking district in each trip.

By noon there'd been cast 140 ballots, up sharply from the 116 ballots in the same election a year earlier. Most of these early 140 votes could be presumed to have been cast for the estimable young man. As for CPD, without having his name on the ballot, what chance did he have? His backers, in spite of their having been ambushed into such a lurch, kept their serene façades static. And this was some wonder, since on the surface the election appeared right up to four P.M. to be just another perfunctory village confirmation of an unopposed slate. No doubt, the trick replacement of the unaware George Washington V had it in the bag.

Then, as the clock overhead in the tall tower on the Central Fire Station struck four P.M., and with a mere hour before the closing of the polls, came the first whiffs of some winds of change. Almost at once, though, the whiffs turned, into a good solid blow. They came just after the shoe factory's closing gong. They came from the Flats. They came from Turtletown, Cannawanna, and the south side of the Susquehanna River. They came from all four corners of the village. They helped rack up a total vote of 562, the largest in ten years! And amazingly, these last-minute ballots were my father's votes. Although by some December 16 hocus-pocus his name had been blocked from the ballot, to the effect that by four P.M. on the January election day, even the most astute pundits not in on the act considered his election a veritable impossibility, now, one hour later, the final rush put the unaware George Washington V in office with write-ins. He had 322 votes. The estimable young man fell far short, with only a 181-vote total.

Clandestinely, what may have happened was this: E. Burt's crowd, looking ahead to 1942, may have been merely trying to hamstring CPD should he again run for the treasurership at *county* level.

But more perceptively, Boilerplate as an expert manipulator of human beings, working through layers of intermediaries, had seen a fine opportunity to exploit the perhaps unexpected ambushing of CPD to the effect that the estimable young man wriggled into his expected spot on the ballot. But politics makes strange bedfellows, and Boilerplate's very good friend was Heetreet, the operator of a local engineering firm and a smart, well-heeled string-puller of a Democrat (who'd gained my father's confidence as detailed in Volume I). Working with his political lieutenants on the Flats, in one instance, lots of workers from the shoe factory were thus lined up to keep the counterattack secret until, for my father, they struck critical blows. But consider this: the political occultists' surmised objective—obviously unrealized by all such good village swing voters—was to freeze my father politically at *village* level by making him think that he'd fought his way back to the treasurership when, actually, the clandestine warriors had planned for him to innocently play their own game. Another clandestine mission was to make it look as though the unaware George Washington V, although he'd been a registered Republican for a score of years, was sponsored by the Democrats in the village-level office (thus attempting to further alienate his substantial half of the county Republicans should he again run for county treasurer, the next chance coming up in 1942).

Why so much mention of this surmised pair (Boilerplate and Heetreet) of strange political bedfellows? They will turn up as crucial political manipulators (but customarily of low profile) in later volumes. At such time they will also display expertise in targeting another Republican and party of interest in this saga for some real slick dirty tricks, then causing the target to temporarily attribute any politically manufactured miseries to the Democrats. But just now, in the aftermath of my father's surprise victory, to keep their hand from showing, and playing it by the rules applicable to such a secrets business, these Old Boy-types of puppeteers who likely worked under their guiding secret sponsorship now saw to it that an available, advisable, and customary cover story, that they'd likely programmed and had helped create, was provided.

When the young Republican cocktail-crowd ladies, still in a state of surprised shock, commenced to look outside of their silk-stocking district for reasons, they soon discovered that they'd been knocked off their assumed prerogative (of substituting on the ballot their political pet, the estimable young man, as their candidate for the treasurership) by another lady. This other lady had organized the mobile, mechanized voting forces that rode roughshod with perfect, last-minute timing over the opposing cocktail-crowd ladies from the silk-stocking district. This other lady who'd KO'd the cocktail crowd had given them a dose of their own secrecy and surprise while displaying a manner quiet and sagacious. It was obviously effective. Her few political captains were from male ranks. These cohorts of both ladies and gentlemen contributed to and put across my father's last-minute, surprise write-in victory. Who was this other lady?

This surprise legendary holder of the controllership of the village-level balance of power had been for almost a year CPD's secretary. She worked expertly for his combined operation of the village treasurership and his secretary-treasurership for the countywide cooperative fire insurance company. She had outgeneraled the cocktail-crowd ladies from the silk-stocking district. She had created what one of the Yankee Tier's astute newsman termed "An FDR-type landslide vote."

My father's secretary, who'd swung the election his way, was Miss Jane Dunne, a brainy Irish lady who, had the economics of the day allowed it, would have made a brilliant lawyer-CPA. But the only ones presumably in on the know. . . . . . that a psychological pattern of entrapment had now been slickly set to confine, attempt to confine or relegate, first my father, and, eighteen years later, your Virginian as an unaware George Washington VI, to a *village*-level, fish-in-the-barrel-type political job. . . . . . were Boilerplate (a Mr. Republican) and Heetreet (his surrogate in the Democratic party). . . . strange political bedfellows generally unrealized because of their very low profile, yet, at the same time, probably the only two locals who were great enough men to be trusted by the top cop in the City of Washington with so great a political-genealogical secret.

Rustikins Puts in a Plug

It was the second Wednesday of the new year, now nearing the end of the hocus-pocus shindig into 1941. It was also the morning after Tuesday's FDR-type landslide for CPD (the unaware George Washington V) in the village of Owego.

When I arrived at work, Bosso Collins put down his copy of the Binghamton morning daily and graciously congratulated me on my father's spectacular write-in victory for Owego village treasurer. Naturally, I was elated.

The next day, Thursday, just two days after the write-in, while your Virginian was almost twenty-three years of age, he was pitching in, giving his best shot to his still brand-new job as understudy in the Norwich purchasing department. As I dug in on my mission to work my way out of the double bind, its fetters, with each and every passing day, got looser. Had I been allowed to come back on Saturday to study the job on my own time, I could have speeded up this double-bind-beating process. But any overtime, on my own time or not, was just now against the rules and regulations. Although my offer had thus been turned down, nevertheless I was beginning to see the light. So I expected good results from the limited forty hours to this effect: in a matter of days, I'd get on top and stay on top of all of the purchasing department's tricky paper work.

Midmorning, sensing some new arrival at the reception window, I looked up. Through the porthole in the thick glass pane I saw a familiar-looking face. The gentleman putting in his appearance was one of the leading socialities from my home town. . . . . Rustikins.

As mentioned, Rustikins was a native of the Midwest. General Custer being one of his heroes, he'd graduated from Culver Academy during the tough depression days. By the mid-thirties, Rustikins, making his living off the economy, struck it lucky. His springboard was a public relations contact point at a Southern resort. There Rustikins had met and married one of the Yankee Tier's loveliest heiresses. By depression standards the fund was adequate. Nevertheless, Rustikins, a gentleman of great promise, showing that he had no inclination to accept an early retirement, went to work in the world of finance. Quick on the trigger, even though the remnants of the depression kept it a tough life, Rustikins succeeded at landing a job as a customer's broker, marketing equities. Although the remuneration just then was not any too rewarding, Rustikins was building up a raft of contacts on which to exercise his burgeoning financial expertise.

When I'd been in college, the greathearted couple, Rustikins and his lovely wife, had always been kind to us hitchhikers. More than once they'd given us a lift across the hump from the Susquehanna Valley to Cornell's Cayuga watershed in the comfort of their steel-gray Packard. While Rustikins was not a tennis player, he was one of the game's great local enthusiasts, giving great moral support to participants such as Tobin, the Eagle, and your Virginian.

And when the drug store cowboys observed thirtyish Clark Gable-type of a Rustikins operate, for the native Michigander, the locals had nothing but admiration. Being one of such fans, out into the lobby I now stepped to extend my warm greeting to Rustikins.

"What are you doing here?" asked Rustikins, who acted just as surprised to see me.

Quickly I explained my recent acquistion of the clerk-receptionist's position as an understudy to become assistant purchasing agent. Naturally I left out that business about my being currently under the paper-work gun—the double bind.

Rustikins said: "Oh. I didn't know that." Then, although he was one of the imported kingppins of the home-town silk-stocking district cocktail crowd, as well as one of the supportive contemporaries of the estimable young man who'd so recently been moved up front in the unsuccessful attempt to supplant my father, Rustikins was quick to let loose some real friendly words: "That was some village election we just had the day before yesterday back home. I was sure glad to see your father win that write-in for the village treasurer's post. That FDR-type landslide was a real good show and I'm glad that your father got it."

"Thanks, Rustikins," I said, and with no small mental reservation. I had some slight but fleeting suspicions that Rustikins and his wife, as prominent socialites of the silk-stocking district, would have voted with the cocktail crowd, which meant against my father, and that, in case my father should run again in 1942 at *county* level for the county treasurership, Rustikins probably had been in 1939 and would be again in 1942—when my father's next chance would come up—voting for if not working openly for the E. Burt opposition.

Our pleasantries by now having been quickly and fully swapped, to Rustikins (who had considerable stubble sprouting from lack of a quick shave, the delay being attributed to a pleasant evening reviewing old times with a couple of his former military school-mates on whom he'd just stumbled), I asked: "Just what can I do for you? Whom did you want to see?"

Rustikins named our company president, whose office was just up an easy flight of stairs. "I'll phone his secretary and tell her that you're here," I said. But just as I turned to start to leave the lobby to do the telephoning inside, I hesitated and being much interested in the market, asked Rustikins: "Are you still a customer's man for that big stock brokerage house?"

"I'm a salesman," said Rustikins, as he displayed a certain amount of nervousness. Then he mentioned the name of his employer.

Sounding a little like a firm of big-name stock brokers, it was a new one on me. Thinking that maybe Rustikins would know what was good, I asked: "Do you people sell stocks?"

"No," said Rustikins.

"What then?"

"We sell advice, investment advice." Rustikins dropped the big name of an investment counseling firm based in Manhattan, as your unaware George Washington VI was promptly impressed by Rustikins' having had the ability to have tackled so difficult a field—that noble one in which he sold intangibles.

Quickly, for the astute and imported big brother-type of operator, I stepped back inside, got on the phone, got Rustikins the appointment, and returned to the lobby: "The president will see you at once. He says for you to come right up," I told Rustikins, as I wondered whether Rustikins was about to deliver to the company's top Boss some nice choice stuff about your Virginian, such as that good one back at college over Deke's haymaker that had boomeranged, along with details of the 1939 last-minute whispering campaign that had let E. Burt nose out my father for the county treasurership.

A half-hour later, his mission wound up, Rustikins descended the flight of stairs from the company prexy's impressive executive suite. To say goodbye, Rustikins tapped on my window. He was upwards of thirty-five while I was going on twenty-three years of age. Once again, but this time to see the imported idol off, I stepped out into the lobby.

"Deanie, I put in a plug with the company president for you," said Rustikins as we shook hands.

As mentioned, being one of Rustikin's many fans, I said, "Gee. Thanks. I sure appreciate what you've done for me, Rustikins."

"Think nothing of it. Anything for a home town boy," said Rustikins, and then he was gone. He'd grown up near a major inland waterway where he'd also picked up some sea legs and nautical leanings. In the Navy, later on, his being a man of substantial inherent abilities would eventually pay off with a lieutenant commandership. And over the long run he'd become a very successful top-drawer customers' man for a gargantuan, big-name brokerage firm. And with his military school education, when it came to the selection of equities, he was now showing the upstate smart set, including the Hamilton College gang, just how to fatten their capital gains.

Back at my desk the next morning, I couldn't help but jump to this conclusion: that plug for me that Rustikins had made to our prexy must have been just great! Maybe I'd now manage to work myself out of the double bind in which I'd lately found myself. Bosso Collins, the purchasing agent, still wasn't about to let me work overtime at catch-up. I looked at the clock and then pitched in for another good old college try at getting all of my paper work caught up so that by quitting time Friday night, maybe, for once, I'd beat the double bind.

But when I returned to my desk after a pleasant TGIF lunch at the big boarding house on the east side of town, before I could take my seat and pitch in at beating out the double bind over all of that paper work, Bosso Collins, who'd just been huddling with the company prexy, intercepted me. Showing me the way through a big oak door from the purchasing agent's office and into the office of the temporarily unoccupied executive secretary's office, Bosso Collins sat down behind the flat-top desk and indicated that in front of it, I too should also take a chair. Once I'd done so, with the reddish tones in his cheeks heightened by an obvious hike in his blood pressure, Bosso Collins, mincing no words, said: "We're letting you go. You're all through."

In disbelief, I asked: "You mean that I'm fired?"

"If you want to put it that way." Ex-Bosso Collins knew how to make an unaware George Washington VI feel like a fish in a barrel.

"How come?"

"I've been reminding you that you haven't yet been able to regularly keep caught up on recording items on the file cards. I've had to call in the bulk-sales executive's secretary to finish your filing. So this is it," said *Ex*-Bosso who, for his future aide, may have actually required some sort of a highly intelligent mouse. And maybe your unaware George Washington VI just hadn't been sufficiently drab and quiet, outright ownership of a new car perhaps having been a minus instead of a plus?

But after rolling with a little emotional jolt, I digested the nice little shockeroo quickly. At least on the surface, this nice little ambush was the logical outgrowth of the double bind. So I asked: "When do I leave? Right now or at the end of the afternoon?"

"Whichever way you like," said *Ex*-Bosso Collins.

Exercising my option, I announced: "Then I'll leave the customary way, with the outgoing crowd punching out at the end of the afternoon." Finally, I couldn't help reminding Ex-Bosso: "This certainly is a surprise. You made me promise to stay here for at least six months. The term has a long way to run," I averred. Then, while not pressing my rights under the employment contract (because a local Cornell friend had already tipped me off and already I had something better in mind), for an added parting shot, with some reasonable amount of gruffness, but with no mention that I'd been impressed by the quinine syndrome, I reiterated, "At the time I was hired, you told me that you expected me to stay with the company at least several months. I took you at your word and I was just getting ready to buy a hundred shares of stock in the company."

The pharmacal company's shares, listed on the big board, were selling well below ten. They were a steal. Nobody had to tell me. It was simply one of those things for which I displayed a knack for knowing. All that had remained was for your Virginian to get up his nerve and make the purchase. The money, left over after I'd purchased my new Chevrolet in Michigan several months earlier, was just sitting in the bank drawing some low rate of interest.

Curiously, *Ex*-Bosso Collins, after some decades and by then a very well-heeled purchasing agent, would retire to. . . . . . . of all places. . . . . . Virginia. Yet, here came the echo of words that he'd let loose during the knife-and-fork hiring session just a few weeks earlier. Then, my having had my new Chevrolet paid for had triggered some little bewilderment. But now, on the occasion of this one-P.M., early afternoon firing session, my having let out my intention to buy some Norwich Pharmacal stock stirred up a repeat. While making me feel as though I had one-upped him, on this firing occasion *Ex*-Bosso Collins let out with the same preceding plaintive hiring note, "But I don't see where you get the money."

Winding up this hocus-pocus shindig that had been introducing the new year of 1941, it commenced to look as though perhaps yesterday, to the company's prexy, Rustikins had given your Virginian a little bit too perfect a plug!

Chapter 10

Aiding USA To Become Arsenal For Democracy

A New Line Of March

As though my primary mission were to one-up those who'd conjured up the close-out of the hocus-pocus shindig dragging in this otherwise first-rate new year, early in the morning I left Norwich with a proverbial dull roar, quickly toned down by the foot or more of snow that soon started buffeting me at the higher levels along this shortcut.

Under winter's cold bright blue sky, the white landscape was flooded with almost enough sunshine to make you snowblind. By the quickest and shortest snow-covered dirt road across an extra tall hill, I was spinning the wheel of fortune for a better job.

Now that Norwich had so dramatically etched itself in the past, as you might gather, there was also no thought of my going back to Monkey's. It was a good thing that they hadn't reacted to their last chance by giving your Virginian some practical recognition in the form of a small raise. Had they done so, I'd have been stuck on a slower boat. Sewell Avery, at the time of my resignation, had completed eight years as the big chain's chief. The company's common stock totaled up on the market to $200 million, contrasted to $500 million for Sears Roebuck. Avery would stay for fourteen more years, during which stretch the competition would lose all semblance of a contest. Just after the mid-sixties, Monkey's common stock would be valued at $400 million—a double in just under three decades. But Sears would be worth $9 billion—up eighteen times during the same twenty-seven years. So how come your Virginian had never thought of switching to Sears? My former college roommate, Si Glann, who was now completing his third and last year in law school, had first come up with this telling preachment: "That time we spent working in respective retail stores for Monkey's taught us a lesson, to wit: To keep the heck out of any chain store business for the rest of our working days." While Si had already embarked towards the final solution—studying law, my contrasty current mission was an experiment in stepping down to blue-collar life that would pay a lot better. Next targeted was an industry that would be entirely different from either merchandising, from which I'd resigned, or pharmaceuticals, from which I'd just been ambushed with walking papers.

On my new line of march to the office of the next personnel director, my car was bucking deeper and heavier snows in an attempt to surmount a high ridge. As I pressed forward gingerly in my Chevrolet business coupe, and without benefit of chains, it looked as though the foot of fresh snow was going to see me at any moment going out of control and then sliding and slithering into a ditch. But fate was on my side. Every minor emergency worked itself out. When a skid would seem ready to do its worst, at the last moment I'd regain control and my wheels would scratch out further footage up and over the tall height of land that separated the Norwich sector of the Chenango valley as it was being kissed goodbye for the Unadilla valley. Inside the light blue Chevrolet coupe, my skis were cocked kitty-corner from left rear to front right. In case my car should slide off a steep bank, I was getting ready to instantly hug the floor in case car and all might roll over. Naturally, had I realized the risks generated by all of this lack of traction, I would have taken some longer water-level route that would have been mostly along safer and more easily negotiated paved roads along valley floors. But now that I was committed to roads too treacherous for a turnaround, I just kept pressing upward in these upstate New York hills. It continued to be a ticklish situation. Iciness under the heavy snow conditions on the shortcut got worse and worse. Then I passed the Guilford turnoff. This triggered a turn of the tide. Like magic, in front of me, from a side road, the rear of a lumbering snowplow appeared. The impossible first became possible and I could now sense that I was going to make it. Thanks to the plow, I was no longer sweating out a sudden slide into a ditch, or, worse yet, down a steep bank. Gradually reducing my altitude by several hundred feet, I followed the very effective snowplow downward as it wound and turned with the road. At East Guilford I popped out onto a paved road on the valley floor. My time-saving gamble had paid off. I proceeded down a slight grade on the first-class state highway to the confluence of the Unadilla River with the Susquehanna. At the intersection, a left turn put me on an easier track in the dominant valley of the Susquehanna. Upstream a relatively short distance, I crossed the river bridge, passing quickly through downtown Sidney, and finally, in the residential district, I knocked on the door of my father's former business partner.

Glad to see me were Byron Dutcher and his wife, Harriet. Commencing in late 1919, and operating until September 1927, Mr. Dutcher had been my father's partner in the very successful feed business in Owego. At Sidney, Byron had first tried his luck as sole proprietor of a feed mill. But after a short stint, he had switched to the realty business, and now was one of Sidney's well-established landlords. After hearing me out, he enhanced my new line of march with an introduction by telephone.

Thanks to this first-rate connection, not long after lunch with these good friends of the family, I was being interviewed for a job by Mr. Van Name, personnel director of Scintilla Magneto Company.

A bit now about my new thinking as I adapted myself to the ongoing international developments. Old values such as had been expounded by Howard Lee Davis in *The Young Man in Business* were still operative, yet now relegated to the back burner while I played by ear the mythical supplement: how to proceed when a peacetime conscription bugle was slowly getting ready to blow?

After getting away as rapidly as possible from that can of worms on this last job, on which the real motive for my having gotten the old heave-ho would forever remain a mystery, and also on which the company's termination records of such hair-trigger torpedoing would mysteriously disappear, I'd decided to forget checking back in with my college job placement bureau. Instead, I was now going myself, cold turkey, to dig in on the current job market. In line with my new do-it-yourself philosophy, no longer would I be playing low man in a Cornell-Dartmouth densification situation and feeling therein like some indentured servant who might, by some stroke of luck and by virtue of his extra hearty application to his trainee's job, just happen to generate a nice raise accompanied by a promotion in rank, provided he exercised great patience for a sufficient number of years. From now on I'd commence asking myself just what it was that most interested me that paid the best. But now that I was hooked on writing I'd opt if necessary for lower pay to get the kind of employment that would enable me to live the best possible artistic life before going to war.

Sure, I'd like to be a writer—but writing, as I was rapidly in the process of discovering, wouldn't pay off—then I would go hook up and pitch in at some job that did pay. While thus keeping from starving, from "how-to" books as well as from practical experience, I'd teach myself to write. While financial independence would remain a distant objective, should I now get stuck in the manufacturing industry, any writing skill that I might now develop, including the unrealized possibility of becoming a technical writer, would be a big plus. But why not cook up some fictional yarns and then save up some do-re-mi from selling them to magazines such as the *Saturday Evening Post* (SEP)? With the proceeds I'd buy some stock. If none were available in the employer company (Scintilla, for instance, was a unit of Bendix.), then the raft of stocks on the exchanges of America would be my oyster from which to pick and choose. In other words, make money at Scintilla and invest it in Norwich or even in much larger Bendix. And these are mere examples of great investment opportunities, with ITT remaining in speculative buying range, from which springboard you'd be able to outdo percentagewise the more conservative companies. But now for making the green with which to do it.

At this time of national crisis, I knocked at the door of a very important factor in one of America's most vital industries. . . . . . an operation that was now furnishing magnetos for aircraft. Just a few short months ago, at Coventry, the *Luftwaffe* had knocked out Britain's magneto works. For a major compensating factor for the loss, magnetos were now being turned out by the recently expanded factory in the hills of upstate New York.

The Breathing Spell

In accordance with my job application, I was hooked up at once out on the big floor, one of the various production supervisors named Ed Herman assigning the post. Under the tutelage of one Wadsworth, at one of the older Warner and Swasey machines out of row on row of similar turret lathes, a semblance of an inside track had come my way from my having observed a color movie on the Warner and Swasey Number Three in operation, such a flick having been featured during one of my very few courses in the engineering school while I'd been a student at Cornell. The movie had left me with the hunch that one day I'd operate one of those machines. Now that such a time had arrived, I caught on quickly. In contrast to Norwich, here at Sidney, no seemingly concocted double bind surfaced. Instead, some extra special priming on my own time, a chance for some warranted catch-up that had been refused at Norwich, helped out like this.

Afternoons, before checking in for the night shift on the big floor, I attended an emergency class in a specially put-together trade school at the old Sidney High School building. Instructing us on how to keep 'em cutting and how to turn top views, end views and side views from blueprints into precision magneto parts was the veteran tool and die maker—Jim Morrow. Just as I was getting my land legs, I got an ache, all from my having been putting off periodic inspections by a dentist. At once, I commenced to roll with the punch. A local dental surgeon soon yanked it. Then, feeling tough, I lost no time getting with it at the afternoon trade school. Thanks to this gutsy hanging tight, I soon had learned enough to step out from under Jim Morrow's wing, graduating to the tune of some full-time, on-the-job metal-working teachings by two of Scintilla's top-drawer set-up men—George Yarter and Ed Knight. With one of the unique production machines, a Warner and Swasey lathe, as mentioned, I commenced locking horns. As we helped open up the brand-new extension, quotas of precision metal magneto parts were soon being met.

Over Britain, the Germans, having lost the daylight battle, were enjoying a free hand at night. By January 23, a stalemate in the European war was predicted by Col. Charles A. Lindbergh in testimony on the lend-lease bill before the house foreign affairs committee. He suggested a negotiated peace to end the conflict.

Naturally such a feature, as it was headlined in the *Bingo PM Bugle* for the popular daily's various circulation areas including Sidney, prompted some war-related comments along our production line. As the inside story now came out, during the preceding fall, when the *Luftwaffe* had leveled Coventry during the ten-hour attack that had commenced early evening November 14, 1940, such German bombs had also destroyed Britain's only aircraft magneto plant. Making all of us machinists feel very important, our plant in the small upstate village of Sidney, together with one other American manufacturing establishment (said to have been American Bosch), had been left to fill the gap.

But at the outset of a certain evening shift, the regular operator warned: "Don't touch the machine until we get the word." Suddenly I realized that when there should have been a solid and steady humming, all motors were silent. For a pay hike, the men were on the verge of a strike. All machines on the big floor remained idle. The peppy purring was a misser. But it wasn't long and you could feel the message come down the grapevine. OK to start work. A pay hike would be added to the small brown envelopes in which the neatly folded green was tucked.

Additionally, Scintilla machinists counted their blessings. The dozen or so recruits turned loose on their respective lathes with your Virginian hadn't been on the job very long when the head office let loose a clerk with a clipboard. Proceeding from recruit to recruit he asked this one and that one: "You want a deferment?" What an out from peacetime conscription! Every metal-sculpting recruit answered in the affirmative. While my good friend Phil Smith had left in January and was now starting the day in a far-off infantry camp by donning wrap leggings, and while Hugh Hogan (now on a Sidney construction project) was slated to ship out in March, particularly in your Virginian's case, this unexpected deferment gave me a much-appreciated breathing spell.

But before long, two hours down the valley in my home town,

the local mothers would soon be complaining about the deferment. But Mother would tell them: "Evans (your Virginian's middle name and his mother's maiden name) is taking just as much risk getting hurt running a machine for the defense effort as though he were drafted in the peacetime army."

That would hold the Yankee Tier critics, but only as long as the United States could keep out of the war. And should war actually come, it looked to me as though I'd be unable, in any event, to resist the temptation of getting some material-generating experiences to write about, first by volunteering, and then, as Negley Farson had put it, by much more than paying my dues for this current breathing spell by finding the ways and the means to get overseas with the army as rapidly as possible.

Some Salient Atmospherics

What were the atmospherics of these opening days of 1941? The national feeling was one of growing apprehension. You could still scrounge up lots and lots of reasons why the United States was most likely to keep out of the war. Yet here were some of the highlights that hadn't come to light, along with those that had surfaced early on and not long after the hocus-pocus opening of the new year.

The successful British raid on the Italian fleet in Taranto harbor on November 12 had crystallized a Japanese concept. But in the Pacific, as Layton's book *And I Was There* would eventually point out, after the U.S. commander had expressed his concern, he'd soon be told that analysts in Washington had determined that antitorpedo nets were not necessary since the waters of Pearl Harbor, unlike Taranto's, were too shallow for making an effective aerial torpedo attack.

But making the headlines, FDR, in his annual message to Congress, declared that the United States should act as arsenal to supply all necessary war supplies to democracies defending themselves against aggressor nations. And to help play such catch-up, your Virginian was now getting his oar in by manufacturing parts for the vital magnetos.

Furthermore, FDR presented to Congress a $17 billion budget minimum, including almost $11 billion for defense. From the viewpoint of the United Kingdom, weapons, ships and planes, but no armies from the United States, were asked by Winston Churchill in 1941. (No one paid much attention to the inference that such armies from the United States might well be wanted in 1942.) In the City of Washington, FDR was inaugurated for a third term.

Although we all could still play ostrich and hope that somehow or the other the European war might peter out, the probabilities were constantly being heightened that the United States might soon become an active participant. The nation's new preparedness policy made the springboard for my new line of march an easy one. On the same day that I arrived in Sidney, and with no knife-and-fork test being necessary, I obtained a job as a machinist, lined up a place to stay at a local boarding house and went to work the same afternoon on the night shift. Some practical recognition went along with the new post. This estimated forty-two-dollar weekly minimum was a substantial increase percentagewise over the hundred a month I'd been making with Monkey's, and the sixteen dollars or so a week that I'd been making a day earlier with the pharmacal company. Telling Scintilla that you'd just been handed mysteriously the old heave-ho from Norwich, so it seemed, gave you a big extra plus with the administration at the magneto works. Very soon after my arrival at Sidney, the forward view was so bright that I sent word downriver to some good friends in my home town, Owego. Spike Lowry and Junior Dingle would have to count me out on the ski trip that I'd organized for the upcoming weekend to Old Forge in the Adirondacks. Although the Indian Princess would be going along, magnetos were in such demand that there was to be no skipping of a single, solitary night shift even though such a weekend of skiing—the world's second best sport—would have given our batteries a very acceptable charge. Instead, I found strength flowing in as an industrial laying on of hands was bestowed by the purring motors of a multitude of capital-goods machines manned by workers destined to "keep 'em flying." Nothing like helping FDR lead the U.S.A. to act as arsenal to supply war materiel to democratic nations fighting off aggressors!

Yarter's Perspicacity

Our set-up man, George Yarter, liked to preach, "I don't get paid for what I do so much as I get paid for what I know."

Aside from the plant-wide deferments, the Scintilla machinists had this additional food for thought: Our establishment that manufactured for the Armed Forces a wide variety of magnetos was far beyond the widest reach of the *Luftwaffe*. Air raid shelters here in upstate New York were nonexistent. Otherwise, same as Coventry, Sidney would have been a prime target. None the less, Hitler-generated headlines kept the metal-cutting pros on edge.

At about this time the Nazi chief announced in his pet historic Munich beer cellar that he was planning a gigantic U-boat war against Britain. Not much later he told an audience of Nazi heavyweights that no help could save England. And Hitler's preachments of what seemed to be the military and naval realities of the day kept making us face up to this this question: To get rid of this ever-present threat of war, should the European conflict be settled by a negotiated peace?

Your Virginian, for one, didn't know the answer. For sure, I was one of the many Americans to whom dislodging the German Army from the Atlantic coast of France seemed to be an impossibility. Letting my thinking all come out to our astute set-up man, George Yarter, I said: "In World War I, France held out and we could land an army. But now that Hitler's got France, in World War II the United States will never be able to get an army ashore again for the necessary foothold to fight on the Continent." And I mentioned the saying of one of my former landlords back in Ann Arbor. Before coming to the States, he'd been a peacetime conscript in the German Army. Regarding any Allied attempts to land on the Contininent, he'd emphasized, "They'll get their noses burnt."

"Don't you kid yourself, Ben," came back Yarter's prophetic reply. "Right now we are working like beavers getting ready. Maybe it will take us a couple of years. But when that time comes we'll go over there and burn a hole right up through from the Atlantic coast of France, and we won't stop until we get to Berlin."

Were Yarter right, this meant U.S. involvement in the war. But we were still at peace.

"So when is the United States going to get into the war?" I asked Yarter the sixty-four dollar question.

He just shrugged. Perspicacity even had its limits. But from then on, to your unaware George Washington VI, although the solution was still imperceptible, the impossiblity got started at taking on an ever increasing aura of chances for success.

Columbine Momentarily Reappears

Thanks to the long hours at defense work, when I got an end-of-month weekend home to Owego, it was a short one. Adding a flashy facet, my little sister announced: "One of your old coed girlfriends is visiting old friends on the campus during winter vacation from her graduate course on the East Coast. Why don't you take a spin to Cornell to pay your respects?"

Motoring right over to a sorority house on the fringe of the campus, when a demonstration of progress on some more-substantial professional course might better have turned the trick, I laid some cut flowers at Columbine's feet.

Our last encounter had been at the World's Fair on Long Island. Generally speaking, I continued to develop my new-found role: Focusing my attentions in turn on various and sundry mademoiselles to the effect that such pressure would perhaps trigger for them a proposal from some much better catch, such as a legal eagle, blacktop spreader, tinker, tailor or slicer, the sawbones having the inside track. That latter sort of certificate was what your Virginian would soon have been equipped with had he followed his original plan, going for a premed course at Harvard, September 1934. Without such inside track, and with my spies' indicating that Columbine was going to fall for the current fad, it was no use crying over spilt milk. Yet, there was more than one way to skin a cat. No sour grapes about it. Now that I was aiming to become a writer, Columbine, were we yet to get together, might well become an anchor inspiring me to exploit my current deferment. And had such become the case, it would have prevented my eventually sailing on some fated Stars and Stripes voyages that would generate literary material for this saga. Now, back to the current realities.

A week after Columbine had departed to continue the pursuit of her graduate studies enhanced by the much-better catch-in-waiting, back on the job at Scintilla, I'd been spelling one of the key regulars sufficiently so that some time in February I was assigned to the new part of the big magneto-manufacturing plant. On a production line-type of arrangement, and without my realizing that I was about to become a slave to a machine, I was put in charge of my own Warner and Swasey Number Three, shared with a co-worker on the opposite daylight shift. At a neighboring machine, Dick Lombard from Fort Plain in the Mohawk valley was turning out aluminum fittings, while your Virginian from the Yankee Tier was turning steel bar stock into precision parts. On the all-too-short weekends we occasionally got in a quick ski junket to some place such as Nimmonsburg on the north side of Binghamton. All too soon the starting gong would clamor and we'd be back at work. One saving grace was the periodic pay envelope. It would contain in good green upwards of forty dollars a week, with some older hands who were being assigned good jobs on piecework fishing out as much as a hundred a week. For this, the tail end of the depression years, except for all of that sweating and grinding your bit against delay, we were earning our first real gravy and it was time to spend some on a seeming frill. Actually it would turn out to be one of the many important elements of genealogical evidence being presented in this volume of my saga to you all. Of course, such a picture might still retrieve the primary favors of the lady Columbine.

From his neighboring production lathe, Dick Lombard announced: "There's an itinerant photographer who has set up temporary shop in the big front parlor in one of the big houses in the residential section. He's already taken pictures of a bunch of us. He knows how to make you come up looking like a movie star. But the photographer says that he's about ready to leave town, has to be some place far away a couple of days hence. We told him that we'd tell you and although he's in a hurry to hit the road, he said that he'd wait."

The photographer, a fortyish man with intense dark eyes and just under six feet in height, acted like a real pro. From his confident instructions on the sitting and his expert placing of lights, it was obvious that he had the know-how. His name would soon be forgotten except that he mentioned being a member of the Holland family of Texas. Aside from that, he insisted that I pay him in advance even though he was immediately leaving town. Taking the gamble, I sweated out the mail. As promised, the photo portriats of your unaware George Washington VI came on schedule. The excellent results gave a needed puff to my ego. On the fancy mounting of one of them endorsed in pencil appeared the word "Paramount." No photographer's name was stamped or otherwise caused to appear on either the front or the back of the photo portraits. So top-drawer photographer thus vanished into limbo. And while putting it all together for my saga, I can't help but wonder whether some of the interests, including the government, occupying choice acreage of George Washington's vast estates, had gotten curious? For instance, the "new airport" on the Potomac was soon to have its official opening. Part of it had been filled in on the frontage of George Washington's Four Mile Run tract. When it came to a deferred machinist squirreled away at Scintilla, one who was an unaware contingent *per stirpes* titleholder by the laws of descent and distribution, did the backers of the itinerant photographer want to to see some looks like George Washington's that you can't hide, of an unaware George Washington VI who'd just turned twenty-three?

Before long, encouraged by some friends, based on the new photo portraits, I'd drop a line to one of the major motion picture studios to see about getting some work as an actor. Several years earlier, in our high school senior play, I'd successfully played the role of an Englishman—all but forgotten. And before leaving Ann Arbor I'd missed the point. An actor's job might well have gone with the territory, a beautiful niece of a Hollywood producer. And that too was forgotten as I now pursued the self-made-man approach.

From one of the important film executives would soon come a letter leaving the door wide open. But by then, events would commence moving so rapidly that I'd feel as though I were fatefully playing the major role in my own movie, living my own novel. Had I not dropped the acting idea, I might have given some one of my former Poughkeepsie intercollegiate rowing contemporaries, such as Gregory Peck, some competition.

And when a local newspaper published an aerial view of the

burgeoning Scintilla magneto factory, naturally, in case Columbine wanted to shake the croaker and join me, I sent her the clipping along with a photo portrait of your unaware George Washington VI. Did it cut any ice? No. Even the Indian Princess hesitated while otherwise evincing great appreciation for the print. From their viewpoint, much bigger game was in the offing. Yet, besides providing motivational pix, I was glad to do them the favor of dropping them some occasional billets-doux, nice crackly notes that they'd let peek from their respective handbags for the stirring up of their relatively secret swains. And I had no regrets: the reappearance of Columbine, though brief, spruced up my fast-running winter of helping furnish magnetos for Uncle Sam to factor into some of his fighter planes in the ever-growing desperate game of peacetime catch-up with the wartime *Luftwaffe*.

No Letup In Sight

From war developments overseas and related moves at home by midwinter there was no letup in sight. Making it look as though one way or another the United States would soon get into it and thus give me my literary opportunity, here were some headlined developments:

Navy Secretary Knox told a Senate Foreign Relations Committee that he was positive that the Axis would invade the Western Hemisphere if Britain were overwhelmed. General Robert E. Wood of the American First Committee told the aforesaid Senate Committee that a Lend-Lease bill might involve the United States in war in ninety days (say by early May 1941!). A controversial measure soon passed in the House of Representatives by a vote of 260 to 165. It would authorize FDR to transfer military equipment to Britain. The resignation of Joe Kennedy became effective in early February when FDR named John G. Winant to be United States Ambassador to Great Britain. Around mid-February a bill raising the national debt ceiling from $49 billion to $65 billion was approved by the Senate. "Britain is in desperate and immediate need of United States help," declared Harry Hopkins on his return from a four-week trip to the United Kingdom. Getting less attention in the Pacific, Japan officially offered its services to end all wars, blaming the United States and Britain for the continued conflict. A large Australian army landed at Singapore. Japan's mediation offer was rejected. Summer Wells, Undersecretary of State, told the press that the United States was interested in deeds rather than in words. The fortification of the naval base at Guam was voted by the House of Representatives. The white race must cede Oceania, the Japanese foreign minister told Japan's governing body. Oceania he defined as a huge area in the Pacific capable of supporting six hundred million persons.

Pressing the U.S. buildup, FDR asked Congress to appropriate almost $4 billion for the Army. He also placed export bans on certain strategic metals and commodities. The war department sent two squadrons of planes to the Philippines and six squadrons to the new Alaskan base. Illustrative of the new nervousness gripping the nation, the government completed secret removal of $8.5 billion in gold from New York City to subterranean gold vaults at Fort Knox, Kentucky.

When March rolled around, Nazi U-boats during the preceding week had sunk twenty-nine ships, the London admiralty would soon admit. The United States requested Italy to close two consulates here and to restrict the movements of Italian consular agents. The Senate passed the Lend-Lease bill by a vote of 60 to 31. It was signed by FDR on March 11. FDR urged Congress to appropriate $7 billion to speed arms to the democracies. A naval bill asking almost $3.5 billion for building of a two-ocean navy was passed by the House of Representatives. FDR in a radio speech told the nation that the American people would have to make sacrifices in order to defeat dictatorships. The *Bremen*, 51,000-ton German liner, was reported ablaze. The United States and Canada signed the pact to develop the St. Lawrence Seaway.

In southern England, Plymouth was shattered by the *Luftwaffe*. Throngs in Sidney cheered arrival of seven United States warships. The Grand Coulee in the state of Washington started operation two years ahead of schedule. The British cut the meat ration to six ounces weekly per person. Their Mediterranean fleet battered Italian naval units in a fierce engagement off Cape Matapan, Greece, sinking three cruisers and two destroyers and crippling a 35,000-ton battleship. French shore batteries in Algeria fired on British naval units attempting to intercept a French convoy believed laden with war supplies for German units in Africa. Germany and Italy protested against the recent seizure by the United States of sixty-five Axis-controlled ships docked in U.S. ports.

At home, the Department of Justice issued warrants to arrest 100 Nazi and 775 Italian seamen on charges of sabotage. With such heightening tensions keeping things spinning, the month of March 1941 ran out while we all kept right on fattening Uncle Sam's arsenal for democracy.

April Fool

At hand was April Fools' Day. It was time, in some small way, to play it. When my turn had recently been switched from night shift to days, that bit about getting up at dawn at Owego for a quick run to make it in time for the daylight shift a good two hours up river at Sidney turned out to be a bit too much. When I had forgotten my identification badge, I was let in to a special section to await security clearance at Scintilla. No problem. . . . except that I missed more than an hour's work at my money-making machine.

Once wasn't enough. A week later it was again around five A.M. when I left Owego in my Chevrolet business coupe scooting for Scintilla, about sixty miles up the watershed. After I parked my car and approached the portals for commencement of the seven A.M. daylight shift, I was still half-asleep. When I reached up to the collar of my work shirt and checked for my badge, again it was a misser. To get out of again losing time on the job, what to do in a hurry?

Pouring through the gate with the crowd, I reached up with the right hand and jerked open the collar of my topcoat. The guard at the sentry box nodded. In to work I went, and with hardly a thought that I'd left my identification badge on the dresser sixty miles downriver. But by thus fortuitously finessing my way in, I'd saved some substantial pay that I'd have otherwise lost while going through the awful drag of waiting with a bunch of other such unfortunates for security clearance.

When it came time to make arrangements to home to the nearby boarding house for lunch, I had to take steps to get equipped with advance plant reentry authorization. It was then that my successful caper leaked. Leaving for lunch break, I stopped in at the security office, arranging for a temporary ID card. From the outside guard post, a nervous security supervisor was called in. "How'd you get in without a badge? Who was the guard who passed you?" he asked.

"It was very clear on this Monday morning and I'd just driven rapidly upriver for sixty miles. I was half-asleep. I can't tell you which guard it was," I protested.

So went late March and early April. Although April Fools' Day was coming up on the morrow, my requested temporary identification pass was soon issued to cover my lunch break as well as my entry the next morning. That same afternoon my regular badge would arrive by special delivery. While that would be no joke, as I said, I actually still had been rubbing sleep from my eyes when I'd made it through closely guarded Scintilla portals without a pass. But the roar of the heavy motors out on that big floor, once I entered the plant, made me come alive as though I'd just downed a couple of cups of black java.

For a Monday morning greeting, Ed Knight, the set-up man now servicing my machine, was waving a new blueprint. "You're going to make some shafts for some magnetos that are slated to become part of some Packard motor torpedo boats," he announced. "But we've got to be careful that we don't spoil the job."

Soon, out of sizeable bar stock, we were taking one of the major cuts and then the other. Once we commenced slowly sculpting machined shafts, the time arrived for that unpopular man from the office to make the time and motion study. With his clipboard and stopwatch he timed separately the two major cuts. Not long after he'd soon posted the official rate, we rerigged the machine. The two major cuts were now taken simultaneously as I personally saw to it that the cutting oil squirted steadily and simultaneously at the point of each smoking bit by which the respective thin ribbons of steel were being peeled off. Still being careful not to spoil the job, while meeting all production quotas, when George Yarter came by to see how things were going currently as well as how they'd been progressing on leave, I got off some sought-after punch lines. "She said, 'Come on, big boy. What about a tip?' "

"How did you respond to that?"

"I had just dropped off my desk radio to Monkey's to get some new tubes. Looking ahead to the pickup, I just had enough left to pay for them."

"Well. . . . did you give her a tip?"

By now some nearby machinists were lending their ears. When I told Yarter, "I reached into my picket and got a dime."

"You gave it to her?"

"She took it."

From up and down the production line, up went a synchronized hee-haw. But my work just then was all caught up. So after turning out another quota-meeting batch of shafts, the straw bosses had to have their little joke. One of them handed me a note to take to the supply room. When I handed it in, from the insiders there came a suppressed laugh.

It seemed that there were two principal types of cutting oil. One was regular for cutting steel bar stock, and the other was milky-looking and soluble for cutting aluminum. My mission had been to fetch some regular. But the note from the straw boss to the man behind the wicket of the supply cage had specified: "virgin oil". . . . . . laugh. . . . laugh. That would have been the milky, and not applicable to the particular job on my lathe on which steel, not aluminum, was being machined.

When my daylight tour wound down and it came time to return to the night shift, that was no April fool. You all might think that working nights would give you some great afternoons on the tennis court. But energy would be a misser. What an awful feeling dragging your tail in through the starting gate to hook up on the night shift. Big surprise! Only minutes after we started hiking between the white lines on the official path that led through the old section, by the time we reached the new part of the plant, the energy that had been missing for tennis boiled back with a bang for lathe operations. But to help the U.S.A. serve as an arsenal for democracy, we were taking our medicine, working our turn evenings, all of this to help keep 'em flying for the Allies.

Parts for magnetos, beyond a doubt, were required for putting together currently needed war equipment. And what about the draft? There was no particular hurry to beat it out by enlisting. Winston Churchill in a broadcast emphasized that Britain needed United States tools and war supplies rather than United States soldiers. By the same token, I could easily surmise that at this stage, the U.S. Army didn't want too large a flood of recruits.

As our helping Uncle Sam play catch-up continued in the aviation industry, too bad that the war itself couldn't turn out to be an April fool. But with the pressure that we could feel for the burgeoning demand for magnetos, fat chance.

The Turbulence Fails To Abate

Back on the night shift, sparkplugging us to keep 'em cutting were the shockers that kept blazoning the headlines. The big question was this: How much longer would it take for the year-and-a-half-old war to actually involve the United States?

During early April, the United States asked Italy to recall her naval attache from Washington. Nazi-Italian armored units in Libya forced British troops to evacuate the port of Bengasi, and Aduwa fell to British troops in Ethiopia.

At the end of the first week, Nazi armies invaded Yugoslavia and Greece. Adding a semblance of a seesaw, Addis Ababa capipulated to the British Army in Ethiopia. By April 7, the RAF bombed Sofia, Bulgaria. London severed diplomatic relations with Budapest. The German Army made fresh gains in the Balkans while on April 9, the RAF bombed the heart of Berlin, damaging the state opera house and other buildings. German and Italian forces in Libya captured six British generals and 2,000 men but in Italian Eritrea, the British took the port of Massawa. Winston Churchill appealed to the United States for aid in keeping open the Atlantic sea lanes.

On April 10, the U.S. revealed an agreement with the Danish envoy in Washington to protect Greenland against aggression, giving the U.S. the right to build bases on the island. The German high command announced the taking of 80,000 Greek prisoners and 20,000 Yugoslav prisoners. The Turks ordered the evacuation of Istanbul. The USSR denounced Hungary for invading Yugoslavia. Nazi-occupied Denmark soon declared void the agreement signed between the U.S. and Danish envoy in Washington.

On April 13 came the announcement that the USSR and Japan had signed a neutrality pact. While *Britannica Book of the Year* furnishes much of this data, in later decades, Layton would point out in *And I was There* that to assure Hitler that Japan intended to launch a diversionary assault against Britain in the Far East, Foreign Minister Yosuke Matsuoka undertook the long trans-Siberian railway trip to Berlin. But he hadn't been told that Prime Minister Konoye was involved in a conflicting secret diplomatic initiative to reach an accord with the United States aimed at pulling the rug from under a potential Anglo-American Alliance in the Far East.

Konoye hoped to reach such an agreement before Matsuoka's return. But these hopes foundered when the army refused concessions over the China issue, and the foreign minister returned with promises to keep to Hitler plus the aforesaid neutrality pact with the U.S.S.R. "Japan can straighten out the Far East and Germany will handle Europe," Stalin had promised the diminutive Matsuoka at Moscow's central station. "Later, together, all of us will deal with America."

Thanks to Layton, your Virginian extracted the foregoing, just to show you all that the anti-American forces, were they to keep their composition, were even worse than current headlines indicated.

German-Italian mechanized troops drove the British back across the Egyptian frontier, taking the town of El Sollum. Nazi troops occupied Belgrade. In Greece, British troops retired to a new defense line. The German high command claimed that the Yugoslav army was virtually destroyed. In the United States, the secretary of war gave Americans subject to conscription (such as your Virginian would be, were he to allow his deferment to fall in) a globe-trotting clue. Bearing out the quinine syndrome, Mr. Stimson said that the Army should be prepared to fight anywhere.

By April 17, the entire Yugoslav army surrendered as German tank divisions methodically drove back Greek and British armed forces. On the Egyptian frontier, the Axis drive easterly stalled and the British got a slight breather.

Giving civilians a hint of shortages to come, the United States motor car industry voluntarily agreed to cut production by one million cars beginning on August 1, 1941. Retaliating for a heavy mid-April raid on London, the RAF pounded Berlin.

By April 19, the British landed strong forces in Iraq to guard the Mosul oil fields. According to *Pravda,* the purpose of the recent Soviet-Japanese pact was to thwart Anglo-American efforts to draw the USSR into the war. A U.S.-Canadian pact for producing war materials for Britain was signed by Prime Minister Mackenzie King and President FDR. The Nazis reported that British armies in Greece were fleeing in evacuation ships. The immediate extension of United States neutrality patrol areas in Atlantic waters was announced by FDR. On April 28, Colonel Lindbergh resigned his commission as a reserve officer in the United States Air Corps, declaring that FDR's recent remarks questioning his loyalty left him "no honorable alternative."

Winding up April, the Russian press reported that twelve thousand German troops, equipped with tanks and big guns, had landed at Abo in southern Finland.

As the turbulence failed to abate, it become clear: Yarter was right. At Scintilla, we were going to have to work our tails off to rearm the United States and then burn a hole right up through the defenses of the Nazi-held Atlantic coast of Europe.

But for at least a year, the catch-up game looked up a long steep hill. From Plymouth, British authorities evacuated women, children, and aged after a series of fierce raids by the *Luftwaffe*. On the brighter side, the British succeeded in evacuating 48,000 of the 60,000 troops originally landed in Greece, Winston Churchill told Commons.

Chasing Away the Corn

Back to the big floor, where the electric motors were filling the atmosphere with an energizing hum and magnetizing our best pocket watch as we slaved at our turret lathe, another saving grace of this new line of march was the breathing spell, as previously mentioned, that the deferment was giving me. Whatever the draft number I'd drawn, had it not been for my defense job, there was a slim chance that I'd have been called up towards the end of winter with the second draft, or more likely in the third draft, slated for summer. But by my now doing it Scintilla's way, no bugle was even threatening to blow.

In contrast, Phil Smith had shipped out as mentioned in January. One popular Owego chap, Hugh Hogan, who'd also traveled to Sidney to find employment, had been working on a housing

construction project (when he too could have been making magneto parts to the tune of a deferment). By now, the draft board had
booked him to leave in March. For his last few months as a civilian, he homed downriver. Winding up his civilian days, he worked
for his father, also on construction. And the last time I saw him I
asked, "How come? You were right there in Sidney. Why didn't
you hook up at the magneto plant?"

Hugh wanted action. And, as he would soon discover, the para-
troops were looking for his type.

Down at Fort Eustis, another home-town boy, Splanaway, eight
years your Virginian's senior, after graduating from law school in
1937, had been clerking for Boilerplate. Leaving with the March
contingent of conscripts, by late winter of 1941, he surfaced with
an outfit in Virginia. Most of Splanaway's group shipped out from
its coast artillery training base at Fort Eustis to such colorful and
romantic spots of adventure as the then relatively unknown coast
artillery installation monikered Corregidor. But, at the last moment, when it would come to Splanaway's number, something happened. He was retained as cadre to help garrison his original post
on the East Coast. Boilerplate's understudy, on leave from the ex-
judge's Yankee Tier law office overlooking Lake Street, would soon
be thanking his lucky stars.

Actually, had chaps such as Phil Smith, Hugh Hogan and
Splanaway wanted to become writers, they were already in a day-
to-day process of generating lots of literary material. In contrast,
during off hours from your Virginian's job in the defense plant, in
one corner of his bedroom at the boarding house, your unaware
George Washington VI had set up a mini-office where he could get
behind his full-size Underwood and knock out some fiction. My
objective was to write some melodrama, maybe another *Wings* or
Dawn Patrol. But first, as advised by the experts in *The Writer's
Digest*, to improve my skills, I'd base my fiction on my current experiences. The story was "Night Shift," in which I saw saboteurs
operating against the nearby O&W railway trestle, and using small
aircraft to drop stuff *Luftwaffe*-style on the roof of our vital production lines. Factoring in a babe for reader interest, I named the
peppy redhead Marta.

My first problem soon surfaced. Sylvia, my contemporary sister, home in the Yankee Tier for a weekend, soon advised: "You've
obviously got lots of colorful material from your own experiences

incorporated in your story. But rid your copy of clichés. Then maybe your stuff will sell."

When I pressed for further details, honoring my request for some boiled-down criticism, my sister said, "Corn."

When you'd got through college barely passing your few English courses, there was nothing like having your Johnny-come-lately literary problems pinpointed so early on by such an expert! My sister, who'd been an English major, by now had become a Philadelphia proofreader for a book manufacturer. Yet, in spite of such early warning, my creative literary progress seemed slow. Off duty and afraid that I might miss something, I found it tough to stay away from the sugar bowl crowd working on the mademoiselles, when I should have been gluing my pants to the seat of a chair and conjuring up a scenario on my typewriter. But any letdown would soon be electrified by international and national developments that seemed to be saying, "Get ready to exploit the better stuff certain to become available. "So I kept plugging at the necessary preliminaries, self-instructing by doing.

Little did I realize that what I really needed was a crash course in wartime military journalism. But with no clues other than hunches from headlines as to just what might be in store for your unaware George Washington VI, there was no way under current circumstances to go out and get some formal instruction. Were I ever to get an induction notice but beat it by enlisting, and then get shipped overseas, I'd have to fly by the seat of my pants while endeavoring to write another *What Price Glory*.

So now, thanks to sister Sylvia, I was on the lookout for the intrusion of any corn, and I was all primed to consign it automatically to the dustbin as I got on with my aspirations of writing some melodramatic fiction, a play for Broadway, and, more feasible, some short fiction for the pulps or the slicks, making a debut in *SEP* my prime objective.

May: It's Still Downhill

Early in May, Italy annexed Ljubljana, capital of Slovenia—a Yugoslav territory—and the area surrounding it. FDR and Hitler swapped preachments. FDR declared that the United States was ever ready to fight again for its existence, while Hitler boasted that Germany and her allies could defeat any possible coalition in the world. Secretary of War Stimson urged the United States to use its navy to escort war supplies to Britain.

By May 6, eleven American fliers engaged in ferrying planes from Canada to Britain were reported to have been among 122 persons lost at sea when their ship was sunk by a torpedo. The United States banned all exports to the USSR of machinery or equipment needed for defense production. Haile Selassie returned to the Ethiopian throne he'd lost in 1936 to Italian armies.

On May 7, the House of Representatives voted 266 to 120 to seize foreign vessels tied up in American ports, while the House of Commons gave Winston Churchill a 447 to three vote of confidence.

The next day, waves of Nazi bombers swarmed over Britain concentrating on the Hull area. The British reported shooting down fifty of the raiders in thirty hours. Somehow or the other, Axis planes managed to extend their range sufficiently to raid the Suez canal zone. By May 9, three hundred RAF planes poured tons of bombs into Hamburg and Bremen. A day later, the *Luftwaffe* blitzed London, while the admiralty disclosed that 1,443 merchantmen had been sunk since the beginning of World War II. But the big political news was this: also on May 10, Rudolf Hess, Hitler's personal deputy, flew to Scotland and made a parachute landing near Glasgow. Thanks to a broken ankle, he was rushed to the hospital, where he was held incommunicado.

The next day, May 11, the *Luftwaffe* dumped 100,000 bombs on London, destroying the House of Commons chamber and damaging Westminster Abbey, Westminster Hall, the Egyptian section of the British museum and Big Ben. . . . . . . Boing. . . . bong. . . . boing! Hermann Goering got a cigar!

Two days after Hess dropped in on Scotland, the Germans stated that the Nazi leader was suffering from hallucinations and a mental disease. Admiral Darlan, Vichy vice-premier, conferred with Adolf Hitler. On May 13, the Germans declared the northern part of the Red Sea a war zone.

During mid-May, twenty-one flying fortresses completed a secret mass flight from the West Coast to Hawaii, FDR, concerned over Franco-German collaboration, appealed to the French people not to support the Petain policy. The United States Coast Guard, acting on FDR's orders, seized every French vessel, including the giant liner, *Normandie*, in U.S. harbors. The Bolivian government decreed expropriation of the Lloyd Aereo Boliviano, a German airline operating in Bolivia. Completed five months ahead of schedule, the 35,000-ton battleship *Washington* joined the fleet. In Africa, the key town of El Sollum on the Libyan border was stormed and recaptured by the British.

The politicos usually don't tell you all, but if you all believe that the basis of most all wars is economics, a ray of light now appeared. A postwar reconstruction program giving all nations access to raw materials and banishing nationalistic trade barriers was suggested by Secretary Hull in a radio address. Unfortunately, the idea was soon pigeonholed and the war between the haves and the have-nots picked up some more momentum.

From the British viewpoint, the war news was still very much downhill even though an Italian force of 7,000 surrendered to British forces in Alagi, Ethiopia. The Nazis, keeping the pot boiling, launched an aerial invasion of Crete, landing 7,000 parachute troops from gliders. Winston Churchill admitted that a serious battle was underway for mastery of the island. The German foreign office asked the United States to withdraw its diplomatic representative from Paris. A submarine, presumably German, sank the U.S. freighter *Robin Moor* in the South Atlantic. War could come most anytime.

Slotting In Some Social Life

As the possibility of our involvement in World War II heated up, we took advantage of the good spring weather and commenced making the most out of our skimpy weekends off.

A fine coed who'd been a freshman when I'd been a senior turned up. Over my short weekends, we went places and did things, watching the gliders soar at Harris Hill, while making sketches from the top of Turkey Hill.

Spring Day at Cornell rolled around. From Sidney by way of the old Catskill Turnpike, hurdling some hills on its remaining dirt stretches, I timely made that good campus scene. Taking in just enough of that unreality, I switched to another version. Down the hill I made my first return to the boathouse world. Since my coed friend was involved in the customary campus play that could keep running in spite of a storm, it was Sunday morning when I took up my observation post in front of the big bakery at the southeasterly corner of Lake Cayuga. Across the finish line came the eights. Although for four years running, ending two years earlier in 1939, I'd been an active participant, and primarily as a member of the varsity heavies, in substantially every crew race, whatever I now saw seemed relatively insignificant. Not only had the threat of war become the major factor in my life, but I got busy helping another lady friend inveigle her swain to pop the question.

Taken with my two years of postcollege work, primarily as a merchandiser with Monkey's, next picking up the quinine syndrome with Norwich, and now turning out magneto parts for Scintilla, this rowing sport that had once put Cornell on the map had a dangler—live and kicking and very clever dirty trick.

Now that the kangaroo aspects of the selection of a commodore at the end of my junior year had faded into oblivion, a spinoff of the political ambush was quietly cooking back on top of the hill in the Cornell University Athletic Department (CUAA). Some anonymous operative had scrubbed from the operating card files almost all of my four years of rowing records. Instead of showing my actually having rowed on the heavyweight freshman crew for the season ending June 1936, and the respective heavyweight varsity crews for the seasons ending June 1937 and June 1938, my clandestinely phonied down records at CUAA merely indicated that I had rowed only during my senior year, and then solely on the *junior* varsity, also known as the *second* varsity or the jayvees.

In addition, many of the news items covering my rowing participation would be scissored from the pertinent issues of *The Cornell Daily Sun* before they would be microfilmed for the University library.

As it would appear thirty years later, the facts of my varsity participation were always at the CUAA, but buried. When I would claim my senior-year varsity letter (based on two years in the varsity four-miler and one year in the jayvee three-miler at Poughkeepsie), Bob Kane would see to it that the basis of the long-delayed Major "C" award would be dug out of the old minute books.

The moral of the story: wherever you, my readers, have played on some college team, you should go back early on as well as later on and check up. I didn't. Thanks to the distraction of both the impending war and my new-found kewpie doll, now in June 1940, I never got the bright idea of following through to see to it that my rowing records at CUAA were intact in the operational card files.

Actually, while trusting implicitly the staff of the university athletic department, I was still playing it cool by ignoring the jay-vee letter that the then-preemptive commodore Jovial John had repeatedly suggested I go and pick up. Proffered for my senior year of rowing services to the University, the shunned item was a major "C" with a small "JV" inside. Actually for such senior year, because I'd met the requirements of participation at Poughkeepsie for three years, I had earned and was thus entitled to another varsity letter that would have been added to the two preceding varsity letters that I'd earned during each of my sophomore and my junior years. But this can of worms that had arisen mysteriously in the form of a surprise kangaroo court (for selection of commodore-elect) at the end of my junior year, tainting my senior year with a carry-over of such lack of fair play, once started, kept right on wriggling.

In a way, were I to be mysteriously shot down from a good job later on in industry (or even, for that matter, in the Armed Forces) because some personnel man had bought, without checking first with me, my clandestinely phonied down rowing record at CUAA, this silent downward switcheroo had created an invisible threat to my career. Should I try to make another go at it with big business, the unrealized scrubbing of practically all of my officially operative tally sheets would be an ever-present but unseen danger any time I would find something new to pitch into with the objective of becoming a substantial executive with some major industry.

With a war coming on, the mademoiselles commenced paying better attention, to the effect that a major dating problem with all of us potential conscripts lucky enough to have a good-paying job and a car was this: keeping our wires from getting crossed. And that perplexity, at the finish line of the crew races, got new impetus from cuties amongst the crowd. Most distracting just now as the chippy-chasing season of May roared towards June were the other tie-ins. Various dollies from one end of the Yankee Tier to the other, even working out with the various and sundry lovelies who played marvelous partners at checkers a hundred miles down the line in Pennsylvania, joined in to keep the romantic mishmash perking. And now that I was back on campus momentarily with former classmates on the verge of graduating from law school, who'd ever have thought of dropping in at the CUAA to investigate and maybe thus discover early on that phonying down that had taken place there of my rowing records? While I slept on, the anti-George Washington VI political occultists, inspired by the exploiters of George Washington's vast estates, continued to get away with one of their simplest and thus most economically effective cuts, chops and slices, one that would continue to do secret damage for more than three decades!

But keeping me from getting hep, what a distraction—a real kewpie doll of a rowing fan who lived right along my Owego-to-Scintilla path. After a storm had delayed the crew races to Sunday morning, I just had time to get back to work on the evening tour at Sidney, from whence I looked forward to seeing her on the following Saturday evening.

While I'd been taking so short a holiday, certain startling flashes had emanated from the front. The *Hood*, 42,500-ton British battle cruiser, was blown to bits by the 35,000-ton German battleship *Bismarck* between Greenland and Iceland. U.S. convoys aiding Britain would be regarded as a "plain act of war," German Grand Admiral Erich Raeder announced to the press. Britain threw a giant naval dragnet around the northeastern Atlantic in the quest for the *Bismarck*. A fifteen-minute test blackout was staged in Newark, New Jersey. Releasing a bit of pressure from your 23-year-old Virginian's age group, a new draft of all men who reached twenty-one after the first registration (of October 1940) was ordered by FDR. An estimated million youths would be affected. Au revoir to my new-found kewpie doll. Again I was looking forward to slotting some more social life into this long-hours defense-plant regimen. On May 27, the Tuesday after Spring Day, the *Bismarck* was sunk four hundred miles off the French coast, after a running sea battle with the British.

To the tune of such startling news bulletins, FDR stepped up the pace. A bit short of throwing the fat in the fire, the President proclaimed an unlimited national emergency to place the U.S. on a war footing. The administration at Scintilla reacted by extending our already-overworked overtime.

Chapter 11

The War Footing Under An Unlimited National Emergency

The Big Red Traffic Ticket

In spite of the long, money-making hours at Scintilla, until now I saw myself as having a comfortable excess of the old vinegar, as I continued to make the most of all-too-short weekends. Thanks to Harry Prew's haberdashery in Binghamton, my bolt of Burberry's fine wool herringbone material (purchased during last summer's traverse of the Province of Ontario) had been made into a made-to-measure suit, double-breasted and the first extra-long threads ever to properly drape my six-foot, four-inch frame. And during a marvelous date, kewpie doll approved. But came the next weekend my wires got crossed.

From the campus, the coed phoned. I was drafted to join a special luncheon at the Dutch Kitchen. But when I phoned a cancellation due to overwork to the kewpie doll, she must have smelled the rat and bounced back into the now more grasping arms of her swain. Once again I'd stirred up some competition, with a good friend as the beneficiary of highly hiked odds for wedding bells.

Now back to my coed soulmate. On the first Saturday of June, after a quick trip across the old Catskill turnpike, I joined a number of students and their respective dates for the extra special luncheon at the Dutch.

Little did I realize just how fatigue could sneak up to top off the recently extended long hours helping Uncle Sam play catch-up under our current unlimited national emergency that had placed us magneto-makers on a war footing. Until the wee small hours I'd been out dancing the mad fandango. And my favorite coed saw to it that the Tom Collinses kept coming. While I'd endeavor to limit intake to a couple, more would slip down the hatch, leading up to some great new but still scoreless holds and bear hugs with my fascinating date atop the popular lovers' leap on Turkey Hill.

Fatigue finally striking home at two A.M. was what put the quietus on all of those park-and-spark operations on top of the mount. Without my realizing it, my scores of miles of driving, while laying the basis for the catch-up of our national arsenal, was running down my battery. Playing the final end of both candles, I had returned my fascinating date safely to her dorm. Not long thereafter, ten miles down the road, I couldn't remember passing Danby, nor after another such count, Springdale, when, thirty miles or so down the general route of the erstwhile horse-drawn railway, I had just crossed Monkey Run and was entering the silent dark northerly portals of my home town of Owego. Around a quarter of a mile into the picture, I could gaze down at a lower level where the distant lights of the business district sparkled but dimly as they beckoned. Just minutes inside the village's north line, and around Cemetery Hill to the left, my nice comfortable extra-long bed was waiting. But first, just inside the village's dark portals and with the business district still far ahead, a village traffic cop appeared. Under my nose he was waving a great big traffic ticket. It was twice the size of a Montgomery Ward catalog and it was bright red! The shock awakened me! Just inside those northern approaches, I found myself driving down the wrong side of the road! Fortunately preserving us to eventually be able to set down for you all this yarn on paper, there was no such cop. Furthermore, the state highway during such wee small hours just happened to be empty. Soon, safely home, there was just time to grab some sleep and then hightail it the sixty miles or so back to my good-paying machinist's post at Scintilla. Illustrating the added difficulties of our now having to tackle our metal-working tasks under the full national emergency that had placed us on a war footing, a surprise package was waiting—a slave-to-machine gimmick that would physically dwarf the dramatics of the big red traffic ticket.

The Slave-To-Machine Double Bind

At the outset, this next gimmick, a slave-to-machine sort of thing, didn't have a semblance of a potential double bind. From a stand beside my lathe some trays of cast iron gear blanks greeted me upon my return to the evening tour. Ed Knight was in the process of setting up my machine. But not a word about the composition of our next target! Surprisingly, that metal in those blanks was going to be tricky. Kennametal and carbide-tipped bits or other specially designed cutting tools had either not yet been developed or, due to the war in Europe, were not obtainable, and if on hand in the tool crib, had not been assigned by the engineers and thus would not be applied to this job.

In the gear blanks, from the cooling after the casting process, diamond-hard zones of amorphous carbon had crystallized in such a way that unexpectedly they talked back at inconvenient moments to the bit. Just when I would really get going good at turning out finished product, one of such zones of extra hardness would knock the tip off the extra large bit that had been engaged in cutting the outside diameter. Simultaneously the gear blank would be wrenched from its chuck. Other times it would be jarred enough in the chuck to throw off the inside diameter. Eventually, some lines of a poem that I'd write for the benefit of some small-town politicos would read: "With a gear blank in a chuck and some buried diamond muck, / You will sweat and grind your bit against delay. . . ."

And once a tip was thus broken, this particular extra large bit, that had its sizeable top spot amongst the various tools doing in turn their thing on the turret lathe, would have to be ground down. Such size factor would in turn require a proportionately longer time as I'd sculpt with the grinding wheel the big bit's new cutting edge. Such a bit-grinding nuisance soon turned this machining of all of

these specially dredged up but otherwise very important gear blanks
into an awful drag.

Thanks to this ongoing wrestling with the curious nature of the
metal, all chances of making extra money on piecework vanished.
The hard spots of carbon in the gear blanks turned the metal-cutting job into straight time. Although this far outweighed my former
salaries with Monkey's and Norwich, the aspiration to outproduce
the time and motion study for extra pay found itself muffled.

While I was now making between forty and fifty dollars a week,
a machinist at a neighboring lathe, shaping easier-to-cut aluminum,
was making between sixty and ninety dollars a week. This little
bonanza came across to him as a veritable surprise package when
he carefully opened and peeked at the contents of his little brown
pay envelope.

But my realization that I was helping keep 'em flying kept me
plugging. . . . that was, until I got the idea that some of the straw
bosses, who'd heard one too many yarns about some simply great
successes at checker-playing on some short prewar weekends off,
were now having a good chuckle while grabbing glances from a
distance at the rare college man of the line, as he locked horns
with the amorphous carbon. But additionally, there was a critical
factor that they couldn't see, yet I could feel—this further irritant
that emerged.

To put the icing on the cake, while I can think of a couple of
other spots where a wart could have sprouted for more convenience
and extra special practicality, one of such doohickies complicated
the galling buried diamond muck by snatching a foothold on the
middle of the ball on the bottom front of my left foot. Its perks I
could feel as I threw levers on the Warner and Swasey Number
Three. In a mean sort of way, this unwanted visitor kept me feeling all bright-eyed and bushy tailed.

The wart had had its relatively unseen birth a year earlier back
at Monkey's. There the Dartmouth part of the Cornell-Dartmouth
densification had showed up sporting some brand-new brogues with
double soles that had inspired the Cornell half to play catch-up.
Making do with my Jarman wing tips, I took them to a cobbler.
Over his contrary advice, I instructed him to attach double soles.
It was a beautiful job but the shoes squeaked. So the cobbler put
nails in the soles in such a way that the squik-squawk, squeak-
squawk stopped. Left over was an unseen mini time bug. The

friction on the skin on the ball of my left foot from one of the bent-over shoe nails now, several months later, had caused this nice little teaser of a wart to sprout. It muted my gung-ho attitude here at Scintilla, where I was helping christen the brand-new building that had so recently been stuck on to the old part of the plant. Exacerbating the wart part of the war footing, we all had gone on sort of a super overtime. As mentioned, it was something like six-day weeks and around ten hours a day. All of those long hours on my dogs didn't help. And that wart on the bottom of my left one seemed to get worse as the zones of hardness in the gear blanks also kept serving notice that they too were going to stick.

By now I was playing doubles with management a few after-noons a week on Byron Dutcher's tennis courts. From the recrea-tional set, a kindly production manager took a turn at the pesky gear blanks. No help. And any suspicions that the straw bosses were having some fun went poof when the machinist ahead of me on daylights indicated that there was nothing to it. Furthermore his work product on display passed my inspection.

Putting the finishing touches on the emerging double bind, George Yarter, one of our key set-up men and a dedicated machin-ist, when he occasionally left his regular post in the old part to see how his former recruits were doing in the new part, would ask: "Do you like your job?"

The answer of course just now, anyway, just had to be, "Yes."

What got under my skin about it was this: what if the United States did get into the war? The various chaps who'd opt to keep their deferments by staying out here on the big floor to keep 'em cutting for the magneto manufacturer, so that the fine-tuned de-vices could then keep 'em flying for the nation's fighter pilots, would periodically be asked: "Do you like your job?"

How to challenge such a double bind? As soon as I got ready, chuck the deferment even though oncoming headlines would keep making my potential for going to war greater than ever. Which op-tion would become the lesser of two evils? What if Scintilla should eventually replace all draft-age men with women? Be that as it may, I wasn't getting in enough tennis. An idea commenced to shape itself in my mind. To beat the slave-to-machine double bind, why not start looking for some lesser-paying job, deferment or not, then live at home with a view of getting the best out of my remaining months of civilian life?

What To Do With A Deferment?

Under the unlimited national emergency in the United States, a deferment's value commenced to take on new life as we took in the wartime headlines from overseas. But, . . . under the circumstances, . . . what to do with this effective put-off?

After the prime minister of Ireland had warned Britain not to apply conscription to Ulster, Winston Churchill abandoned the plan to apply conscription to Northern Ireland. The Nazis captured the capital of Crete and were in the process of ousting British warships from Suda Bay. Near French Tunisia, the RAF attacked an Italian convoy. By May 29, the British started to evacuate Crete and the next day Anglo-Greek resistance collapsed.

Good news: For once the politicos demonstrated that they knew not only how to start but also to stop a war. In Baghdad, an armistice was signed ending the month-old war between Britain and Iraq. Four big bombs were mysteriously dropped on Dublin.

On June 1 came the announcement: the British were abandoning Crete. The next day Hitler and Mussolini conferred at the Brenner Pass. Hardly noticed on the home front, Charles Evans Hughes retired as Chief Justice of the United States Supreme Court. Also during early June, the British Labor Party at its 40th annual convention voted to continue the war until the Axis was crushed. The RAF bombed Beirut in preparation for an invasion of the French mandated territories of Syria and Lebanon. Axis planes staged their first air raid over Alexandria, Egypt. Rumors that the British were seeking peace were branded by FDR as falsehoods deliberately circulated by the Nazis. He also signed a bill authorizing the United States to requisition foreign ships lying idle in the nation's harbors. The British and the Free French successfully invaded Syria.

Until recently, there had been shocking indications of collaboration between the Nazis and the Soviets. But by June 11 there came some winds of change. Maybe we would no longer have to suspect that Russia and Germany might team up against the United States. Some relatively unnoticed headlines indicated that the massing of Nazi troops on Soviet frontiers was increasing tensions between Germany and the USSR. What to do about my deferment? How to get the best out of our remaining days of peace? Be a sport. Take a chance. Get a lesser-paid job closer to Owego and live at home, where I could play tennis occasionally with the Indian Princess. Chuck the deferment.

A Job Switch Gets Christened

While all of our attentions over war worries were focused on what was going on between Germany and Russia in Europe, the wart on the bottom of my left foot was turning into a slow burn over those gear blanks which kept locking horns with the hard spots of carbon—that buried diamond muck. Nevertheless, with most of such repetitive operations, I eventually got onto overcoming the obstacles and machined out finished parts to the effect that practically all of them (except those few that got wrenched out of the chuck) got the nod of approval from one of Scintilla's esteemed inspectors such as Royal Cooper. As I kissed off with fine tolerance batch after batch of work product, I felt a solid sense of achievement. Yet, as mentioned, the time had come. Very discreetly, I commenced to job-hunt.

In later decades, there would still be an old application form kicking around in my files, one for Bell Aircraft at Buffalo. Probably I filled it out but never got around to sending it in. With a war coming on, I wanted to stay in the Yankee Tier.

Sure. On one occasion or another I tried IBM. But their response always had a twist to it that would forever keep me from investing in their stock (even though it would turn out to be one of the best available opportunities). This time, as coached by some of my colleagues at Scintilla, I applied to be a model maker.

Through the wicket, Whitey Marinus, a very important cog of punch-card personnel, perused my filled-out application form, then said, "I see what you are trying to do."

In contrast, Slim Emerson at Link Aviation Devices, without my having realized it, may have been looking for some raw material to develop into a technical writer. When he learned of my aspiration to become an author of fiction, after mentioning his similar interest, he asked, "What's the difference between a story and an incident?"

While I likely came up with some explanation that I had soaked up out of *The Writer's Digest*, for the enlightenment of the reader, the dictionary indicates that a story is a strung-together series of events aimed at entertaining or informing, while the latter runs from a mere occurrence, through a minor event in a novel or a play, to an apparently minor conflict between parties that may have serious results.

So within easy commuting distance of Owego where, during off hours, I'd be able to implement the writing angle of my new line of march, I wound up with this new job on the north side of Binghamton, this time as an inspector, still in the aviation industry, but where magnetos would give way to a different flight-simulator phase. Slated to check parts going into the famed Link Trainer, I was to report to work in the plant on the north side of Binghamton on Monday after the Fourth of July.

While I would be making less money than at Scintilla, I would be off the production grind. And I could bet that my deferment would soon fall in.

In order to get this job, I had taken the liberty of skipping the final day of the six-day work week at Scintilla. Were there any medical facilities at the plant? First aid would have been a must. But I hadn't seen fit to make inquiries about treatment for my wart. So besides getting the new job at Binghamton, only twenty miles easterly, I was able get that pesky wart treated by Kennedy F. Rubert, our family doctor, who'd served as a lieutenant colonel during World War I in the U.S. Army Medical Corps. Taking his time with the acetic acid, Doctor Rubert poked away at the nuisance growth with the tip of a glass rod until he was satisfied. In due course I'd learn that the good doctor's treatment had turned the trick. But in the meanwhile, I was still walking around on a sore foot.

Back at the plant the week's first evening tour (also referred to as the night shift) was just commencing. My Warner and Swasey turret lathe greeted me. The operator from the day shift had just left and I prepared to get going again on those tricky gear blanks in which the metal had a few too many difficult-to-cope-with extra-hard, bit-busting areas. Just as I'd finished donning my apron and had locked the first raw gear blank in the chuck, Ed Knight, the currently assigned set-up man and one of the straw bosses, came a-hurrying down the production line. "Ben," he said, "before you go to work you have to go down to the far end of the line and see Jim Green."

He was the shop foreman, who knew how to build a magneto from the sparks on up. Just outside of his small glassed-in office the wiry five-footer looked up at your slim six-foot, four-inch unaware George Washington VI and demanded: "On this night shift we work six nights a week! Where were you for when we were winding up last week's schedule?"

Thinking that I'd be laughed at if I brought up the wart, I made a mistake. Instead of peeling off my left shoe and displaying the healing hole that had been so recently occupied by the wart, I said weakly: "I had a headache."

Averred the bossman: "Your headaches are my ass aches!"

It was then that I got up the nerve and told the bossman that I had latched on to another job down the Susquehanna valley and within easy commuting distance of home. "It starts in two weeks. But if you want me to stay here and work until then, I will," I volunteered.

"There," said the bossman. "You didn't have a headache after all, did you?"

"No," I replied weakly, still failing to explain that I'd been handicapped by the soreness from the wart on the bottom of my foot while I'd been locking horns with those tricky gear blanks.

"Well," said Jim. "You're going back to the old plant with George Yarter as your set-up man. We'll see how you make out."

It was time for me to grab my tool box and return to my January location. Back there I'd be working with old hands such as Don McGinnis and my original tutor, Wadsworth, hooked up for the duration. And from the viewpoint of the administration, I wouldn't be contaminating any of the recent recruits with my deferment-shunning, job-switching wanderlust. But nobody would have paid much of any attention anyway. All minds were focused on the news. German armies launched an invasion of the U.S.S.R. on three huge fronts stretching from the Baltic to the Black Sea; Nazi panzer units penetrated Russian Poland. Now that I was ensconced in the aviation industry, such was the makeup of the headlines that christened my first lateral move.

Scintilla Epilogue

Back with the regulars, but this time assigned to my own older machine, a test awaited me. I learned that instead of having to struggle with those freakish gear blanks, I'd be reverting to working with more manageable bar stock. George Yarter, playing it tough, walked up and handed me a blueprint. "Here it is. Go to it," he ordered.

"Aren't you going to set it up?" I asked.

"You're going to set it up," said Yarter.

Taking the blueprint, I said: "Oh."

Fading back to another position, Yarter kept peeking my way out of the corner of his eye. I proceeded to grind the necessary bits and set up the job. The part called for this time by the print was a little smaller in diameter but thicker than a silver dollar. The array of tools that I positioned soon was cutting outside and inside diameters. I put on a chamfer and faced the front, then cut off the part as designated on the print and faced its back. It was a relatively simple job but it was a Big First: with no help from the set-up man, your Virginian, back in that old part of the plant where, some few months earlier; he'd received his first trial, making it look easy had successfully set up his own machine.

Now that I was on the last two weeks of my deferment, I'd just gotten nicely started at spewing out accurately finished parts; in Europe, the mishmash on the Eastern Front commenced to boil over on the hot stove. Leading up to it, around mid-June FDR ordered the immediate freezing of all assets of Axis or Axis-occupied countries. Somehow or the other Japan was not included in the order. Italy retaliated by freezing United States funds in Italy. The closing of all German consulates, travel and propaganda agencies was ordered by the State Department. Secretary Ickes banned shipment of a quarter-million gallons of lubricating oil bound for Japan. Germany and Turkey signed a ten-year friendship treaty. Vying for some attention on the home front, Joe Louis KO'd Billy Conn in the 13th round of a close bout. Getting even for some recent walking papers that had been handed their officials, Germany and Italy expelled United States consuls in reprisal. Finland ordered a general mobilization. FDR branded the sinking of the

Robin Moor as an act of piracy and as a German effort to intimidate the United States. He placed a curb on oil shipments from the Atlantic coast to all countries save the Allies and Latin American nations. The Ford Motor Company signed a union shop contract with the United Automobile Workers (CIO). The United States ordered the Italian government to shut all of its consulates in U.S. territory. Damascus, capital of Syria, fell to British and Free French forces. As mentioned, on June 22, Hitler had attacked Russia. Economic and technical support was promised the USSR by Winston Churchill. Any state that fought against Hitler would have British aid, he added.

Now, back to Scintilla's ace machinist. While I'd been making a go of it without his services, my set-up man, George Yarter, had been inspecting operations on neighboring lathes but, as mentioned, had kept glancing furtively my way. Time ran out. On my own I kept 'em cutting. The expected summons from your Virginian for Yarter's help never got served. I'd ground all cutting tools, anchored them in place on the turret, and once everything was in place I kept right on turning out precision finished parts that passed inspection. Were Yarter surprised, his innocent look never once gave it away and your Virginian was even more surprised at his own success.

Eventually Yarter cast aside his mask. Moving alongside, he offered: "Ben, if you keep right on working like you have been working for the past week, you can stay right here and work."

Translated, this meant: "If you don't want to fight in the upcoming war, we like your production and you can stay right here where it's safe and make money."

But I told Yarter: "I like this company. Anyone who's had a hand in helping fashion parts going into a precision product such as a magneto earns a sense of accomplishment and can feel proud of himself. But I've recently figured out what I really want to do."

"What's that?"

"To be a writer."

"But you can't make a living at that like you can here at Scintilla, and you'll lose your deferment," said Yarter.

"I've thought of that. But my plan is to work where I can live at home, thus support myself while I'm training myself to write. Then, if war comes, one way or another, if only to get the raw material about which to write, I expect to be in it."

Yarter shrugged and walked off. He didn't again inquire as to whether I liked my job.

At the end of a daylight shift, my six months with Scintilla came to an end and I moved on out through the good offices of Mr. Van Name, the personnel director. Back in early January, my father's former business partner had phoned Mr. Van Name to tell him that I was coming in for a job interview, one that had been successful. So now, when it now came to saying goodbye, I explained my qualms. "I appreciate this job, but now that I have obtained a new one within easy commuting distance of home, it will give me some extra time to work at my sideline of writing. I hope that you don't begrudge my making the switch?"

But Mr. Van Name was very gracious about my situation. Out of six months on the production line, I'd missed only that one evening tour, and then it had been on account of the painful wart on the bottom of my foot. The personnel manager said: "No, we don't begrudge your leaving, and if you should later decide that you want to return, just let me know. When I was a young man I switched jobs frequently before I finally wound up here at Scintilla as personnel manager. Those different jobs I held gave me a better understanding of my current position. I can see things better from the viewpoint of the workers. So I happen to believe that for a young man such as you, it's a good thing to knock around a lot and try out different jobs."

Although Howard Lee Davis, author of *The Young Man in Business*, probably would have disagreed, my views just happened to coincide better with those of Mr. Van Name. With my resignation as a turret lathe operator I'd finished the first phase of my new line of march. To such sound of a different drummer I was now committed to the extent that as soon as the draft board would get caught up on their paper work, my deferment would be scrubbed and I'd soon be reclassified 1-A. After that, your Virginian shouldn't have very long to wait before the conscription bugle would trigger my enlistment. But while waiting, now to give some off-hours priorities to helping Owego live out its last prewar days as a tennis town.

Chapter 12

Link's Furnishes the Final Link

The Tune of a Couple of Missed Boats

This timing of my switch from Scintilla to Link's coincided with a couple of missed boats. Had I commenced premed studies at Harvard in September 1934 (my original professional aspiration), by now I'd be commencing my post-medical school internship. And should war break out, I soon would be an army medic.

And had I become a double registrant in Cornell Law School in September, 1938, along with Si Glann, Ralph German, and Norton L. Penny, right now I'd be sweating out the results of my bar exams. Although the military didn't go out of its way to find suitable slots for lawyers, had I already garnered this certificate, certainly it would have been the better course . . . . except that either of the foregoing paths of endeavor would have knocked me out of some two volumes worth of experiences as well as material still to be generated for upcoming volumes.

Keeping me from crying over these two missed boats, headlines kept blazoning colossal military events that were transpiring on the Eastern Front. From the outset, the Nazi panzer divisions were getting the upper hand. Following the lead of her Axis partner, Italy declared war on the USSR. Turkey proclaimed her neutrality. As the successful German motorized divisions kept cracking Soviet lines, Finland entered the war on the side of the Nazis, but only in a "defensive capacity" according to President Risto Ryti. By now, to us potential conscripts, it had become clear: were the Soviets to eventually hold, the war in Europe definitely was not going to peter out. While we still hoped that it would simply dry up, we had no choice but to enjoy the best of this current summer that might be our last.

Sure. Thoughts occasionally surfaced. Start now at age twenty-three to study for a profession. But what an excuse! Take these epic events, especially on the Eastern Front. What was going to be the spillover effect? The situation provided the excuse. Why knock yourself out studying for a profession? Before this thing would be over, you'd likely be called away from your books to go to war.

Helping muffle ambition were irrelevant excuses against using the family treasury such as, "You've already had more than my brothers got." (Some of my mother's brothers had worked in the coal mines.) Of that last argument, its author, making the most of what might well turn out to be her last chance, was now feeding me with garden-fresh cooked vegetables and fine cuts of roast beef, pork chops, etc. as though there were no tomorrow. After all, who knew where I might be a year hence. In muddy Europe? In the tropical Pacific taking quinine to ward off malaria? In our personal estimates, Asia currently took a back seat while the quinine syndrome still signaled that part of the war would take place in the tropics.

Were the United States soon to be drawn in, it looked as though the action was going to take place across the Atlantic. But we had these other contrary clues. Implementing the quinine syndrome, now that I was part of the Link Aviation work force, I picked up an interesting lead. With a view of learning how to build one of their own, Japanese technicians had taken a Link trainer apart but couldn't put it back together. When they sent for a Binghamton technician to fly to Tokyo and help them out, the request was rejected.

As current events now commence to illuminate the background of our saga, although previously mentioned, I would like to again stress *Britannica Book of the Year* as perhaps the principal source of such tight-knit items. More detailed events have been gleaned from *The Broken Seal,* by Ladislas Farago. And by the time of final drafts of this volume, two new books are called to the readers' attention: *Infamy,* by John Toland, as well as *And I Was There,* by Rear Admiral Edwin T. Layton, U.S.N. (Ret.). Where items are spelled out, I will endeavor to add pertinent credits. Explanations and assessments provided by these three books enliven the atmospherics under which your unaware George Washington VI was now living, and with the ever-present thought that his deferment that had previously been granted at the request of Scintilla was due to fall in.

Although students of military science well understood: for sure, trouble was due from the Orient. Yet, the expected source of the war was forseen to arise out of Europe, and with little or no real trouble to come from the Japanese. Telling the reader some of that which we didn't then know, Lieutenant Commander Alvin D. Kramer, chief of the translation section of ONI, zeroing in on pertinent intercepts, tells us now what was going on in the Japanese imperial conference: Germany had asked the Japanese to move against the Soviets but the Japanese had decided not to comply. Instead they would proceed with operations to strengthen their military position in French Indo-China. Finally the Japanese resolved to intensify their air operations in China.

After all, in World War I, the Japanese had been on our side! Making it look as though they might now at least keep off our backs, on the Fourth of July, Ambassador Nomura, in a personal letter to Secretary Hull, injected some serenity as follows: "I am glad to inform you that there is no divergence of view in the [Japanese] Government regarding its fundamental policy of adjusting Japanese-American relations on a fair basis."

The danger from the Tokyo sector of the Orient was thus muffled and it was under the gun that emanated not from Japan, but rather from Europe, that we tried to make the most of these seemingly halcyon months. While I worked on my fiction-writing sideline, and with a view of enhancing my skills to use any upcoming war for my raw material, I kept operating on an assumption that war would not come, and if it did, I'd forget my having missed out on med school or law school, and now make the most of these still-halcyon days, while I got ready to enlist.

Early July: Some Pertinent Developments

Local belles, much admired from days last past, yet always off on tangents leading toward the bigger guns, appeared on local beaches, where the subject of matrimony frequently took center stage.

When my cousin, Robert G. Dean, who'd already been called up from New Milford, Pennsylvania, with the reserves and who was also a great-great-grandson of Israel Dean, came to visit and put on a diving exhibition, one of the bathing beauties present couldn't get over just how much these two unaware George Washington VI's looked alike.

Bob and I had the same problem with these young ladies. There was this good recurring question: Whether or not to get hitched before Uncle Sam beckoned, so that you'd have someone to come home to? All in all, it looked as though we'd get snatched singly by Uncle Sam. And conscription, so the odds were shaping up, would beat out any matrimonial instincts.

Tilting the odds towards still sleeping single, just before the fourth, General Marshall, United States chief of staff, asked for immediate legislation to extend the military service of conscripts and national guardsmen and to permit the use of United State Armed forces *beyond* the Western Hemisphere. Just after the Fourth, the occupation of Iceland by United States naval and marine units was announced by FDR. The Nazi war machine was stalled on five principal sectors of the Russian front by Soviet counterattacks. Maxim Litvinov, former Soviet foreign commissar, exhorted the British to hurl their full weight against the Germans in the west.

An announcement from the German foreign office branded the United States occupation of Iceland as a "stab in the back." But the parliament of Iceland approved by a 39 to 3 vote the Reykjavik government's agreement permitting the occupation.

By July 11, additional appropriations totaling $3.3 billion for the Navy and the Merchant Marine were asked by FDR.

Belfast authorities confirmed the presence of United States technicians and laborers in Northern Ireland. Successfully, German mechanized units resumed their drive into the USSR. Behind the scenes, the government of Japan (as such secretive developments would later surface, thanks to the *The Broken Seal*, by Ladislas Farago) *almost* decided to join the Nazis on the liquidation of the Soviets. Arguments at once developed. The few days of vacillation eventually commenced to crystallize into a decision to move southward instead, and maybe, simultaneously, *eastward*. And little did we suspect Japan's designs on the United States. To all of us, the Nazis were the only potential enemy. Rather than trying to read current events between the lines, your Virginian continued to live out these halcyon weeks, using spare time for writing fiction, to wit: "Night Shift."

A Hero Of The Day

For the first time since graduating from college, I was living at home and commuting to work. Destination was Hillcrest, on the north end of the east side of the city of Binghamton, the actual site of Link Aviation Devices. From Owego, the one-way trip was less than thirty miles. There was no night shift to contend with. When I drove my own car I could go play tennis with my new Hedley racket that I'd purchased from Joe Berry, the lawyer who had his own law office in Binghamton and who ran a sporting goods store as a sideline. Just then the Binghamton Tennis Club had some fine clay courts where it was easy to get a game with a first-rate partner. What a way to spend some great late afternoons!

When there was no evening social engagement requiring that I drive my own car, for some reasonable weekly fee, LeRoy Kelley, an Owego neighbor and fellow worker from an adjoining department at Link's, would screech to a stop in front of my house early mornings, usually behind schedule. Then, making it up, piercing the foggy layers from the nearby Susquehanna River, there would ensure a wild, 70-mph ducking in and out, a passing of cars upriver on Route 17, skirting downtown Binghamton, crossing the Susquehanna and roaring north on Brandywine. Finally, on foot, from the company parking lot on the north end of the city, we'd sprint to punch in moments before the eight-A.M. deadline.

Just the way I wanted it, I was still with the aviation industry.

At Link's, I wasn't making as much money as at Scintilla. And my deferment was momentarily due to fall in. But at home, with our fine garden including strawberries, raspberries, and sweet corn, economically, as my father had hinted just before I'd hopped the Lackawanna flyer for Monkey's two years earlier, I was better off back here in the Yankee Tier.

As mentioned, my new job was a switcheroo from machinist to inspector's bench. The parts that I inspected before they went into a Link trainer, generally speaking, because of their relationship to that particular kind of organs on which you pumped with your feet to get the music-making wind—Link's original product—did not require the built-in precision in the sense of the close tolerances that had been required on the parts that had been fitted in to make up magnetos. At Scintilla we had met the challenge of producing to close tolerance to help ensure that our airmen wouldn't fall out of the sky. Here at Link's on trainer parts, the tolerances weren't as tight. But a knowledgeability was mandated as to the many parts that made up our final product, the simulated flying machine. So I sat at an inspection bench with Gordon V. Gallagher and Carl J. Kolly where we checked this new and more exotic flow of parts against prints.

Appropriate comments dripping with background color and philosophical angles were provided by the keepers of the time cards recording the flow of parts from manufacturing through inspection and on to assembly. Fred used to buy for a song bushel baskets full of old-fashioned pocket watches from New York City dealers, then peddle them upstate in the boondocks. A still older chap named Buda was good for comments on politics and religion. . . . "Nobody knows how I vote." Or, "Show me and I'll believe."

From a nearby production department an actual Englishman came over to inspection to greet his American counterpart. "My father fell during the retreat from Mons." His illustration from the last war kept us focused on news items that were trying awfully hard to lead us into the next.

Now, back to aviation devices; in spite of the lesser danger to the users of the end product, we all still had plenty of incentive to do all that we could to keep 'em flying. Link trainers were an important part of pilot training for national defense and we all kept learning all we could with a view of becoming better inspectors of this entirely different family of aviation-related parts.

There was a first-rate cafeteria where plant management sat down for lunch at tables in one corner, the workers at tables in the other three corners. The bosses took themselves seriously yet not too solemnly. They ran a tight ship, but it was a friendly, philosophical production rarely witnessed. This was because just about every member of the administration was also a licensed pilot flying part-time on his own and often on business with the company plane. Giving us a chance to participate vicariously, Gordon V. Gallagher presented the most recent yarn. "Slim Emerson was at the controls on a takeoff with Link's twin-motored executive aircraft from the Old Airport at Endicott. One motor conked. Bravely doing the inadvisable, almost the impossible, and at a dangerously low altitude, Slim did a U-turn on a dime and then, saving a possible washout, successfully landed our fancy company plane back at home base."

News of this quick-witted salvor's job ran through the plant like wildfire. Just before he turned back to the task at hand, Gordy Gallagher looked over from his slot on the inspection bench and dubbed Slim as the hero of the day. Our acclamation affirmed it.

Introduction To A Hot Pilot

When the time clock beckoned us to get back on the stick at Link's, today it was a case of, "Say hello to one of the Yankee Tier's best young hot pilots." Bob Stimming dropped into my inspection department to keep in touch with a fellow Tiogan. Hailing from north of Owego, occasionally he had his parents drop him off during early morning hours at 443 Main so that he could ride with me to work. As a holder of a pilot's license, he was the kind of flier management liked to assign to help put the finishing touches on the Link trainers almost ready for shipment. When the Girl Scouts arrived for an educational visitation and tried out the controls, Bob gladly taught them how to keep out of tailspins.

One day we made a dicker. I'd pay the rental fee for an hour's real flight in a Taylor Cub, while Stimming would handle the stick. From the administration building at the Old Airport at Endicott, I phoned my parents downstream less than ten miles at Owego. "Get out in the back yard and I'll wave to you," I instructed them.

It wasn't long and out of the side window (we were in a vertical bank and dropping rapidly) my eyes were sweeping the area below at the rear of our Owego house and barn. Then I saw them. From several hundred feet below, my mother, father, and sister Peggy were seen looking up from our rear lawn and hailing us. Then came the unexpected aftermath. Immediately to the north of our back lot loomed Sa-sa-na's Mountain (also known as Cemetery Hill). Next thing Stimming and I knew, our Taylor Cub was caught in the mount's downdraft. We were a hundred feet below the crest. For the first delicate, seesawing moments, it looked as though our single-engine craft was going to shake hands with the tall timber just below the top of the big bluff. A monument dedicated to Sa-sa-na and marking her grave was ahead and the tip of the white granite spire soon flashed by off starboard. Even then the treetops were still ticking by not far from our starboard wingtip. Little did I realize the danger until it was almost too late. But Stimming, at the first sign of trouble, had reacted instantly. Even though he had opened up the throttle, long branches of tall trees still reached for our starboard wingtip. For ten to fifteen seconds, a very brief interval that seemed like an hour, Stimming fought to maintain a straight course as our aircraft drilled forward on a course parallel to the fat steep face of the mount.

It was a fight of wills, the Cub's motor against the mountain's suction. Gradually our light plane shook itself loose and we cruised out across the valley floor on which the village of Owego spread itself out.

"Wow! That was a close one!" I shouted over the motor's roar.

Stimming, keeping his cool, shrugged. "That was nothing. Nothing at all. There was nothing to it," he answered calmly. His only admission that it had been a close one was this: From now on, but with one slight exception, Stimming kept the light plane climbing. The showplace where the Indian Princess lived in the village was far below. Stimming was impressed. We turned on the southeasterly leg of a triangular course across the Pennsylvania line to Quaker Lake. Twenty minutes later I spotted the Indian Princess sunning herself on the dock before her family's summer place. Stimming, to give both of us a much closer gander, buzzed the boathouse. The Indian Princess returned our wave. Sadly, we had no pontoons and it was time to head safely back to the Old Airport at Endicott.

Since Stimming had opted not to go to college, he didn't have the two years required to apply for the Aviation Cadets. But his head was so jampacked with practicalities that eventually, when the army would learn of Stimming's exploits, they'd develop him into a hot pilot of troop-carrying gliders. The all-American boy would then star in combat.

The First Major Far East Crisis Boils To A Head

In contrast to our halcyon life in the Yankee Tier was the mid-July war news that managed to get by the censors. Distracting us from this year's first major crisis in the Far East as it boiled to a head, headlines blazoned a breaching of the Stalin Line at all decisive points as announced by the German high command. An armistice to end the war in Syria was concluded between the British and Free French forces and the Vichy command. Great Britain and Russia signed a mutual aid pact agreeing not to sign a peace pact except by mutual consent. Moscow admitted the loss of 250,000 men, but claimed that the Nazis had lost 1,000,000. Thirteen German troopships, two destroyers and a tank-laden barge were sunk in the Baltic, Moscow also announced. In federal court in Brooklyn, thirty-three persons were indicted for acting as German espionage agents. Smolensk, 230 miles short of Moscow, was claimed by the Germans. An estimated 9,000,000 men were locked in battle on the Russian Front.

We paid lesser attention to the Orient. In Japan, the cabinet resigned that had been working under Prince Fumimaro Konoye, who promoted rapprochement with America while trying to play ball with the Axis. FDR issued a blacklist order freezing funds of 1,800 Latin American firms having Axis ties.

At home, Yankee Tier sports fans focused on Joe Di Maggio of the New York Yankees as he established a record, hitting safely in fifty-six consecutive games. The second draft lottery to determine the order in which an estimated 750,000 youths twenty-one years old would be conscripted was held in the City of Washington.

By July 18, in Tokyo, Japanese Premier Konoye formed a new cabinet, the third headed by him. But keeping the spotlight, the

Germans announced the "disintegration" of the Russian Front. Stalin assumed the post of defense commissar of the USSR. Bolivia nipped a subversive plot by Axis agents. The U.S.A. called upon private shippers to transfer an additional one hundred oil tankers to Britain, which launched a "V for Victory" drive in Axis-occupied countries.

On July 21 came word that FDR was urging Congress to keep trainees in the Army for more than the statutory year limit.

July 22, German-Finnish forces pressed a drive on the Leningrad front while Moscow admitted Nazi gains in the southern Ukraine sector.

A day later Vichy yielded to Tokyo's demands for military bases in Indo-China.

Over the weekend of July 25 and 26, Layton in *And I Was There* would eventually explain: . . . . twenty-four hours after Japanese troops entered Indo-China, the State Department announced the freezing of all Axis funds in the United States—and therefore trade with the United States. But FDR, heeding State's advice, allayed the navy's concerns reinforced with Churchill's fears that the American sanctions might force the Japanese to run amok, when the president personally reassured [Admiral Kichisaburo] Nomura [who had traveled in April to become Japan's new ambassador] that he did not yet intend the blanket embargo on trade to include oil exports. Nonetheless, Interior Secretary Ickes and anti-Japanese hardliners in State (led by Far East desk head Dr. Stanley K. Hornbeck) seized their chance to interpret the freeze order as an oil embargo, later interpreted by *The New York Times* as the most drastic blow short of war.

On the same day, the army announced the recall to active duty of General MacArthur as commander in chief of U.S. forces in the Far East. This signaled the start of a major reinforcement in the Philippines as a strategic deterrent against a Japanese southward move to grab the oil reserves of the Dutch East Indies.

Passing unnoticed by our gang of analysts in the work force at Link's, strategic doctrines of both the Rainbow 5 war plan (which envisaged dealing with Germany in the Atlantic and holding Japan in the Pacific) and a twenty-year-old policy *not* to make any major commitment of American forces west of Hawaii, were thus reversed.

Layton would point out that neither the army nor our already overstretched fleet at Hawaii would be able to defend the Philippines with untrained troops at the end of an exposed and insufficient ocean supply line.

Now back to gleanings from *Britannica*. By July 26, FDR placed the Armed Forces of the Philippines under U.S. command. Japan froze U.S. and British assets (as Britain had acted with the United States in freezing all Japanese assets). U.S. defense agencies froze all stocks of raw silks. Britain announced the termination of its British-Indian Burman trade treaties with Japan.

On July 27, all possible U.S. aid to the USSR was pledged by Harry Hopkins, lend-lease coordinator, in a broadcast from London.

A day later, the Dutch East Indies suspended that government's oil agreement with Japan in a general order freezing all Japanese assets.

By July 29, in the Smolensk area, the Red Army claimed that it had dislodged the Nazis.

Near the end of the month, the USSR worked out an agreement with the Polish government-in-exile. It ended an existing state of war and the USSR agreed to recognize the Polish frontiers prior to the Soviet-Nazi pact of September 1939.

Winding up the first major-crises month of 1941, the USA accepted Japan's prompt apology for the bombing of the American gunboat *Tutuila* at Chungking, China. And the RAF, in the first direct military support given by Britain to Russia, attacked the Finnish port of Petsamo and the Nazi-held port of Kirkenes in Norway.

But as Farago would indicate, by early August some nice choice information was being withheld for security reasons by top federal analysts. A complete revelation of the recent Japanese imperial conference as intercepted for the U.S. high command by a unit led by Lieutenant Commander Kramer enabled him to present these conclusions: Japan would not go to war against the USSR in the north. Japan would intensify preparations for "the southward move." Japan would immediately begin to arm for all-out war against Britain and the United States to break, as Kramer quoted from one of his actual intercepts, "the British-American encirclement."

But between the Sugar Bowl crowd at Owego and Link's work force at Hillcrest, thanks to all of those great distractions rising from the battlefields of Europe, how little notice did we all take of the more dangerous implications of this first major crises of 1941 in the Far East that might well go on to generate the real thing!

A Scoffer Reverses Himself

Had the still-secret information surfaced about the behind-the-scenes jockying around between the USA and Japan, it would have read more like fiction. And that's what your unaware George Washington VI was endeavoring to write during evenings and weekends—some of the real marketable stuff.

When Slim Emerson's request to see some of my copy was met, while he didn't expect the slick magazines to commence calling for more, he did realize that I hadn't been joking about this aspiration to write.

Had we been Pacific-oriented, we might have conjured up an imagined yarn that would have mirrored current events. But now, as I got out and dusted off, as mentioned, my old textbooks left over from college classes in English, I found myself also inspired by various how-to features fished out of *The Writer's Digest.* Therein the professionals offered practical advice to beginning writers. Just as Rome wasn't built in a day, I soon discovered that it took lots of time and sweat to knock out some short fiction, let alone try to sell it right crack off the bat to *The Saturday Evening Post (SEP).* Using my recent experiences in the magneto factory as a basis, my first objective was a far cry from the Pacific. I commenced to flesh out and polish up my previously written yarn entitled "Night Shift," detailing an imagined attack by saboteurs on a vital East Coast defense plant. After my current position at Link's, while I was thus moonlighting on my own account, a good supper at home followed by a sundae at the Sugar Bowl with a couple of local maidens would chase away my fatigue from the day's work at the factory. After making the most out of such abbreviated social contacts, I'd vanish into my third-floor office. A whole new life behind the typewriter commenced. For at least two hours evenings, I'd dream up various short story outlines, decide on the direction in which to concentrate any leftover energies, and then plug away behind the Underwood, gradually building up a manuscript. It was then that I learned that the unaware George Washington V was downstairs scoffing at the unaware George Washington VI.

My very loyal younger sister soon passed along the word that below in the living room, my father was having a considerable snicker over my literary efforts. Accompanying his characteristic terseness were a few well-timed scoffs. While I thought that he was nuts, his snickers behind my back continued for around a week. Then my father broke down and in a rare moment took the initiative and made what was for him a rare apology and confession.

"I've been thinking it over about your sideline of writing. Maybe you heard of it and didn't like my scoffing. But now I want you to know that there's nothing so unexpected about your having this literary aspiration."

"How do you figure?" I asked, and with no little display of amazement at the reversal, and on his own motion!

"My father, who was your grandfather, Frederick Wellington Dean, he was a writer," announced my father.

"He ran for Congress against McFadden in 1914?"

"Yes. Besides being a farmer, produce shipper, and beekeeper, he was also a writer."

"What sort of stuff did he write?" I asked.

"He wrote agricultural features for newspapers and journals in New York City, Newark, New Jersey, and Pittsburgh, Pennsylvania," said my father. "Part of the time he exposed brokers who charged farmers both a commission and a markup when marketing their produce."

This about grandfather's writings was all news to me. But I managed to comment: "That figures. Then the knack must have leapfrogged you." I brightened up.

Keeping his options open, Dad explained, "Maybe I just haven't gotten around to it yet." (As I would get hep decades later, he'd already kept a diary for a year. Reflecting his experience during the early nineteen-twenties, one of his many years in the feed milling business has been polished up and factored into Volume I of this saga. And in later years, Dad would write a memo of his early days in grammar school at New Milford.)

"Then I take it that there are to be no more little snickers about my new literary sideline here at home?"

"That's right. There's probably no money in it for you. But since you're making a living working days at your regular job, if you hit the jackpot, it will be all gravy. In the meanwhile you'll have to do as you think best." Astoundingly, the unaware George Washington V had not only reversed himself, but also he'd given my literary sideline the laying on of hands.

The War News of Early August

Making me even dizzier than my father's confession of confidence was the war news of early August. Since most all of us saw no immediate threat from Japan, it was of seemingly minor portent when Undersecretary of State Welles assailed Vichy's cession of Indo-China bases to Tokyo.

At home, the U.S. ordered a rationing of rayon to avert dislocation of 175,000 silk mill workers. A voluntary curfew on gasoline sales from 7 P.M. to 7 A.M. went into effect in 13 Eastern states. A tax bill topping $3 billion was voted 369 to 40 by the House of Representatives.

Conflicting claims from the front: the German high command claimed the capture of 895,000 prisoners in the Russian campaign and estimated Soviet casualties at 3,000,000 dead and wounded. The Soviet information bureau put German casualties since the beginning of the Russian campaign at 1,500,000, while estimating Russian losses at 600,000.

On August 7, a bill to extend army service to thirty months passed in the U.S. Senate by a 45 to 30 vote.

By August 8, twenty-five Soviet divisions were trapped in a Nazi pincer movement in the Ukraine, according to the Germans. Vichy military observers estimated Nazi losses at 1,500,000 and Russian losses at 2,000,000 in the first 48 days of warfare on the Russian front. Into all three major fronts of the Russian theater, the Nazis hurled large masses of men and material. And in the Odessa and Krivoi Rog sectors of the Ukraine, Red Army units there were reportedly being pocketed by the Germans.

By August 12, a bill extending army service to thirty months was approved by a single vote in the House of Representatives, the final ballot being 203 to 202.

As *Britannica* would brief it: in a historic meeting aboard a British battleship "somewhere in the Atlantic," FDR and Churchill agreed on an eight-point declaration of war and peace aims and pledged themselves to the common goal of "destroying Nazi tyranny." Decades later, a more detailed explanation of this one of the most consequential, but little understood, meetings in history (that was held in foggy Placentia Bay on the bleak southern coast of Newfoundland), aboard *Prince of Wales*, Monday, August 11, would eventually be provided in Layton's books. There was at least one indication of an unwritten alliance. Layton would also point out that the Atlantic Charter wasn't signed (constitutional issues being involved), all of this being a bit over the heads of most all of us potential conscripts waiting for the draft board to get itchier. Yet we realized that more than ever before, something was up!

A Culver Cadet Sidetracks A Winnah!

Two years earlier when I'd left for Monkey's at Ann Arbor, I'd expected an occasional house-sponsored outing. There were none. But factored in with Link's putting a lot of guys in a simulated sky, here and now, in August 1941, came the real thing.

So far as I know, your Virginian was just about the only college graduate amongst Link's crew. If any of my coworkers had so much as a year in a university, in these days before SUNY Binghamton (after which a big percentage of mothers' sons and daughters would eventually sport a college degree), I never heard of it.

But halls of ivy or not . . . . did these chaps ever know all about college-town horseplay! Heading the list was one that would have nonplussed the class of '39's mischievous Mercer. It one-upped the antics I'd either witnessed or participated in five years earlier during that Mercer-sparkplugged clownery at Sheldon Court.

Here it was, mid-August 1941. In perfect Saturday afternoon weather, the company picnic took place in a glade off the Colesville Road where the professional proprietor served up delicious corn on the cob, steamed clams, broiled chicken . . . . you name it.

Along with our ducats went all of the draft beer we could drink. And therein was this new angle. Who was the best shot? You could sling a glass of beer, not the container, just the stream of beer, across a couple of loaded picnic tables, and hit a target broadside. Naturally there were countershots. Soon, long streams of catapulted beer were making a constant pattern of cross fire over the heads of chowhounds lining the picnic tables. But just what sort of trouble might break out? If anybody knew, it was your Virginian. In College Town just four and a half years earlier, as result of Deke's surprise blow that had boomeranged, having been involved in the worst of the results, I now kept to the sidelines while staying alert for backfire. Suddenly I felt a sense of relief. Outing from the kitchen area and taking the center of the stage, the older-generation proprietor huffed and he puffed as he rapped for attention. His telling lecture that emphasized the strong possibility of serious personal injuries influenced a halt to the horseplay.

When the boys promptly settled down, the program chairman kept things moving by announcing the next prize—a greased pig.

Cocking his ears was my pilot friend Stimming. After our near collision with the high side of Sa-sa-na's Mountain, this graduate of the school of hard knocks saw a good chance to conquer a much smaller nearby butte. But first he found some fortuitous special private counsel. An esteemed older licensed pilot and member of Link's administration, when he took note of the avid interest in the far blue yonder that Stimming now evinced, advised: "Listen carefully. What I'm about to tell you is worth a small fortune. The way to catch the greased pig is to goose him with the index finger of one hand while wedging the wrist of your other hand in his mouth. No one else here knows that trick. Now let's see you grab that porker."

Another gent expecting to be a strong contender was Fred Livermore, former member of the Owego Free Academy all-conference undefeated football team. But since he now was just finishing up his last full course of sweet corn, he was out of earshot and missed the tip.

Soon the greased pig was let loose. From the start line two dozen contenders, wild Indian-like, focused their sprints on the pig that went up and over the nearby butte and out of sight. Hot on the porker's heels and leading the van disappeared Stimming, but with Fred Livermore barely off the pace. Then came the waiting period when the low hill screened out observations of the real action.

Eventually, from the other side of the small butte, who came back across the flat floor of our bowl in the hills with the pig? None other than Stimming, the winnah!

While Fred Livermore who'd been first to grab the pig was wondering just how it had gotten through his fingers, for the better-coached Stimming, the two-pronged attack had worked.

"This catch is worth half a week's salary." Sticking out his chest, Stimming displayed the pig to his many admirers. Translated, such economic gain would soon become the crux of our chapter. It would be a foot in the door for a down payment on a brand-new Culver Cadet, that red-hot, low-winged monoplane then sizzling on the private aviation market.

After taking delivery, as a first-time owner of his own aircraft, Stimming was welcomed into the inner sanctum of Link's stable of hot pilots. Did your Virginian get a lift? No. Circumstances decreed that Stimming would commence living in a different world. No wonder. Not only was the countdown to potential conscription moving at much too rapid a rate, but also an army captain would soon inveigle Stimming into flying him to the City of Washington on important government business. During the final half hour of the flight, an argument ensued. Who was going to land the plane? It was unusual for our all-American boy to lose an argument. But this time rank carried the day. When the captain won, he washed out the landing gear of the Culver Cadet. This meant that for the next few weekends, the taproom at the Ahwaga with its lining of customary mademoiselles and their escorts, the program being presided over by Dwight Decker, would be minus Stimming's much-valued company as he found the ways and the means to get to Washington and get his plane repaired. Although we all missed Stimming, we had no choice but to grin and bear it. The Culver Cadet had sidetracked the winnah!

Some Late-August Headlines

Winding up the month of August, flashes from the Eastern Front depicted German panzer divisions reaching the coast of the Black Sea near Odessa and Nikolayev. RAF bombers set fires in Berlin and blasted the Krupp works in Essen. By mid-August 300 of such heavy bombers blasted three German cities. The Nazis announced a twin drive on Leningrad coupled with a new offensive in the central sector. The fall of Nikolayev, a Soviet naval base on the Black Sea, was admitted by Moscow.

Great Britain and the USSR jointly warned Iran to curb infiltration of Nazi "tourists" and technicians. An Anglo-Soviet trade treaty was signed. The ferrying of combat planes to the British Near East via Brazil and Africa was announced by FDR. Drifting across newsprint inked with yarns of the heavy military operations, especially in Russia, came news of some seeming disruption of the rights of Americans in the Orient. Rising to the occasion, United States Ambassador Joseph Grew protested against Tokyo's refusal to allow the departure of a group of U.S. citizens stranded in Japan.

On the home front, by August 18, the United States ordered a census of all foreign-owned property. The next day the War Department announced a measure to release conscripts and national guardsmen from active duty after 14 to 18 months of service.

Also by August 19, the German Army hammered Russian forces falling back toward Leningrad while other German units laid siege to Odessa. Marshal Budenny, commander of Red Army units in the Ukraine, was reported to have blown up the huge Dnieper dam. The Nazis claimed advances at Leningrad, Kiev, and on the lower Dnieper.

In Paris, two alleged communists were executed and scores were arrested. Back on the home front, a 26.6 percent cut in passenger motor car production was ordered from August to December of 1941. North of Leningrad, Finnish troops announced the capture of Kaekisalmi. Prophetically, on August 24, Churchill told Japan that Britain would side with the United States in the event of trouble in the Far East. Berlin announced that twenty-five merchant ships in a British convoy were sunk by Nazi U-boats and surface craft. On August 25, Soviet and British troops simultaneously marched into Iran. The British occupied the vital southern oil fields while Red Army units to the north marched into Tabriz. Hitler's legions captured Dnepropetrovsk in the Ukraine, where Moscow confirmed the destruction of the huge dam.

By August 28, in swift reprisals for the wave of sabotage sweeping France, the Vichy government had three men executed on the guillotine. Hitler and Mussolini held a five-day parley on the Russian front. Tallinn, the capital of Estonia, fell in bitter fighting to the Nazis. Making it look as though maybe the war in Europe wasn't quite so serious, the U.S. War Department announced plans to release 200,000 men from the Army by December 10, 1941, with special consideration to be given to conscripts and national guardsmen over 28 and enlisted men with three years of duty.

W. Averell Harriman, U.S. minister to London, was appointed by FDR to head the U.S. delegation to the Anglo-American-Russian conference in Moscow.

Back in France, firing squads in Paris shot eight men on charges of espionage and terrorism.

By August 30, the Finnish Army captured Viborg, taken by the Soviets after the Russo-Finnish war of 1939–1940. On the Russian front, as August came to a close, Soviet forces launched heavy counterattacks against Nazi positions in the central sector and along the Dnieper River in the Ukraine. Providing headlines that sold lots of late-August newspapers, the war in eastern Europe was hotter than ever.

Petula Steps Out On Center Stage

In Binghamton there was an ongoing mixed bag of midsummer dates that got us by very nicely from quitting-bell tennis to late evening dances, with the dark of the night usually being finessed at the faddish fast-food stop monikered the Pig Stand.

Then came race track time at Saratoga. As we had prearranged it, with a royal inspector friend from Scintilla, there was a good dog-days junket to the glittering show at which no fringe benefits with neighboring mademoiselles got left out. After a couple of royal bets on which the jockey wouldn't let his nag come in, over at the swimming pool at the spa, we got acquainted with Senorita Sanchez, my first envisioning up close of a Cuban bathing beauty, one still ensconced in Manhattan with her distinguished-looking folks as they were all present on holiday. But, alas, during the rush of events, we would never again manage to further this fine swimming-pool receptiveness to win friends and influence people.

Easing the pain, Carl Kolly invited me to spend a Saturday

evening with some friends back at the Triple Cities, at his father's tavern. When I stuck to lemonade, I thought that I was safe. But such a flavor, much to my unawareness, served to disguise the gin. After one too many, I barely managed to stop for all red lights as I homed for fifteen miles westerly through Johnson City and Endicott.

In the morning, I went down to a Labor Day breakfast with a couple of visitors from Philadelphia. My sister Sylvia and her friend Swede, a navy officer on leave from the battleship *North Carolina*, indicated that they had been impressed by my heavy-footed return. Said Sylvia, "When you flopped into bed, like a ton of bricks you shook the whole house."

After hearing about Swede's brushes with some U-boats, your unaware George Washington VI headed for the tennis court to quickly dry out in a game of doubles organized by Don Davis, the erstwhile member of the Cornell varsity tennis team, Vinnie Richards having been a teammate.

With that Cuban beauty at the spa out of sight but not out of mind, a replacement would fatefully forestall my early trip to Manhattan to track her down.

Out on the shop floor, at my inspector's bench where I was checking trainer parts for accuracy, some days I felt a little underemployed and bored. Some days I wished that the United States would declare war and get it over with. This was one of such slow days. From behind my bench, I looked up with surprise. Parading the plant with some Yankee Tier society girls was my tennis-playing associate, the Owego Eagle. What had gripped the young ladies in his entourage—especially a beautiful redhead—with some nice little but obvious fever was this: For almost a year, the Eagle had been Owego's spearhead in the war. On the preceding December he'd enlisted in the RCAF where he'd quickly won his wings flying fighter aircraft. Just now, in civvies and home on leave, he was getting rested up before returning to Canada to go through some advanced flying training and then head for England, where he'd eventually be participating in fighter sweeps over the Nazi-held part of the Continent.

On this particular afternoon, none other than the company owner, that famed inventive genius, Ed Link, was giving a Cook's tour to the Eagle and his scintillating companions. Just beyond my workbench, one lovely brunette caught my eye. Right before the Eagle returned to his Aylmer air base with the RCAF, he let loose the necessary data about his date's good friend. So I promptly called up this other doll whom my eye had singled out from the Cook's tour, and got a date.

A big-name band was wowing the couples jampacking the pavilion at Johnson City. Just then one unaware George Washington VI encountered another. Up sashayed an army lieutenant and proferred a hand. It was cousin Robert Glenn Dean, also a great-great-grandson of Israel Dean, and, as to facial features (but not as to stature), also a look-alike of George Washington.

Although cousin Bob was only a scant two years older, being an only child must have helped, and he had graduated from the University of Florida, where he had been a double registrant, getting his undergraduate and law degrees in a total of six years. By now he was a member of both the Florida and Pennsylvania bars. Having taken advanced ROTC, he had an inside track on pilot training, troop carriers being his assignment. In my civvie threads, with my double-breasted Burberry's suit, white shirt, silk tie, and white shoes, I easily held my own. Yet so great was my surprise at seeing Bob in his impressive officer's uniform topped of with pilot's insignia that for the moment, while I was commencing to introduce Petula, his name escaped me.

Failing to understand my hesitancy, the two tiny but beautiful Polish girls in his company pointed their fingers and cried out, "Look at him. Look at him. See how tall he is."

At six-feet, four-inches, I loomed over cousin Bob by several inches. But I managed to hold my tongue just long enough to collect my wits and make the introductions. Forgetting all of the feminine giggles and finger-pointing, it was strike up the band. Dancing with Petula was just out of this world. And I wrote off all of these cute little squeals. This ongoing war footing under our unlimited national emergency could account for almost anything.

But with Petula, headlines of war took a back seat and the ever-present threat of the draft board to lower the boom seemed nonexistent. Learning to hate the potential enemy in Europe would have to wait for this Petula and your Virginian to finish watching Errol Flynn cavort on the screen in *Custer's Last Stand*. Afterwards, in one of the Yankee Tier's other silk-stocking districts, "Follow Flynn" was the motto as we topped off the evening with a raid on Petula's family refrigerator. The timing for this new romance couldn't have been a better buffer. My favorite straw blonde, Columbine, as word had it, was getting more and more involved at graduate school with her favorite slicer, now completing his internship.

But so what? With your Virginian on the outside track with the birdie two hundred miles away on the East Coast, this Petula was at least momentarily in hand in the Yankee Tier, and, much more than a consolation prize, soon had nipped Columbine from my noggin's deepfreeze to the effect that it was goodbye, straw blonde, and hello, brunette whose daddy was an old friend of father.

These were the good halcyon days in the Yankee Tier, where we were still well-insulated by the Atlantic from the Four Horsemen of the Apocalypse, confined to headlines now being generated on the Eastern Front. At home, Petula continued to hold the center of the stage, that was until she soon shuffled off to Buffalo, en route by rail for a year at some extra special finishing school in the Midwest, leaving your Virginian to concentrate on his fiction writing.

Launching A Nice Try For The Aviation Cadets

At Link Aviation Devices deferments weren't dished out the way they were to the slaves of turret lathes, milling machines, etc. making highly precise operational parts for the magnetos of fighter aircraft engines, etc., as such "stay home and work your tail off" ducats had been practically forced on us when I'd been hooked up at Scintilla.

When my deferment fell in during the last half of summer, the fateful postcard came as no surprise. The draft board had finally caught up. After my having been deferred at Scintilla, I greeted this new notice with a laugh. As expected, I was reclassified as 1-A. This meant that any time now, the bugle could blow. I'd be getting one month's notice to ship out on the Lackawanna with the next contingent of conscripts. But not just yet, if you please, Uncle Sam.

From his post, where he was tagging another Link Trainer for shipment, Stimming turned and, seeing the 1-A, enviously declared, "With your more than two years of college, if I had that qualification, I'd already be in the Aviation Cadets. That's the way to go."

Thanks to such an extraordinary dose of aviation atmospherics that you absorbed every time you turned around at Link's, why not let Ed Link, the great inventor, put another guy in the sky? Never mindful of the eventual obvious danger, I put together my application for the Aviation Cadets. Recommends were quickly typed up and signed by Attorneys Abacanocus and Young Dingle, along with Kennedy F. Rubert, who, as mentioned, was the family doctor who'd served in World War I as a lieutenant colonel in the medical corps.

When the draft board got notice of my application for the Cadets, they instructed me to go right ahead, become a fighter pilot if that's the way I wanted it. In accordance with the practice, the board then temporarily called off its dogs.

For flying training, in the federal building at Binghamton, it soon came time to take the physical. After failing to find a hernia, an Army Air Corps major demonstrated that I was deaf in one ear. But promptly restoring my hearing, the magician poked masterfully with some fancy nickle-plated instrument and extracted painfully a plug of wax that looked like a twenty-two bullet.

Now for the critical part of the exam. Into my eyes went the customary dilating drops, and I donned dark glasses while awaiting dilation of the pupils so that the major could peer inside with his bright light. Simultaneously asking questions and making notes (as though pinch-hitting for a shrink), he took me by surprise: "Have you ever had a piece of tail?"

I wondered, "Are the wowsers lowering the boom on all candidates who said, 'Yes,' " And out of such perplexity came some hesitancy. With all of the checker-playing that had been going on, should I let it all come out? But what was the secret policy of the Cadets? For my first post-college job, Monkey's had made it clear. They had expected a trainee to get married and settle down. What if a guy had been laid but wasn't married? Were the Cadets, Monkey's-like, going to hold such a sideline against such an applicant? Wondering whether I might be bucking up against some wowsers-in-brass-hats who unexpectedly had infiltrated the military, I held back. This made the major suspicious.

"Take your glasses off," he commanded.

In a jiffy the major found himself looking into a couple of

piercing, burning orbs. "What's this all about?" I tried to conceal my irritation.

"You ever ding-donged [I cleaned it up] a woman?" The major pressed.

"Suppose I have? What's that got to do with flying one of your crates?" (I almost told him that a few years earlier, and within a stone's throw, at a since-padlocked checker-playing parlor, the doll had said, "Come on, big boy. How about a tip?")

"That's OK," said the major. "We just want to be sure."

"You want to see for yourself?" I asked (thinking that perhaps the major too could get fixed up simultanously, on down the line sixty or so miles where babes as pretty as chorus girls lined up to be selected as checker-playing partners.)

"That's all right," said the major. "You pass."

"Thanks," I said, and with a sense of relief that maybe, after all, the wowsers weren't running the Aviation Cadets, because were war going to soon become the real thing, I expected it to be the wild life just like I'd inferred it to be from such flicks as *Hell's Angels, Dawn Patrol,* and *Wings.*

But then came the vision test. Twenty-twenty was the watchword. My readings of the charts were close enough so that I thought that I'd make the grade. And while the major alerted me as to a potential vision problem, he didn't turn thumbs down then and there, so I headed back to Owego thinking that because the exam board had withheld judgment, perhaps the notice I'd soon get from Washington would include my instructions to proceed to an assigned air field for pilot training.

Some More Hustle For The War Footing

Providing plenty of hustle for our war footing, in early September, Berlin reported that Nazi troops had entered the suburb of Krasnoe Selo, only twenty miles from Leningrad. Hitler and Mussolini decided to unite all Europe into a single "harmonious cooperation of all European peoples," according to *Il Duce's* newspaper. At Smolensk, the Red Army was counterattacking successfully while units of the German Army were driving toward Kharkov in the Ukraine.

Keeping the spotlight directed on the Atlantic, a U-boat attacked the U.S. destroyer *Greer* en route to Iceland with mail. The *Greer* counterattacked with depth charges. U.S. plane production in August 1941 reached a record high of 1,854. FDR authorized the use of lend-lease funds to supply Polish troops in Canada.

Back on the Eastern Front, long-range German artillery shelled Leningrad while the Red Army there staged a counterattack. In warmer climes, British submarines torpedoed five Italian vessels, including a liner and a cruiser, in the Straits of Messina. By September 6, a furious battle was developing at Leningrad, while other units of the Red Army farther south still held Kiev and Zaporozhe.

Momentarily, we forgot the unlimited national emergency when Robert L. Riggs won the U.S. men's singles title. But the overshadowing threat from Europe soon made tennis begin to look sort of insignificant. With the advent of cool fall weather, your Virginian got ready to hang up his Hedley tennis racket and work harder than ever during spare time, writing some fiction that he hoped would sell. But it was difficult to conjure up anything that could outdraw the daily headlines.

In the Red Sea, the U.S. freighter *Steel Seafarer* was bombed by an unidentified plane. An Allied force landed on Spitsbergen and destroyed coal mines and a radio station. German forces were attempting to ring Leningrad. A successful RAF raid that killed twenty-seven persons in Berlin was branded by the German press as a terroristic criminal assault.

On September 9, the State Department announced that the *Sessa*, a U.S.-owned freighter under Panamanian registry, had been torpedoed and sunk just after mid-August 300 miles southwest of Iceland. Senator Nye charged that a small group of motion picture producers born abroad had been injecting pro-war propaganda into films. FDR ordered the Navy to shoot first if Axis raiders entered American defense zones. But he said that there would be no shooting war unless Germany continued to seek it. The *Montana*, a U.S.-owned freighter, was torpedoed in waters 260 miles southwest of Iceland. By September 11, Charles A. Lindbergh charged at an America First rally that certain specified groups, along with the FDR administration, were pressing the United States toward war. U-boat strength was still very much on the increase. The German high command announced that twenty-two ships out of a convoy of forty had been sunk in the Atlantic. (Read all about what it was like, folks, in *The Cruel Sea*. Also see *Infamy*, by Tolland. At page 66: since early 1941, Captain Laurance Safford had suspected that Naval Cipher No. 3, used for high-level communications between the British and the United States, pertaining to convoy-and-routing as well as anti-submarine warfare, was being "read solid" by the Germans. But so far, his superiors had not taken his warning seriously.)

More evidence of the unlimited national emergency: In Louisiana, Texas, and Mississippi, Red and Blue armies clashed as U.S. war games involving more that 400,000 troops got underway. And the ominous trend augmented by this heightening of preparedness continued. Back in the City of Washington, FDR gave Edward R. Stettinius, Jr., broad powers to speed arms shipments to the Allies. The Navy announced that all contracts for the 2,831 ships needed for the two-ocean fleet had been awarded. In Paris, the execution of ten more hostages was announced by German military authorities. In Russia, units of the German Army widened the bridgehead on the east bank of the Dnieper. The RFC contracted to swap $100 million of U.S. goods for an equivalent in Soviet metal ores. The American Legion passed a resolution backing FDR's foreign policy, and approved use of U.S. forces on foreign soil if war should become unavoidable. FDR asked Congress for a new appropriation of almost $6 billion under the lend-lease program. In the Atlanlic, we were already in a sort of *de facto* war. *Pink Star*, a U.S.-owned freighter under the Panamanian flag, was sunk between Greenland and Iceland. In Russia, a Nazi panzer spearhead entered Kiev while, 200 miles to the south, other German Army units captured Poltava. In the first seventy-one days of fighting, the Nazi high command reported total casualties of 402,865 dead, wounded and missing.

Other flashes adding impetus to the war footing recorded a September raid by a fleet of Italian mosquito boats on Gibraltar, where three British supply ships were claimed to have been sunk. In Russia, Nazi panzer divisions, reaching the Sea of Azov, cut off Crimea and reportedly trapped 150,000 Red Army soldiers under Marshal Budenny. By September 23, FDR disclosed the U.S. plan to arm its merchant ships. Two days later, the Red Army was hurling great masses of troops at Nazi concentrations east of the Dvina River, three hundred miles below Leningrad. The first anniversary of Japan's adherence to the Tripartite Pact fell on September 27.

Japanese Foreign Minister Teijiro Toyoda announced that the Rome-Berlin-Tokyo Axis aimed to create a New Order for the world. Claimed by the Nazi high command was the capture of 665,000 Russians in the Kiev battle. *I. C. White*, a 7,052-ton U.S.-owned tanker under Panamanian registry, was torpedoed and sunk in the South Atlantic. Fourteen U.S. merchantmen were launched in a nationwide "liberty fleet day" celebration. Then on September 27 came an event that was relatively unnoticed, but which would have far-reaching consequences: Reinhard Heydrich, Nazi chief of security police was named Reich protector of Bohemia-Moravia.

In the United States, but only for the moment, the heavyweight championship was more important. Joe Louis KO'd Lou Nova in the sixth of a scheduled fifteen-rounder. Back to the national emergency: W. Averell Harriman, head of the U.S. mission to Moscow, pledged fullest U.S. support to the USSR. Reporting British gains in military strength, Churchill warned that the Nazis still held the initiative in all military fields except air. In response, the war footing, already cranked up, kept rolling.

Goings-On With The Japanese

What was going on in the Orient? In later decades, Layton would point out in *And I Was There*, a major reorganization had been underway since April 1941 involving the creation of a First Air Fleet effectively marshaling more than two hundred carrier-based planes under a single commander.

Yet by early September, little were the worries that we at Link's had concerning possible trouble from the direction of Japan. While we didn't hear much talk about their military aircraft, their pilots were certainly, so went our current thinking, no sweat. This was because the still uninitiated members of the plant's "hot-pilots' club" averred that the Japanese were too nearsighted to handle effectively their fighter and bomber aircraft. Furthermore, the PR focus was on the Russian Front. Yet, let's see what Farago, in *The Broken Seal*, and other previously mentioned authors, would eventually have to say.

In the Orient by September 5, Premier Konoye, as well as Emperor Hirohito, seemed shocked to realize that the powerful military had placed war preparations ahead of diplomatic negotiations. In mid-September, Admiral Yamamoto, at the indoor war games at the Naval War College, presented his "Plan Z" for the attack on Pearl Harbor. (Layton would point out that in the southern Honshu city of Kagoshima, naval planes were buzzing low over Yamagataya department store to make bombing runs on target vessels in the bay, the site having been selected for its topographical similarity to Pearl Harbor. Off the nearby naval base of Kanoya, at the tip of Kyushu, the obsolete battleship *Settsu* was anchored in Ariake Bay as a target for dive-bomber pilots. Off the rocky coast of Shikoku, two-man midget submarines fine-tuned their act.)

On September 18, an attack by four men that might have been fatal narrowly missed Konoye in such a manner as to deliver an unmistakable message. The war party (the military clique) wanted him out. He needed some helpful concession at once from the United States in order to remain in office.

On September 24, a radiogram from Captain Ogawa (whose organization operated in Hawaii) was intercepted, setting up a grid system for requested extra special accurate reporting in spy messages of the positions of U.S. warships in Pearl Harbor. As Layton (to whom reference is made for fascinating details) would later stress, diplomatic intercepts by Washington were not being forwarded to Pearl Harbor.

On September 29, Ambassador Nomura in the City of Washington was pressing Secretary Hull to agree to a FDR-Konoye meeting in Juneau, Alaska. In contrast to the war party (referred to by the ambassador as "some people in Tokyo"), it was indicated by Nomura that Konoye was sincerely anxious to see his efforts for a rapproachement succeed. In U.S. intelligence circles, intercepts of internal bickerings amongst Axis partners then took the spotlight from the Ogawa spy request that a grid scheme be used to report the warship status in Pearl Harbor.

By October 3, an exchange of messages indicated that Secretary Hull, in all practical effect, had told the Japanese to clean up their act before the United States would sit down and talk. But the Japanese were suspicious that the United States simply wanted from them a policy statement in order to condemn it.

In contrast, by early October in the Yankee Tier, we were getting in our last few sets of home-town tennis and attending football games weekends thirty miles northerly at Cornell. But at Ariake Bay on the *Akagi* (the crack unit of the First Air Fleet), a large group of officer pilots were told by Admiral Yamamoto that they would fly to destroy the American fleet at Hawaii and named the date. "Plan Z" had been adopted.

Konoye offered to meet FDR almost anywhere to straighten things out. But FDR sent word that he was not ready for such a meeting. In Washington, Ogawa's grid request fell into a deferred category of intercepts. But Col. Rufus S. Bratton, chief of G-2's Far Eastern Section, from all intelligence sources commenced plotting Japan's march to war. He began marking all hinted deployments. He stuck a marker on the Pearl Harbor spot on the map. It was October 13. Just a few days later, on October 16, shortly before the deadline that had been given Konoye by the military clique to conclude negotiations with the United States, the premier resigned with his entire cabinet. The war party took over. The new premier named by the emperor was General Hideki Tojo. While extending the deadline until October 29, he jacked up preparations for war.

For A Commission In The Air Corps: Down But Not Out.

Word came in the mail. I was turned down for flying training with the Aviation Cadets. They spelled out the solo reason. So what about that disqualifying touch of nearsightedness? In later decades I told my tough-luck story to an air force chief of staff. Very drily, he replied, "I hid my glasses for years."

But no such clue was available at a time when it could count for your Virginian. Too bad. But the Owego Eagle, before he had so recently left for his RCAF base in Canada, hadn't coached me. Since I didn't regularly wear glasses, the problem that would prove to be a roadblock to the wide blue yonder had given no warning. Otherwise I'd have timely memorized the eye charts.

But I wasn't yet through. When the draft board gave me the go-ahead to work on some interesting ground-duty alternatives, I applied for the one that would see me situated closest to combat where I still might have a chance to learn to "hide my glasses" with a view of getting into actual flying training. The commission that next beckoned: armaments officer. Nearsightedness was no handicap. Once again I was completely qualified except for a different old bugaboo. This time, instead of the eye exam, it was college algebra. In the summer of 1938 I'd been knocking myself out scholastically with Columbine cheering me on. My objective: to get into the first year of law school as a double registrant during my senior year as an undergraduate. That college algebra course had been one of the prime factors that had knocked me out of the box. Overlooked: I hadn't thought to first go back and review my high school algebra courses that I'd passed with flying colors. And it was such overconfidence that had pulled the rug. But with the year of 1941 running out, and with national defense the issue, perhaps my old prof could patch things up?

During that college summer session of 1938, I'd grown dizzy watching Cornell's genius with numbers chalk up a full blackboard and erase it only to chalk it full up again and erase it again and repeat, so fast that it made your head swim. But now in late 1941, thinking that I could get this same mathematical wizard to conjure up a way to get me into armaments training, I paid him a little visitation on the Cornell campus.

I was sitting in front of the desk occupied by Professor Wallie Abraham Hurwitz, who was said to have checked the computations on the Panama Canal. Quickly I spoke my piece. My expectations heightened as I could discern a friendly reaction. But my pitch couldn't quite turn the trick.

"I admire your spirit and your patriotism for a worthy cause," said the professor. "But in your case there is nothing, *retroactively* that I can do to patch up your record for you. Other than that, while I wish you the best of luck, I can well appreciate your interest in the Armed Forces. . . . ." the mathematical wizard dismissed me.

At least I'd given it my best shot, the old college try. And still, with the Cadets, as I soon was briefing the draft board, there were a few other possibilities. While these remaining opportunities didn't sound as close to the action as armaments, there were meteorology, photography, communications, etc., etc. and etc. . . . . I continued to sweat out conscription.

I never thought to take a trip to the City of Washington. Operating on pure intuition, and without realizing the why and where-fore of it, an unaware great-great-great-grandson of George Washington might well have gotten himself a commission. . . . and without any recommend by Sewell Avery.

But following the regular route, and much appreciative of the restraint being exercised by the county draft board, as I kept right on furthering my applications for these additional available opportunities with the Air Corps, your unaware George Washington VI was down but not out.

October Events Take On A More Dangerous Tone

Regarding the military-secrets category of all of this sort of stuff, to us 'uns back in the Yankee Tier, it was a case of what we didn't know, temporarily, wouldn't hurt us. Yet there was plenty that we did know that kept us at the ready to pick the right moment and then enlist.

As always, because of their high profile in the press, it was still the Germans from whom we Americans expected trouble. Highlights in October opened with a delayed dispatch from Reykjavik. A new force of U.S. Army units landed in Iceland under the command of Major General Charles H. Bonesteel.

Appearing before the American Bar Association, Secretary of Navy Knox said that the United States and Britain should police the world for at least one hundred years after the defeat of the Axis to ensure peace enforcement.

The German Army launched an intensive drive against Moscow along a 375-mile front. A year earlier the Battle of Britain had been in full swing. In the first big raids against the United Kingdom since the start of the Russian campaign, the *Luftwaffe* blasted five English towns. In German-occupied Europe, fifty-seven Czechs were executed by Nazis for alleged terrorist or treasonous activities. Mayor Otakar Klapka and a number of the city council members of Prague were numbered among the unlucky ones. Back in the German homeland, Hitler told the people that the German Army had broken the backbone of Russian resistance.

At the last minute, British authorities called a halt to a scheduled exchange of some 3,000 German and British war prisoners. Charles A. Lindbergh told an America First rally in Fort Wayne, Indiana, that FDR was leading the U.S. along a road which might involve suspension of congressional elections in 1942. Soviet troops had made an 18-mile advance in the Ukraine sector, Moscow announced. Norwegians were warned by Nazi Commissioner Terboven to accept Major Quisling's New Order or be annexed to the Reich. The Soviets announced German losses at 3,000,000 dead, wounded and missing; and Russian losses at 230,000 killed, 720,000 wounded and 178,000 missing. Panama's cabinet forbade the arming of ships flying the Panamanian flag.

By October 7, on the Russian Front, German Field Marshal Fedor von Bock's forces drove to within 130 miles of Moscow. Field Marshal Karl von Rundstedt's armies seized ports of Mariupol and Berdiansk on the Sea of Azov. The Finnish government rebuffed Britain's demand to cease war on the USSR. The Red Army admitted the loss of Orel.

FBI agents arrested George Sylvester Viereck on charges of withholding information from the state department concerning his activities as an agent for Germany. (Aside from that, in the roaring 'twenties with Paul Eldridge, he'd co-authored *My First Two Thousand Years.*)

On October 9, FDR asked Congress for immediate authority to arm U.S. merchantmen. Arnulfo Arias, the Panamanian president who'd banned arming of that nation's merchant ships, was ousted as chief executive. The cabinet selected Ricardo Adolfo de la Guardia as his successor.

By October 10, German panzer divisions reached a point 105 miles south of Moscow. The British War Office disclosed that shock troops known as Commandos were being drilled for invasion maneuvers. A U.S. naval vessel discovered and disposed of a German radio station operating in Greenland, the Navy Department announced. As the German Army pushed closer to Moscow, women and children were evacuated. In the Vyazma sector the Germans advanced. The Red Army admitted that Bryansk had fallen, Vyazama (130 miles west of Moscow) being taken the next day. One hundred miles northwest of Moscow, the German Army soon occupied Kalinin.

Just after mid-October, 500 miles south of Iceland, the U.S.-

owned freighter *Bold Venture,* flying the Panamanian flag, was sunk. Southwest of Greenland, the U.S. destroyer *Kearny* was torpedoed and damaged while on patrol duty.

More on the Orient: The day after Japanese Prime Minister Konoye and his cabinet resigned and Tojo took over, the U.S. Navy Department ordered U.S. merchant ships in Asiatic waters to put into friendly ports.

The bill permitting the arming of U.S. merchantmen was passed in the House of Representatives by a vote of 259 to 138.

By October 17, U.S. Ambassador Laurence A. Steinhardt and other envoys to USSR left Moscow. The recapture of Orel was reported by the Soviets. Their strong counterattacks blocked Nazi thrusts in the Kalinin and the Moshaisk sectors. And on October 28, in forming a new Japanese cabinet, Tojo took over portfolios not only of the prime ministry but also the war and home ministries. Shigenori Togo was made foreign minister.

In the Balkans hundreds of Yugoslav rebels were executed in an effort to stamp out the revolt of the Chetniks, Serb patriots.

By October 19, the damaged *Kearny* reached port with eleven missing and ten injured. The U.S. merchant ship *Lehigh* was sunk in the South Atlantic by a submarine.

On the Eastern Front, Moscow and adjoining areas were placed under a state of siege. The Germans captured the port of Taganrog in the Donetz basin. By October 20, the Moscow diplomatic corps reached Kuibyshev (Samara), temporary GHQ for foreign envoys in the USSR. Secretary of Treasury Morgenthau disclosed that the U.S. had advanced $30 million to the Soviets against their promise of gold delivery. Panama's new government revoked the ban on arming merchant ships.

October 21, at Nantes, France, the Nazis executed fifty French hostages in reprisal for the slaying of a German officer by two unidentified civilians. Fifty more hostages were slated to be executed unless the slayers were apprehended by midnight October 22. Also on October 21, the Soviets announced that the Red Army had stopped all German drives on Moscow. A day later the Germans seized one hundred more French hostages after the slaying of a Nazi major in Bordeaux. On October 23, German authorities ordered the execution of one hundred French hostages in reprisal for the slaying of the Nazi commander of Nantes.

Having a bearing on all of the would-be fliers and air corps aficionados still working in civvies at Link Aviation Devices, on October 23, the U.S. War Department announced plans to expand the air force combat groups from fifty-four to eighty-four and to increase air force personnel to 400,000 by June 30, 1942.

In France, the terror increased. On October 24, the fifty French hostages were shot by the Germans at Bordeaux. The next day the German Army captured Kharkov and launched a new drive against Moscow. But on October 27, heavy rains bogged it down.

On October 28, Senator Taft of Ohio charged that FDR had tricked the United States onto the road to war. Mussolini boasted that the coalition of Bolshevism and its European and American allies would be shattered by the Axis. The U.S. destroyer *Reuben James* was torpedoed and sunk while on convoy duty west of Iceland. Seventy-six crewmen were missing. Also off Iceland, the U.S. naval tanker *Salinas* was torpedoed but proceeded to port under its own power. On the Russian Front, by the end of October, German units pierced the outer defenses of Tula, and Marshal Boris Shaposhnikov was renamed chief of staff of the Red Army.

And back here in the Yankee Tier, while there were still hopes that the war might not involve the United States, those of us (of the ripe age for conscription) who'd managed to mull over even a small fraction of the foregoing knew from the more dangerous tone that it was only a matter of time before we would be tapped by Uncle Sam.

Last Update On Doings In Tennis Town

Now that Scintilla wasn't taking so much starch out of me and I could muster up some leftover energy (thanks to the physically less-demanding job at Link's), as hoped, tennis took on new dimensions. At Joe Berry's place, I had recently replaced my old Davis Cup racket with a new Black Knight model. Since returning a year earlier from Monkey's, I had perfected my serve. And now that my latest job was located in the Binghamton area, I not only continued my customary competition on Don Davis' clay court at Owego (that included some occasional fascinating sets with the Indian Princess), but now added play at the Binghamton Tennis Club.

On this current switch from Sidney to Owego, Saturday night social life beckoned. But all we needed was just one successful night out on the town. When the hangover was balanced off against the good feelings needed to play Sunday tennis, it was the week-end partying that got the gate.

Came time for an open tournament. After the Owego Eagle and John Tobin, Clark Fitts was the most recent village champ. But when the scope of players included aspirants from Ithaca, for the clay-court action at Binghamton, Bob Boochever came down and bested Fitts with a telling series of overhead smashes that closed out the final set.

Now back to our annual closed local tournament. In this last peacetime update on doings in a tennis town—Owego—Young Dingle (against whom your Virginian had never played) not only wasn't any too fast on his feet, but also had done practically all of his playing out of town, thus unobserved; either at his family farm at Dingledale, or else at his college fraternity house. So when I drew him in a quarter-final round of Owego's annual tournament, who won? Taking me by surprise, it was Young Dingle.

When the Eagle still ducked playing me at singles, and when Tobin always had a tough time pulling out a win, usually by the use of surprise drop shots, my defeat by Young Dingle was some sort of a recognized anomaly that never got replayed.

Later on, Johnny Tobin, to knock Young Dingle out of the tournament, kept manuevering him from corner to corner, eventually bouncing a drive just out of Young Dingle's reach.

Consolation prize: At an informal game of doubles, Jimmy Patton and your Virginian easily defeated two local stars, the Eagle and Tobin.

As part of the opening scene in Volume I, it was Jimmy Patton who had proclaimed that Israel Dean was the son of George Washington. But since our mutual pick-and-shovel experience during June 1934, so many fascinating scenes of distracting action had transpired (Volumes I and II) that now, on the winding up of current events for a potential explosion into war, once again I remissfully failed to quiz Patton, for instance: "Did you hear about this Israel Dean thing from your [native Kentuckian] father?" Or, "When you were going through Centre College, is that what they told you?"

With winds of change calling for our early shipment through the conduit of the Armed Forces to far-flung ports of call, here again, your Virginian lost another chance to elicit some political-genealogical evidence from his good friend, Jimmy Patton. Yet the light would eventually get turned on. And then we wouldn't forget. It was Patton who had first broken the political-genealogical ice.

During the formal part of these annual village-level tennis contests, we took turns acting as umpire. When your Virginian inadvertently called some of the Indian Princess' shots in, returns that the preponderance of the bystanders thought to be out, the gallery took it with a grain of salt.

And when it came to the question of whom your Virginian could best at tennis: During early season (thanks in earlier years to all of that rowing at Cornell, and more lately to the demands of the turret lathe at Scintilla), not many of our first-line players. But during the last good October weather, I could usually win every set against almost all of Owego's potential conscripts; waiting for the bugle call, who cared? That's how we all felt.

A Plug For *Britannica*

In spite of the trend toward war for the United States that these October highlights exposed, there were still lots of ostriches around who still hoped that the United States by some lucky chance would somehow manage to keep out of it. Helping us think that peace for the U.S. was still possible, around the end of October came an impressive flow of discharged soldiers.

Included were the over-twenty-eight draftees such as Splanaway, and the one-year volunteers who'd just completed their hitch. Making the biggest impression on Owego in the heart of the Yankee Tier was Splanaway. Homing from Fort Eustis, he again commenced serving in civvies as Boilerplate's aide in one of Tioga County's most prestigious small-town law practices. But taking the current spotlight for the returning one-year volunteers, to a position at my right on our inspection bench at Link Aviation Devices, John J. Krisko said how-di-do-di.

Since Krisko had just racked up a year's experience with the infantry, right crack off the bat, just in case that I might soon wind up with the footsloggers, I commenced picking Krisko's brains. As the steady stream of parts for the famed Link Trainer passed under our respective noses for inspection, simultaneously I got some updating on the military-training lectures that I'd previously soaked up from Major Tarbox of the ROTC when I'd been at Cornell. Currently, subjects ranged from military mapping to coding and decoding (with the latest available hand-held gizmo) messages for operations in which, so far as I could see, on an infantry advance into enemy territory, the most exciting job was held down by the ever-popular point man (eventually to inspire the subtitle, but in a postwar political sense, of Volume Six of this saga).

And in appreciation, I got ready to compensate Krisko with some thumbnail sketches of worldwide military geography. To refurbish and update my noggin with some new geographical facts about the far-ranging military situation, I clipped a coupon from a newspaper advertisement, filled it out and mailed it. Within a very short time a salesman knocked on the door at 443 Main Street. During the dark of the midautumn evening, he made his pitch in the parlor. Take my father, who feigned disinterest while tuning in from his nearby den. For instance, he didn't believe in buying books to build a family library. Most all tomes that he'd ever OK were books that had been mandated for required courses in high school and college. Demonstrating some then unrecognized evidence that he was an unaware George Washington V, clearly, he had oft stated, "If possible, hang on to all of your old high school and college books. In later years, they will help you look things up in a hurry."

On the other hand, he would make me wonder how on earth he could ever be a great-great-grandson of George Washington. When I had suggested that he buy *Encyclopaedia Britannica* for the family, he had automatically turned thumbs down. But by now I was finally recovering financially (from my seed-money confiscation), even scoring an improvement over my balance sheet position of five years earlier. Now that I was once again ahead, I listened closely to what this traveling salesman had to say. Without giving this city slicker too much of a hard time, I signed on the dotted line, agreeing to pay in installments, while my father's ears wiggled with seeming disapproval.

Including its mahogany case, my big purchase was soon delivered by express. With it came the option to buy at some reasonable yearly figure the *Britannica Book of the Year*. Your Virginian, again as mentioned, gives credit, in particular, to the "Calendar Of Events" in the respective yearbooks. As gleaned from them, the reader can attribute a large part of the briefing that has been and will continue to be delivered when deemed warranted, as concisely as possible, on current events.

Now, back to our inspection bench at Link's. It was covered with heavy brown paper. From the latest stories in the press, taken together with my background studies out of the *Britannica*, to my coworkers at Link's I'd deliver thumbnail lectures, including colorful details and exotic names of far-away places, etc. elaborating about goings-on in the various war theaters or those in which war seemed to be about to erupt, such as Southeast Asia and the Southwest Pacific. At the same time, on the brown paper covering the inspection bench, in broad strokes, I sketched strategic and tactical maps of areas of current as well as potential military campaigns, the Singapore area in particular. All of these geographical pointers were submitted, especially in return for the ongoing cluing that John Krisko was delivering on just what modern U.S. Army infantry life was like.

Grouchily, our immediate straw boss was watching. Interrupting, he would approach and order: "Say, you can't mark up that inspection bench."

But by now, under the exciting cloud of this seeming, undeclared war that involved all of us, we all, on the thick brown paper, Krisko, Kolly, Gordon Gallagher, and your Virginian, kept right on illustrating our points geographically with soft lead pencils, sketching war maps as we saw fit. Since we simultaneously did our inspection work acceptably, and since the paper was expendable, our straw boss eventually toned down his squawks as I continued to ring in geographical factors gleaned from the *Britannica*.

When headlines of overseas military operations, troop movements, etc., reached out and touched some exotic far-away area, for us four military aficionados, more background details were required. So again and again I'd come to work, morning after morning, primed for delivery during any rest period in the workday of the latest encyclopedic spiel that made all four of us itch to go to war. If for nothing else, *Britannica* provided lots of the impetus, as we all hungered for a dangerous voyage.

The Draft Board Gets Itchier

Back in the Yankee Tier, from all of the heightening danger mirrored in the wartime events across the seas, even though some of the developments were still secret, the draft board was truly feeling the vibes coming down from the top. So long as we were not at war, the board let me know that my still-pending application for some training other than flying with the Aviation Cadets would keep me from getting called up, provided that I kept the board informed. But they made it clear: at any old moment, the situation could change.

As though to beat some deadline that I could sense was in the offing, I was knocking myself out evenings writing fiction. Were I to enlist, I first wanted to sell a yarn to the *SEP*. But like The Man said, "You want to make money now at writing? Then write now the way you'll be writing after you work at it for ten years."

Testing my literary stuff on friends at the Sugar Bowl, I'd pass my most recent manuscripts to chaps such as Junior Dingle. Attorney Young Dingle's older brother was about four years my senior. Same as my status had been with Scintilla, the older brother was now deferred as the junior partner of Heetreet in their local engineering concern that was under contract to manufacture war materiel.

Amongst my manuscript readers on the lower end of the age scale, there was Freddy Andrews, still in high school and a great fan of fighter pilots. During the preceding decade, his father, had served as DA. Prior to that, during World War I, he'd been trained to become a fighter pilot only to have been cut off from combat by the Armistice.

My various and sundry Sugar Bowl friends liked my fiction stories. But that wasn't good enough to put the stoppers on the rejection slips from seasoned magazine editors. Still I kept plugging, even though the early November headlines kept one-upping the material on which my literary products were based.

North of Moscow, German troops advanced in the Kalinin area. The Soviets admitted that Nazi spearheads had entered Tula. FDR placed the entire Coast Guard under the Navy Department. General Sir Archibald Wavell reached Singapore. The Germans captured Simferopol, the Crimean capital. Secretary Hull indicated that the United States had been exerting pressure on Finland to end its war with the USSR. The Reich rejected a U.S. request for almost $3 million for the torpedoing of the *Robin Moor* in the South Atlantic on May 21.

Fiorello La Guardia was reelected mayor of New York City, defeating William O'Dwyer. British ships seized six vessels in a Vichy convoy as they attempted to run contraband for the Germans in the South Atlantic. Nazi divisions captured Theodosia, the Crimean port near Kerch. Women hurled eggs and tomatoes at British ambassador Lord Halifax in Detroit. On November 5, the Japanese government announced that veteran diplomat Saburo Kurusu was en route to Washington on a mission to establish a basis for peace in the Pacific areas. In later decades, Layton would explain that the arrival of such a special envoy gave specific warning that this was a last-ditch diplomatic effort and that if it were to bog down, relations between Japan and the United States would be on the brink of chaos.

As revealed by the State Department, on the basis of an exchange of letters between FDR and Stalin, the United States was loaning $1 billion in lend-lease aid to the USSR. Maxine Litvinov was appointed as the new Soviet ambassador to Washington. Stalin urged the creation of a second front and forecast the inevitable doom of Hitler. German casualties were put at 4,500,000 and Russian losses at 1,748,000. Nazi propaganda minister Goebbels warned the German people that they would face an inferno if the Reich lost the war.

In Atlantic equatorial waters, a U.S. cruiser seized the *Odenwald*, an Axis raider disguised as a U.S. merchant ship. After eleven days of bitter debate, the Senate voted 50 to 37 to permit the arming of U.S. merchantmen and to permit the entrance of U.S. ships into war zones. The Red Army launched a counteroffensive from Kalinin to Volokolamsk.

On November 8, Hitler declared that German warships would fire on U.S. vessels only if attacked. The admiralty in London claimed the destruction of eleven Italian merchantmen in the Mediterranean by a British naval squadron. Nazi authorities announced that twenty Czechs had been executed for attempting to disrupt

Vienna's food supply network. By November 10, Churchill pledged to the United States that Britain would declare war on Japan within the hour if Japan and the U.S. should go to war.

A day later, Finland rejected the U.S request that it stop military operations against the Soviets. (It didn't come out, but your Virginian thinks that the relatively unpublicized issue was the great nickel mine at Petsamo.) By a wide margin, Manuel Quezon was reelected president of the Philippines. On November 12, Churchill told the House of Commons that the Battle of the Atlantic was turning in Britain's favor.

Counterattacking Red Army units made new gains in the Tula sector. But Nazi forces reportedly captured some coast positions south of Kerch in the Crimea. Just before mid-November, the British aircraft carrier *Ark Royal* was torpedoed and sunk by an Axis submarine about twenty-five miles east of Gibraltar. U.S. marines were ordered by FDR to pull out from garrisons in Shanghai, Peiping, and Tientsin.

On November 17, the new Japanese premier, Hideki Tojo, set as terms for peace in the Pacific: hands off China, lifting of the economic blockade against Japan, and the end of military encirclement. FDR and Saburo Kurusu, the special Japanese envoy, conferred on the Japanese crisis.

Also just after mid-November, the German Army claimed the capture of Kerch, key city in Crimea. Hitler placed conquered Soviet areas under the civil administration of Alfred Rosenberg, chief Nazi ideologist. FDR asked Congress for $7 billion in supplemental appropriations for the Armed Forces and for defense housing. He also signed the measure repealing the Neutrality Act. On November 18, British forces launched a surprise sea, air and land offensive into Libya, advancing fifty miles in the first day's operations. Japan's special emissary Saburo Kurusu and Ambassador Kichisaburo Nomura asked Tokyo for further instructions after a three-hour parley with Secretary Hull.

The Soviets admitted that the situation was grave in the Crimea as Red Army units withdrew from Kerch. An accord was reached between the U.S. and Mexico. It covered peso stabilization, the Mexican road program, silver purchases, payment of U.S. claims and attempted settlement of the oil dispute. Ten miles south of besieged Tobruk, British desert armies captured Rezegh. The sixth major offensive against Moscow in three weeks was halted at Volokolamsk and Tula. Anzac troops captured Fort Capuzzo, Italian stronghold in Libya. Berlin announced the capture of Rostov. Anzac forces recaptured Bardia on the Libyan coast while a tank battle was taking place at Rezegh. The U.S. consulate in Saigon was wrecked by a bomb, but there were no injuries. Lend-lease aid was extended to the Free French movement. British forces reportedly captured Gambut in Libya. The German Army reached a point just thirty-one miles west of Moscow.

At Owego, even though I was awaiting the results of my latest Aviation Cadet application for a commission in a branch other than flying, I could sense that the Tioga County draft board was getting itchier.

Good Old Owego

While this Aviation Cadet application for training other than flying dangled, evenings we'd hang out at the taproom of the Ahwaga Hotel, where Dwight Decker held court. Between sessions, my college friend Phil Smith showed up in a corporal's uniform, so I proceeded to pick his brains as rapidly as possible about America's modern infantry (just in case that's where I'd soon be fated to get the opportunity to exploit my ROTC training). When the yarn-swapping was well launched, who else showed up? Still another old acquaintance, one who had already starred in the opening and closing of the first section of Volume I of our saga. Now taking a quiet bow in the uniform of a second lieutenant, then elbowing up to the bar for a beer, was none other than the Lace-Curtain Waterboy. But his balking with the bucket way back in June 1934 by now was all forgotten. On the surface, everybody was having a good time.

After closing the bar, Phil and I were winding up the evening with a hamburg, coffee, and pie (for just two-bits) at the Boxcar on North Avenue. My erstwhile college friend, whose job it was to wise me up about what I too might soon be putting up with in the military, said: "Did you see what happened back there in the taproom? That looey and I are both members of well-known Democratic families. But you couldn't mistake his tone and his attitude."

"What about it? I missed that one," I said.

"Because I'm wearing an enlisted man's uniform with corporal's stripes and he's wearing officer's duds, he snubbed me."

"As important members of our county's minority party, you're both in the good graces of FDR."

"Well, that didn't help. I thought you'd like to know how it works."

My college friend, whose mother was a member of the Ball family, like some good distant but unaware cousin, clued me in on the type of situation, just now merely good old Owego, but later on a taste of goings-on in the military that might soon be coming up for your unaware George Washington VI.

Right across the street was the Elks Club. As mentioned, a year earlier, they'd initiated my father as a member of the so-called General Pershing class. Included at the time was the Hawk, who now commenced to exploit the Taproom-Elks axis.

Same as your Virginian, old friend Hawk was still in civvies but was engaged in a more speculative occupation—selling real estate while still sweating out conscription. For a double-barreled evening he would take turns at the Ahwaga taproom, then trot across the street for the Elks Club. When he'd return, sounding like real big stuff, he'd say: "I just lost five," or. . . . . "I just lost ten."

To an envious twenty-three-year-oldster such as your Virginian, such club life seemed to mean an opportunity to match wits with the big boys who played poker and blackjack, sometimes until dawn. One morning when I caught my ride to work at Link's, LeRoy Kelley handed me a paper. "Here's an Elks Club application. Let me submit it for you."

Since it was about time for me to catch up with Hawk, I went along with my self-proposed sponsor. But a fortnight later, when I boarded the sedan for the customary fast ride from Owego to Hillcrest, I noticed my application sitting between us on the front seat. "I've got to return this to you." Kelley pointed it out and I picked it up.

"How come?"

"You know why." Kelley didn't bother with the details.

I shrugged. Back home, I was speculating whether or not some ancient academy horseplay when it backfired had lasting detrimental effects . . . . or whether the surprise rejection was just one more notch in the abnormally high level of political tricks that we targets, unaware of secret political-genealogical motives, rolled with as ordinary punches. It's still a whodunit.

Later on, my mother (a frequent conduit of more sensitive dialogue between your Virginian and his father) said: "You should have told your father that you wanted to join the Elks. He and his friends could have seen to it."

"But he's already been a member for almost a year. Yet it was LeRoy Kelley who first approached me to join. So it was only fair that I took Kelley up on it."

There was absolutely nothing more for either of my parents to say.

Good old Owego!

The Countdown

While the real fomenting was taking place in the western Pacific, the newshawks' beanbag, as it was getting tossed back and forth, kept our attention focused first on Europe and North Africa, then on the Orient.

On November 25, British tank units recoiled under counterblows of General Erwin Rommel's panzer divisions. But the next day Secretary Hull submitted new proposals for the readjustment of U.S.-Japanese relations to Nippon envoys Kurusu and Nomura, while German troops, driving toward Stalinogorsk, flanked Tula.

Axis forces in the Libyan desert, according to Rome dispatches, captured 5,000 British soldiers, including two generals. On November 27, FDR and Secretary Hull conferred with the Japanese envoys Kurusu and Nomura amid reports that the Nipponese were massing troops in Indo-China. Anzac troops joined forces with one section of the British garrison in Tobruk; New Zealanders recaptured Rezegh. The Italian garrison in Gondar, last Italian outpost in Abyssinia, surrendered to the British after a siege that had lasted several months. By November 28, dispatches from Shanghai reported seventy troop transports to be moving 30,000 Japanese troops southward.

President Manuel Quezon asserted that the Philippines were unprepared for war. On November 29 came the news that the Red

Army had recaptured Rostov. Japanese Premier Hideki Tojo declared that the Anglo-American exploitation of Asiatic peoples must be purged with a vengeance. According to the admiralty, in the Arctic, British submarines sank eight Nazi supply ships carrying troops and supplies to German armies in northern USSR. On November 30, dispatches from Cairo said that British mechanized patrols reached the Gulf of Sidra after a 300-mile advance across the Libyan desert. A state of emergency was decreed in Singapore, and new reinforcements of British and Indian troops reached Rangoon, Burma. Japanese Foreign Minister Shigenori Togo rejected as "fantastic" U.S. proposals for settling the far eastern crisis.

In spite of the foregoing atmospherics gleaned from the passing headlines, life in the Yankee Tier still remained pretty much an extension of a halcyon summer into a fall season in which we swapped views evenings at the Ahwaga Hotel taproom. And this time there were no extrasensory perceptions to tell us what really was going on in the Pacific. Any mysterious vibrations reaching the Yankee Tier were awfully weak and soon muffled. For the reader, additional background is in order. Critically, a study of these developments would be too convoluted a pursuit to be taken lightly. As mentioned, suggested references include writers such as Ladislas Farago in *The Broken Seal,* John Toland in *Infamy,* and Edwin T. Layton in *"And I Was There".* They aptly flesh out this upcoming bare-bones outline for students of this, the final countdown to the real thing.

To these steps toward war, by hindsight, our age group that was ripe for conscription was already a blindfolded captive audience. Going back to November 1, a timetable of events was taking shape in the Orient. Admiral Isoroku Yamamoto was so certain that war with the West had become inevitable that he ordered his primary top-secret operations order printed in seven hundred copies. For openers it called for a declaration of war on the United States. In an unusual move, all fleet call signs were changed. The curiosity was that the Japanese, jumping the gun by a month, didn't wait out the end of the normal six-month period. Nevertheless, Lieutenant Commander Wilfred J. Holmes, a communications expert in Hawaii specializing in traffic intelligence, discovered an entirely new organization of the naval air force and dubbed it as the Japanese First Air Fleet. It was Nagumo's task force exercising at Saeki Bay, but no sooner was it identified than it was lost.

On November 5, an imperial conference took place at which not a single man expected its proposals (representing national policy) to be forwarded through Nomura and Kurusu to the U.S. government to be acceptable. Nor did they expect the crisis to be resolved on Japanese terms. The conference's actual purpose: to issue orders to the Japanese Army and Navy to be ready to fight around the beginning of December.

By November 12, certain intercepts indicated that the pall of war hung heavily over the Pacific. But FDR and Secretary Hull, biding their time, undertook nothing to advise the nation of the utmost seriousness of the situation or to alert the Army and the Navy of the showdown.

On November 15, Saburo Kurusu arrived in Washington. His aide, a young diplomatist named Shiroji Yuki, opened up completely to a British scholar who had been at one time Yuki's teacher. Yuki let it out that Japan was moving toward war. At about the same time, regarding Pearl, Ogawa asked for a ships-in-harbor report, irregularly—but he increased the customary weekly rate for the spy-messages from his ensign on the spot to twice a week.

Radio silence commenced, with changes made to give the impression of reassignment of old calls. By November 17, Admiral Nagumo's *Kido Butai* (literally Mobile Force but more accurately Striking Force, per Layton) had been assembled and the fleet was at sea, en route to Tankan Bay in the Kuriles. Commencing on November 18, Ensign Yoshikawa (Ogawa's man on the spot) increased the intensity and scope of the effort on his secret mission, primarily reporting ship movements in the Hawaiian area. By November 20, Nagumo's striking force completed battle preparations and reached its rendezvous in Hitokappu Bay at Etorofu Island in the Kuriles. Soon thereafter by the impregnable new code, Yamamoto signaled Nagumo: "X-day will be December 8." (This Tokyo time meant December 7, U.S. time). On November 25, the main strike force departed the Kuriles. In Washington, the war council, according to Layton, agreed on terms of a temporary accommodation. Colonel Rufus S. Bratton, moving pins on his secret war maps, graphically displayed the *pattern* of the scattered moves to reveal the deployment of the Japanese forces. He became absolutely certain that war with Japan would break out on Sunday, November 30 (December 1, in Tokyo time).

On a fateful (according to Layton) Wednesday, November 26,

came a volte-face. The Japanese envoys arrived in Hull's office expecting to be handed details of an accommodation based on FDR's formula of "some oil now, more later." Instead, they got only an uncompromising ten-point declaration of absolute conditions that had to be met before the United States would consider resuming trade or lifting its oil embargo.

On November 27, Secretary Hull reported to Secretary Stimson that the note had been handed to the Japanese. As Stimson wrote it down or dictated it, Hull said: "I wash my hands of the whole matter and it is now in the hands of you—the Army and the Navy."

On Saturday, November 29, the SS *Lurline*, flagship of the Matson Line, sailed from San Francisco and Los Angeles on the romantic Hawaiian run. Details of this believed pickup of signals from *Kido Butai* have been written up in the "Postscript" that appears only in the *paperback* edition of *The Broken Seal*.

However, in the later publication, *"And I Was There"*, Layton would suggest *Uritsky*, a Russian ship carrying war materiel from the West Coast to Vladivostok, as such signals' source.

November 29 (but in Tokyo time, meaning November 28 in the United States) was also the last extension of the deadline by Tojo. As November ran out, the last day was Sunday, the thirtieth, the day on which Bratton, in the City of Washington, had predicted the commencement of hostilities. Nothing happened. So it looked as though Bratton had cried wolf once too often. Yet he didn't give up.

Back in the Yankee Tier, no suspicions of the upcoming hostilities found their way through the various news processess into the scuttlebutt at work. For the lot of us, as Link's provided the final link, Japan was still the country of *Madame Butterfly*. Instead of attempting to read the news between the lines, during my spare time I was getting behind the typewriter and knocking out fiction. For sources of techniques displayed by clever movie producers as their productions kept the viewer on the edge of the anxious seat, I studied flicks such as *Swampwater* and *Night Must Fall*. Then, as I made applications, I played on contrasty reader perception with a view of keeping my potential readers well entertained. Finally, downtown at the Sugar Bowl, I continued to pass my latest manuscript around. There, Junior Dingle, Charley Bedell (with whom I had attended a fictionalized Japanese-U.S. war movie—*The Battle—*

at the Criterion Theater on Times Square, back in the fall of 1934), and Freddy Andrews would tell me that I was turning out good stuff. And it would have to be were it to eventually compete successfully with daily headlines mirroring the increasing rate of wartime operations.

Highlights of the *regular* news ran something like this: On Monday, December 1, FDR conferred with Admiral Stark and Secretary Hull on the Japanese crisis. Ambassador Nomura told the press: "There must be wise statesmanship to save the situation." Tokyo decided to continue the parleys after hearing a report from Foreign Minister Togo. Dispatches from Moscow indicated that 102 German planes were destroyed and 118 tanks and 210 guns were captured from the Nazis in the Rostov area. Marshal Petain and Marshal Goering met in St. Florentin in Nazi occupied France.

On Tuesday, FDR asked Japan for an explanation of the movement of troops, planes, and ships into French Indo-China. A British warship squadron headed by the battleship *Prince of Wales* and the battle cruiser *Repulse* arrived at Singapore. According to Layton, its protective carrier had gone aground at Bermuda. But the task force had proceeded under the theory that "bombers were no match for battleships."

In Britain, Churchill asked Commons for authority to draft 3,000,000 more men into the Armed Forces and to require women to join the uniformed services. In Libya, General Rommel's Axis tank units seized Rezegh. In the Donetz area, Soviet forces pursued German units fleeing westerly along the shores of the Sea of Azov. In Trieste, sixty persons charged with plotting to assassinate Mussolini appeared before a tribunal. FDR announced that he had OK'd shipments of lend-lease supplies to Turkey.

On December 2 (Tokyo time), three elements in the covering up of the departure of the "Z" forces were these: Regular radio operators of the carriers were kept home, lending outgoing signals the "swing" presumably known to U.S. monitors. The usual number of sailors showed up on shore leave. But in the Ginza they were soldiers in sailors' uniforms. From Yokohama, the *Tatsuta Maru*, flagship of the NYK line, sailed on schedule for San Francisco. (Under sealed orders, it would turn around five days out and while observing radio silence reach Yokohama without incident).

On Thursday, December 4, according to a dispatch from *Reuters*,

Vichy had just agreed to grant Hitler naval and air bases in North Africa. By a vote of 326 to ten, the House of Commons passed the British conscription bill.

On Friday, December 5, Japan, endeavoring to explain it away to FDR, said that reinforcements to Indo-China were only a precaution against Chinese troop movements along the colony's northern border. An official Tokyo spokesman said that the Washington parleys would continue and that both sides were sincere.

From the diplomatic maneuverings, front line operations seized the spotlight. On the Russian Front, Red Army units in the Don basin swept eleven miles past Taganrog. In the City of Washington, the house passed by a vote of 309 to five a defense appropriation bill authorizing more than $8 billion to expand the U.S. Army to 2,000,000 men.

On Saturday, December 6, the Russians began a counteroffensive along the entire Moscow front. FDR made a personal peace appeal to Emperor Hirohito after hearing reports of heavy troop concentrations in Indo-China. The Philippine cabinet asked all nonessential civilians to leave Manila and other danger zones. Britain announced a declaration of war on Finland, Hungary, and Rumania. The United States ordered all Finnish ships in U.S. ports to be put under protective custody.

While such flashes from the fronts were keeping us all perked up, Petula, who'd been attending finishing school in the Midwest, sent word that she'd be coming home as planned for Christmas. Expecting to then take a breather from my sideline of writing, once home from the day's work at Link's, I headed for my study and buckled down on my various literary projects.

To us 'uns in the Yankee Tier, the events most likely to get the United States involved in the war were seen as emanating from the Atlantic. So now let's take a thumbnail look-see, as gleaned from Farago, at the shenanigans, many of which were going on very much behind the scenes, in the Pacific.

On December 1 in Tokyo (November 30 in the United States), a very brief "Japan-will-declare-war" resolution was passed. It was twelve minutes past four. Japan secretly was *de facto* at war. Yet a pall of doubt hung over the heads of the war-makers. Their objective was to now formulate the declaration and deliver it without jeopardizing their plans by alerting the enemy. Then a Japanese courier carrying the final "General Order" containing minute details of the Hong Kong attack crashed in Chinese-held territory north of Canton. General Sugiyama, the chief of staff, and Admiral Nagano, chief of the naval general staff, soon agreed that due to the danger that the document might have fallen into the hands of Chiang Kai-shek, who would alert London and Washington, they would petition the Emperor at once to approve the final and definite date (December 8, Tokyo time) that they had already set.

On the morning of December 2 (Tokyo time but Monday, December 1, back in the Yankee Tier where we were hacking it with John Krisko, Carl Kolly, and Gordon Gallagher at our inspector's corner at Link Aviation Devices), the two Japanese chiefs of staff described the emergency and asked the Emperor's permission to start the war on X-day (that happened to be December 8, Tokyo time: December 7, U.S. time). The Emperor nodded. This was sufficient authorization and the respective chiefs of staff rushed to their offices to issue final orders. As previously mentioned, the Pearl Harbor strike force was already at sea. It was about a thousand miles north of Midway when Nagumo, the commanding admiral, received Yamamoto's signal. They were steaming in two parallel columns at seventeen to twenty-four knots covering around 320 miles each day directly between two patrolled areas. One was by U.S. aircraft flying eight hundred miles south of Dutch Harbor, the other eight hundred miles north of Midway.

On that same December 2 morning that the Emperor fatefully nodded, in Tokyo and on the same day that Nagumo got the message on the bridge commanding his striking fleet that was a thousand miles north of Midway, it was December 1 in Hawaii, where Ogawa's telegram was intercepted inquiring about torpedo nets and barrage balloons at Pearl. On the *Lurline* as it was about to close out its romantic Hawaii-bound voyage, Second Officer Grogan standing the 4 A.M. to 8 A.M. watch in the radio shack picked up the faintest of signals. Soon thereafter, hearing low frequency 375-kilocycle signals on successive nights, the *Lurline's* radio officer confirmed his original belief that he had discovered a group of moving objects. Use of such low-power transmissions was standard procedure for ships sailing together, so it seemed, regardless of whose navy. But in this case, it is assumed that Japanese intelligence units on the various ships of the striking forces were keeping surreptitious contact and that the fleet admiral didn't know about it. The point is that, thanks to the personnel of the *Lurline's* radio shack, on Wednesday, December 3, a full report that concluded that a phantom force was moving stealthily on Hawaii, and which report was signed by the *Lurline's* radio staff and endorsed by the master of the vessel, was delivered to a proper U.S. Navy unit in Hawaii. But shrugging off insistence of *Lurline* officers that the report be put in circulation to higher-ups, the watch officer put it into a Naval pigeonhole. (See page 388, the paperback edition of *The Broken Seal*, together with contrasting comments on *Uritsky* in *"And I Was There"*.)

In the meanwhile the U.S. Navy's communications intelligence apparatus had been having some woes. The final blow came on Thursday, December 4. The Japanese changed their fleet code. Due to previous moves, it had been the only remaining code through which the U.S. Navy could still cull a smidgeon of information. Curiously, the change, that ordinarily would have been made on the first day of the month, came four days late.

At Hawaii, it was Friday. Ensign Yoshikawa was observing: the fleet was in. Then came Friday night, December 5. An advance expeditionary force of twenty-seven Japanese submarines arrived at its destination, eight and a half miles off the mouth of Pearl Harbor. Then they dispersed to take up preassigned scouting and patrolling positions.

In Tokyo on December 5 (Saturday, December 6 at Hawaii), high Japanese officials were attempting to gage a narrow margin of time so that *the* note would be delivered in Washington *before* the proposed attack on Pearl.

On December 6, one of the last signals from Tokyo gave Nagumo the number and position of the American ships at Pearl on the basis of Ensign Yoshikawa's report of the 5th. His last ship-movement report is on page 308 of Farago's book. Also lately mentioned was the absence of anti-torpedo nets and barrage balloons. Ensign Yoshikawa ventured the opinion that now would be the opportune moment to attack the fleet assembled at Pearl. As Farago stressed in his book: "The absence of carriers darkened Nagumo's mood." The strike force on Saturday night was about 500 miles north of Oahu.

In Europe, on December 7, Hitler issued his *Nacht and Nebel* decree for German-occupied countries. In Washington, Bratton was trying desperately to make contact with General Marshal. He was temporarily out of touch during his customary Sunday morning horseback ride. Back in the Yankee Tier, your unaware George Washington VI was home behind his typewriter. From my viewpoint a big roadblock had just appeared in the road to war, one that might even temporarily alleviate the pressure from the draft board. Some dissident officers who were anti-FDR and anti-British had lifted some top-secret documents from the War Department. This blatant effort to expose our plans to aid Britain was called FDR's conspiracy to sneak the United States into the war. The documents were smuggled to an isolationist chain of big-name newspapers. On December 4, the publications, as the "FDR War Plan," had been made simultaneously under a Washington dateline. Headlines of America's most vital war plans created a national emergency. At Link Aviation Devices, those of us who had been expecting Uncle Sam to call us to the colors now felt as though we could forget it for a few more months. This unexpectedly new and bizarre angle on the ongoing national emergency overshadowed the crisis that was developing way out there in the Pacific. So the clandestine operations by the missing Japanese strike force were the least of my worries early Sunday afternoon when the folks below shouted up to my third-floor study: "Evans! Turn on your radio! There's a surprise attack! The Japanese are bombing Pearl Harbor!"

Momentarily, I shoved the typewriter aside. Writing was temporarily shelved. War had been triggered—not as expected in Europe, but had come alive in the Pacific. The countdown was over. Here was the real thing! I decided to enlist.

Chapter 13

The Real Thing

Ebulliently: "We're At War!"

When most of the Japanese bombers were safely back on their carriers that were headed home to Tokyo, on Sunday evening just a few hours after Pearl Harbor, Junior Dingle, Freddy Andrews, and your unaware George Washington VI huddled at the Sugar Bowl. Seemingly overlooked: Who was going to have to go?

Junior Dingle, who'd suffered at age ten some unfortunate partial lost of sight in one eye while then fussing with his brand-new BB gun, now, as Heetreet's junior partner, turning out important defense products, was doubly deferred. Freddy, whom you all would think was the most eager to ship out to war, was still too young. In the relatively near future, were he to meet the age requirement, then apply and be accepted, my quick guesstimate was that with his family background, he would make a first-rate Aviation Cadet.

As for your unaware George Washington VI, when would he ship out? Well within the next several weeks: this was a foregone conclusion.

So who took the conversational lead? Freddy. This enthusiastic son of a World War I fighter pilot who'd been kept from France by the Armistice was wildly ebullient. "What do you think, Evans? How do you feel? Isn't this exciting? We're at war! Doesn't it make you feel like dancing in the streets?" Freddy whooped it up, aiming his exuberance at the one of us for whom the draft board most itched . . . . your unaware George Washington VI.

Curiously, Freddy, because of some physical indisposition that didn't much show, when he'd become old enough, would stay home with Junior Dingle. Otherwise, as a fighter pilot he might have gone down with a plane to the effect that the country would have lost one of its foremost biographical buffs of World War I fighter pilots. In later years, after he'd become an advertising salesman in Florida, he'd exploit his access to the surviving members of the Lafayette Escadrille such as Jimmy Grey as well as to lingering members who'd served as fighter pilots in combat on the Western Front with various groups of the Army Air Corps. Armed with both notes and tape recordings from personal interviews of aces who'd homed from the Kaiser's war, eventually Freddy, should he ever make up his mind to get behind a typewriter and put in the long hours, would find himself on a springboard with a potential of turning out *Full Circle*-type paperbacks, after the fashion of British Group Captain J. E. Johnson. Were the required gumption to surface, future decades would find Freddy setting further details down on paper of America's contribution to that winged epoch on the Western Front of early military aviation.

So it was that Freddy now carried the ball, while Junior Dingle and your Virginian listened as though watching a flick. To Freddy's ebullience, the two of us responded with sporadic assents such as: "If you say so, Freddy," followed up by one or the other of a "Yes" . . . . . "Yep" . . . . . . "Yup" . . . . or an . . . . . "Arp." But of the three of us, it was only your Virginian who had reason to be wrapped in thought. Running through my noggin were questions such as: How many more evenings would Junior Dingle, Freddy, and I huddle at the Sugar Bowl? Would the quinine syndrome dictate my expected military trip to the tropics? Would I ever get back? That was enough. Three attractive young ladies came up. We moved to a large table for a more calming conversation discreetly targeted on furthering the ongoing angling for potential husbands before they got carted off by a troopship. As the high-

school member of our group, Freddy, when he next raised the hare,
"We're at war!" turned down the volume, thus deferring to the
hunt, while Junior Dingle and your Virginian concentrated on the
tomatoes.

The Fat's In The Fire

Highlight of the aftermath of Pearl Harbor: it all came out; in
Washington the Japanese diplomats blew it. Their note rejected
U.S. terms and said that the United States and Britain were con-
spiring against Japanese interests in Asia. But the note had been
intended to be delivered *before* the strike at Pearl. Yet, due to some
comedy of errors, it was delayed until *after*. The sneakiness of the
surprising raid was a low blow in the eyes of the world. Secretary
Hull thus was justifiably able to give the Japanese diplomats, upon
their making the belated delivery, a first-rate dressing down, turning the day into one of great shame for the enemy.

On Monday, Congress declared war on Japan after FDR denounced their aggression and treachery. The Senate voted eighty-
two to zero. The house voted 388 to one. Britain declared war on
Japan. China declared war against Germany, Italy, and Japan. The
Free French declared war against Japan, as did Honduras, San Sal-
vador, Guatemala, Haiti, and the Dominican Republic.

On the Russian Front, the Red Army broke through at two
points on the Moscow Front and destroyed two German divisions.
From Berlin came the admission that winter had stopped the German drive and that the capture of the Soviet capital was not expected before spring. On December 10, Japanese torpedo planes
sank the 35,000-ton battleship *Prince of Wales* and the 32,000-ton
battle cruiser *Repulse* off Malaya, where Kota Bharu was simultaneously under attack by Nippon ground forces. The Japanese also
landed strong infantry forces on northern Luzon. Soviet troops captured more towns in the Orel sector. British armies in Libya freed
the Tobruk garrison and captured Gambut. On December 11, Germany and Italy declared war on the United States. Congress declared war on Germany and Italy with no negative votes, as both

houses of Congress removed restrictions against the use of U.S. troops outside the Western Hemisphere.

Naturally, I stepped up my contacts with the draft board for the latest word on my status, pending word from the Aviation Cadets on my application for a non-flying commission. Obviously, the declaration of war further heightened the draft board's itch. My remaining breathing space as a civilian might extend another four weeks, or just past mid-January 1942.

Then there was this other alternative: Well before Pearl Harbor, an application for the FBI had crossed my desk and I had submitted it. Perhaps I had taken note of the FBI agents passing the house to visit the office in the garage, where they were making occasional calls on my father in order to get some idea of just what was going on in the various corners of the country. Fatefully timed with Pearl Harbor, I got a notice to appear. While my old friend the Hawk went along for the ride, I drove to Albany, met Mr. Cornelius, then in charge, and with a sizeable group of young aspirants, I took a written exam composed of some few essay questions. What was the real import and objective of the questions? I never did find out. Since they seemed to require answers based on common sense, that's what the FBI's board of examiners got. Afterwards, as instructed, we cooled our heels for the results. As though the applicants had been pre-selected, the decision was unusually rapid. Your unaware George Washington VI was included among those who were turned down. For some coaching did I go home and intercept some of the agents calling on my father? Why bother. There was a war on. I might miss something.

But what if I'd have been accepted. It's likely that this saga would never have seen daylight. Seduced by the FBI's good pay, I'd likely have taken a special agent's position and perhaps have made a career out of it. But its contrasty unavailability presented me with a much more adventurous outlook while I continued to await some constructive reply from the Aviation Cadets for a commission. Some news was due to break. A selection-or-rejection letter would be arriving in the mail. Were I to again be turned down, instead of sweating out the draft, I would take action to go on instant active wartime duty with the Army.

Naturally the war came as a shockeroo. But now that the fat was in the fire, it took me just about a week to get my land legs. When I'd been on my new job for about six months, I made arrangements with the greathearted Slim Emerson to put in a final fortnight with Link's, then enlist. And, still hoping to sell a yarn to some magazine of importance, I allowed myself an additional fortnight during which I would stay at home and spend each full day writing with a view of being able to say that I'd successfully submitted something for publication in some big-name magazine *before* joining up.

Petula Plays Hard To Get

While the home-town belles were tops, now that some of their leading candidates were about to slip through their fingers, they were more interested in matrimony than in merely passing the time with an old pal who was about to enlist. In the contrasty neighboring Triple Cities, Petula, when she got home from finishing school for the holidays, got right to work exploiting the aftershock. Our late-summer dates had perked up her targeted swain to this effect: now that Petula was back in the Yankee Tier, all that the good-looking Irishman had to do was pay extra close attention to business while your Virginian promptly fell into his highly skilled role of keeping the phone hot. Petula's folks would then pin written messages on the family bulletin board where the much-better catch en route to the icebox during after-theater sessions, would spot them.

Orchestrating the arrival of war with this new pattern blocking progress in our relationship, Petula's suddenly playing just a little bit too hard to get was explained by a colleague at Link's who happened to be a member of the Friendly Sons of St. Patrick. Although I was eligible by virtue of my great-great-grandfather, Patrick Dwan (on my father's mother's side), to join that important aggregation, an application had never been shoved my way so that I hadn't had such an opportunity to so successfully impress Petula. Furthermore, this other old hoss who suddenly found himself leading along the rail was a flesh-and-blood mirror of Errol Flynn. What to do in a hurry? Two things. First, I practiced my letter-writing skills on my erstwhile coed friend, Columbine. As expected, when she ripped open the envelope at the mail room of her graduate establishment on the East coast, she merely had to mention in passing the properly composed lines. Her favorite sawbones (same as Petula's swain) promptly saw the light and within a fortnight after Pearl Harbor, the two lovebirds were united in heavenly bliss.

Once such splicing had become a *fait accompli* (the love birds having left on their honeymoon), Columbine had her social secretary drop the announcement in the mail. Its arrival told me that I might just as well do the same for Petula. To help her panic her better-established Errol Flynn-type, I got back on the wire. When I caught Petula at home, she was always busy. And during her absence, the memos of my unsuccessful attempts to make contact emblazoned the family message pad. While this upriver mishmash perked, it had not yet had time to mature to Columbine-style speediness. So as Petula commenced making preparations to entrain post-holidays for school in the Midwest, even though no engagement had been announced, it was the handsome Hibernian who held the upper hand. Your unaware George Washington VI commenced canvassing his wits: How to get Petula to slack off just enough on her current "hard to get" policy so as to come up with just one last date?

P.H. . . . Dingman Was There, Sibley Missing

In this first early-war update of some of Owego's luminaries, going back to the last weeks of peace, Jack Killea graduated from George Washington University. After passing his bar exam, he was admitted to the D.C. bar. A fortnight after that he was appointed as assistant personnel director in the City of Washington for the WPA.

His younger brother, Billy, now a lieutenant, was ordered to active duty with the 3rd Armored Division at Camp Polk. During his junior year he had been cadet captain, ROTC, at the University of Kentucky.

In the Yankee Tier, Senior Rep was appointed as the new Waverly village attorney. He succeeded Robert Cohen, who resigned for a post of assistant in the New York State attorney general's office at Albany.

By early October, an esteemed tennis partner, Spike Lowry, was accepted for enlistment in the U.S. Army Air Corps. Since graduating from Cornell, he had been employed as a draftsman at Ingersoll Rand at Painted Post.

So far, Owego's spearhead in the war was the Eagle. Now taking second place, Adam Schwindle, after completing four years with the U.S. Navy, followed in Eagle's shoes by enlisting in the RCAF. While he didn't have the two years of college to become a pilot for the U.S. Army, he would soon show the world that there was more than one way to skin a cat.

On the small-town political front, Dave Relihan, a leading Democrat, threw his hat into the ring for the post of supervisor, town of Owego. He kicked off his campaign by attacking the local GOP poo-bah through the columns of the village's Democratic weekly.

In Waverly, James R. Flynn announced his candidacy for federal district judge to succeed Frank Cooper of Albany, who recently had resigned.

On the front page of Owego's Lake Street sheet, Hugh E. Hogan, Jr. was pictured in a feature that described the parachutist's life in the Armed Forces. Friend, Don Stocks, was at P.H.

Back to the Eagle: In early November, Owego's spearhead in the war paid his last visit to his home town, then returned to Aylmer, his base in Canada. Since his year-earlier enlistment, he had trained at Victoriaville, P.Q. By the end of Thanksgiving he had arrived in the U.K. at his new base, in northwestern England.

Appearing on the knife-and-fork circuit, Fred Snyder, world traveler, lecturer, and writer, got some coverage from the Lake Street newshawks when he told the local service clubs, "Owego is the first defense line. Schenectady is the No. 1 place to be bombed should the Nazis invade this country."

(But the globetrotter forgot to mention the intervening locale of very sensitive Scintilla at Sidney.)

Men of commerce: John P. Webster was pictured in the Lake Street sheet when he retired from Armour and Company. The traveling salesman was based in Binghamton, his territory stretching across Hudson shores. He was born in the town of Tioga on November 22, 1876. (This meant that he would have been about forty-six in 1922, the estimated time that one Carothers rented an apartment in Owego from my father's business partner, Byron Dutcher.

As Splanaway would eventually recall, Carothers had retired as a foreign service officer who'd served in Mexico. He was reputed to have been part of the Armour family of Chicago.)

How did Owego's Democratic weekly handle Pearl Harbor (P.H.)? A small yarn on the top left of page one announced, "America's At War!"

Who from town was there? James Charles Cameron Dingman. In the Christmas issue of the Democratic sheet, his eyewitness account of the attack on Pearl Harbor was featured on page one. Unfortunately, another of the Armed Forces' early acquisitions from Owego, Delmar Dale Sibley, nephew of Police Chief Earl Sibley, was missing at Hawaii after the surprise blow by *Kido Butai*.

One Last Date

Finally, it came time to say goodbye to Petula, but not in the way that you'd think. Since she'd homed, the Errol Flynn type had been staying on the ball and I hadn't been able to get a date. Yet a semblance of some catch-up surfaced like this: Since Petula would be entraining back to school via my home town on the Lackawanna on a Sunday afternoon, when she had suggested that we should at least have one last date, yet expressed disappointment that there just wasn't time, brightly, I told her: "I'll join you on the passenger train when you come by. Save me a seat. Then we'll shuffle off to Buffalo. You're going to visit at your Aunt Millie's for the night. But first we'll have time to take in a show. Afterwards I'll catch the midnight flyer that will get me home early enough in the morning."

Petula went for the idea. But some linked evenings of first-rate Owego festivities muffled any Christmas and New Year's disquietude over my inability to play instant catch-up. Then came some news from the over-itchy draft board. But when I tried to post up Petula by phone, she was always out. Nevertheless, we kept our one last date. At the designated time I was standing on the Lackawanna station platform in Owego. From the Triple Cities, in rolled the same fast train that had picked me up two and a half years earlier on the Buffalo leg to Ann Arbor to begin my year-and-a-quarter bout with Monkey's. From the freshly arrived express train, passengers were soon debarking, and then those waiting to embark were summoned by the conductor. "All aboard . . . . all aboard," he cried out. Hustling in line with the crowd to the top of the few steep, steel steps, I found a most luscious-looking Petula, with lips like a soft red couch, and wearing a leopard-skin coat over a black and white jumper outfit, looking much the brunette baby doll as she waited on the car's end platform to escort me into the coach. "You're in luck," she said. "There's a big crowd on the train but I managed to save a seat for you beside me." Her words hiked my blood pressure. But then I explained: "Something's happened. As much as I want to, I can't shuffle off with you now."

Outside and above the buzz of the crowd in the coach, I could hear the engineer doing his toot, toot, tooting to call in the flagman. So I knew that I still had the few moments that it would take him to leg it along the westbound track and to commence hopping aboard.

"But you were all for our having this one last date. What's happened?" Petula, and with no little bit of romantic, wide-eyed mistiness, inquired.

"Plenty," I told her, then added: "That's just it, events are moving too quickly. I couldn't get you in time on the phone, and my message was too sensitive for just leaving a note. You were out every time I called. But I wanted to see you this one last time anyway, so here I am, your Johnny on the spot."

"What happened? Did you get a different job?" Petula guessed.

During his last moments on the station platform below, the conductor was getting nervous. "The flagman's just boarding the observation car," he warned me. As I seemed to ignore it, Petula was awaiting my answer. A quick goodbye kiss had to do it. Then I poured it out, "I really wish in the very worst way that I could shuffle off to Buffalo as planned, but with this appearance I'm doing my very best."

"Then you did switch jobs?"

"I'll try to catch up to you in the Midwest. I've got to go to war."

"You're going to go to war?" echoed Petula.

"I've gotta go to war," I reiterated as the conductor came up the steps and we all could hear the choo-chooing getting slowly started. The train was pulling out. Tearing myself away, I managed to get down the few steel steps of the passenger coach and alight, running, on the station platform. Now that the conductor was safely aboard the train, he slammed the coach's steel platform extension, and next snapped shut the lower half of the steel outside door. On the depot's concrete apron, while breaking into a gallop, I kept patting my heart so-long to Petula who, from the upper open part of the platform door of the passenger coach, kept waving a white silk scarf as the Lackawanna flyer, getting smaller and smaller, disappeared in a westerly direction around the bend and out of sight at the foot of the tall Narrows hill. Maybe our encounter was merely a stopgap. Yet, momentarily we'd made our relationship whole with one last date!

Update On Boilerplate And His Law Clerk, Splanaway

It was early January 1942. Surfacing in the village's Thursday weekly were a couple of items that will serve to bring us up to date first on Boilerplate, then on Splanaway. Featuring developments concerning such two local-level notabilities at this time is important because, especially during the last three volumes of our saga, they will serve as dynamic figures in the slippery political background, both of them already having appeared during the opening volumes of this literary production.

In Volume One of our saga, Boilerplate was billed as Owego's PR God No. 1. This continued until the middle of Volume Two, when he was finessed out of his county judgeship during the GOP primary, summer of 1936. Since New Year's Day 1937, not only had Boilerplate (who was several years my father's senior) been successfully carrying on his own law practice opposite the good offices of the Democratic Lake Street weekly, but also he had been serving as a substitute judge in important courts on Long Island.

Splanaway, as detailed, was several years older than your unaware George Washington VI. He had been on the pick-and-shovel gang with your Virginian in the first scene of Volume I. After commencing at Gettysburg, the OFA graduate had gone south for the completion of his advanced education. And in 1937 he had graduated from law school, and then had homed to the Yankee tier. On the recommendation of the high-profile high school shop teacher, Al Hubbard, he had obtained a prestigious position as law clerk for Boilerplate.

While waiting to pass the state bar exam, Splanaway had been serving as acting village police justice. In such a spot, not only had his decisions and his handling of matters generally been looked upon with approval by the heavyweight members of the Owego Old Guard, but also he had gained his moniker and a reputation amongst a small coterie of the more astute pundits. Splanaway was especially skilled at explaining away various political questions that surfaced during the goings-on that were naturally generated as Owego performed its role as a small town in mass society, especially where an unaware George Washington V and his son were striving for some upward mobility.

After this subject update, gleaned in part from the Thursday weekly, the rest from your Virginian's observations and investigations, we now return to the first days of wartime 1942. Villagers read that Boilerplate (no mention being made that he had his residence in the adjoining town of Springdale) had been named by the village fathers to represent the board in a nuisance action brought by a countryman against our municipality. Over the years, this point would resurface. Boilerplate would be acting as attorney for the village, whereas the unmentioned holder of the official post of village attorney was required by state charter to be a resident of the village.

To what sort of a complaint against the village would Boilerplate soon be responding? As the weekly had mentioned in previous issues, an application was being made by a neighbor to abate the offensiveness of a village dump. Although the matter was of relatively minor consequence and eventually would be resolved, nothing appeared in print about the reputed grave of the Indian chief. This was a large colorful rock that excited imaginations of both young and old as it sat, iceberg-like, beside Monkey Run, and attracted attention just below Allen's Glen. The adjoining footpath ran southerly to the top of the mount from which Evergreen Cemetery overlooked the village of Owego on the other side.

As for the reputed grave of a chief, we all wondered: where did that impressive tall stone come from? Either the glacier had dropped off a singular chunk of interestingly shaped float that was larger and a lot more dramatic than any other stones so imported (and unusual for the area when they were), or else the Indians had managed to scrounge up the rock and sink it into place as a monument. And while such chief's grave may seem to be a digression at this point of our saga, better to mention it here than never. According to my own investigation in later years, the dump that had covered it up would keep right on serving as a very thick veil.

Now back to polish off the update on Boilerplate's law clerk. Almost a year earlier, during the spring of 1941, when your Virginian had held a deferment (while turning out magneto parts on a Warner & Swazey turret lathe at Scintilla), Splanaway had been drafted. His orders had seen him soon stationed at Fort Eustis, Virginia, where he had served almost eight months in the coast artillery. But during the autumn last past preceding Pearl Harbor, because he was more than twenty-eight years of age, Splanaway had been discharged, only to see the Jap attack activate his reserve status early on.

On the first Tuesday of the new year, Splanaway got his orders via Oswego. While he was placed on hold, he expected to soon receive travel papers for Fort Niagara. If all went well back home at the county seat of Owego, until Splanaway would eventually get back from secure postings, Boilerplate would hold the fort.

Instant Active Wartime Duty

By mid-January 1942, members of the Owego tennis establishment such as Spike Lowry and Don Munroe had been accepted for pilot training by the Aviation Cadets. Fred Welch, one of the Yankee Tier's best young golfers, was slated for the Air Corps. While they waited for their orders, for your unaware George Washington VI, the time had arrived to leave them in the ruck.

For more than a year, the Owego Eagle had been serving with the RCAF and as mentioned, was now stationed in northwestern England. And for almost four months, still another Owego lad, Adam Schwindle (after putting in a four-year hitch with the U.S. Navy), lacking two years of college for the Aviation Cadets, had also been serving with the RCAF. So for your unaware George Washington VI, how to get on instant active duty?

First, I finished my most recent literary project, intended to be a serial, if acceptable, in *SEP,* mailed it to the editorial department, attention of Jack Alexander, on Saturday, January 17, and on Monday, January 19, with the county draft board's blessing, I drove my car to the federal building in Binghamton, where I signed on the dotted line for the Army Air Corps.

Then I drove home to Owego, stashed my car in a neighbor's garage, had lunch, then took my previously packed suitcase and caught the next train back to Binghamton. While nobody raised the hare over my previously confiscated $500 chicken-money nest egg, my father had silently eyed these enlistment proceedings in such a way that I left with the feeling that I was teaching him an extra good lesson.

Across from the federal building, an old friend of the family, Art Stark, now in charge of nearby Chenango Valley State Park, happened along and joined me for a beer. When I mentioned some slight sense of trepidation, he said, "Your grandfather, Fred W. Dean [the one who ran for Congress in 1914], he was a great fighter. If you're anything like him, your shipping out isn't going to bother you a bit."

It didn't. In the federal courtroom, Captain Goatley, recently of the CCC's, administered the oath while his measured gaze swung back and forth along lines totaling at least one hundred men, as he made sure that all lips were repeating the pledge.

Now, back to the recruiting office. Sergeant Pankhurst made the announcement. In contrast to the kangaroo strategems that had permeated my senior year on the Cornell crew, your Virginian was put in charge of the contingent destined overnight by rail for Fort Niagara. Then I was entrusted with the customary vouchers that I turned in later on when my men picked up their box lunches at the railroad Y.M.C.A.

Then came the long wait for the Westerner-type late train and this time, in contrast to my goodbye to Petula, the shuffling off to Buffalo was for real. At an early hour, we were bussed along the Niagara Frontier to Fort Niagara.

I wasn't there more than a few days when the bussing process was reversed, this time entraining us on another overnighter from the Niagara Frontier to Baer Field, Indiana. On account of my year-earlier tilt with Norwich Pharmacal Company that had given birth to the quinine syndrome, I was certain that I'd quickly be assigned to some Air Corps unit that would soon be operational in the tropics.

Back in the home town, a front page spread on the January 29 issue of Owego's GOP weekly pictured Don Munroe, Spike Lowry, Frederick Welch, and your Virginian, the story stressing that we all were awaiting orders. Actually for your unaware George Washington VI, there had been no such sweating-out process. Once I'd signed up on January 19, 1942, as hoped, I'd gone on some nice contrasty instant active wartime duty.

The Kentuckians

As Volume three of *A Virginian in Yankeeland* is winding up, it's only natural that the reader (after having been enlightened about Monkey's, the quinine syndrome and magnetos, linked by Link's), may well be itching for more evidence that your Virginian actually is the great-great-great-grandson of George Washington on the male line. Thus it's only fitting to let you all in ahead of time on this next happening to be further detailed early in the next volume.

At the recreational hall at Baer Field, Indiana, I would be approached by a group of Kentuckians. "I would like to introduce myself to George Washington." The spokesman proffered a hand.

"What's this all about?" asked the recruit from Owego.

"What's your father's name?"

"Clifford Pierce Dean."

"What's his father's name?"

"Frederick Wellington Dean."

"Who was his father?"

Although I wasn't used to such attentions now being paid to my family tree, I responded, "Pierce Dean."

"That means that Pierce Dean was your great-grandfather?"

"That's right."

"Then Pierce Dean's father would be your great-great-grandfather. What was his name?"

"Israel Dean."

Letting out a whoop, the spokesman for Kentuckians turned to his mates. Pointing a finger one way at me, he yelled in the other direction to his companions. "That's him!" Then back at me he reiterated, "We're going to call you George Washington."

"How do you figure?"

"You're his great-great-great-grandson and you look just like him."

"But I'm a great-great-grandson of Israel Dean."

"Israel Dean was George Washington's son."

I looked at the other Kentuckians. Their nods of respectful silence confirmed it.

Making their position clear, the spokesman boldly reiterated. "Here in this man's army, we all are going to call you George Washington."